ELIZABETH
AND
CATHERINE

ELIZABETH
and
CATHERINE

Empresses of All the Russias

ROBERT COUGHLAN

Edited by Jay Gold

G. P. PUTNAM'S SONS
NEW YORK

To Patricia Ann and our family
ROBERT COUGHLAN

Contents

With *appreciation to many colleagues,*
especially George Hunt, Philip B. Kunhardt, Jr.,
Ralph Graves, Dmitri Kessel, David Maness,
Dorothy Seiberling, Bernard Quint, and Lucy
Voulgaris, each of whom had a part in making
this book possible;

and to

Jay Gold, the editor, who had the optimism
and stamina to see it through from beginning
to end and whose contributions have been
invaluable.

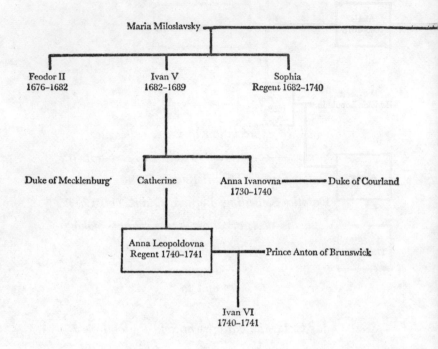

Maria Miloslavsky

Feodor II
1676–1682

Ivan V
1682–1689

Sophia
Regent 1682–1740

Duke of Mecklenburg·

Catherine

Anna Ivanovna
1730–1740

Duke of Courland

Anna Leopoldovna
Regent 1740–1741

Prince Anton of Brunswick

Ivan VI
1740–1741

= Important figures
in *Elizabeth and Catherine.*
Dates show period of reign.

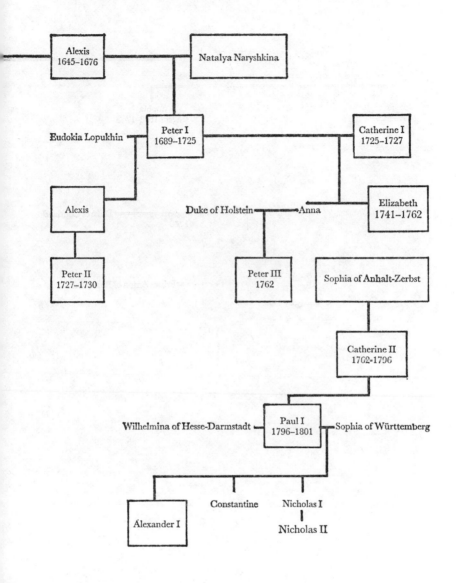

Foreword

THIS book tells the story of two remarkable women who played key roles in the forging of modern Russia. The name and some of the achievements of Catherine the Great are of course known to anyone who has read European history. Elizabeth is far less known.

There could have been no Catherine without Elizabeth. And Catherine would have been a far different person and ruler had she followed someone other than Elizabeth to the throne. Indeed, in a very literal sense, Elizabeth created Catherine the Great of Russia even though they had no blood ties and even though, as Catherine's biographers like to note, her name was not Catherine and she was not Russian. So it is right that Elizabeth take her rightful place beside Catherine in the pantheon of Russian and world history. To show that she belongs there is one of the aims of this book, which does not pretend to be a historiographical work. Rather, it is the carefully researched, factual, and dramatic narrative of two fascinating women who played commanding parts in the shaping of their own times—and ours.

In fact, our times provide an excellent vantage point from which to observe Elizabeth, Catherine, and the nation they ruled. Shortly after the outbreak of World War II, Winston Churchill said: "I cannot forecast to you the action of Russia. It is a riddle wrapped in a mystery inside an enigma." But was it? And is it now?

Russia had at that time seemingly reversed course abruptly and allied itself with Nazi Germany after years of virulent and open ideological antagonism between the two countries. The beginning of the war saw the conquest of Poland by Germany from the west and Russia from the east and a subsequent division of that hapless country between the two invaders. That event was not unprecedented in history.

More: a student of Soviet Russian foreign actions since World War II—in making alliances, in establishing a military presence in various parts of the world, in mounting diplomatic offensives—might well think many of these moves were rehearsed in another time and by another Russia, Catherine's. If for only this reason, the story of her life and reign calls for retelling today.

NOTE ON SPELLING

Knowledgeable readers of this book will quickly discover inconsistencies in the use of transliterations from the Cyrillic. No effort was made to be consistent. The aim was, rather, to make the book as readable as possible for readers accustomed only to the Latin alphabet. When one usage is more familiar than another—czar as against tsar, for example—the familiar form is used. In other cases, the aim was to avoid drowning the reader in a torrent of diacritical marks while giving him words he could at least make a stab at pronouncing.

Many French and sometimes other non-Russian titles will be found. In this regard the book follows the lead of Catherine the Great in her own writings.

Cast of Characters

ADADUROV, BASIL, Catherine's instructor in Russian and one of those involved in the Apraxin-Bestuzhev affair

ALEXANDER I OF RUSSIA, grandson of Catherine II, eldest son of Paul I

ALEXIS, CZAR, father of Peter the Great

ALEXIS, FATHER, chaplain of the Ismailov Regiment of Guards, who gave them the oath of allegiance to Catherine

ANNA, oldest daughter of Peter the Great, who died two years after her marriage to the Duke of Holstein

ANNA IVANOVNA, daughter of Peter the Great's half brother Ivan; she ruled as Empress for ten years during the time between the death of Peter II and the regency of Anna Leopoldovna

ANNA LEOPOLDOVNA, mother of Ivan VI and Regent during his reign, ended by the coup of Elizabeth

APRAXIN, GENERAL STEFAN, commander of Russian forces against Prussia during the Seven Years' War

BERNARDI, an Italian jeweler who was employed by many, including Grand Duchess Catherine, to convey confidential messages

BESTUZHEV-RYUMIN, COUNT ALEXIS PETROVICH, Chancellor of Russia during most of Elizabeth's reign

BEKETOV, COLONEL NIKITA, a onetime member of Elizabeth's intimate circle

BIRON, COUNT ERNST JOHANN, a German who was the lover of Empress Anna

BOBRINSKY, ALEXIS GREGOREVICH, illegitimate son of Grand Duchess Catherine and Gregory Orlov

BRUCE, COUNTESS, principal lady-in-waiting to Grand Duchess Catherine and later to Empress Catherine

BRÜMMER, COUNT, chief tutor of Grand Duke Peter

CARDEL, BABET, French governess of Catherine the Great as a child

CATHERINE, daughter of Peter the Great's half brother Ivan; she became the Duchess of Mecklenburg and mother of Anna Leopoldovna, ruler of Russia as Regent until deposed by Elizabeth

CATHERINE I, camp follower who became the wife and Empress of Peter the Great and titular ruler of Russia after his death

CATHERINE II, born Sophia Augusta Frederica of Anhalt-Zerbst, known to history as Catherine the Great of Russia, wife of Grand Duke Peter (Peter III), mother of Paul I, and grandmother of Alexander I

CHARLES XII OF SWEDEN, military foe of Peter the Great, who ended Sweden's long string of victories at the Battle of Poltava

CHOGLOKOV, M., Chamberlain of Elizabeth's court, and with his wife, one of the "Arguses" assigned to enforce behavioral regulations imposed on the grand ducal couple

CHOGLOKOV, MARIA, chief lady-in-waiting to, and "watchdog" over, Grand Duchess Catherine

CHOISEUL, DUC ÉTIENNE DE, French Foreign Minister, avid art collector, and longtime antagonist of Catherine

CHRISTIAN AUGUST, Prince and co-ruler of Anhalt-Zerbst, father of Catherine the Great

CONSTANTINE, GRAND DUKE, grandson of Catherine the Great, who hoped to place him on the throne of a new "Greek" empire at Constantinople

DASHKOV, PRINCESS CATHERINE, younger sister of Elizabeth Worontsova and ally of Grand Duchess Catherine

DIDEROT, DENIS, one of the foremost *philosophes* and co-editor of the great *Encyclopédie*

DMITRIEV-MAMANOV, ALEXANDER, an "adjutant general" to Catherine

ELIZABETH, EMPRESS OF RUSSIA, daughter of Peter the Great

ERMALOV, an "adjutant general" to Catherine

FALCONET, ÉTIENNE MAURICE, French sculptor who created equestrian statue of Peter the Great commissioned by Catherine II and was for many years one of her advisers in matters of art

FEODOR II, CZAR, elder son of Alexis and his first wife, who reigned briefly after Alexis' death

FREDERICK II OF PRUSSIA, known as Frederick the Great, onetime enemy of Russia, later participant with her in the Partition of Poland

FREDERICK AUGUSTUS II, Elector of Saxony and King of Poland

GEOFFRIN, MARIE THÉRÈSE, hostess whose Paris salon was a gathering place for leading intellectuals and artists

GEORGE, PRINCE OF HOLSTEIN, Catherine's uncle, her mother's youngest brother

GOLITSYN, PRINCE DMITRI, Russian ambassador to France and Holland and one of Catherine's advisers on art purchases

GORDON, GENERAL PATRICK, a Scotsman and senior officer in the Russian Army when Peter I was a youth

GRABOWSKA, COUNTESS PANI, morganatic wife of Stanislaus Poniatowski when he was King of Poland

GRIMM, BARON FREDERICK MELCHIOR VON, international litterateur and diplomatic correspondent, art adviser to Catherine

GROOT, MADAME DE, member of the household staff at Grand Duke Peter's residence, chosen to "initiate him into manhood"

GUSTAVUS II, KING OF SWEDEN, who briefly attacked Russia while Catherine was engaged in fighting the Turks

HANBURY-WILLIAMS, SIR CHARLES, British ambassador to court of Elizabeth in the period before the Seven Years' War and for some time after the war began

HARRIS, SIR JAMES, ambassador of England to the court of Catherine II, of which he was a keen observer and reporter

HOLSTEIN-GOTTORP, ADOLF FREDERICK OF, guardian of Charles

Peter Ulrich (Peter III of Russia) and oldest brother of Johanna, mother of Catherine the Great

IVAN III, CZAR, known as Ivan the Great, who began liberation of Russia from Tatar rule

JELAGINE, IVAN P., aide-de-camp to Count Razumovsky, a friend of Count Poniatowski, and one of those implicated in the Apraxin-Bestuzhev affair

JOHANNA ELIZABETH OF ANHALT-ZERBST, mother of Catherine the Great

JONES, JOHN PAUL, American naval commander during the Revolution, who served with Russian naval forces in the Black Sea during war against the Turks

JOSEPH II, Emperor of Austria-Hungary, with whom Catherine made a military pact against the Turks

KACHINEVSKY, a chorister and onetime member of Empress Elizabeth's intimate group

KARL AUGUSTUS, Prince of Holstein-Gottorp, who was betrothed to Elizabeth of Russia but died before they could be married

KOSCIUSZKO, THADDEUS, Polish nationalist who fought with American troops during the Revolution, led an abortive uprising in Poland against Russian and Prussian dominance

KOSHELEV, MLLE., one of Grand Duchess Catherine's ladies-in-waiting

KRAUSE, MME., maid to Grand Duchess Catherine

LANSKOY, ALEXANDER, an "adjutant general" to Catherine

LEFORT, FRANÇOIS, Swiss soldier of fortune and resident of the German Quarter, boyhood companion of Peter the Great

LEOPOLD II, EMPEROR, successor to the Austro-Hungarian throne after the death of Joseph II

L'HÔPITAL, MARQUIS DE, French ambassador to Russia

LOPUKHIN, EUDOKIA, Peter the Great's first wife and mother of the Czarevich Alexis

MARIA THERESA, Empress of Austria-Hungary

MENSHIKOV, ALEXANDER, lowborn boyhood friend of Peter the Great's, his companion during the Grand Embassy, and a high official in his government

MONS, ANNA, mistress of Peter the Great for many years

NARYSHKIN, LEON, member of the Young Court of Grand Duke Peter and Grand Duchess Catherine and an intriguer who helped arrange some of Catherine's illicit affairs

NARYSHKIN, ANNA, sister of Leon and one of Grand Duchess Catherine's best friends

NATALYA, second wife of Czar Alexis and mother of Peter the Great

ORLOV, ALEXIS, brother of Gregory and ringleader in the plot to depose Peter III in favor of Catherine

ORLOV, FEODOR, brother of Gregory

ORLOV, GREGORY, successor to Poniatowski as Catherine's lover and, with his brothers, an engineer of the coup that brought her to power

ORLOV, IVAN, brother of Gregory

ORLOV, VLADIMIR, brother of Gregory

PANIN, COUNT NIKITA, tutor to Czarevich Paul, son of Catherine

PASSEK, CAPTAIN, one of the Guards officers involved in the plot to enthrone Catherine

PAUL, son of Catherine, who reigned briefly as Paul I

PETER, born Peter Charles Ulrich, grandson of Peter the Great, later Grand Duke Peter of Russia, husband of Catherine, and, briefly, Peter III

PETER I, known as Peter the Great, son of Czar Alexis, father of Empress Elizabeth

PETER ALEXEEVICH, grandson of Peter the Great, named successor to the throne by Catherine I as Peter II, died at fifteen

PONIATOWSKI, STANISLAUS, a Pole who first came to Russia as a member of British Ambassador Hanbury-Williams' entourage and became Grand Duchess Catherine's lover; afterward King of Poland

POTEMKIN, GREGORY, Catherine's lover and in effect co-ruler for many years, and executor of the Greek Project, which established Russia securely in the Crimea

PUGACHEV, EMELYAN, leader of a Cossack rebellion against Catherine's rule

RAZUMOVSKY, ALEXIS, Chamberlain of Empress Elizabeth's household and her lover: the "Emperor of the Night"

RAZUMOVSKY, COUNT ANDRY, Czarevich Paul's best friend and secret lover of Paul's wife, Natalya

RAZUMOVSKY, COUNT CYRIL, commander of the Ismailov Regiment of Guards, the first to swear fealty to Catherine

RIMSKY-KORSAKOV, IVAN, an "adjutant general" to Catherine

ROMODANOVSKY, PRINCE FEODOR, boyhood companion of Peter the Great, later a high officer in his army

SALTIKOV, SERGE, Catherine's first lover and in all probability father of her first child, Paul

SHEREMETOV, FIELD MARSHAL COUNT BORIS, a boyhood friend of Peter the Great and a high commander in his army during the Northern War

SHUVALOV, ALEXANDER, brother of Ivan, and successor to Choglokov as overseer-adviser to Grand Duke Peter

SHUVALOV, IVAN, Gentleman of the Bedchamber to Elizabeth, also probably at one time her lover, leader of one of the "factions" at court

SOPHIA, half sister of Peter the Great, who organized a revolt of the *streltsy* that led to Peter's half brother Ivan's being proclaimed co-czar and herself as regent

SOPHIA, Princess of Württemberg, second wife of Czarevich Paul as Maria Feodorovna

SOPHIA AUGUSTA FREDERIKA, Princess of Anhalt-Zerbst, who became Catherine II

SUVOROV, ALEXANDER, one of Catherine's greatest military commanders

TEPLOV, MME., one of Grand Duke Peter's mistresses

THEODORSKY, SIMON, Orthodox priest who was Catherine's religious instructor

VASILCHIKOV, ALEXANDER, briefly successor to Gregory Orlov as Catherine's favorite

V<small>LADISLAVOV</small>, M<small>ME</small>., successor to Mme. Krause as maid to Grand Duchess Catherine

V<small>OLTAIRE</small>, leading exponent of the Enlightenment and lifelong correspondent with Catherine

W<small>ILHELMINA</small>, Princess of Hesse-Darmstadt; as Natalya, first wife of Czarevich Paul

W<small>ORONOTSOV</small>, P<small>RINCESS</small> E<small>LIZABETH</small>, lady-in-waiting to Grand Duchess Catherine and mistress of Grand Duke Peter

W<small>ORONTSOV</small>, C<small>OUNT</small> R<small>OMAN</small>, Vice-Chancellor of Elizabeth's court

Z<small>AVADOVSKY</small>, P<small>ETER</small>, an "adjutant general" to Catherine

Z<small>ORICH</small>, S<small>IMON</small>, an "adjutant general" to Catherine

Z<small>UDOV</small>, P<small>LATON</small>, last "adjutant general" to Catherine and the cause of her break with Potemkin

Prologue

PETER the Great had been dead for more than fifteen years when the events related in the body of this book begin. But his presence was palpable, as first Elizabeth and then Catherine consciously—even self-consciously—followed his policies and strove to win his goals. Furthermore, Elizabeth was his daughter and in many ways a feminine replica of him physically and temperamentally. The poor, insignificant, German-born princess who came to be Catherine made him her model in many of her pursuits; the inscription she had placed on the magnificent equine statue of him that she commissioned is cryptic but certainly reveals that she closely associated herself with her unsurpassed predecessor. Our story must therefore begin with him.

Peter was enormous, standing close to seven feet tall in his boots. When dressed against the Russian winter in his heavy flowing cape, fur hat, and leather gauntlets, he seemed not merely outsize but twice the size of ordinary mortals. As well as being tall, he was broad-shouldered, big-boned, heavily muscled, and he had the coordination, quick reflexes, and tireless, self-renewing stamina to use this physical machine to the maximum.

He was a restless, hyperactive man driven to keep moving, discovering, challenging, achieving, and, one should add, drinking, carousing, wenching, fighting. Men of normal size and wind had to trot to keep up with him when he walked. He bent horseshoes with his bare hands. He could eat, drink, dance, prank, and debauch all night and waken after a few hours' rest fresh and fit for a hard day's work. None of his friends, tough and robust though most of them were, could keep the pace. In the attempt to do so many were temporarily invalided, and a few simply wore out and died.

He was also an exceptionally handsome man. In repose his face, with its strong regular features, full lips and large, luminous, and slightly protuberant brown eyes, framed by an unruly shock of curly dark hair, had a wild male beauty. But this was marred by uncontrollable spasmodic twitching in the left side of his face and a nervous habit of grimacing and opening his eyes wide, rolling them so that at times only the whites could be seen. Sometimes his arms, legs, or even his whole body would be agitated by spasms.

He was full of incongruities. He combined insensibility with so much sheer brilliance that he was an exhibit not only of a form of greatness, but of how fine a line may separate genius from madness. He was subject to volcanic blind rages, during which he was likely to break anything handy and to batter almost anyone within reach. He was so much the democrat that he served as a foot soldier in his own army and an ordinary seaman in his own navy, advancing himself in rank only when he was truly sure he had earned it. He was so much the autocrat that reverting instantly to his role as Czar when that suited him, he expected instant and total obedience. He mastered twenty-odd trades and skills, from shoemaking to ship carpentry, from watch repairing to dentistry. After visits to an anatomical museum, as one of his biographers writes, "He became so interested in surgery that he considered studying it . . . and, although he could not find the time to do this, he always considered himself competent as a surgeon and readily operated on anyone ill and luckless enough to fall into his hands."

It was almost as if two natures inhabited the same body. He

was a charismatic natural leader who hated to be stared at and fled public attention, a humanist who attached almost fetishistic importance to the values of Western civilization but was gross in his table manners, sometimes dirty in his clothes and person, and disorderly in habits of living. He was usually assertive and fearless, yet he could be so overwhelmed by shyness that when he was presented to stylish European princesses, he put his hands over his face and groaned, "I don't know what to say." He was a man of sentiment, generous, and warmly affectionate with his friends. With his enemies he was ruthless and sometimes could be shockingly cruel.

He had inherited Russia. Almost literally it belonged to him, for in the Russian social order as it then existed everything was suspended in concentric class layers from the central, individual figure of the Czar, or Emperor, whose person was sacred and whose powers were considered God-given. But Peter perceived it as a mean inheritance: shrunken, isolated and vulnerable, deformed in character and crippled by archaic values, lacking status and even any well-defined identity in the world.

His obsessive goal, which became the all-consuming motive of his life, was to restore his inheritance to the greatness and prestige it had once known and at the same time to refashion Russia, its borders, economy, armed forces, social institutions, culture— the whole civilization—into a great and vigorous state respected and feared in the world.

The Russia he wished to restore is known historically as Kievan Russia, after its capital Kiev, nearly 800 miles south of Moscow. From modest beginnings recorded only in ancient, dubious chronicles, Kiev thrived and expanded until by the eleventh century it ruled a vast territory stretching from the Black Sea to the Baltic and from the Carpathians to the Volga. Its nobility had kinship ties with most of the leading dynasties of the West.

Kievan Russia owed its wealth to the fact that it was an aggressive trading state located in a place especially advantageous for trade. The geography was of key importance, and the reason stems from the elementary textbook fact that Europe is a peninsula of the Eurasian continent, bounded on the south by the Black and Mediterranean seas, on the west by the Atlantic, and on the north (apart from the unusable Arctic Ocean) by the Baltic Sea. The northern Baltic water boundary is not quite as long as the southern one; its easternmost extension, which is the Gulf of Finland, ends just beyond the line on a map that marks longitude 30 degrees east. Accordingly, if that line is taken as the neck of the peninsula and measured, the distance from sea to sea is more than 920 statute miles. However, to travel between those same two points by boat, sailing clear around the European peninsula, would be a matter of some 5,500 statute miles, about six times longer. Of course, even so, for a merchant with the problem of getting cargo from one point to the other the greater distance might not be decisive, because hauling cargo across 920 miles of land could turn out to be four—or forty—times as difficult and dangerous. The decisive fact was that the land route was really, in all practical effect, a water route, with the advantages thereof.

Several navigable rivers in this northwest corner of Russia flow north into the Baltic, and following them upstream to their sources, early travelers found the southward-flowing Volga and Dnieper. The Volga never gets to sea water; it veers southeast and ends in the landlocked Caspian Sea. But the Dnieper, a mighty stream fed by a far-branching system of tributaries, draining about a third of Russia, flows into the Black Sea. And so the Dnieper plus the northern rivers and lakes—save only some not very long or difficult overland portages—make a navigable north-south watercourse across the land of Russia, a logical and natural route for commerce between the Baltic and Black Sea regions.

This happy miracle of geography and geology accounted for the existence, growth, and expanding prosperity of Kievan Russia, which owned the whole thoroughfare. It was famous in the world as "the route from the Varangians to the Greeks"—the "Varangians" being the Norse and other peoples of the Baltic region, the "Greeks" being the Byzantines with their empire and great capital of Constantinople.

Kievan culture and its religion were derived primarily from Byzantium, then the biggest, richest, strongest, most energetic, and highly civilized nation of Europe. It was also the greatest trading nation.

A plague of civil wars, changes in the nature and patterns of

European trade, and many other factors combined to destroy Kiev's economic and political primacy in little more than a century. But it was still an important city when a frightful blow fell. In 1240 an army of Tatars, fierce nomads from the central Asian plains, swooped down on Kiev, captured and destroyed it, and massacred its inhabitants. An Italian traveler passing that way a few years later wrote: ". . . we found lying in the field countless heads and bones of dead people; for this city had been extremely large and very populous, whereas now it has been reduced to nothing: barely two hundred houses stand there, and these people are held in the harshest slavery."

By then, so lightning-fast had the Tatar assault and the Kievan collapse occurred, the Tatars had devastated many other cities and populations, had won control of the entire country, and had withdrawn into the southern steppe, which they kept for themselves, as the domain of the Golden Horde. They established their capital in the lower Volga town of Sarai, site-to-be of the twentieth-century city once known as Stalingrad, latterly Volgograd. From there, for some 250 years, they held the rest of Russia as their fiefdom. There the Russian princes and dukes sent their annual tribute payments.

Russian national sovereignty dates from the year—1480—that Czar Ivan III, known as Ivan the Great, defied the Tatar Khan by withholding tribute. By then Tatar power had weakened enough that Ivan's gamble succeeded, but it was so far from finished that Tatar rule in the south, particularly in the Crimea, choking off the southern end of the great trade route "from the Varangians to the Greeks," remained one of the excruciating facts of Russian life for centuries more.

As the Russian-American historian George Fedotov has written: "Kievan Russia, like the golden days of childhood, was never dimmed in the memory of the Russian nation. In the pure fountain of her literary works anyone who wills can quench his religious thirst; in her venerable authors he can find his guide through the complexities of the modern world."

In short, for the people of later Russian eras Kiev was the Lost Paradise. And the "Russian character," that famous opaque conundrum that so continually fascinated European visitors and

Russian novelists, seemed to have a special susceptibility to grieving for lost glories. There were few Russians who were unaffected by this nostalgic golden dream of Kiev—and Peter, a Russian of Russians, mystic and idealist and obsessed patriot, was decidedly not one of those. The Kievan legend was in his bones.

Peter was born on May 30, 1672, in the Terem Palace, the royal residence within the Kremlin, the "high town," the walled and fortified central area of Moscow, capital of the Russian state.

Russia was then, if one included the parts of Siberia it controlled, by far the largest nation in the world. But it was still blocked off from both the Black Sea and the Baltic Sea. All the eastern perimeter of the Baltic was held by Swedes, Germans, and Poles. The northern shores and hinterland of the Black Sea were held by the Tatar Khanate of Crimea. Always formidable, the Crimean Tatars had become even more so when they accepted the suzerainty and protection of the Ottoman Turks, who in the sixteenth century had conquered Byzantium and taken over the empire's territories.

The capital of this vast, hemmed-in nation where Peter was born was a great sprawling city, as large in area as London, though its population was only about 100,000. It was far and away the most populous city in the realm, 99 percent of which was rural, but small by comparison with Western capitals. There were some 40,000 to 50,000 buildings, of which at least 1,500 were churches. All figures of this sort were variable, for the city was built almost wholly of wood; houses, churches, the palaces of the nobles, even the defensive wall that encircled the city were made of logs, stripped or rough-hewn for the rich structures but otherwise with the bark left on. Hence, fire was a continual menace. Thousands of houses and shops and churches burned each year, and it was not uncommon for a quarter or a third of the city to be wiped out in a single conflagration.

It was a strange, exotic city, depressing in its squalor but exciting in its splendors. The raggle-taggle street crowds parted at the approach of a rich boyar, with his high fur hat, his glossy full beard, and his long gown of sumptuous brocade or damask—a costume taken from medieval Byzantium. As one came toward the center of the city, there were many of these nobles and many important functionaries of the church in lavish vestments, mounted on horseback or being drawn in carriages or richly carved and decorated sleighs, accompanied by a retinue of underlings, men-at-arms and servants. These were veritable processions, for the number of attendants was a measure of status; so were the costumes, the jewels, and gold chains, even the height of the hat.

The ultimate degree of magnificent display was by custom attached to all public or official appearances of the Czar. When Peter's father, Czar Alexis, rode the streets, he was accompanied by a thousand horsemen. And "at the presentation of the credentials of the Holstein envoy," as Ian Grey relates, "the Czar sat in a long robe embroidered with pearls and precious stones, wearing a fur cap on top of which rested his crown, while in his right hand he held a golden sceptre. Handsome young nobles stood on both sides of the throne, dressed in long coats of white damask, with caps of lynx-skin, white buskins, and with chains of gold over their chests; each held a silver axe as though in readiness to strike."

The high ceremonial appearances of the patriarch—Muscovy had obtained its own patriarch, and complete autonomy for its branch of the Greek Orthodox Church in 1589—were somewhat less grand but even more ornate in costume and ritual. When Czar or patriarch went forth, and on other holy occasions, the church bells rang and the city and all the sky for miles around were filled with the sound, for there were belfries everywhere. The city was known as "Moscow of the forty forties"—the city of the 1,600 belfries.

Czar Alexis, a good and kindly man—he was called "the gentlest Czar"—was a pious ruler. Prayers at 4 A.M. in his private chapel were followed by matins in one of the churches in the royal palace; then, in late morning, a two-hour mass in a Kremlin church; then an evening service, and nightly prayers in his chapel. During Lent and other high religious festivals he spent nearly the whole day in church, prostrating himself full-length hundreds of times during the intricate rituals of old Byzantium.

It is a superb irony that Alexis, gentle, pious apostle of the past, was the father of Peter, the great iconoclast, the apostle of change. Those of his generation who lived on into Peter's reign may well have seen it as God's special favor that Alexis did not live to see the idols broken. Those of Peter's own generation who shared his work and ambitions may equally have thought it a blessing that Alexis died before he could exercise any influence on his son.

It was Ivan the Great who may be said to have set the stage for Peter's drive to refashion Russia in a modern image. In addition to challenging the Tatars' right to exact tribute from the descendants of Kievan Russia, Ivan brought Western specialists into the country to help it rebuild. He had no choice but to look abroad for architects and engineers, for the technical knowledge no longer existed in his own country. The Italians he hired had to teach again what the Byzantine architects had taught the Kievan Russians almost four centuries earlier. And the same situation existed in almost all fields. The long isolation had so withered progress in the arts and sciences that the reborn state was centuries behind the West, and as this realization slowly, partially penetrated the consciousness of the Czars and their advisers, they perforce recruited foreign experts.

First and mainly they hired military officers, European soldiers of fortune. With the increasing technology of war these warriors made possible, there had to be an armaments industry, so other foreign specialists were hired to open mines, foundries, smithies, and factories for explosives.

The foreign influx grew, not from choice but from need, and was always kept under careful strictures. Even so, the influx and the signs of spreading Western influence caused increasing alarm in the church, among the conservative boyars, and the general population. To protect the foreigners, a special settlement was established for them on the outskirts of Moscow. It became known as the German Quarter because most of the foreigners Ivan settled there were Baltic German mercenaries hired to train and officer the then newly created *streltsy*, the first Russian standing army. The popular name for this suburb, the German district, was "the foreign ignoramus quarter."

In the mid-seventeenth century, in the wake of street battles between foreigners and Muscovites, Czar Alexis issued a ukase that no foreigner could thenceforth buy a house in Moscow proper. The German Quarter thus became a kind of ghetto—but a spacious and pleasant one. By the 1670's and '80's it had a population of some 15,000 to 20,000, predominantly Dutch, English, Scotch, and German, but with some French, Swiss, Italians, Poles, Irish, Scandinavians, and others. All being strangers in a strange land, they submerged their own national biases and lived together in remarkable amity. They made the quarter a pretty town of broad, paved, treelined streets, with neat brick houses built in the Dutch gabled style, each usually with its well-tended garden. There were churches, schools, and the other civilized necessities and amenities: shops that stocked European goods, tailors and dressmakers who made clothes in the current Western fashion (couriers arrived every few days with books and mail), and even musicians and actors.

This foreign quarter was to prove crucial to the education of the boy who would become Peter the Great.

Czar Alexis died when Peter was four and was succeeded by the older son of Alexis' first wife, who briefly reigned as Feodor II. On his death Peter was proclaimed Czar under the regency of his mother, Natalya, Alexis' second wife. He was then ten. Three weeks later, his scheming half sister, Sophia, wanting power for herself and her side of the family, instigated a palace revolution by the *streltsy* in favor of her fifteen-year-old feebleminded brother Ivan, who had been passed over in the succession.

Peter stood with his mother, Natalya, on the Red Staircase leading to the Facets Palace in the Kremlin and watched, immobilized with terror, as men of the *streltsy* seized first their own commandant, then his mother's chief adviser, then others of his supporters, and flung them from the top of the staircase to be impaled on the halberds of other guardsmen below, who savaged and dismembered their bodies, painting the courtyard with blood. For three days the carnage went on as the *streltsy* ransacked the palace for Natalya's brothers, whom he loved, and others whom Sophia denounced to them.

Afterward Peter developed the spasmodic twitching and strange rolling of the eyes that afflicted and disfigured him all his life. And from that time on he hated the sight of this palace, which contained his throne room, and the sight of the Kremlin and stayed away as much as official duties allowed. He was never fully to trust any of the *streltsy* again.

As a result of this revolt, Ivan was proclaimed co-Czar, Sophia became Regent and *de facto* chief of state. (In other words, as historian Joseph Reither has noted, Peter "became half-czar along with his half-witted half-brother.") Peter's mother, Natalya, fearing to stay on in the Kremlin, had withdrawn with him and his younger sister to a modest estate in the village of Preobrazhensky near Moscow. There he spent his boyhood and early youth, returning to Moscow only for state ceremonials.

Easily visible from the hilltop estate, and only two miles away, lay the German Quarter. Naturally it aroused his curiosity, which turned to fascination as he found there were men there who could teach him things he wanted to know and about which he was frustratingly unable to learn from any of his countrymen. He was precociously intelligent, and his eagerness for knowledge was whetted by the lack of any formal curriculum except reading, writing, arithmetic, and religious studies, and so little of the first three that even in his teens he read and wrote with difficulty and knew only addition and subtraction. But from the age of twelve, with the help of skilled craftsmen enlisted from the German Quarter, he was learning trades.

The records show that he first ordered a set of stonemason's tools, a few months later printing equipment, then a set of carpenter's tools, then equipment for a smithy. When he was sixteen, the Muscovite ambassador to France brought him an astrolabe, an instrument for measuring altitudes and distances, but could not explain how it worked. To find out, Peter again had to turn to the German Quarter. A Dutchman there, Franz Timmerman, could teach him, but to do so first had to teach him elementary geography, geometry, and the rest of his arithmetic. Peter hired him as his tutor. A man of parts, Timmerman instructed him also in cabinetmaking, the manufacture of fireworks, and the sciences of fortification and artillery fire.

One day, as Peter and Timmerman were exploring the outbuild-

ings of one of the Romanov ancestral estates, they came across
the decaying hulk of a small sailboat.

The Kievan Russians, of course, had known the elements of
sailing, but this was another of the lost skills, like the uses of stone
in architecture. The only boats Peter knew were the flat-bottomed
riverboats that had to be rowed, and he was thunderstruck when
Timmerman told him that this craft of English or Dutch design
could move not only with wind, but actually against the wind.
Peter was eager to try it. Timmerman produced a friend from
the quarter, another Dutchman named Karsten Brandt, who re-
paired and rigged the boat and showed Peter how to handle it. At
Peter's insistence, Brandt subsequently took him to a large lake
some 50 miles north of Moscow, to teach him how to sail.

This was the beginning of a lifelong fascination with ships and
the sea, the beginning, in fact, of the Russian Navy and of the
idée fixe that led to the founding of Peter's naval base and sea-
port which grew into his capital city, St. Petersburg. There, many
years later, he brought the little sailboat and installed it in a special pavilion, with solemn ceremony, as "the grandfather of the
Russian Navy."

From earliest childhood Peter had loved playing soldier, and he
had unusual facilities for his games; he could call on the Kremlin
arsenal to lend him equipment or to manufacture special items
to order. When he was ten, he ordered a pair of full-scale, horse-
drawn cannon, quite realistic except that the barrels were made
of wood lined with iron. For his eleventh birthday he gave himself
real cannon.

Some time before he had begun organizing his playmates into
small-boy "armies." So long as he lived in the palace, his "troops"
were the highborn sons of courtiers. But at Preobrazhensky the
"court" was miniscule. So Peter sought out the sons of the grooms
and servants and tradesmen for his games and then soon called
for volunteers from all the boys of the village and of a neighboring
one named Semenovsky. Thus he filled his play armies with a
cross section of the Muscovite social hierarchy, from young princes
to street urchins, and so he learned a truly revolutionary lesson:
He learned to judge people not on the basis of their origins and
titles but by their qualities as individuals.

The play troops grew in numbers and in military proficiency as Peter grew in years. By the time he was seventeen he could muster close to a thousand youths and young men in two fully equipped and smartly trained regiments named the Preobrazhensky and the Semenovsky, for the two villages where they had their headquarters. They were no longer play troops. They were to become the solid, dependable core of Peter's army.

Now word reached Peter that Regent Sophia had ordered him assassinated. He panicked. Coatless, he fled on horseback from Moscow to the monastery-convent of Holy Trinity-St. Sergius, one of the holiest places of Russia and a citadel—actually a town in itself—for those in need of refuge. There a few of his closest associates found him and persuaded him that he could mount a coup against his half sister. He had the two play regiments he could rely on, and messages were sent out to other military commanders to ask for their help. Enough was forthcoming.

When Peter rode in triumph into Moscow, the streets were lined with members of the *streltsy*, kneeling in fealty and to signify their request for pardon for what they had done in the revolt of seven years before. Peter's half-witted half brother, Ivan, renounced all claims to the throne. Peter sent Sophia off to a nunnery for the rest of her days.

That year he followed his mother's wishes and married a girl she had selected for him. Eudokia Lopukhin was a girl of the conservative nobility, young, reasonably pretty and altogether well meaning, but she lacked spirit and imagination and suffered from incurable banality. She could not understand Peter's ideas and motives; to the extent that she did, she disapproved. After she produced two children, the ill-fated Czarevich Alexis and another boy named Alexander, who died in childhood, Peter had little more to do with her. Eventually he divorced her.

The most profound influences on Peter during the early years of his life were people from the German Quarter. General Patrick Gordon, a cultivated Scotsman, senior officer of the army, became a surrogate father, on whom Peter could lavish the affection that he had never had a chance to bestow on his own father.

François Lefort, a Swiss soldier of fortune then in his early thirties, was like a beloved, understanding, fascinating older brother to Peter. Through Lefort, Peter met the daughter of a German wine merchant of the quarter, a beautiful blonde named Anna Mons, who was to be his mistress for ten years.

Lefort was an habitual two-fisted drinker, although not an alcoholic. Peter, at the age of eighteen, took to strong drink and all-night carousing as if these had been invented for him. Lefort was an antic rebel against the Calvinism of his native Geneva, where the spirit of perdition hung as heavily as the traditions of Orthodoxy in Moscow. Abetted by Lefort and other irreverent friends, Peter's sense of humor produced slapstick travesties of Orthodoxy's elaborate ceremonials and, for that matter, of the Byzantine pomp and circumstance of czarist court life.

He formed a mock hierarchy from patriarch to priest, complete with vestments and rituals, which he convened for riotous evenings as the Universal Joking and Drinking Assembly. One of his former tutors presided as "Prince-Pope" or "Prince-Patriarch." As the corresponding head of state, Peter appointed a somewhat solemn and conservative friend, Prince Feodor Romodanovsky, as "Prince Caesar" or "King" and insisted that all address him as "Your Majesty." Peter himself, serving as a "loyal subject," deferred to Romodanovsky and faithfully reported to him about his plans and activities. In place of the Kremlin court, which he allowed to wither, he formed what was known simply as the Company, consisting of people he liked and trusted, Muscovites and foreigners.

The first important act of Peter's reign was a campaign against the Turkish bastion of Azov, near the mouth of the Don, an attempt in a renewed war to break through to the south. This campaign was successful, but only temporarily. The Turks were still the strongest military power in the world, and they refused to accept the loss of Azov. They would not make peace or even accept a truce. Peter was faced with the prospect of a long, expensive war in which, if Russia had to fight it alone, he could not be at all sure of the outcome. He needed allies, and therefore he decided to send a Grand Embassy of his most trusted advisers to the major capitals of Europe to construct a coalition against Turkey. And then he decided to go along himself. He would not go as the Czar, but incognito, as a member of the embassy suite, one of the thirty-five young men who had "volunteered" (at his command) to study Western European technical and military skills. His name would be Peter Mikhailov.

It was one of the great pranks of all time, undertaken with the most serious purpose and having the most serious results. As the English historian Thomas Babington Macaulay said, Peter's trip began "an epoch in the history not only of his own country, but of . . . the whole world."

On March 9, 1698, the Grand Embassy left Moscow. It must have looked more like an army than an embassy. It had a baggage train of a thousand wagons, some loaded with food and supplies, some with gold, silver, and bales of sable furs for the purchase of the many items Peter had in mind and others that predictably he would discover—and did, in vast variety, including parrots, monkeys, and two little black boys. Other wagons were left empty to receive these purchases. Besides hostlers, grooms and servants, there were some 250 people attached to the embassy.

Peter wanted the knowledge of the West, and he approached it the way a famished man might approach a banquet table, wanting it all. During eighteen months of travel on a route that took him through the Swedish Baltic provinces, Prussia and other north German states, Holland, England, Austria, and Saxony, his interest remained omnivorous and insatiable.

In Riga he was nearly shot by a Swedish sentry who discovered him measuring the depth of the moat around a fortress. Visiting mills and factories in England, he was impatient with mere explanations of machines and processes; he wanted—and got— models, working drawings, exact procedures and specifications. On his first night in Dresden he was suddenly overtaken by a great desire to see the city's famous museum of art and science. Although it was past midnight, the museum was opened for him, and the curator and Prince Fürstenberg, his official host, were obliged by courtesy to spend the rest of the night roaming the halls with him.

He stayed for four months in Amsterdam, going through the whole process of shipbuilding, from the laying of the keel to launching, and was duly awarded a certificate of proficiency as a practical shipwright.

Politically the Grand Embassy was not a grand success. In Prussia, Frederick III showed no interest in Peter's plan for an anti-Turkish coalition but urged him to join in an alliance against Sweden. In Holland the States-General was politely equivocal, going only so far as to indicate it might help the Muscovites with naval equipment to some extent sometime in the future. In England, where Peter went in January, 1698, King William III, William of Orange, was a perfect host. He presented Peter with a beautiful twenty-gun yacht, had his portrait done by Sir Godfrey Kneller, the most admired portrait painter of the realm, staged full-scale fleet battle maneuvers for his benefit, cordially agreed to let English technical experts of all sorts take service in Moscow, and gave him every facility for seeing English life and institutions: Parliament, Oxford, the Greenwich Observatory, Woolwich Arsenal, the Mint, the Tower of London, Windsor Castle. He also arranged for him to continue his studies of shipbuilding at Deptford and gave him and his companions the use of a splendid estate adjoining the naval yards, Sayes Court. (Here, incidentally the house and magnificent gardens were left half wrecked. The damage to the holly hedges was apparently caused by Peter's being pushed through them full-tilt in a vehicle new to the Muscovites, the wheelbarrow.)

But King William, far from wanting to join in fighting the Turks, was in fact trying to secure peace between Turkey and its current major enemy, the Austro-Hungarian Empire. The reason behind this was that Louis XIV of France was preparing to install his grandson on the throne of Spain and the other powers were preparing to prevent it. The outcome was one of Europe's longer and bloodier wars, the War of the Spanish Succession. William wanted to stabilize relations with the Turks so that all available strength could be concentrated against France. It was another penalty of Russia's isolation that Peter had come to Europe without a proper understanding of this situation and the obstacles it would present to his mission.

He went on to Vienna. There, too, negotiations for help against the Turks became clogged. The Austrian Foreign Minister at last said plainly that a peace conference was in the offing and advised Peter to join it. With this Peter finally had to admit to himself that the Grand Embassy was a failure.

He was preparing to go on to Venice, where he might still find support and which he wanted in any case to see, when a courier arrived from Moscow with a message from ("Prince-Caesar") Romodanovsky, whom Peter had made governor of the city during his absence: Four regiments of the *streltsy* had revolted and were marching on Moscow.

This news reawakened in Peter the most horrid memories of his life. He canceled his trip to Venice and left hurriedly for Moscow. A few days later in Poland a message reached him that the revolt had been put down and the leaders executed. He paused long enough for meetings with Frederick Augustus of Saxony and Poland and then went on to Moscow. He arrived after nightfall. Avoiding the Kremlin, he passed through the city without attracting attention, tarried awhile in the German Quarter with Anna Mons, and went on to Preobrazhensky—home after seventeen months and seventeen days.

The news of his return spread in the capital overnight, and next morning the patriarch, Romodanovsky, and all the other dignitaries of the court came in a swelling throng to welcome him back and pay homage. When they prostrated themselves before him—a relic of the Tatar era, copied from the court of the khans and incorporated into czarist ritual—he bade them rise and kissed them. Then, when they were all assembled, he took a pair of long shears and passed from one to another, cutting off their beards, sparing only the patriarch and two old boyars. Peter went about his work silently smiling. They submitted to it as martyrs, too shocked for words. The remaking of Muscovy into a modern state had begun at that moment, because the beard was a symbol of Muscovy's medieval Byzantine past. Peter's defoliation of the dignitaries was thus a dramatic way of serving notice that the long era of addiction to the past was finished.

Later he made a similar assault on that other most conspicuous symbol of old Muscovy: the flowing, full-sleeved, ornate gowns of the boyars. At a banquet he again produced his shears and went around snipping surplus material from the sleeves. "See, these things are in your way," he said. "Get gaiters made of them." Later he issued ukases prohibiting long beards and requiring caftans and coats to be knee-length.

These were tokens of the scores and hundreds of changes that Peter now imposed with a rapidity that left most of his subjects dizzied and scandalized. There were storms of resentment. An interested observer, the Khan of Crimea, wrote to his patron, the Sultan of Turkey, "The Czar is destroying the old customs and faith of his people; he is altering everything according to German methods and is creating a powerful army and fleet, thereby annoying everyone; sooner or later he will perish at the hands of his own subjects." But Peter survived, using the traditional awesomeness of his authority as Czar for all it was worth, reinforcing it with the awesome force of his own personality and by the calculated use of sheer terror.

He destroyed the *streltsy*. A thousand or so were executed in Red Square, and more than a hundred were beheaded over an open trench at Preobrazhensky in a macabre bloodletting. Peter himself wielded an ax. Many others were hanged on gallows specially built near the nunnery where his half sister, Sophia, was serving her unwilling devotions. Finally, three were hanged and left to swing from a gallows built directly outside Sophia's window. In this horrible fashion the horror on the Red Staircase was avenged. When he had finished, Peter disbanded what remained of the Moscow *streltsy* regiments and exiled the men and their families to Astrakhan, Siberia, and other far-off places. Later he disbanded all the other *streltsy* regiments in the country.

He was equally ruthless with individuals who stood in his way. He dominated the state, the church, and his 15,000,000 subjects with a degree of tyranny never achieved by anyone before in Russia. He wrenched old Muscovy, groaning and protesting, from its vapid dreaming of a false past and resurrected the spirit that had animated Kievan Russia. This was the true result of Peter's journey.

Failing to assemble an anti-Turkish coalition, Peter resignedly made peace with the Turks on the best terms he could get. He had to give up Azov, as well as Turkish forts his troops had taken on the lower Dnieper, and to put aside temporarily his hopes for regaining an opening to the Black Sea.

So he reversed the direction of his ambition: He set out to regain access to the Baltic, the other end of the old Kievan Russian trade route. The lands there were held by the current descendants of some of those same "Varangians" who had explored the rivers and helped found the earlier Russia: the Swedes. The Swedes' young King, Charles XII, only eighteen years old when Peter invaded his Baltic provinces, turned out to be an astonishingly gifted military leader. Moreover, he was as vital and bold in character as Peter and had an equal sense of patriotic mission. He had inherited one of the major empires and one of the strongest fighting forces of Europe. He was proud, willful, and fearless —so much so that he was in the thick of every battle he fought, exposing himself to danger with such contempt and such invariable success that he soon had a reputation of being indestructible and invincible.

When the war began—history knows it as the Northern War— he moved with dazzling speed against Peter's allies, the King of Denmark and King Frederick Augustus of Saxony and Poland. He knocked Denmark out of the war entirely, smashed Frederick Augustus' invasion of the Swedish Baltic province of Livonia, moved on to defeat Peter's forces catastrophically in their first encounter. Then he turned back to Poland and Saxony to settle accounts with Frederick Augustus. He planned to return to finish off Peter and the Muscovites at his leisure.

Peter and his generals, rallying within the year, won a series of victories over Swedish forces in the eastern Baltic and won control over the territory of the Neva River. On an island in the delta of the Neva, on May 16, 1703, Peter started work on a fortress and port to be named after his patron saint, St. Petersburg—or, as he called it in Dutch, the language he now used often in preference to Russian, Sankt-Piterburkh, or Peterburkh.

It was a most unlikely place to build a city. Neva is a Finnish word meaning mud. The low-lying delta, with a number of islands formed by the river as it divides and subdivides in a maze of watercourses seeking the sea, was marshy land at best, afflicted by fogs and rain, and subject to periodic unpredictable flooding when storms turned the river into a torrent which inundated the islands and made them mud. The islands were inhabited only by a few Finnish fishermen who subsisted precariously and left whenever the waters rose. The Swedes had built a fortress there and another one upstream near Lake Ladoga. They had held these posts tenaciously against many Muscovite attacks in the past because the Neva and Ladoga gave them the best access to the interior. In the days of Kievan Russia, most of the goods that went out to the world from Novgorod, the northern anchor of the Dnieper route, went by way of this lake, this river, and through this delta. In building a fortress and port there, Peter was in effect reestablishing Novgorod and moving it to the Baltic shore.

Across the main branch of the Neva, facing the fortress, he built his Admiralty—the second great landmark of the city of the future. Army fortress, naval base, commercial port—the marshy settlement, filled in with dirt carried from the mainland by thousands of workmen in bags, or even in their own blouses, soon had its own dynamics of growth. Peter began to see it as a potential Amsterdam, which also had been retrieved from the sea. He had canals dug; he planned three main semicircular canals and many smaller, connecting ones.

Peter's first house in St. Petersburg, built in two days after he began to work on the fortress, had only three small rooms: a bedroom, dining room, and study. It was of pine boards painted on the outside to make it look as if it had brick walls and tile roof, like a little Dutch house.

Having secured his outlet to the Baltic, Peter would have liked nothing better than to make peace. He would have given up all his other gains and even paid compensation if he could have kept St. Petersburg, the Neva, and Ladoga. He tried every tangent and intermediary he could think of to persuade Charles.

Charles could not be persuaded. He expelled Frederick Augustus from the Polish throne, followed him into Saxony, and imposed an ignominious peace on him. Then he turned again toward Russia. Peter decided on a policy that combined prudence with ruthlessness: He would retreat, avoiding pitched battle indefinitely until a time and place of his choosing, but while retreating, he would "scorch the earth," leaving nothing for Charles'

advancing army—no villages for shelter, no livestock for the troops
to forage, and no fodder for the animals. Thus he would make
Charles dependent on an ever-lengthening supply line from his
bases in Poland and Saxony.

Peter applied his tactics without let or remorse, burning and
destroying, retreating, harassing the Swedish flanks methodically
for hundreds of miles. Advancing northeast toward St. Petersburg, then veering east toward Moscow, Charles decided to
turn south to the steppes. There, he calculated, he could rest his
troops and animals and receive reinforcements and supplies. It
was a fatal mistake.

Peter intercepted and defeated the reinforcements and captured the supply train they escorted.

That winter was the coldest within memory. All Europe froze,
and in the normally temperate southern steppe, where there was
no natural protection at all, it was said that sentries froze in their
tracks and birds in flight fell from the sky, lumps of frozen
feathers and blood. To spend a night in the open was almost
certain death. To walk even a few miles in the open was to invite
frostbite and gangrene. Both armies suffered, but the Swedes
suffered more. Though they were northerners, they were not prepared for the weather and had no means of getting protective
clothing. When the spring rains began, the steppe turned into a
muddy gumbo and the rivers flooded, immobilizing both armies,
but again to the main disadvantage of the Swedes, whose forte
was quick maneuver. Swedish supplies were thinning dangerously.
Charles' generals urged him to retreat as soon as the ground became passable. His pride would not permit it, and instead, he
moved even farther south to lay siege to a commercial center
and fortress town where he expected to find provisions. This was
a place called Poltava.

For Peter, the time had come. The Battle of Poltava, a decisive
one in world history, began at nine in the morning of June 27,
1709; by noon the power structure of Europe had been changed.
The Swedish Army was shattered, and with it Sweden's long-held
position as the dominant power of the north. That role passed to
Russia. Peter this day indeed projected his country into the affairs

of Europe "like a launched ship," as Pushkin wrote, "accompanied by the noise of . . . firing guns."

Although *de facto* commander in chief during the battle, he had served with the nominal rank of colonel, having advanced slowly in grade from bombardier. He now allowed himself—on petition from his troops and officers—to be promoted to high rank, on the basis of merit demonstrated in battle. He became a lieutenant general in his army and a rear admiral in his navy, which pleased him very much.

Charles had managed to escape with a few of his men to Turkish territory. Being as temperamentally incapable as Peter of admitting defeat, Charles made difficulties for Peter as long as he lived, which was close to another decade.

And Peter found that by defeating the invincible Charles and upsetting the power structure of Europe, he and Russia were now suddenly the objects of universal nervous fears, which gave rise to all manner of maneuvers, secret alliances, and shifting cabals to limit and neutralize Russian strength. To be part of Europe was to be part of European power politics. Thus it was a long time— actually another dozen years—before his great victory brought him peace. However, with the capture of the Swedish fortresses at Riga and Vyborg—"two strong pillows for St. Petersburg," he wrote—and other eastern Baltic towns during a massive mopping-up operation accomplished during the next year, he could consider the fledgling city he called "paradise" reasonably safe and could take time to make it even more paradisiacal.

In 1712, to build the human resources of his city with the same intractable, ruthless, driving determination with which he created the land itself and the structures on it, he ordered 1,000 men of the lesser nobility to come with their families from Moscow to St. Petersburg. They were to build houses on the mainland side of the Neva and live there. A similar order went to 500 merchants and 500 shopkeepers. Another commanded the migration of several thousand workers skilled in a wide assortment of trades and crafts. The orders were issued in April. The men and their families—the total number of persons unknown, but by reasonable guess perhaps 20,000 or so—were to move and settle in before winter. The men were not consulted; they were drafted, having been specifically and individually chosen by the Senate, a council of ten eminent men formed the year before by Peter to help him govern.

With the Senate in Moscow, however, and Peter avoiding that city as much as possible, liaison was poor, and the Senate functioned inefficiently. Therefore, in that same year of 1712, he ordered the senators also to leave Moscow and reestablish themselves permanently in St. Petersburg. He also declared St. Petersburg the capital of Russia.

To make it easier to drain the resources of Moscow toward St. Petersburg, Peter directed Farquharson, a Scots engineer and mathematician he had recruited in England during the Grand Embassy, to build a direct highway between the two cities. It was a huge undertaking, but at the cost of vast labor, expense and hardship it was done in a few years. Such was the human cost that by the time St. Petersburg and all the rest of Peter's projects had been built, he had lost more lives than he had at Poltava.

Also in the year 1712, in a special public pronouncement and a special church ceremony, Peter acknowledged his marriage to a young peasant woman called Catherine. He had in fact been married to her for five years. She had been his mistress for five years before and had already borne him eight children, five of them before the secret marriage that he now made public.

Almost nothing is certain about Catherine's origins. Probably she was born illegitimately in 1684 or 1685 of Lithuanian peasant stock in the region later called Estonia. Her family name, or at any rate the name she used, was Skavronskaya. Her given name was Martha. Her mother died when she was only three, and she grew up in East Prussia in the Swedish fortress town of Marienburg in the household of a scholarly Lutheran pastor, Ernst Gluck. Pastor Gluck had a large family and took in Martha as an act of charity, although later, as she became old enough, she earned her keep as a servant girl in the house and nursemaid for the younger children. It is indicative of her position that while Gluck himself was a linguist and man of intellectual attainments and had a resident tutor for his own children, he did not think it necessary to teach her anything except the catechism. So to the end of her days she remained illiterate.

In 1702, the second year of the Northern War, Marienburg fell to Russian troops commanded by Peter's old friend Field Marshal Count Boris Sheremetov. Pastor Gluck, accompanied by his family and household, managed to cross to the Russian lines before the surrender and to present himself to Sheremetov with an offer to serve as a translator. During this interview, it is related, Sheremetov's manner was gracious, but his attention was distracted by Martha. She was then a little past seventeen, a beautiful, dark-haired, dark-eyed girl with a pert nose and lively expression, rosy lips and a fine, full figure. Sheremetov asked about her and learned that she was only a servant. The outcome was that he sent the family Gluck to Moscow (where, the next year, Peter gave Pastor Gluck money to found a school and an aristocrat's mansion to house it). But Sheremetov informed Gluck it would be necessary that Martha stay on with him, as he had need of a housekeeper.

She remained with Sheremetov, sharing his military campaigning and his bed, for the next six months. Then Alexander Menshikov saw her, and he began trying to get her for himself.

Besides their admiration for Martha, the two men had a few other things in common. Both were in their forties at the time, making them some twenty-five years older than she and a dozen years or so older than Peter. Both had joined Peter's cause when he was still the boy-Czar, both were charter members of his Preobrazhensky Regiment, both had already served him brilliantly, and both were among his few most trusted colleagues.

Beyond these similarities, it would be hard to think of two men more different. Sheremetov was the product of a great boyar family with a lineage easily as aristocratic as the Romanovs'. Menshikov's antecedents (like Martha's) were so dim that two centuries of scholarship have failed to establish the date and place of his birth and his parentage.

Menshikov was illiterate. Through a long life and fabulous career, he learned to read a little and to write his name and a few simple, useful words and expressions.

Sheremetov was a man of honor and personal integrity, with a strong devotion to his Czar and his country—a robust, energetic, hard-driving field commander who could take his hardships and pleasures as they came, but who eschewed pleasures that interfered with duty. Menshikov was thoroughly corrupt. Peter was often angry with him, and sometimes furious. Discovering him in some particularly florid instance of wrongdoing, Peter was known to cuff him, kick him, knock him down, or even thrash him with a heavy stick. Yet Peter could not do without him. Peter always addressed his communications to Sheremetov formally (in a kind of Dutch) *Min Herr General Feltmarshzal*, but when he wrote to Menshikov it was to *Mein Bruder*, "My brother."

When Menshikov visited Sheremetov's headquarters a few months later, the two met as equals. It was then that Menshikov encountered and was smitten by the lovely young woman we will henceforth call Catherine.

It was said that Menshikov bought her. And it is easily credible that money changed hands, for by law she literally belonged to Sheremetov as a prize of war, if he claimed her. Further, her peasant origins and her status as a house servant with the Gluck family would have made her, in the Russian view, the equivalent to a serf, and serfs were chattels. But Sheremetov was very fond of her and would not have parted with her without her consent.

When he did, it is known, it was with considerable feeling of irritation. From the circumstances it would appear that Menshikov wooed her and that she responded, in effect making her own choice between the sophisticated, somewhat austere aristocrat and the earthy, charming, illiterate plebeian, with whom no doubt she could feel far more at ease.

Menshikov and she lived together for some months. Menshikov was on the move, on various assignments from Peter, with his own staff and headquarters. She accompanied him as circumstances allowed. Some time in 1703, Peter arrived unexpectedly at Menshikov's headquarters of the moment. That evening at supper, it is related, he noticed her among the several women who served the officers' table. His orderly at the time, a Breton soldier of fortune named De Villabois, reported this historic first encounter: "The Sovereign looked at her often, questioned her, found her intelligent and finished his jesting with her by saying that when he retired to bed it must be she who carried the torch to his room. It was an order without appeal, although delivered with a smile."

In the course of a robust, intensely active life filled with opportunities for dalliance, Peter had had many experiences of just such a casual nature as this night with Martha promised to be. He was a bachelor. He had begun the liaison with Anna Mons before his brief marriage to Eudokia. He continued it until approximately this time. In his fashion he was faithful to Anna, and he assumed that she was completely faithful to him despite his frequent long absences. He was shocked when he discovered she was having an affair with the Prussian Ambassador, Kaiserling—shocked and, moreover, deeply hurt, for he thought of her as his wife in all but name. The outcome was that he left Anna Mons, taking away the large estate and diamond-framed miniature portrait of himself but letting her keep the palace and the large treasure of jewels that he had given her.

Some months after encountering Catherine, during which he shared her with Menshikov, he took her for his own. And regardless of the simple carnality of their relationship at the beginning, it is altogether evident that it developed into love.

By all accounts, Catherine was exceedingly good-tempered, "obliging and civil to all, and never forgetful of her former condition." She was also merry, kind, loving, forgiving. She had native intelligence and practical common sense. She was entirely womanly, and in a guileless and natural way she knew and used all the womanly resources with a sure sense of the suitable time, place, and circumstances. She could be soft as velvet, seductive, and yielding. She could also be tough as iron.

She went with Peter on some of his campaigns, most famously in 1711 when the Turks, egged on by Charles XII, the Khan of Crimea, and some European powers, renewed their chronic war with Russia. Peter hurried south with too small an army and insufficient preparation and found himself surrounded by an overwhelmingly superior Turkish force, faced with catastrophe. Catherine shared the hardships of the march with him, kept her own courage, and encouraged him in a singularly bloody battle which cost many thousands of lives on both sides. Instead of showing fear of her own grim prospects in the event of Turkish capture, she became a source of reassurance and good hope for Peter and his despairing generals. Catherine's stalwart behavior in that time of crisis earned Peter's everlasting admiration and gratitude. His losses were great, but he survived with his army to fulfill his hope, as he wrote to General-Admiral Stefan Apraxin, that "this loss will lead to great strengthening in another quarter, which will be an incomparable gain to us"—St. Petersburg and the Baltic. And for this he always gave the major credit to Catherine.

She had the even more remarkable courage to stand steady in the face of Peter's wild, demented rages, when he was quite capable of any kind of cruelty and destructive violence. What was even more remarkable is that she had the power to calm him. And she knew how to forestall these tantrums, for usually they were preceded by a violent headache. When she recognized the signs she would take him aside, sit with him, draw his tormented head to her bosom, and gently stroke his brow until he fell asleep—to awaken there, perhaps hours later, with the pain and the nightmare gone. She was "the friend of his heart," his *Ekaterinoushka*, his "little mother."

And so, when Peter built a winter palace and a summer palace and a summer garden in St. Petersburg, they were for Catherine, as well as himself. She became Peter's mistress in the spring or summer of 1703, shortly after he founded the city. Possibly Peter built his first little three-room cottage for her. At any rate, she was there with him from time to time, though her usual residence was Moscow, in Menshikov's house, a large domicile Peter had given Menshikov.

Peter made the house his home whenever he was in Moscow, as did Menshikov. There Catherine bore her first five children. It was after the first birth, when she was received into the Orthodox Church, that she dropped the name Martha and was rechristened Ekaterina, or Catherine.

As often as Catherine's pregnancies and the fortunes of Peter's wars permitted, they were together in St. Petersburg. There, in November, 1707, they were married privately in the Cathedral of the Holy Trinity, the first sizable church built in the city and always Peter's favorite and personal place of worship. During the next two years, he was almost continually in the field against Charles XII.

It was in February, 1712, that Peter made public his marriage to Catherine, and in that spring that the Summer Palace was finished and ready for occupancy. They moved in—their first home as acknowledged man and wife. Of the five children, two had survived, Anna and Elizabeth. For these little girls, suddenly elevated to the status of princesses, the Summer Palace was their first real home.

Peter was soon led to the countryside by Catherine. He was absent for some months during 1714–15, and when he returned, she told him she had found a place not far away from the city, yet so pleasant that she felt sure that when he saw it, he would want to build a summer home there. The next day she took him to her "discovery," eight miles down the coast, where he found a delightful park and large villa. "This is the place which I told you about," she said, "and here is the country palace which I have built for my master." She took him then to a point of land from which he could see the spires of St. Petersburg in the distance. He was immensely pleased and so touched that he made the palace her personal property, and it became known as the Catherine Palace.

These were pleasant and rewarding family interludes in Peter's crowded life. At about this time, however, another family matter came to a climax of a far different sort. This concerned Peter's son, Alexis.

When Peter forced Alexis' mother into a convent he kept the boy with him. The Czarevich had various tutors, including some priestly ones. Somehow it happened that he grew up estranged from all his father's hopes, ideals, goals. His intellectual interests and tastes were theological. He married and had two children, Natalya and Peter. After his wife, a German princess and sister-in-law of the Emperor of Austria, died in childbirth, Alexis drifted into debauchery and idleness, though Peter had appointed him governor of the city of Moscow.

Peter's reforms had made all kinds of enemies for him, among the nobility, in the church of course, and among the Old Believers of the lower classes. All these dissidents, and more, began to look to Alexis as their leader against Peter and the new Russia he was building.

Peter was enraged by Alexis' disinterest in government, his distaste for soldiering. In the fall of 1715 he wrote his heir a long letter reciting a lengthy list of his inadequacies and shortcomings and threatening to disinherit him. Alexis in his reply offered to renounce his rights to the throne.

In this dilemma Peter apparently decided that Alexis would have to forswear his rights and retire to a monastery so as to diminish his threat as a potential center of rebellion. But Peter also apparently decided to play for time. Alexis abruptly changed his mind. Invited to join his father in Copenhagen, he fled instead to Austria, to his brother-in-law.

Now Peter was forced to act, and he acted draconically.

Alexis was coaxed back to Russia with promises of amnesty. In the Cathedral of the Assumption in Moscow, he publicly renounced his claim to the succession and agreed to denounce those who sided with him. (These included his mother, with whom he had been in correspondence.) Nevertheless, he was imprisoned in the Fortress of Peter and Paul—the first political prisoner to be immured there. This happened on June 24, 1717. On the same day, a court of more than 100 members convened by Peter ordered that Alexis be executed for treason.

Before that could happen, he was put to torture, first by the knout and then by the rack.

The latter was applied to Alexis two days after the guilty and death verdict of the court. Peter was present. The archives of the fortress are laconic in describing what happened: "The rack was applied at eleven o'clock. . . . That same day, at six o'clock in the afternoon, the Czarevich gave up his soul."

The war with the Swedes had gone on interminably. Finally, consistent Russian victories and shrewd, tireless diplomacy brought hostilities to a close on August 30, 1721. For Peter this was the end of twenty-one years of physical and emotional ordeal which had severely weakened his giant frame and several times had brought him close to death.

For Russia, this was the end of the quest of centuries, a secure outlet to the Baltic and to Europe.

Peter was traveling when the news of the treaty arrived from his plenipotentiaries. He hurried back to St. Petersburg, sailing into the harbor amid a din of celebration. Followed by a great throng, he walked from the wharf to the Cathedral of the Holy Trinity to give thanks. After the service General-Admiral Apraxin and the other senior officers of the navy petitioned him to accept a new rank in their service, the highest of all. With the final victory won, and thus with a good conscience, he did so, becoming Admiral of the Red Flag. The following month, on petition from the Senate and representatives of the nobility and the church, he went again to Holy Trinity to hear his Grand Chancellor, Count Gavril Golovkin, a friend from earliest childhood and an original member of the play troops, declare: "By your untiring labors and by your sole leadership, we have stepped forth from the darkness of insignificance and ignorance onto the road of glory and have joined in equality with the civilized states of Europe . . . how can we render our proper gratitude? . . . We take it upon ourselves in the name of all ranks of the subjects of Your Majesty, humbly to pray you . . . to take this title . . . Father of the Fatherland, Peter the Great, Emperor of All Russia!"

Two years afterward, by ukase Peter shared his acclaim with Catherine. His declaration said: "Our best beloved spouse, consort, and Empress Catherine has been a great support to us . . . also in many military operations, putting aside womanly weakness, of her own will she has been present with us and has helped in every way possible . . . and so, for these labors of our spouse, we have decided that by virtue of the supreme power given us by God she shall be crowned. . . ."

As if to give the coronation of the sometime waif, peasant serving girl, and camp follower all the emphasis that history and tradition could convey, Peter held the ceremony not in his beloved St. Petersburg, but in Moscow—in the Kremlin—and repeated in every detail the old customs. The coronation procession began from the Red Staircase. Catherine's coronation gown and the dresses and finery for the grand round of festivities were ordered from France. Her cape was embroidered in gold with the

Byzantine-Russian double eagle. Her gold crown flashed with precious gems. It was Peter himself, when the moment came in the service at the cathedral, who lifted it and placed it on her head.

After the end of the Northern War there was time and inclination for the pleasures afforded by St. Petersburg's natural assets. The canals gave the city a special quality of textural contrast and lovely vistas. And there were the bridges, eventually some 600. Peter wanted the Russians, landlocked for so many stagnant centuries, to know the sea and to use it skillfully as their forebears of Kiev and the Dnieper route had done. He had other reasons for wanting Russians to know and use waterways: He needed men for his navy, and the only alternative to boats as transportation was horses, which had to be fed with imported fodder, using up shipping space the city could use for other needs.

Peter therefore issued a ukase that every able-bodied citizen must have a boat. In case of need, boats were supplied at public expense. One and all, Petersburgers were to be sailors. Further, all privately owned boats were subject to official inspection periodically and, if found wanting, were made shipshape at the owner's expense. Anyone visiting the Winter Palace or Summer Palace was required to arrive and depart by boat.

It was in 1723 that Peter brought his own first boat, "the grandfather of the Russian Navy," to St. Petersburg. The whole fleet, anchored in the harbor in battle order, saluted with guns and flags as the little boat went by with Peter at the tiller and his four senior admirals manning the oars.

Peter's favorite diversion in these last years of comparative calm was to sail on the Neva or lead a party of friends in their boats down the coast to the Catherine Palace or to Peterhof, his first home in St. Petersburg. In the summer, on special Sundays and holidays, all Petersburgers assembled in the harbor in their boats, some 5,000 sailboats, rowboats, vessels of every size and sort. While orchestras played and bunting flew and vodka flowed, they sailed on the Neva, led by Peter and Catherine.

In November, 1724, sailing in rough seas along the coast near St. Petersburg, Peter spied a ship that had gone aground and was in danger of capsizing. He hove to, leaped into the frigid water, and directed the maneuvers that saved the ship and its crew. He was still convalescing from an operation; the exertion and exposure brought him down with a raging fever. But by Christmas he felt well enough to insist on leading a band of musicians and carolers through the streets of St. Petersburg. Then he had a relapse, and on January 28, 1725, he died. He died in Catherine's arms; it was she who closed his eyes.

Peter's later years had been haunted by a series of tragedies in his own family. These were not only the source of great personal sorrow for him, but a threat to his achievements and the stability of the nation, for they left the matter of the royal succession in utter confusion.

Alexis, the son of his first marriage and heir to the throne, was dead. Alexis' son, Peter Alexeevich, could have taken his place as heir apparent. But Peter made the boy's position wholly equivocal by decreeing that the old rule of succession from father to son was void and that the Emperor could choose the person he decided was best qualified to succeed him.

Perhaps he still hoped for a healthy male heir from Catherine. She had already given him four sons—two were named Peter, and two named Paul—but all had died in infancy or early childhood. The death of the second Peter in 1719 at the age of three and a half had been an especially cruel blow, for he was a handsome child and Peter had idolized him.

Of the eight daughters Catherine bore, only the two eldest, Anna and Elizabeth, lived to adulthood. Anna was affianced to the Duke of Holstein-Gottorp, the nephew of Sweden's late King Charles XII, Peter's old adversary. The Duke had a strong claim on the Swedish throne; for Peter, he represented a way for establishing his daughter and her descendants as Sweden's rulers and ending any further Swedish threat for some time to come. Peter had also tried to negotiate a marriage between the younger daughter, Elizabeth, and a prince of the French royal house in order to make secure the alliance with France he had formed during his visit there. Nothing had come of this, and at his death Elizabeth still was not spoken for.

Other possible heirs were the two daughters of his half-witted half brother, Ivan, with whom as a youth he had been half-Czar. Compounding the confusion, their names were Catherine and Anna. Finally there was his own Catherine, crowned by his own hand as Empress.

Peter's actual intentions were never to be known. In the last hours of his life he asked for pen and paper and started to write: "Give all to"—but the next word, the word that would have set the course of history, was only a blurred, incomprehensible scribble. His fingers could not hold the pen. He could still speak, faintly; he called for his daughter Anna so that he could dictate the testament to her. But by the time she reached his bedside his power of speech was gone, and he lapsed into unconsciousness.

The issue was decided within a few hours, principally by the initiative and quick maneuvers of Menshikov, who hurried to rally the officers of the elite Guards—the Preobrazhensky and Semenovsky regiments, the old "play troops"—to Catherine's support. She was immensely popular among the guardsmen, who saw her as the perfect soldier's wife and the perfect helpmate for their beloved hero, Peter. Menshikov's work bore fruit immediately: The Guards demonstrated in Catherine's favor, and Grand Admiral Apraxin, on behalf of the Senate, proclaimed Catherine I sovereign of all the Russias "according to the desire of Peter the Great."

Thus, the illiterate former servant girl became the ruler of the largest empire in the world. But being clearheaded, she knew that she was incompetent to rule. And since she was very fond of Menshikov and since he had been Peter's closest adviser, she left the decisions of rule very largely to Menshikov. And thus in turn the semiliterate former pie vendor became the most powerful man in Russia. In effect, the former lovers reigned and ruled together.

This utterly quixotic turn of history, however, turned again, as sharply and unpredictably, only two and a half years later, when Catherine died. As her successor she had named Peter's grandson, Peter Alexeevich, and as regent until he was old enough to rule (he was still only eleven) she had appointed a committee of eight known as the Supreme Secret Council. Menshikov was the leading member of the council. The selection of young Peter Alexeevich, the regency, the whole apparatus had, in fact, been conceived by Menshikov as the foundation for what he planned to be the climax of his career. He produced a forged will of Catherine's which made him, in effect, the boy's guardian and sole Regent. For all practical purposes, he was the country's dictator. He even removed the boy from the royal palaces and took him to live with him. He then capped the coup by announcing the betrothal of his daughter, Maria, to the young Czar.

In all this there was only a single flaw, but it was fatal: Peter Alexeevich disliked Menshikov and made a confidant of young Prince Ivan Dolgoruky. The Dolgorukys were a numerous family of the boyar aristocracy whose members had served the state—and their family interests—in high positions for generations. A Dolgoruky prince was commander of the *streltsy* at the time of the massacre of the Red Staircase, and for his attempts at restoring discipline he had been the first man they pitched over the side onto the halberds. Another, the Russian envoy to France, had brought back the astrolabe that led the youthful Peter I to Timmerman and thus eventually to his interest in boats and the sea.

The family had served Peter I loyally, even while they, like most of the old aristocracy, covertly but deeply resented Menshikov. With Peter II's attachment to Prince Ivan and with two of their family members on the Supreme Secret Council, they had the leverage for a successful coup. Menshikov was arrested, stripped of all his honors and properties, and exiled to northern Siberia, where he died two years later, in November, 1729. Almost simultaneously the Dolgorukys announced the betrothal of Peter II to one of their own young princesses. But in only a few months they, too, were undone. Early in 1730, Peter II, not yet fifteen, died of smallpox.

He had been the last of the male Romanovs, and he had died without issue and without naming a successor. The council, seeking a way to keep power in its own hands, and the old aristocracy, hopeful of reversing many of Peter the Great's reforms and regaining its old privileges, combined to deny the throne to Elizabeth, even though she was the only surviving child of Peter I. (Elizabeth's older sister, Anna, had died only two years after her marriage to the Duke of Holstein.) Elizabeth had been Peter's darling, his special delight, the treasure, pride, and hope of his later years—as everyone well knew. She became both a delightful toy and a play companion for him; he lavished little-girl fineries on her and was pleased to show all her innocent unclothed charms to the world in a small nude statue that Carlo Rastrelli did of her at about the age of five in the classical style and identity of Cupid.

But Elizabeth's loyalty to her father's memory and her own self-willed nature made her, from the council's viewpoint, a dangerous person, and ironically Peter I himself had given them the means to pass her over when he voided the old law of succession and based the selection on merit as defined by the sovereign, in this case the council.

The available candidates still included the two daughters of Peter I's half brother, Ivan V. An offer was made to the eldest, Anna, who was known for her amiability, generosity, love of luxury, and conservative instincts. To make sure she would merely reign and not rule, however, the council imposed terms that left her powerless over taxes, expenditures, the military forces, and virtually everything of any consequence. She was widowed and childless; a further condition was that she not remarry.

Anna accepted and was duly enthroned and delighted her sponsors by moving the royal court and the government "colleges" back to Moscow. The prophecies that St. Petersburg would wither away without Peter seemed on the way to fulfillment.

But then the old, ingrained Byzantine heritage of double-dealing and instant opportunism came to the fore in Anna as it so often had in past rulers and so often would in future ones. Soon after settling on the throne, she declared that the restrictive terms were contrary to the will of the people. She tore them up, abolished the council, and proceeded to rule as an autocrat. Her unofficial prime minister and constant adviser was her lover, the German Count Ernst Johann Biron. Since Anna had no enthusiasm for most of Peter's policies, since Biron was preoccupied with acquiring wealth and honors for himself, since many of Peter's men survived in office and quietly worked toward the goals he had set, Anna's ten-year rule was a mixed interregnum—somewhat reactionary, somewhat debilitating to the national spirit and character, but on the whole a continuation of Peter's essential policies of Westernizing Russia and increasing its influence in Europe.

When Anna died in 1740, she named as her successor the grandson of her sister Catherine, the older daughter of Ivan V. The new Czar, Ivan VI, was just two months old. As regent to rule on his behalf, Anna named Count Biron. Within a month this coup by Biron led to a countercoup with the indispensable support of the Guards regiments: Anna Leopoldovna, the infant's mother, became Regent; Biron was stripped of his titles and wealth, put to torture, and exiled to Siberia.

By this juncture, however, the Guards and many Russian officials were in a mood to get rid of the whole "German party" in the government. The new Regent, half Russian by blood, had been born and reared in German Mecklenburg and had married the Duke of Brunswick. The infant Czar would be German in everything except name and in due course would grow up to sire a Germanic successor and found a Germanic dynasty. There was a welling up of patriotic nostalgia for the days of Peter the Great.

Much as Peter admired and used individual foreigners and foreign methods, he manifestly did so in the interests of Russia. Much as he relished the ways of the German Quarter, spoke Dutch, built Dutch and Italianate buildings and French pavilions set in French-Dutch gardens adorned by Greco-Roman-Italian sculptures, he always remained essentially a Russian. He had now been dead fifteen years, and even among many of those who had hated him in his lifetime there were second thoughts, mellow regrets, the sense of a disturbing void in the life of the nation. The process of apotheosis was well along: Anti-Christ was merging with the figure of the Messiah, and the hero was on his way to becoming a national saint. These sentiments found their natural catharsis in the person of Peter's daughter Elizabeth.

I

A Gallery of Elizabeths

"SHE is a beauty the like of which I have never seen . . . an amazing complexion, glowing eyes, a perfect mouth, a throat and bosom of rare whiteness. She is tall in stature, and her temperament is very lively. One senses in her a great deal of intelligence and affability, but also a certain ambition."

Thus the Italian ambassador, the Duke of Luria, who obviously took a deep interest in such matters, described Elizabeth in her early twenties.

She resembled her father in a good many ways, not least in her ability to meld complex, sometimes opposite, sometimes grotesque character traits into a personage both viable and forceful, and which, bewildering as it often was to others, she was able to carry off with what seemed to be perfect inner assurance. Not surprisingly, considering how much she had been admired and indulged, among these traits were personal vanity, a voluptuous delight in beauty, adornment, the harmonies of form and color, and an impatient refusal to let cost or other mundane difficulties stand in the way of satisfying her desires. In time, when she was Empress, she was to have a wardrobe of 15,000 dresses, with matching accessories; she was also, for her imprudence, to be refused any further credit by a Paris milliner.

Nor was it surprising that her nature was dramatic. In her life she had many roles to play and never failed to rise to a part and play it superbly, with such inventiveness and conviction and with such a large interchangeable repertory that it became difficult to know her personal feelings or to predict the actions of the public character. Hence she often seemed capricious. Certainly she was willful. Above all, she was romantic and fanciful. And on two matters at least, she was entirely consistent and left no doubt about the depth of her sentiments. She was devoted to the memory of Peter and Catherine and her sister, Anna. And she loved Russia.

Elizabeth had been eighteen when Catherine I died; it was she who wrote down the will and signed it for her. Since then her status at court had greatly changed. During the rule of Empress Anna, she was virtually exiled and spent most of the reign living at a small estate in the country, leading a robust country life among the peasants and, much of the time, dressing in well-fitting feminized male costume. Tall, abundantly healthy, and voluptuously formed, she was as much a woman as Peter I had been a man. The male raiment only emphasized her womanliness, while suggesting that she was competent to ride a horse, deal with an empire, lead an army. Having been forced from the court, she adopted country life with almost aggressive enjoyment, and the costume was part of her role, a sign of her disdain for court finery.

Perhaps from living this role so fully, she was not particularly ambitious to assert her claim to the throne. This changed, however, with the accession of the infant Ivan VI and Regent Anna Leopoldovna, when rumors and speculations began to reach her that the Regent planned to force her to renounce her claim and enter a convent.

Thereupon Elizabeth took a house in St. Petersburg and a new role: Sweetheart of the Guards. She flirted with them, lost money to them at cards, entertained them, flattered them, reminisced with them about the days of Peter the Great, dazzled them with her charms—set off by the most luxurious and feminine of costumes—and within the year had conquered them utterly.

Her activities did not, of course, escape the notice of Regent Anna. The two women, each pretending cousinly affection, eyed each other, as it were, from their bastions, calculating the moment to strike. The fact that under both Annas, Russian foreign policy was pro-German in the constantly shifting struggle for supremacy in Europe was a help to Elizabeth, for the Germans were not popular.

On a night late in November, 1741, Elizabeth came to the Preobrazhensky barracks. While the guards were strapping on their battle gear and forming ranks, she went to a private chamber. When she reappeared, she too was in full guard's uniform, with a coat of mail over her bodice and her blond hair flowing from underneath a plumed helmet. She was in her role—magnificently. Reverently, as she stood before them, the guards whispered an oath of allegiance to her.

Then, as silently as possible, their forms hidden in the darkest hours of the dark November night, with Elizabeth leading the way, they went to the Winter Palace. There was no opposition, no bloodshed. The surprise was so complete that Elizabeth herself had to rouse Regent Anna from her sleep, touching her shoulder and saying, "Wake up, sister. . . ."

The coup had taken perhaps two hours.

Elizabeth Petrovna, Empress and Autocrat of All the Russias, reigned and ruled for twenty-two years. Historical judgments of her have been as mixed as her character, as mixed as the times, as mixed as Russia itself. "As was to be expected"—in the obiter dicta of one scholarly authority—"Elizabeth, ignorant, dissolute, bigoted, and lazy, was incapable of improving the state of the country." Another eminent authority, however, has remarked: "Fortunately, Elizabeth had inherited some of her father's genius for government . . . and she developed a keen political and diplomatic sense"; further, the successful diplomacy of her chief minister, Bestuzhev, "would have been impossible but for the steady support" she gave him in the face of continual intrigues against him at court; further still, her "unshakable firmness was the one political force that held together the heterogeneous jarring elements of the anti-Prussian combination" of Russia, France, and Austria in the most important of her foreign ventures, the Seven

Years' War. To still another authority she was "indolent, easygoing, and disorganized, although by no means stupid" as well as being "kind . . . handsome, and charming." To yet another she possessed "outstanding intelligence, ability, and force of character."

There would seem to have been a veritable gallery of Elizabeths, one to suit every taste and predilection.

Here we are mainly concerned with her role as the discoverer and importer, surrogate mother-in-law, terrifying and revered model, and somewhat inadvertent benefactress of the girl who became one of the most remarkable rulers who ever lived, known in history as Catherine the Great.

As a beautiful, abundantly healthy, and life-loving but unmarried woman, Elizabeth was the object of continual prurient speculation and salacious gossip. The number 300 has somehow become fixed in tradition; allegedly this was the exact number of the love affairs she carried on during her lifetime. Actually there is clear historical evidence for only 5—a considerable discount.

In childhood and girlhood, as the beautiful, vivacious, intelligent daughter of the Great Czar, her life had, it seemed, an inescapable logic. She would have droves of eager suitors, foreign and domestic. She would marry young, having made her choice on the basis of personal liking, possibly even of love, but foremost and decisively for well-calculated reasons of state, and—surely—it would be a brilliant marriage. For a long time the thought was in Peter's mind, and hence it grew in Elizabeth's too, and seemed more and more natural, that her groom should be King Louis XV. They were very near in age, he a year younger. Meeting Louis when he was seven, Peter had been delighted to find him bright, healthy, and handsome. Overflowing with affection, the giant Czar scooped up the little King of France in his arms, hugged him, and kissed him soundly on both cheeks—somewhat to the consternation of the King's attendant ministers and courtiers, but causing Louis not the slightest loss of composure.

With this match in mind or, failing that, perhaps some other young Bourbon of high rank, Elizabeth acquired flawless French, a thorough grounding in French history and literature, and the graces and manners of French society. As a natural result, she grew up a Francophile in all things. Probably her major contribution to the overall objective of Peter's revolution—the remaking of Russia as a modern European power—was the infusion of French specialists and French influences which she encouraged throughout her reign.

However, the French marriage was blocked by the force of some erratic new current in the troubled waters of European diplomacy. Other possible candidacies in other countries were examined; again, at the critical moment, there was always a reason to prevent a definite betrothal.

Finally, when Elizabeth was sixteen, she was betrothed to Prince Karl Augustus of Holstein-Gottorp. Politically it was a useful and certainly respectable alliance. The Holstein-Gottorps were an old and aristocratic house with ties to many of the royalties of Europe and even with potential claims to some of the thrones. Moreover, there was the fact that Elizabeth had fallen wildly in love with Prince Karl Augustus.

A few days after the betrothal he died.

This tragedy was soon followed by a host of other tragedies and troubles: Peter's death, then Catherine's, then the accession of Empress Anna and the effectual banishment of Elizabeth from court. Her position as Peter's daughter and potential heir to the Russian throne, always her great asset in the diplomatic marriage mart, had now become an almost insurmountable barrier to marriage. No noble house of Europe could allow a son to pay suit to her, for this would be interpreted as an unfriendly act toward Empress Anna. In effect the same held good for the Russian nobility. Marriage to a commoner would cost Elizabeth her title and could undermine her property rights and her claims to the throne. Her position was hopelessly equivocal.

Elizabeth's response was, in effect, to reject what she could not have, matrimony, and with it all the attributes, including moral respectability. She formed a liaison with a trooper of the Semenovsky Regiment of the Guards, then with a coachman, then with a waiter. A few years before her coup d'état, she met a handsome young Ukrainian peasant who, because of his fine bass voice, had been brought north by a St. Petersburg nobleman for a church choir. Elizabeth took a fancy to him, hired him for her own choir in her private chapel, made him the Chamberlain of her household—and her lover.

This was Alexis Razumovsky, a genuinely good and simple-minded man, untroubled by education or personal ambition. Evidently Elizabeth was devoted to him, and there is a possibility that at some point she actually married him in a secret ceremony, making him her morganatic spouse.

In any event, she loved him deeply and left no possible doubt of it in the minds of her courtiers, among whom he became known as the Emperor of the Night. She made him a prince and a field marshal and gave him every other honor that she, as Empress, had to bestow. The Emperor of Austria, as a courtesy to the Empress of Russia, made him a count of the Holy Roman Empire. His titles and benefices and dignities were more than he could possibly remember, or really cared to.

European and Francophile though she was, Elizabeth remained in heart and soul Russian with a close sense of personal identification and involvement with the landscape, the people, and the past. And so, much as she loved St. Petersburg, she was strongly drawn to Moscow. She went there for her coronation, of course, as sentiment alone would have required, descending the Red Staircase and following the processional route of her father when he was a boy of ten and of her mother when she herself was a girl. But instead of staying for only the normal month or two of coronation ceremonies and festivities, she spent a year.

During her reign Elizabeth returned so often to Moscow that the city, which for decades had been undergoing progressive, deadly atrophy, enjoyed a temporary revival as the court, the embassies, and high officials perforce followed the Empress in a massive train. Peter, for good reasons, had hated the Kremlin. His daughter, a product of the new world he had created, could enjoy fully the sheer visual drama of this product of the earlier meeting of Italian, Russian, and Byzantine culture under the annealing royal auspices of the first Czar, Ivan the Great, and his Byzantine consort, Empress Sophia. No actress could have asked for a more dramatic setting, and no hostess for a more exciting amphitheater for her triumph. No romantic Russian patriot could have found anywhere such a rich and ample mixture of the elements from many times and places that made up the Russian past and formed the Russian character.

For these sentiments, as well as for the mystical part of her nature, the churches of Moscow and the region afforded Elizabeth a perfect catharsis. While in Moscow, feeling surfeited at a certain point with her gay court life, Elizabeth would go to one or another of these churches for prayer and contemplation. There were dozens in and around Moscow that she found and liked during her personal reconnoitering. And now and again, increasingly as the years went by, she would be overtaken by such a surge of piety that she would gather a modest entourage of a few score of servants and ladies of the court and, with suitable escort from the guards regiments, make an extended pilgrimage to one of the major outlying holy places such as the vast walled fortress-monastery of Holy Trinity-St. Sergius, where Peter had taken refuge from Regent Sophia and rallied his regiments and other allies to overthrow her. Refreshed by her devotions, Elizabeth would return to Moscow and soon to St. Petersburg, to the frivolities and worldly pastimes for which she was better known.

It was one of the oddest turns in Russian history that the great Russian Empress we know as Catherine the Great—who took Peter the Great for her hero far more than any did who were linked to him by blood, who was heir to his ideas and executor of his plans—was in fact not Russian at all but German, born and reared not Orthodox but Lutheran, and christened not Catherine but Sophia. Until the age of fourteen she was only Princess Sophia Augusta Frederika of Anhalt-Zerbst, one of the most minor of the minor principalities that were strewn across the German landscape. She was not pretty. She had no money. Her prospects, at the most optimistic, were mediocre. The possibilities of her becoming the grand historic figure she became, Catherine the Great, were so implausible as to be ludicrous.

How could it have happened?

The answer to this goes back initially to Peter the Great himself. Further to ensure the safety of St. Petersburg and Russia's access to the Baltic, he had arranged the marriage of his older daughter, Anna, to the Duke of Holstein-Gottorp, who was the nephew of his old enemy, Charles XII of Sweden, and prospective heir to the Swedish throne. Anna died of tuberculosis only a year later, leaving a three-month-old infant son, Charles Peter Ulrich, named for his great-uncle Charles and his grandfather Peter.

When Charles Peter was ten, his father, the Duke, died, and his claims to Sweden passed on to the boy, who for the next several years was educated with that destiny in mind. As the only surviving male descendant of Peter the Great he also was potentially heir to the Russian throne. During the reigns of the two Annas this was only hypothetical, since they, of course, were determined to keep the succession in their own family line, the line of Ivan the half-wit.

Elizabeth's coup d'état turned the boy's life upside down. For Elizabeth, being unmarried and, so far as is known, childless despite her various liaisons, being devoted to the memory of her parents and her sister, Anna, and needing an heir to the throne, immediately chose Charles Peter.

Thanks to Peter the Great, the Russian throne manifestly was far more important than the Swedish, as the boy's guardians decided on his behalf. His Swedish rights were transferred to a cousin, who ultimately became the King of Sweden. Charles Peter was brought to St. Petersburg, where Elizabeth formally declared him heir apparent, made him a Grand Duke, and changed his name to Peter Fedorovich. Grand Duke Peter Fedorovich—the future Czar Peter III—was by then fourteen years old, and thus it was already necessary to think about a bride for him.

Automatically, given Russia's new position as a great power, every little princess in Europe was potentially an applicant for this marriage. Vast and intricate diplomacy was set afoot. To his dying day King Frederick II of Prussia—Frederick the Great—believed that it was he who engineered the outcome and won the victory. But in fact, had he done nothing at all, the result might have been the same. In making her choice of the future Czarina, Elizabeth was motivated, just as she had been in choosing the future Czar, by deeply sentimental and romantic memories that went back to her girlhood.

She had briefly been betrothed, as we noted, to Prince Karl Augustus of Holstein-Gottorp—a cousin of the Holstein Duke who married her sister, Anna, and begat Charles Peter. She had never ceased cherishing and grieving over the memory of this first lost love; the mention of his name or the thought of him always brought tears to her eyes. (That she consoled herself as well with so many other men suggests that these emotions had become incorporated in a role, part of her repertory. But even if so, that would not mean they seemed any the less genuine to her.)

Prince Karl Augustus had had a sister named Johanna Elizabeth, who at the age of fifteen had married a Prussian army officer, Prince Christian Augustus von Anhalt-Zerbst. Their first child, a girl named Sophia, was born in 1729. Thus she was just a year younger than Charles Peter of Holstein, the newly made Grand Duke Peter of Russia. Had Elizabeth's prince lived, this girl would have been his niece and Elizabeth's niece by marriage. Thus the marriage between the young Princess and Grand Duke would, so to speak, unite her most treasured memories and dearest personal attachments and would give her in surrogate fashion the children and grandchildren for which she yearned. And she, as a wedding present and perhaps in some sense a devotional offering to the dead—to Peter and Catherine, to Anna and Karl Augustus —could give the throne of Russia.

So Princess Sophia, fifteen, accompanied by her mother, Princess Johanna Elizabeth, set out for Russia in the winter of 1744. Empress Elizabeth was on one of her visits to Moscow at the time, bringing the Grand Duke and most of the court with her, so that city rather than Petersburg was their destination.

En route they stopped at Berlin, where they were entertained by Frederick. Johanna tried to keep Sophia out of sight as much as possible—perhaps because of her plainness. The King would have none of this; even when told first that Sophia was ill and then that she had no court dress, Frederick insisted on giving a state dinner and borrowed a dress from one of his sisters for the little girl from Anhalt-Zerbst. He sat next to her at table, having carefully seated her parents elsewhere in the room, and held an animated conversation with her that she remembered for years afterward.

The time and place for this journey could not have been more inconvenient. To travel from Prussia to Moscow in the dead of winter was an ordeal. But to Elizabeth the succession was a matter of supreme, even obsessive importance, and she was impatient. She knew a great deal about Sophia from reports of her agents and relatives and had even had a portrait of her copied and brought to Russia. But she had never met her, and she would not make her decision final and official until she had formed a personal judgment, a womanly judgment, of the girl who was to carry on the dynasty and ultimately to take her own place. So Sophia was still, in some degree, on trial.

Her mother, Princess Johanna, was just as impatient. Indeed, one feels she would have undertaken to cross the North Pole, if necessary, to make the trip. Vivacious and attractive, pleasure-loving and extravagant, shallow, ambitious, and conniving, she felt that she deserved far better than her poor Prince with his insignificant domain could give her. She relished the high connections she had through her family and took pains to cultivate them, paying them visits, writing them letters. When Elizabeth, who might have been her sister-in-law, emerged suddenly as Empress, she was elated and wrote at once to express her happiness— and to remind the Empress of herself. And when Elizabeth made young Charles Peter of Holstein heir to Russia, she realized instantly what this could mean and thereafter did everything she could to nourish the possibility.

Actually Johanna had never liked Sophia, whom she considered plain, rather shy, and lacking any notable signs of brilliance or special talent. Thus, she could and did regard the invitation to Russia as a personal triumph of her own diplomacy.

As for Sophia herself, she was thrilled and as impatient as either of the older women. She knew very little about Russia, its people or the life there. She knew that it was powerful, rich, and exotic. She had heard much of Peter the Great, who by then had become a romantic and awesome legend in all the Baltic lands. She knew from her mother (who had never met Elizabeth) that the Empress was beautiful, wise, generous, and splendid and bore deep affection for her family. But what mainly was in her mind was that she was on her way to becoming a queen. Sophia was easily as ambitious as her mother—and incomparably more intelligent. The combination made her extraordinarily perceptive and effective on her own behalf.

II

Empress Catherine Remembers Princess Sophia

LONG years later, when she had become Empress and was on her way to greatness, she wrote a partial autobiography. What she meant to do with it is a mystery. The manuscript covers her first thirty years and stops in midsentence in the middle of a most delicate and crucial conversation with Empress Elizabeth. No one knew it existed until after she died, when it was found in a sealed packet in her library at the Winter Palace. It is a richly rewarding document, full of information and colorful impressions about Russia and Europe during one of history's most effervescent eras and fascinating in its candid revelations of her own character and the foibles of the history makers, diplomats and other intriguers, crowned heads, seducers and noble mistresses, and mixed notables among whom she lived.

In addition and apart from this manuscript, she had a habit of writing memorandums and notations to herself: reminders, anecdotes, insights, ideas and sudden inspirations, items of self-criticism and self-congratulation, character sketches, fragments of old memories—all sorts of serious and random jottings, some of them evidently intended for use in the later, never written chap-

ters of her memoirs. Further, she had a very large official correspondence, and in an age famous for the volume and polish of
personal correspondence she was among the most prolific letter
writers of all.

All in all, hers was an enormous literary output, and one way
and another it supplies, in her own words, a narrative of most
of the important episodes of her long life. Naturally, it needs
additions to fill gaps, interpolations for clarity, and, since neither
her contemporaries nor later historians found her judgments in-
fallible or her behavior blameless, an admixture of critiques, dis-
sents, and other viewpoints for proper balance. However, not
only was she a good reporter with an eye and ear for significant
detail and a fluent, lucid style, but she was also an honest one. At
any rate, she made a point of being honest with herself, and even
in those private intrigues and political strategies in which prudence required the use of deceit she regarded truth as the ultimate weapon. As she reminded herself in one of her notes, "I
have discovered that in life honesty alone can pull you out of a
difficult situation." Accordingly in the pages here that deal with
her rising career and achievements, she will be found telling most
of the story herself.

Elizabeth and her court were at the Annenhof Palace at the
far end of Moscow. "After we had passed through all the state
apartments," wrote Catherine, "we were brought to the room
where the Empress held her audiences. There, on the threshold of
her state bedchamber, the Empress appeared before us. Certainly,
it was quite impossible on seeing her for the first time not to be
struck by her beauty and the majesty of her bearing. She was a
large woman who, in spite of being rather stout, was not in the
least disfigured by her size . . . her head, too, was very beautiful.
On that day she wore an immense hoop of the kind she favored
when she dressed up . . . on great occasions. Her dress was of
silvery moiré with golden braid, she wore a black feather erect at
one side of her head and many diamonds in her hair."

Writing this when she herself had been Empress a dozen years
or more and had the wealth of Russia at her disposal, Catherine
still remembered the costume exactly, and with good reason:
Young Princess Sophia owned three dresses. They and her under-

things and shoes and stockings and indeed all her worldly goods, which she had brought along to Russia with her, did not fill even a small trunk.

"My mother curtsied and thanked her for all the favors she had bestowed on our family; after this the Empress entered her bed-chamber and asked us to follow her; chairs were arranged there for sitting down, but neither she, nor consequently anybody else, sat down."

Elizabeth was too excited by this sentimental and portentous occasion to think of resting. At one point she was so overcome with emotion by the resemblance between Princess Johanna and the dead Prince Karl Augustus that she left the room to hide her tears—so Johanna wrote to her husband. Catherine says: "She talked at great length to my mother and looked at me very attentively."

Both accounts treat the presence of Grand Duke Peter as merely incidental. As Catherine related, "While she was talking to my mother, the Grand Duke talked to me. He took us both to our apartments, had supper with us, as did his Court and many other people. . . . I was on the Grand Duke's left. . . . During supper the Empress came to the door of the apartment to watch in-cognito how we were progressing.

"The next day, February 10, Friday of the first week of Lent, was the Grand Duke's birthday. There were great celebrations. Towards 11 A.M. we were told to come to the Empress's apart-ments. We did so—there were large crowds in all the anterooms through which we passed . . . the Empress emerged from her room in full dress. She wore a brown robe embroidered with silver and her head, neck and bosom were covered with jewels. The Master of the Hunt, Count Razumovsky, followed her." This was Alexis Razumovsky, Elizabeth's lover, "Emperor of the Night."

Catherine, writing these lines from the perspective of ripe expe-rience, paid Razumovsky a compliment in commenting, "He was one of the handsomest men I have ever seen in my life. He car-ried on a gold plate the insignia of the Order of St. Catherine." Peter the Great had founded this order in honor of his Catherine, Elizabeth's mother. It ranked with the Order of St. Andrew as the highest honor the throne could bestow, and for Elizabeth, of course, it had the strongest personal associations. "The Empress handed me the order, then conferred the same honor on my mother; after that she kissed me."

Elizabeth made a yearly pilgrimage during Lent to Troitsky—or Holy Trinity-St. Sergius—Monastery near Moscow, holy to the memory of Peter I. Now this ritual time had come again. Hence, a few days after the arrival of the princesses, the Empress "came to take leave of us in our apartments. That day she wore a dress with long black velvet sleeves and all the Russian Orders—the ribbon of St. Andrew and St. Alexander round her neck and of St. Catherine on her left breast."

In a manner of speaking—save for her mother and countless court attendants and officials and servants—Princess Sophia and Grand Duke Peter were alone at last.

They were not strangers. As second cousins in a large but close-knit noble family, they had been aware of each other's existence from earliest childhood. Indeed, in the speculative planning for marriage that began almost literally from the moment of birth among the aristocracy, Charles Peter Ulrich of Holstein was seen as the natural target of choice for Sophia, though it was equally easy to see that the odds were against her, considering her inferior station and, as she grew old enough to be scrutinized for personal assets, her plainness.

"I do not know if I was actually ugly as a child," she writes, "but I know that I was often told that I was and that because of this I should try to acquire wit and other merits that until the age of fourteen or fifteen"—that is, her first year in Russia—"I was convinced that I was a rather ugly duckling and tried much more to acquire these other virtues than rely upon my face. It is true that I have seen a portrait of myself painted when I was ten, excessively ugly—if it was a good likeness, then I was not being deceived."

It was her father's friend and general factotum, a man named Bolhagen, she relates, visiting one day with her French governess Babet Cardel, "who roused in me the first stir of ambition. In 1736"—she was then about seven—"he was reading a gazette in my room which recounted the marriage of Princess Augusta of Saxe-Gotha, my second cousin, with the Prince of Wales, son of

George II of England." (From this union there ensued George III and the American Revolution.) "Bolhagen said to Mlle. Cardel: 'Really, this Princess has been much less carefully brought up than ours; she is not beautiful either, but there she is, destined to become Queen of England! Who knows what future faces ours?' He then proceeded to preach to me wisdom and all the moral and Christian virtues which would make me worthy of a crown, if it were my fate to wear one.

"The idea of a crown began running in my head then like a tune and has been running a lot in it ever since."

She met Charles Peter three years later, when she was ten and he was eleven. His father had just died, leaving the boy in the guardianship of a cousin, the Bishop of Lübeck, Adolf Frederick of Holstein-Gottorp. The bishop was the eldest of the numerous brothers of Princess Johanna, in whose head the same tune ran and who took the first opportunity to pay him a visit and introduce Sophia to the presumptive heir to the Swedish crown. Apparently they got along well.

In the memoirs, Catherine recalls that although "He was pale and looked delicate," he was "good looking, well-mannered, and courteous; in fact . . . was considered a prodigy." Adding: "My mother, who was then very beautiful, fascinated [him] and he danced attendance on her, but envied me my freedom. As for me, I hardly noticed him, for I was too busy frolicking around without any supervision. . . . The hints that my uncles and aunts, also our closest intimates, dropped here and there led me to think, however, that my name and his were being coupled. I felt no repugnance at the idea: I knew that he was one day to become King of Sweden, and the title of Queen rang sweet to my ears, child though I was. Thereafter all those surrounding me teased me about him and gradually I got used to the thought that he was my destiny."

III

... And Grand Duke Peter

O F all the sad, miscast, and foredoomed figures who have crossed the pages of royal history, Charles Peter Ulrich of Holstein, Grand Duke Peter, was one of the most unfortunate, inept, and finally one of the most tragic. The frailty that Princess Sophia noticed was constitutional. This grandson of the giant Peter I and his peasant Catherine, son of a sturdy military father (the Duke loved soldiering and his Holsteiner troops were among Europe's best), was prone to all sorts of illnesses and retarded both physically and emotionally. In other circumstances he might have grown up finally to be a nondescript youth and man who would have found a small niche in life and lived his years without doing much of either good or harm to himself or others. But what favorable potentialities he had were stunted and twisted by circumstances that could not have been better designed to bring out the worst in him. Without a mother, with a father who had no time and little feeling for him, he was a child who never knew love or warm affection.

To prepare him for the role he was supposed to play as King and military leader, his father turned him over at the age of seven to a staff of tutors and military officers, who kept him busy from morning to night with languages, religion, history, mathematics, and other matters, including military training. The last was the only part of his regimen he liked.

He was fitted out with uniforms and drilled with his father's elite regiments and stood make-believe sentry duty. His proudest moment—very likely the proudest of his whole life—came when his father personally promoted him from sergeant to lieutenant. As for the rest, it was simply too much for him, try as he might. His trying depleted his fragile resources, and beneath a façade of conformity to the expectations of others a deadly erosion began. His limited intelligence slowed, he looked for escapes, and sometimes his frustrations discharged in flaring temper tantrums.

By the time Sophia met him again in Russia, according to the memoirs, "it was rumored that he already had a great inclination for drink and that his tutors had difficulty in preventing him from getting drunk at table. He was hot-tempered and rebellious, and disliked his tutors, especially Marshal Brümmer, a Swede by origin."

Brümmer deserves notice; it was his historic role to corrode the boy's personality beyond all help. For some years he had been the *Oberhofmarschall,* or High Chamberlain and General Manager, of the ducal court. To the Bishop of Lübeck, who was too busy to give his important ward much personal attention, it seemed only logical to entrust Brümmer, who obviously had enjoyed the late Duke's confidences, with the direct, day-to-day responsibility for him.

Brümmer was a martinet, a brutish disciplinarian, and something of a sadist. When the young Duke had not done well in his work, Brümmer would come to him in the dining hall and belabor him so fiercely for his errors and sins, shouting and threatening, that the boy could not eat and sometimes even vomited. Brümmer might punish him by denying him any food all day, then making him stand in the dining hall with a donkey head hanging around his neck, watching his tutors and courtiers eat. A favorite physical punishment was to make him kneel for hours with bare knees on hard dried peas. The result of these abrasive methods of making him learn was that he learned progressively less, his mind refusing information as his stomach refused food.

It was a miserable life, but at least it was led among surroundings that he had always known and contained some pleasant memories. Then, suddenly, he was removed to Russia. He was adopted by an aunt he had never met, expected to speak a language he had failed to learn, made heir to a country about which he knew little and cared less. The only familiar face was that of the atrocious Brümmer, who accompanied him as his instructor and general manager of his affairs. The boy was dreadfully homesick. But there was no escape. A year and a half after arriving in Russia, the miserable, incompetent, and by then deeply neurotic boy collapsed in an illness for which the doctors could supply no clear diagnosis and no cure. For months he lay near death.

The nearly fatal episode terrified Elizabeth. Death had cheated her often enough in the past; all her elaborate plans and sentimental hopes depended on his surviving, marrying and begetting, and the business of finding the right bride for him could not be delayed. By early winter it was evident that he was returning to his normal degree of health. At her urgent command Brümmer wrote the letter which, arriving on January 1, brought Sophia to Russia.

"The Grand Duke seemed glad to see my mother and me," she wrote in the memoirs. "I was in my fifteenth year and he showed himself very assiduous for the first ten days. In that short space of time I became aware that he was not greatly enamored of the nation over which he was destined to reign; he was a convinced Lutheran, did not like his entourage, and was very childish. I kept silent and listened, which helped to gain his confidence. I remember he told me among other things that what he liked most in me was that I was his second cousin and in that capacity, as a relative, he could talk freely to me; after this he confided that he was in love with one of the Empress' ladies-in-waiting who had been expelled from Court . . . he would have liked to marry her, but he had resigned himself to marrying me as his aunt wished it. I listened to these disclosures with a blush, thanked him for his premature confidence, but privately observed with astonishment his imprudence on a number of matters."

For her own part Sophia, prudently calculating how best to please the Empress, began studying Russian and the Orthodox religion with such dedication that she even got up in the middle of the night to review her lessons. As a result, she caught a chill which developed into pneumonia. Her mother disagreed with the doctors about her treatment: ". . . and there I lay unconscious between my mother and the doctors, arguing, with a high fever and a pain in my side so acute that I could not help groaning, for which I was admonished by my mother who expected me to suffer in silence."

The doctors reported to Elizabeth, who rushed back from Holy Trinity, ordered Princess Johanna from the sickroom, and took charge of the case. Sophia regained consciousness in her arms. "I remained between life and death for twenty-seven days, during which . . . my mother was not allowed into my room. . . . At last the abscess which had formed in my right side burst . . . and from that moment I began to recover. I realized at once that my mother's behavior during my illness had antagonized everyone towards her. When she saw me *in extremis,* she wanted a Lutheran priest brought to me; I was told that, profiting by a moment of consciousness, they had asked me whether this was what I wanted, and that I had replied: 'To what purpose? Better send for Simon Theodorsky, I would like to talk to him.'" (Theodorsky was a liberal and learned Orthodox priest, her instructor in the religion it behooved her to join; her presence of mind was remarkable.) "He came and talked to me . . . in a manner that satisfied everyone; this raised me in the eyes of the Empress and of the whole Court."

In fact, it was a lucky illness, for the outcome was that Sophia entirely won the heart of Elizabeth, whose motherly instincts were satisfied at last in caring for this "adorable child." Elizabeth showered her with affection, attention, and lavish gifts. The first of these was a diamond-encrusted snuffbox worth a fortune. "At last on April 21, 1744, my birthday, I was strong enough to appear in public for the first time. . . . I was mortally pale. I appeared to myself ugly as a scarecrow and did not feel at my ease. The Empress sent me a pot of rouge that day and ordered me to put some on." The date of the betrothal was set officially for the end of

June. Sophia's victory was won. More than that, as she reports, Elizabeth had begun to care for her more than she did for her peculiarly disappointing and unobliging nephew.

On June 28 Sophia was received into the Orthodox Church in great ceremony. She dropped her name, which as the name of Peter the Great's wicked half sister had unpleasant connotations for Elizabeth, and became Ekaterina, or Catherine, a name which of course had the dearest connotations. The next day, the feast day of Sts. Peter and Paul, the betrothal took place, and Catherine became Grand Duchess of Russia.

The ceremonies were held in the Kremlin. "In the evening," Catherine wrote, "we went incognito to the Kremlin, an ancient castle which served as a residence of the czars. I was given a room at the top, so high that one could barely see the people who walked at the foot of the wall. The next day. . . . The Empress' portrait, framed in diamonds, was brought to me early in the morning, and shortly afterwards the portrait of the Grand Duke, also encircled with diamonds. Soon after he came to take me to the Empress who, wearing her crown and imperial mantle, proceeded on her way under a canopy of massive silver, carried by eight major-generals and followed by the Grand Duke and myself. . . .

"We descended the famous flight of stairs called *Krassnoe Kriltso*"—the Red Staircase, which had held such morbid memories for Peter the Great—"crossed the square and walked to the cathedral, the Guards regiments lining the road." (This was the coronation route; the regiments were those founded by Peter the Great.) "The Empress took the Grand Duke and myself by the hand and led us to a platform carpeted with velvet in the center of the church where Archbishop Ambrose of Novgorod exchanged our rings. . . . Guns were fired after the service. At midday the Empress lunched with the Grand Duke and myself on the Throne in the hall of the Facets Palace. . . . Afterward we returned to the Palace beyond the German Quarter where we were living."

Thirty years afterward she still remembered and felt it worth stating that "the ring the Duke gave me cost twelve thousand rubles and the one I gave him fourteen thousand."

Having spent her life until then in relative poverty, Catherine had an acute appreciation of jewels and luxuries. She also seems to have been born with the eye of an appraiser, and she took naturally to the prevailing Russian attitude that the giver without gifts is bare. In the part of her memoirs covering these early years, there are so many notations of gifts received, often with precise or reputed worth, that the pages form a kind of running inventory. The main source of this marvelous flow was Elizabeth.

During this first year of Catherine's life in Russia—the first of what would be a lifetime, for she never again set foot on foreign soil—so many things went so well, worrisome problems tended so to melt away, that she seemed to herself to be living in a magical Russian fairy tale. It seemed reasonable that the remaining problems would fade away too in due course, leaving an ending filled with enchanted bliss.

Not only had she won Elizabeth, but Elizabeth had won her. "My respect for and gratitude to the Empress were extreme," she wrote. "I looked upon her as upon a goddess, without a flaw." Further, "I tried as much as I could to win the hearts of the people with whom I was to spend my life"—and with her friendliness, tact and manifest good sense she made a conquest of the Court and the population around it. Even the hardhearted abominable Brümmer became fond of her and tried to enlist her influence to make the Grand Duke study more and behave better. She declined, of course, for the approach she had taken to Peter's affections was to be his friendly companion and trusted confidante. And this, too, had worked out well. He did not "fall in love" with her, but undoubtedly he liked her very much indeed and wanted to marry her. Etiquette required that he write a formal request to her father for her hand, and when the Prince of Anhalt-Zerbst replied giving his consent, Grand Duke Peter danced for joy and ran about to read the letter aloud to members of the court.

As for her feelings about Peter, in her memoirs she wrote: "I cannot say that I either liked or disliked him . . . but to tell the truth I believe that the Crown of Russia attracted me more than his person. He was sixteen, quite good-looking . . . but small and infantile, talking of nothing but soldiers and toys. I listened politely . . . and he enjoyed talking to me for long periods of time. Many people took this for affection . . . but in fact we never used the language of tenderness . . . he had never even thought of it, which did not greatly incline me in his favor. Young girls may be as well brought up as you could wish, but they like sweet nonsense, especially from those from whom they can hear it without blushing."

Yet Catherine herself at fifteen was in so many ways a child—a bright child, to be sure—that Peter's childish ways could not have surprised or distressed her greatly. She loved playing blindman's buff with her maids and ladies-in-waiting; she loved dancing, dressing up, roughhousing, joking, and bantering, a good deal of it girlishly silly. Most of the time her mind operated on about the same level of inanity and inconsequence as Peter's and, for that matter, of their teen-age companions, the noble maidens who attended Catherine and the noble youths who attended Peter and who constituted the Young Court.

Writing of Peter many years later, she tended to be self-serving, but the fact was that in this first year they got along together extremely well. She felt a little superior, perhaps, for at sixteen he still liked to sit in his bed and play with dolls, nevertheless she was fond of him and had good times with him.

If Elizabeth had wanted them to marry the next week, Catherine would have agreed gladly. And Elizabeth would have liked nothing better: tomorrow, next week, next month, as soon as the wedding preparations could be arranged.

Only one problem remained. But it was insuperable. Fragile, retarded, lately weakened still more by his illness, Peter simply had not grown up enough for marriage. He was sexually immature, incapable of fatherhood. Since the production of an heir was the urgent reason for the marriage, his sexual incompetence removed the urgency. The doctors advised waiting several more years. Elizabeth halfway believed that marriage itself and the intimacy of the nuptial bed would be an effective natural cure for Peter's condition. However, reluctantly she decided to wait a year.

In her disappointment, Elizabeth embarked on a pilgrimage to Kiev, taking with her Catherine and Peter, Catherine's mother, her own faithful and essential Razumovsky, and a host of others from the court. The carriages and supply wagons made a procession half a mile long.

The road distance from Moscow to Kiev was then some 800 miles. And it is an index of Elizabeth's fervor that this sybaritic, passionate, extravagant, and pleasure-loving woman, whose foibles were the gossip of Europe, covered the greater part on foot, marching along in the dry dust, carrying a holy banner, sweating, singing, and praying with a small group of like-minded zealots from her court and household. Razumovsky, whose ambitions were modest in heaven as on earth, kept her company but rode in the comfort of a fine carriage.

Catherine and Peter and scores of others from the court followed in a separate convoy equipped with all possible traveling luxuries. Peter, a staunch Lutheran beneath his thin official veneer of Orthodoxy, thought the pilgrimage was nonsense but made the best of it by converting the trip into a lark for Catherine and himself and their young friends. One of the big wagons had been fitted out by Catherine's mother as a caravansary so that eight or ten people could live and sleep in it. "When this vehicle was ready," wrote Catherine, "we remained in it the whole time and apart from my mother, the Grand Duke and myself allowed only the most amusing and entertaining among the entourage to join us, so that from morning to night we did nothing but laugh, play and make merry."

They found Empress Elizabeth and her weary devotees encamped on the east bank of the Dnieper opposite Kiev, a site that offered "an admirable panorama" of the city. Having mortified the flesh at Holy Trinity and Kiev and numerous way stations and having thus purged herself of all sin and any sinful thought, Empress Elizabeth returned with her heirs and court to Moscow for a season of pleasure.

That fall in Moscow, Catherine remembered, was an exciting round of entertainments, dances, masquerades, operas, comedies, concerts, balls, dressmakers, shopping, games, visits, gossip, frivolities, extravagances. She found herself being liked and admired. She found herself—it was hard for her to believe—becoming pretty, even with the beginnings of an elegant, unusual but striking kind of beauty.

Most gratifying, Grand Duke Peter was noticing her much more and, it seemed, in a new way. Writing of that brief happy interval, she said, ". . . the Grand Duke loved me passionately . . ." but then, she continued: "In November the Grand Duke caught measles, causing such anxiety to the Empress and everybody else. . . . During the illness he grew taller and stronger, but his mind was still very immature. He spent his time in his room playing soldiers with his valets, flunkeys, his dwarfs, and his gentlemen-in-waiting. . . . He exercised them and drilled them, but kept this as much of a secret as possible from his tutors . . . he confided his childish pranks to me and it was not my business to restrain him. I let him do and say what he liked. When this illness was over and the winter had settled in, we left Moscow for Petersburg, my mother and I traveling in one sleigh, the Grand Duke and Brümmer in another."

Halfway to Petersburg, "The Duke fainted in my room in the evening . . . and developed a high fever during the night." The next day Brümmer told her that Peter had symptoms of smallpox. "As I had not had it my mother quickly dragged me away . . . it was decided that we should proceed at once to Petersburg. . . . A messenger was sent to the Empress who had gone ahead and was already there. We met her a short distance from Novgorod. She had heard about the smallpox and was on her way back to join the Grand Duke . . . she remained for the duration of his illness."

Elizabeth conducted herself in the matter as a true heroine. She was proud of her beauty. Sometimes this pride led her to do outlandish and glaringly neurotic things, such as crossing a crowded ballroom floor and slapping the face of a woman wearing a costume that resembled hers. Now, without the slightest hesitation, she exposed her beauty to destruction for the sake of this nephew with whom she had long since become deeply disappointed. She stayed on with him night and day for six weeks, personally performing all the work and onerous necessities of the sickroom and nursing him back to health. At last, early in February, he had recovered enough that she could bring him to Petersburg, to the Winter Palace.

Catherine wrote: "As soon as we heard of her arrival we went to meet her and found her about four or five in the afternoon in the semi-darkness of the great hall. In spite of the obscurity the sight of the Grand Duke filled me almost with terror; he had grown very much in stature but his face was unrecognizable—his features were coarser, his face was still swollen, and one could see beyond doubt that he would always remain deeply pockmarked. His head had been shaven and he wore an immense wig which disfigured him all the more.

"He came up to me and asked whether I found it difficult to recognize him. I stammered a few wishes for his convalescence, but in fact he had become horrid to look at."

He was seventeen a few days later. That summer they were married.

IV

A Wedding
That Redeemed a Vow

ELIZABETH was determined to make this the most splendid wedding Russia had ever seen: a wedding, moreover, that by magnificence and fine taste would advertise to the Western nations, in their own terms, the wealth and power and advanced civilization of the Russia created by Peter the Great and nurtured now by his daughter. She had her ambassador in Paris send her a minutely detailed report on the recent wedding of the French Dauphin and Spanish Infanta. This was the basic model, which she then embellished with her own whims and fancies, adorned with special luxuries to outshine the original, and adapted for the particular glory of Russian tradition and of her father's memory. The preparations commenced in March, the wedding was in August, and for six months the other affairs of state languished, documents went unsigned, questions of war and peace and national economy were left in limbo while Elizabeth devoted herself to this, the event that would bring to fruition her years of planning and searching.

As for the two principals, Grand Duke Peter and Grand Duchess Catherine, Elizabeth's attitude toward them was a loose amalgam of tender affection and somewhat abstracted expectation that they would, of course, perform properly and on cue in the great pageant for which she was impresario, designer, director, patroness, and star. She arranged everything, and she assumed that everything was to turn out as she had arranged.

While the couriers, artists and architects, jewelers, music directors, coachmakers, ecclesiastics, courtiers, and supernumeraries came and went on a thousand crucial errands, she moved restlessly here and there among her palaces, which were already in various states of disrepair because of a program of building and remodeling she had undertaken. There were prenuptial festivities and ceremonials and, of course, exercises of public piety which Elizabeth adored and which her subjects adored in her as a characteristic of her Russian nature. The Empress and the Duke and Duchess took communion at the Church of the Virgin of Kazan, the largest mainland church; again, the Empress and the Duke and Duchess and members of the court walked in procession from the Winter Palace along the Nevsky Prospect all the way across the city to the Alexander Nevsky Monastery for vespers, followed by a court supper.

The Duke and Duchess, neither in full health, were wearied by all this, but they were mesmerized and swept along like two small corks in flood. In her memoirs, Catherine recalls the wedding day: "When my hair was dressed, the Empress came to place the Grand Ducal crown on my head and told me I could wear as many jewels as I wanted, both hers and mine. She left the room and the Court Ladies continued dressing me. . . . My dress was of silver moire, embroidered in silver on all the hems, and of a terrible weight. At three, the Empress, with the Grand Duke and myself in her carriage, drove in a great procession to the Church of the Virgin of Kazan where we were married by the Bishop of Novgorod."

The royal carriage was drawn by eight horses, each led by a liveried groom, and was flanked by footmen and guardsmen. A hundred and twenty splendid carriages followed, each drawn by six horses and attended by clouds of uniformed lackeys. With the Guards regiments in dress uniform and ecclesiastics in ornate vestments and all the great and noble of the realm wearing their finest raiment and jewels and decorations, the procession was a brilliant and awesome, vast and gorgeous spectacle. The English ambassador reported to his government: "The procession infinitely surpasses anything I have ever seen." It started at the Winter Palace, skirting the Admiralty gardens, where tables were piled high with food for the populace and the fountains ran with wine, and up Nevsky Prospect to the church.

Afterward, at the wedding feast in the Winter Palace, the newlyweds sat on a dais with the Empress; Peter sat on her right and Catherine on her left, the three of them a symbolic step above all mankind. "By the time we rose from the table," Catherine relates, "the weight of the crown and the jewels had given me a headache." Reluctantly, since she thought it might be a bad omen, Elizabeth allowed her to remove the crown while the room was cleared for the grand ball; then it was put back on her head.

The next day, "after receiving congratulations from everybody in the Winter Palace, we went to dine with the Empress in the Summer Palace. She had brought me in the morning a cushion covered with a magnificent set of emeralds and had sent the Grand Duke one of her sapphires to give me; in the evening there was a ball at the Winter Palace and two days later the Empress came to dine with us there. The wedding rejoicings lasted ten days"—and ended then in a scene both so gala and reverent that it stirred the hearts of everyone, Russian and foreigner.

As had happened on a few great occasions before (and now, as events turned out, was happening for the last time), the little boat that had been Peter the Great's first vessel—"the grandfather of the Russian Navy" it was called—was taken from its shrine in the Peter and Paul Fortress and placed on the deck of a larger boat which was draped entirely in crimson. Escorted by a flotilla of naval vessels carrying the senior officers of the fleet, Empress Elizabeth, and the new Peter and Catherine, the crimson boat with it precious relic, which bore as its cargo a portrait of Peter the Great, sailed up the Neva past the Admiralty, the Winter Palace, the Summer Garden, and on beyond to the Alexander Nevsky Monastery. There the bishop sprinkled the little boat with holy water. The double-eagle flag was unfurled and hoisted to the top of its mast. Elizabeth stepped forward and kissed the picture of her father. It was as if this were the redemption of a vow, the consecration of the grandson and his Baltic bride to the dynasty and work of Peter the Great.

It was a scene that Catherine never forgot.

V

The Imprisoned Newlyweds

THE wedding was a marvelous success: "... the gayest marriage that has perhaps ever been celebrated in Europe," Catherine's mother wrote to her husband, who had suffered a disabling stroke and had stayed at home in Zerbst.

As a personal union, however, the marriage was a grotesque failure. In all her elaborate plans, Elizabeth had steadfastly ignored the biological imperative of a fruitful marriage: the existence of at least some physical attraction and at least some emotional rapport in the relationship. Between Peter and Catherine there was none of either. The smallpox and Catherine's involuntary revulsion, which he sensed, apparently had shattered any weak confidence Peter may have had in his ability to be a man with her. He withdrew into his own pastimes and avoided her, except to take vengeance by telling her how much he admired other women or to imply that in marriage he intended her role to be entirely uncritical.

"I was well aware of his lack of eagerness, and of his lack of affection, too; my pride and vanity suffered. . . . The nearer my wedding-day approached, the more despondent did I become, and often found myself crying without quite knowing why." She remained outwardly amenable and tactful, "in order that he should at least consider me a loyal friend to whom he could say anything without risk," but inwardly she had begun to feel contempt and dislike for him. Contempt for his "childish occupations, incredible at his age—he even played with dolls." Dislike for his callousness: "The Grand Duke found great amusement in instructing me in military exercises, and owing to him I can handle a rifle with the precision of an experienced grenadier. He made me stand at arms with my musket, on duty at the door of the room between his and mine. Hope for the crown, not of the celestial order but very much on earth, sustained my spirit and courage."

On the wedding night, after the grand ball, "the Empress took the Grand Duke and me to our apartments. The ladies undressed me and put me to bed. . . . Everybody left me and I remained alone for more than two hours, not knowing what was expected of me. Should I get up? Should I remain in bed? I truly did not know. At last Mme. Krause, my new maid, came in and told me very cheerfully that the Grand Duke was waiting for his supper which would be served shortly. His Imperial Highness came to bed after supper and began to say how amused the servants would be to find us in bed together. Mme. Krause questioned us the next day on our marital experience, but she was disappointed in her hopes."

Nor, as the fortnight of celebrations wore on, "did my dear husband pay the slightest attention to me but spent all his time playing soldiers in his room with his valets, performing military exercises and changing their uniforms twenty times a day. I yawned and yawned with boredom. In the very first days of our marriage I came to a sad conclusion about him. I said to myself: 'If you allow yourself to love that man, you will be the unhappiest creature on earth; with your temperament you will expect some response whereas this man scarcely looks at you, talks of nothing but dolls and such things, and pays more attention to any other woman than yourself; you are too proud to complain, therefore, attention, please, and keep on a leash any affection you might feel for this gentleman; you have yourself to think about, my dear girl.' This first scar made upon my impressionable heart remained with me forever; never did this firm resolution leave my noodle. . . ."

Elizabeth, who assigned their servants, as well as ladies- and gentlemen-in-waiting to Catherine and Peter and thus kept herself closely informed, waited first fretfully, then with growing exasperation, and finally with sheer outrage. Childish contrariness, spite, impertinence, perversity, unfaithful adventuring with others— she could not be sure which, if any or all, might be impeding the consummation of the marriage, but she was determined to overcome it, whatever it might be. After a month or two she began to take steps, progressively harsher, to enforce her imperial will on the insubordinate couple. And thus opened a fantastic siege that was to last for almost nine years, climaxed by a fantastic denouement—and the birth of a child.

Elizabeth's tactics changed Catherine's character, transforming her from a wide-eyed naïve innocent to a woman of the world, with important consequences for the world. It was in this time that she acquired her education and her intellectual fiber.

As for her naïveté, she described it in a delightful and fairly startling scene that occurred a few weeks before the marriage, the night before the holy day especially dear to Petersburgers, St. Peter's Day. "I remember that on the eve of that feast I suddenly had the fancy to have all my ladies and maids sleeping in my room. For that purpose I had my mattress as well as theirs stretched out on the floor and that is how we spent the night; but before we went to sleep we had a prolonged discussion on the difference between the sexes. I am certain that most of us were extremely innocent; for myself I can testify that though I was more than sixteen years old, I had no idea what this difference was; I went so far as to promise my women to question my mother the next morning about it; they agreed that I should do so and we went to sleep. Next day I put the question to my mother and was severely scolded."

Presumably she had gone to the marriage bed little more enlightened; as for Peter, although he had at least the usual juvenile vocabulary and no doubt some of the prurient fantasies, he was still, at seventeen, more pubescent than adolescent, lingering physiologically as well as mentally in childhood, and he came to his astonishingly uninformed bride with only the vaguest ideas of what was involved in the occasion or what procedure he should take.

Thus Elizabeth's initial dilemma was that she was dealing with a pair of actual innocents. She could not imagine such heights of guilelessness. Assuming, consequently, that their sexual energies were somehow being misdirected, she began by removing all other likely targets, so that ultimately through lack of more attractive alternatives they would discover each other. No sooner did either show any particular liking for any servant, court attendant, or acquaintance—of either sex—than the person was sent away from court. Guards were posted outside their bedroom (from the first night, they always had slept in the same bed) and at other well-selected sentry stations in their apartments to be sure that no one could enter or leave without being observed. To make observation easier, their private apartments were reduced in size until finally they had only two rooms each to themselves. They were forbidden to write private letters. Their allowances were reduced to a pittance. Their lives were regulated by the Empress, who insisted that they accompany her and her court on her steady perambulations among her residences. They could not leave the palace of the moment without the express permission of Her Majesty. On the other hand they were not allowed to speak directly to her about anything whatever unless first spoken to; all messages were to be transmitted back and forth by the "Arguses" and "Harpies," as Catherine called them, who were assigned by Elizabeth to act as their guardians and advisers, or more truly their jailors.

The Grand Duke had been given as a residence the vast showplace of Oranienbaum that had belonged to Prince Menshikov in Peter the Great's time. Sometimes he and Catherine were allowed to go there instead of trailing, unrecognized, unseen, in effect invisible to her, in Elizabeth's entourage. But at Oranienbaum the jailors were if anything even more severe, on the safe assumption that without access to the Empress' permission the answer to any request should almost always be no.

It was a nightmare world in which Catherine once thought of killing herself. Then, rallying her reserves of character and sense, she decided to make the best life she could under circumstances of misery. She found her main solace in books. She read vastly, omnivorously, discovering dimensions of pleasure and satisfaction she had not dreamed of as she moved from the works of Plato to the works of Voltaire. The latter became a hero to her. And thus the great iconoclast, chief philosopher of the rights of the individual and subverter of the divine claims of church and state, sowed the seeds of liberalism and ultimately of revolution in the most autocratic court of Europe. Much later Catherine and Voltaire were to have an extraordinary relationship of mutual admiration and mutual benefit.

Her pleasure in the intellect caused an even greater estrangement between her and Elizabeth and the court. With her native wit and intelligence fortified by knowledge and fertilized by thoughts from great minds, she recovered from her girlhood difficulties and became a conversationalist—when she could find anyone to converse with, usually a foreigner. She acquired a reputation for mental vivacity and self-assurance which annoyed Elizabeth, who several times during the years accused her—in a manner indicating it was a very sore point and a grave charge—of thinking herself "cleverer than anyone."

Elizabeth herself, for all her devotion to her father's memory and commitment to his policies and for all her considerable intelligence and taste, had practically none of his intellectual curiosity. Accordingly she had very little real comprehension of his methods and ideas. She functioned, often with great effectiveness, on quite another plane, that of the emotions, but she was mentally lazy and preferred the company of people who could be as easily satisfied as she with superficial pastimes.

Catherine was increasingly bored by these and wrote of the incessant cardplaying and gambling: "This entertainment was essential at a Court where there was no conversation, where everybody cordially hated everybody else, where slander took the place of wit and any mention of politics was reported as lèse-majesté! Intricate intrigues were mistaken for shrewdness. Science and art were never touched on, as everybody was ignorant of those subjects; one could lay a wager that half the Court could hardly read and I would be surprised if more than a third could write."

Catherine's skills as a diplomat, dissembler, blackmailer, and driver of discreet hard bargains, manipulator of foes and rivals into friends and allies—all these arts first developed as she strove to protect herself. Her chief maid, Mme. Krause, was the sister of Elizabeth's chief maid and manifestly was a spy as well as a tyrant who reduced the other girls of Catherine's staff to speaking in whispers. But, Catherine writes, "I discovered that she had a great liking for the bottle," and often "my entourage managed to make her drunk, after which she went to bed, and I was delivered from this formidable Argus." In the course of this treatment, Mme. Krause mellowed and developed such fondness for Catherine and Peter that she eventually became an ally.

A more difficult case was Maria Choglokov, cousin of Elizabeth, who was imposed on Catherine as her chief lady-in-waiting—"a great blow to me, for this lady [was] uneducated, malicious, and full of self-interest. . . ." As for the other reason for her assignment as Catherine's chief lady-in-waiting: "The Grand Duke took me aside, and I could clearly see that he had been given to understand that Mme. Choglokov was being appointed . . . because I did not love him. . . . She had the reputation of being very virtuous, because she adored her husband; hers had been a love marriage" and conspicuously fruitful. Madame Choglokov had already produced six children, with the certain expectation of more to come. ". . . and such a good example thrust in front of my eyes was obviously meant to inspire me with the desire to emulate it." Catherine, who feared and hated her, remarked: ". . . but for this particular function it was not sufficient to be malicious and malevolent. I cannot understand how anybody could have believed that this woman could in any way make me feel more tenderness for him. I told him so."

It was all the less likely because Choglokov, the object of Madame Choglokov's adoration and intemperate desire, was "an arrogant and brutal fool . . . stupid, conceited, malicious, pompous, secretive, and silent, with never a smile on his lips," and had nothing to recommend him but his wife's devotion. But Elizabeth, who loved her family, made him Chamberlain of her court. (She also made him a Count and thus his wife a Countess; but Catherine, writing her memoirs in French, never acknowledges these titles and always referred to them by the abbreviations M. and Mme.) As Elizabeth's majordomo he made himself "an object of terror to everyone." Before long he was put in charge of the Grand Duke's household. Catherine wrote: ". . . even Mme. Krause . . . trembled when she heard of this grim choice.

"There were, however, methods . . . by which this pair of Arguses could be not only put to sleep but won over." In time, "everybody around us tried to mitigate the rigor of the political imprisonment to which we were subjected. Most prominent amid these conspirators was Count Hendrikov, Mme. Choglokov's brother, a kind and outspoken man."

But meanwhile, the Grand Duke led a constricted, miserable life, and Madame Krause, not the most prominent but the first of those "conspirators," warmed by the bottle and by a certain affinity for Peter because she too was a Holsteiner, "mellowed so much that she conspired to deceive the Choglokovs, who had become everybody's pet aversion. She went further: she procured toys for the Grand Duke, dolls and other childish games which he was mad about; in the daytime we hid them inside and under my bed. The Grand Duke was the first to go to bed after supper and as soon as we both were in bed Mme. Krause would lock the door and the Grand Duke played until two or three in the morning. I had no choice but to take part in this unusual entertainment, nor had Mme. Krause.

"Often it made me laugh but more often it irritated me and interfered with my movements, the whole bed being covered with dolls and toys, sometimes quite heavy ones. I do not know if Mme. Choglokov came to hear of these nocturnal amusements, but one evening towards midnight she knocked at the bedroom door: we did not open at once because the Grand Duke, Mme. Krause and I were too busy hastening to remove the toys from the bed and found the blankets very useful to hide them under. When we eventually opened the door, she was indignant at having been kept waiting and told me that the Empress would be furious to learn we were not asleep at such a late hour. Then she left us, grumbling at having discovered nothing more."

Not long afterward, "through the medium of Mme. Choglokov, a strict order was issued by the Empress, forbidding anyone to

enter the Grand Duke's and my apartments except with the permission of M. and Mme. Choglokov, and ordering the ladies- and
gentlemen-in-waiting of our Court to remain in the antechamber,
and neither to cross the threshold, nor to speak to us otherwise
than in loud tones. The same order applied to the servants, on
pain of dismissal. The Grand Duke and I, reduced to a life *à deux*,
protested to each other as we exchanged ideas about this prison
which neither of us deserved."

Among the few diversions allowed them were hunting and riding. Catherine relates: ". . . with nothing better to do and with
tedium spreading more and more at our Court, riding became my
dominant passion." The best facilities were at Oranienbaum,
"where I spent thirteen hours out of the twenty-four in the saddle
. . . the more violent that exercise the more I enjoyed it, so that
if a horse ever broke away I galloped after it and brought it back."

Elizabeth forbade her to ride astride for fear this might interfere
with pregnancy, so "I invented for myself saddles upon which I
could sit as I wanted. They had the English crook and one could
swing one's legs to sit astride; the pommel, furthermore, could be
screwed off and one of the stirrups raised or lowered as required.
If the grooms were asked how I rode, they could truthfully say:
'In a lady's saddle, according to the Empress's wish.' I switched
my leg only when I was sure that I was not going to be observed."

In either posture she rode magnificently, and she had numerous
riding costumes, always of silk. She was acquiring great elegance
and assurance and a certain delicate, attenuated beauty. One
costume, which she wore while putting the boastful wife of the
Saxon ambassador in her place both as an equestrienne and a
clotheshorse, she described as a "habit of rich sky-blue material
with silver braid and crystal buttons, which looked exactly like
diamonds. My black hat had a string of diamonds round it."

It was the riding, not the hunting, that she liked, whereas with
Peter, as usual ("never did two minds resemble each other less than
ours"), it was the opposite. "In the country he collected a pack of
hounds and began to train them himself; when he grew weary of
tormenting them, he began to pick at the violin. He did not know
a single note, but had a good ear and showed his appreciation of
the music by the strength and violence with which he drew sounds

from his instrument . . . mercilessly. This mode of life went on in town as well as in the country."

In the autumn of 1747 "came the order for us to move to the Winter Palace, where the Grand Duke and I were forced to remain inseparable. . . . To procure more amusement for himself during the winter, the Grand Duke had eight or ten hunting dogs brought from the country and put behind the wooden partition which separated the alcove of my room from an immense vestibule at the back of our apartment . . . the stink of the kennels penetrated into our room and we both slept in this putrid air."

A year later: "The Grand Duke had only two occupations. One was to scrape the violin, the other to train spaniels for hunting. So, from 7 o'clock in the morning until late into the night, either the discordant sound which he drew very forcefully from the violin or the horrible barking and howling of the five or six dogs, which he thrashed throughout the rest of the day, continually grated on my core. I admit that I was driven half mad. . . . After the dogs I was the most miserable creature in the world."

And still the next year, during one of the enforced sojourns in Moscow: "One day I heard a dog whine piteously for a long time. I opened the door of my bedroom where I was sitting and I saw that the Grand Duke was holding one of the dogs in the air by its collar, while a young servant of Kalmuk origin held its tail; it was a poor little English King Charles, and the Grand Duke was flogging the dog as hard as he could with the handle of a whip. I tried to intercede for the poor animal but this only increased the blows. I retired to my room in tears."

Here, perhaps, was a projection of the sadist Brümmer at work disciplining his helpless young pupil with torments to make him behave, do his work, come to heel, lead the pack. However much he may himself have deserved pity (and Catherine, often loathing him, could still pity him), Peter could be truly interesting only as a case study in psychopathology. Even Elizabeth was forced against every inclination to admit this to herself and finally in confidential terms to some few others. Much later, when Catherine had access to the state archives, she found among Elizabeth's papers the angry, tragic judgment: "My nephew, Devil take him, is a monster!"

VI

The Inescapable Need for an Heir

OF course, it can be argued that in Grand Duke Peter, both Elizabeth and Catherine had got what they deserved, for each had thought of him not really as a human being with his own interests but as a mechanism for attaining her own self-centered ends. He had been forced into his role; he was entirely unfit for it and unhappy in it; he hated the whole intricate, impenetrable web of circumstances that had brought him into the situation and kept him there. He careened from one infatuation to another, with women of the Empress' court or Catherine's or women encountered in the royal entertainments and royal travels. And "as was his custom," Catherine wrote, "he did not fail to confide in me at once."

Peter was still impotent not only with his wife, but also with all women. How much this condition was due to psychological factors and how much to physiological ones is never made clear by Catherine or anyone else in a position to report reliably on those intimate matters although, as will be related in a moment, there is reason to think that he needed, and finally got, a surgical correction.

In any case, his incompetence, it is reasonable to surmise, contributed powerfully to the growing alienation he felt for everything Russian and his increasingly obsessive admiration for all things German, especially for Prussia and, above all, for his native Holstein. For in the Russian character—as generations of foreign visitors have reported with amazement—extremes of pious self-abasement were matched by equal and opposite extremes of erotic self-indulgence.

Elizabeth was the apotheosis of Russian piety and carnality. On the one hand, her piety (and her patriotism: Russia must have dignity in the eyes of the world) shocked and outraged her as any puritanical maiden aunt when members of her establishment were discovered *in flagrante* and caused public scandal or gossip. On the other hand, her court throbbed with eroticism, always there, just beneath the surface of propriety, manifesting itself at every good chance and in a constantly changing maze of sexual intrigue. But Peter could only pretend to play seriously at this intrigue. He was a monstrosity who must often have been driven to perceive himself as a monstrosity. Naturally enough he took refuge in a realm of fantasy—which in this case had a geographical counterpart that actually belonged to him, his legal patrimony, Holstein. His homesickness became pathological.

Catherine, who did not understand it, described his condition disdainfully but with almost clinical exactness: "This Prince had an extraordinary passion for the corner of the world where he was born . . . day after day he told us cock-and-bull stories about it . . . and was angry when he noticed our incredulous glances. Who would have guessed that the passion he had . . . gradually turned this Prince into one of the greatest liars the world has ever seen? In the end his blindness went so far that he was convinced at the bottom of his heart that the lies he invented and repeated were indisputable truths."

Peter's fantasies of the magical realm (where in fact, of course, he had spent the later years of his childhood in misery and terror) were nourished by his having become, through a number of political convolutions, its legal ruler, not long after his marriage. He was Duke of Holstein, as well as Grand Duke of Russia. As Duke he could dismiss his old tormentor, Brümmer; as Grand Duke, subject to the will of the Empress, he was forced to send home as well various Holsteiners who had come to Russia with him and whom he liked. As Duke he was allowed, however, to import Holstein officials through whom he ruled his homeland; as Grand Duke he was not allowed to visit there or indeed to leave the borders of Russia at all for any reason.

So his fantasies grew, and not surprisingly in the circumstances they soon incorporated a German savior-hero, Frederick the Great, who had made Prussia the preeminent German state and one of the most formidable military powers of Europe. His attitude toward Frederick became worshipful, and this became the common gossip of the court and hence of all the courts of Europe. Even Frederick, although naturally delighted that the heir to the Russian throne should insist on fitting so well into his own plans for Prussia's future, could not help being amused at such a truly Quixotic fixation and remarked, "I am his Dulcinea."

Peter began dressing in Holstein uniform. He imported Holstein soldiers to serve as his honor guard. Finally, he brought in a whole regiment which he billeted at Oranienbaum and delighted in marching up and down. His native city of Kiel, he declared loudly, had more merit in it than the whole Russian Empire. He brooded much over the loss of the duchy of Schleswig, which had been part of the Holstein dominion but had been taken over by the Danes in his grandfather's day. When he became Czar, he implied, he would turn loose the terrible combined military strength of Holstein and Russia to retrieve the lost duchy. And, of course, he would bring Russia to the side of Prussia as a firm and faithful ally.

In any circumstances all this would have been unseemly, to say the least, in a Russian Crown Prince. What made it far worse was that Elizabeth had come to power in a revolt against the too-conspicuous German influence at court during the reign of the two Annas. Furthermore, Elizabeth's foreign policy was becoming steadily and ever more vigorously anti-Prussian and pro-Austrian in response to the rise of Prussian power near Russia's borders and—a much more touchy matter—on the shores of the Baltic.

Elizabeth's policy, which she referred to and believed to be

"Peter's policy," was nurtured and administered by her trusted Chancellor, Count Alexis Petrovich Bestuzhev-Ryumin. By the end of the decade of the 1740's—that is, Elizabeth's first decade on the throne and some six years after the wedding of Peter and Catherine—there was a strong probability that Russia and Prussia were headed for war as Frederick the Great pursued an aggressive, expansive policy at the expense of countries bordering on his. In these developing circumstances, Grand Duke Peter's fervid affection for Frederick passed unseemliness and became outrageous, manifestly disloyal to national policy and not far, perhaps, from being actually treasonable.

For Bestuzhev the situation presented an incredible dilemma, filled with the gravest potential dangers to the national welfare, as he saw it, and certainly not less to his personal welfare. Elizabeth was in her forties, and her health was not reliable. The energies spent in living so many kinds of life, playing so many roles so ardently, had weakened her robust body and, as became progressively evident, eroded her nervous system. Bouts of neurasthenia, violent rage, deep melancholy, nagging incapacitating fear, insomnia, intervals of utter lassitude, self-pity, and self-indulgence, including gluttony that made her swell to elephantine proportions —all testified to her decline. Her death would bring Peter to the throne, and this event, besides saddling Russia with a mental incompetent, inevitably would bring a reversal of the anti-Prussian policy. If she died while the two countries were at war, Russia's military forces would be controlled by a Czar who was the self-declared friend of the enemy.

All this helps illuminate the strange situation in which Catherine found herself and the events that enabled her to escape from it and finally to secure the throne for herself.

Because of her family's close ties to Prussia and Frederick, Bestuzhev had originally advised against the marriage. Elizabeth's strong sentimental feelings far outweighed her doubts. Catherine arrived in Russia to learn soon that she had, as her personal enemy, the most influential man in the government. And what an enemy to have! He was cunning, devious, adroit, utterly opportunistic and utterly ruthless in pursuit of his aims, and seemingly omniscient. His spy service, within Russia and abroad, was a marvel of its time and a model for the future. He used it time and again to discredit his enemies at court by producing evidence of their intrigues with foreign governments, particularly Prussia.

Those disgraced included some of Elizabeth's close associates and personal friends. Also among them, of dire consequence for Catherine's position, was Catherine's mother. Correspondence from the French ambassador, intercepted by Bestuzhev, showed that Frederick had asked her while in Russia to help undermine Bestuzhev and bring a pro-Prussian faction to power. Elizabeth was furious and sent the misguided princess packing to Anhalt-Zerbst as soon as possible after the wedding.

Elizabeth had been so shaken by these revelations of deceit in her own circle, even her own family, that she relied more and more on Bestuzhev's judgment and soon raised him from Vice Chancellor to Grand Chancellor, the equivalent of Premier or Prime Minister. For fourteen years he directed the affairs of Russia, foreign and domestic, on her behalf. Although it would ordinarily seem unnatural that the chief servant of the throne would use the full weight of the state security apparatus to keep the chosen and legal heirs to the throne under minute surveillance and semi-imprisonment, and do so moreover with the full knowledge and approval of their loving aunt, the Empress, under the given circumstances it was understandable, plausible, and even, in a way, natural.

To what extent the specific miseries inflicted on the Grand Duke and Duchess were Bestuzhev's inventions, and to what extent Elizabeth's, has never been certain.

Catherine, who had adored Elizabeth and taken her as an ideal and who had received Elizabeth's lavish and surely genuine affection until some months after the wedding, could hardly believe that her benefactress could so easily become her tormentor. For a long time she blamed Bestuzhev for everything. She hated him and feared him, and although it was many years later that she wrote her memoirs, those feelings were still vivid enough to lead her to enter them on page after page of the section describing those miserable early years.

If it is true, on the one hand, that Elizabeth was fully aware of the harassment and punishments, and that all were applied with her consent, it was Bestuzhev who drew up the codes of behavior for the grand ducal couple and the regulations for their household and submitted these to Elizabeth for approval. Accordingly, there is every logical reason to think that the startling events that now began to occur were set in motion by Bestuzhev with Elizabeth's knowledge, at least to a point, and with her approval or at least tacit consent.

The year was 1751 or 1752—that is, some six or seven years after Peter and Catherine's marriage, with the prospect of war with Prussia now very clear, and with it, equally clear, the patriotic and personal dilemma confronting Bestuzhev. Even the cleverest, most pragmatic diplomat needs room for maneuver, and with Peter as the heir to the throne there was no room, no opening at all in which to seek a solution through "the art of the possible." So an heir must be created; further, to avoid putting the nation into turmoil, the heir must be, or convincingly seem to be, a legitimate offspring of the dynasty.

In short, the grand ducal couple must produce a child.

The strategy of the past years not having worked, it must be discarded and a new strategy invented. This, to be sure, is in part surmise, but it is the only rational explanation for what happened.

VII

An Heir Is Created

ATTRACTIVE young men had been banished from court at the first sign of being attracted to Catherine or of Catherine taking any pleasure in their company. Now the grand ducal household suddenly acquired not just one, but two gallant charmers, both of them noblemen of the highest aristocracy: Leon Naryshkin and Serge Saltikov. They were close friends, bons vivants, full of young energies and fond of parties, dancing and witty conversation. They were endowed with all the civilized attractions Catherine had been missing in male company for so many years with Peter.

She writes: "Mme. Choglokov, who never abandoned her favorite occupation of watching over the succession, took me aside one day and said: 'Listen to me, I must really talk to you about this quite frankly.' I was naturally all ears and eyes. She started in her usual way with a long dissertation on her affection for her husband, on her wisdom, on what had or had not to be done to secure love and facilitate conjugal relations, and then suddenly declared that there were certain situations of major importance which formed exceptions to the rule.

"I let her say all she had to say without interrupting, unaware of what she was aiming at, slightly surprised and wondering if she was setting a trap for me or whether she was sincere. While I was deliberating this, she added: 'You will see how much I love my country and how frank I can be: I have no doubt that in your heart you have a certain preference for one man over the other; I leave you to choose between Serge Saltikov and Leon Naryshkin, and if I am not mistaken it is the latter.'

"To this I cried out: 'No, no, not at all.' And she went on: 'Well, if it's not him, it can only be the other.' I remained silent and she added: 'You will see that I shall not be the one to create any obstacles for you.' I feigned the simpleton to such a degree that she scolded me for it. . . ."

Catherine had every reason to suspect an ambush. So too did all the other characters on their individual behalf—from Bestuzhev to that chosen instrument of state, Serge Saltikov, to the household servants—who were involved in these improbable adventures. Conspiracy and intrigue were so much the norm at Elizabeth's court even in small matters that in such a matter as this every action and word had to be calculated against the possibility of treachery. Consequently everyone dissembled to everyone else; everyone played a part in a double game. Some, including Madame Choglokov, Serge Saltikov, Bestuzhev, and even Elizabeth appear to have been engaged in a triple or quadruple game.

The action had elements of a French bedroom farce, a seduction scene staged in a crazy-house hall of mirrors, and a mystery drama in which half the clues had been deleted or distorted and for which crucial specific revelations in the third act were not written in but deliberately left blank for each spectator to fill in with his own preferences. Aware, accordingly, that the proceedings are beyond the competence of scientific historiography and that Catherine's memoirs for all their occasional contradictions and obscurities and evasions are incomparably the fullest and most reliable source, one cannot really improve on Catherine's own remarks except to shift some into what seems to be a somewhat more logical sequence.

Like all young men of the high aristocracy, Serge Saltikov in his early twenties had served for a while in one of the numerous ceremonial court offices. As Catherine relates, briefly and without warmth, he was part of the Grand Duke's entourage during a visit to Tsarskoe Selo that Elizabeth ordered the Young Court and the ladies-in-waiting of the Old Court to make while she herself was helping Count Razumovsky celebrate his birthday at one of his country estates. Tsarskoe Selo was still being built—or rebuilt, for "it was like the task of Penelope; the work of today was all destroyed on the morrow . . . demolished and rebuilt in all six times . . ." and in its unsettled condition offered few pleasures. "In Tsarskoe we tried to entertain ourselves as best we could. . . . The swing was a great resource." It was a grand, fanciful, high-arcing swing. "It was on the swing that Mlle. Balk, lady-in-waiting of the Empress, won the heart of M. Serge Saltikov. . . . He proposed marriage to her next day. She accepted and they were married soon afterwards. In the evenings we played cards; after that there was supper."

Two years had passed. Saltikov was twenty-six, and after only occasional dutiful visits to court and at necessary ceremonies he had reappeared, attending court "more assiduously than ever," as Catherine observed. And, what was truly remarkable, cultivating close friendship with the two chief Arguses, M. and Mme. Choglokov. "As the latter were neither clever nor amusing, or even amiable, his attentions could only have had some secret purpose." Madame Choglokov once again was pregnant—a seventh blessing from Choglokov and still more bountiful example for Catherine. But "she was often ailing . . . pretended that I alone was able to entertain her, she wanted me to visit her all the time, in summer and winter. Serge Saltikov, Leon Naryshkin, Princess Gagarine and a few others were usually at her house. . . ." Thus the scene was set for friendship, attraction, and whatever else might develop.

Yet there was the equivocal figure of Choglokov. Was he part of a conspiracy? How much? Whose representative? He was still Argus, guardian-jailor-protector of the Grand Duke. Yet, as Catherine relates, he had quarreled violently with Bestuzhev. Or was that a deception to throw the Grand Duke and Duchess off guard? Tacitly it was agreed to accept him in his familiar role of ogre and treat him with corresponding care.

"Serge Saltikov devised for Choglokov a peculiar way of spending his time. . . . I do not know how he discovered in this heavy-minded and unimaginative man a passion for writing lyrics which made no sense at all. Once this became known, every time anyone wanted to get rid of M. Choglokov he was asked to write new lyrics, and he would at once eagerly go and sit down in a corner of the room, usually near the stove, and start writing them, which took him the whole evening.

"His lyrics were usually warmly praised so as to encourage him to write fresh ones. Leon Naryshkin set them to music and sang them with him; in the meantime, conversation in the room became unrestrained and one could say anything one wanted.

"During one of these concerts, Serge Saltikov gave me to understand the reason for his attentions. At first I did not reply to him. I asked him, when he reverted to the subject, to explain what he expected to get from it. Then he began to draw so joyful and exciting a picture of the happiness he expected that I said: 'And what about your wife whom you loved so passionately two years ago when you married her and with whom you are supposed to be still in love and she with you—what will she say to that?'

"To this he said that all is not gold that glitters and that he was paying a high price for a moment of folly. I did all I could to make him see reason; I hoped I would succeed, for I was sorry for him. But unfortunately I could not help listening to him; he was handsome as the dawn. . . .

"I held firm during the spring and part of the summer."

Catherine had come to Russia, and to marriage, as we saw, innocent not only of carnal knowledge, but of any knowledge of what carnality meant. She was to become, in later years, "the scandal of Europe"—perhaps the most notorious woman of her time and among the most notorious of all time. Her love affairs made history and did so in ways that far exceeded the level of common gossip. Her affairs made political, military, and economic history of the first magnitude. Some of her lovers are associated with events that have loomed even larger in our time than in theirs.

Without prurience, therefore, or as an essay in historical voyeurism, but for essential purposes, it is necessary to examine the transformation of her character and the circumstances that may explain it. Some of these have been made clear enough already; others can be left to emerge in the context of later events. But there is a question that Catherine herself raised in the memoir passages above—manifestly important to her and to our understanding of her—which can be answered only in the immediate context in which it arose. This was the problem of adultery, which, for her, undoubtedly presented a moral crisis.

Later she could be accused with some justification of being hypocritical about her religion, but at this point in her life—conveniently though she had allowed herself to be persuaded to change from Lutheranism to Orthodoxy—she was undoubtedly a convinced Christian with clear convictions about good and evil and the gradations of sin. She knew that fornication was sinful, that adultery, involving as it did the breaking of a commandment, was a cardinal sin. And in fact she never really fully recovered from this ingrained sense of sin; as an old woman, drenched in sinning, she could somehow think of herself as an essentially virtuous victim of circumstances.

And there was just enough truth in this to make her rationalizations acceptable to herself. For good cause, as we have seen, she could begin with Peter's nature and the sham of their marriage. "There was no question in all this of the dear husband," she wrote, "because it was a recognized thing that he was ruthless even regarding those with whom he was in love, and he was in love all the time . . . the only exception being the woman who was his wife." And "Everybody knew that the marriage between me and the Grand Duke had not been consummated."

She was twenty-three, decidedly attractive, charming, intelligent, healthy, and a virgin whose virginity, to quote one of her female biographers, "had been a standing reproach to her for eight years." Even so, this unnatural situation might have continued indefinitely except for the unruly reminders that nature supplied in such abundance in Catherine's own immediate environment. And the gaudiest of these, hence the ones most suggestive of possible emulation, came at a period when she was most vulnerable.

In the autumn of 1749, Elizabeth made an appointment that

resounded through every department of her government and establishment and echoed in every court and foreign office of Europe. The announcement, all the more freighted with possible significance because she made it while on a pilgrimage to one of her favorite monasteries and on her own saint's day, was that Ivan Shuvalov would be her Gentleman of the Bedchamber. The title, to be sure, was a traditional one that carried with it only some honorary and ceremonial duties. But because Shuvalov was attractive and Elizabeth had already given signs of her feelings, it was assumed, and quickly confirmed, that in his case it was to be taken literally.

"This is a great event," Catherine wrote, adding with what could only have been meant as sweetly malicious and ironic humor: "I was glad of the promotion as I had observed him ever since he was a page because he was so studious. He was always seen with a book in his hands."

What of Count Razumovsky, the long-established "Emperor of the Night" on whom Elizabeth had lavished so many honors and palaces and who possibly was her morganatic husband? It soon became clear that he was not actually deposed, but instead reduced to junior rank in what emerged as a co-monarchy, a situation that he accepted with his usual good nature. There were political consequences, for the Shuvalov family seized the advantage to build a powerful faction. But Ivan Shuvalov was as selfless as Razumovsky; the result was a viable *ménage à trois*, sometimes strained but by and large congenial.

The situation was lent additional piquancy by other facts. Ivan Shuvalov's mother, Countess Shuvalov, was one of Elizabeth's best friends; she "had been brought up with Her Majesty and was of the same age; her gay disposition amused the Empress, who at one time could not do without her. . . ." His father, Marshal Shuvalov, had once been Elizabeth's lover, early in her reign, briefly replacing the patient and durable Count Razumovsky as "favorite."

Thus there was a special quality to the Shuvalov affair. Soon, however, complicating factors were added. It had been Razumovsky's fine bass voice, as mentioned before, that had drawn Elizabeth's attention to him. Now, some twenty years later, she encountered a young chorister named Kachinevsky who in splendor of voice and handsomeness might have been Razumovsky's son. Elizabeth, perhaps in nostalgia, added him to her intimate visitors. This made three. And soon there were four.

As Catherine tells the story: "Prince Yussupov, senator and Chief of the Cadet Corps, was commander-in-chief of the town of St. Petersburg, and he remained there while the Court was absent. For his entertainment and that of the important personalities who had remained with him, he had the cadets perform the best Russian comedies of the time, by Alexander Sumarakov, and the French dramas by Voltaire. The latter were spoken as badly as they were acted by these young men, and since the women's parts were also performed by cadets, the plays were, in every sense, manhandled.

"When she returned from Moscow, the Empress ordered that Sumarakov's comedies should be played at Court by these young men. She took great pleasure in attending the performances, and it was soon observed that she watched them with greater interest than might have been expected.

"The theater, which had been built in one of the halls of the Winter Palace, was dismantled and rebuilt in her private apartments. She took a particular pleasure in dressing the actors. She had magnificent clothes made for them, and they were covered with Her Majesty's jewels. It was noticed that the first lover"— that is, the leading man or juvenile lead—"a rather handsome boy of eighteen or nineteen, was, as befitted him, the best dressed; and he was soon also outside the theater wearing diamond buckles, rings, watches, lace jabots and expensive linen.

"When he left the Cadet Corps, the Master of the Hunt, Count Razumovsky . . . immediately made him his Aide de Camp, which gave the young man the rank of captain. The courtiers drew their own conclusions and decided that if Count Razumovsky had taken Cadet Beketov as his A.D.C., he could only be trying to balance the position of M. Shuvalov, the Gentleman of the Bedchamber. . . . So the impression grew that this young man was coming into great favor with the Empress."

Catherine reports that on Easter Sunday, 1750, Elizabeth left church in the midst of the mass, which was for her quite extraordinary. She "had gone to her little chapel and seemed to be in a very bad humor. It was whispered that this choleric disposition was caused by the embarrassment in which Her Majesty found herself among her four favorites, Razumovsky, Shuvalov, Kachinevsky and Beketov." And she adds: "It must be admitted that anyone but Her Majesty would have been embarrassed with less than that. To deal with four men and conciliate them all is not a task that everyone could accomplish."

To Elizabeth's courtiers and officials, the fascination of the volatile *menage à cinque* lay in the play and interplay and possible effects of the political forces represented. Count Bestuzhev, instantly recognizing a threat to his own preeminence in the rise of the Shuvalovs, moved to bolster Count Razumovsky's position by entering into close alliance with him and using his vast resources to undermine—with utmost discretion, of course—Ivan Shuvalov's position and ambush the Shuvalov family ambitions. Kachinevsky, the Third Man, may well have been his secret protégé, an agent provocateur of the boudoir, and undoubtedly he inspired or guided the move that made young Beketov ADC to Razumovsky.

Yet the Shuvalovs' position was very strong. They could compete with Bestuzhev evenly in pragmatic ruthlessness. And they had as their allies great numbers of people of consequence whom Bestuzhev had made his enemies, others who had hurried opportunely to join a rising power, and—a special and powerful fact —foreign sources of support: Frederick of Prussia, of course, and Louis XV of France. For Prussia and France were allies, and Ivan Shuvalov was genuinely an ardent admirer of French culture. He was bound to influence Elizabeth toward French interests. Thus the stakes of the game were actually very high. Indeed, the prizes in this boudoir tournament included the role of Russia in Europe. In the event it was the Shuvalovs who scored first, disposing of Beketov (already, only a year out of cadet school, Colonel Beketov) by bold character assassination.

Again, Catherine: "After Easter [1751] we went to Peterhof [where] something happened which gave the courtiers food for gossip. It was brought about by the intrigues of Count Shuvalov. Colonel Beketov, out of boredom and not knowing what to do during the days of grace he was enjoying (though his prestige had risen so high that at any moment it was expected that either he would yield his place to Ivan Shuvalov or vice versa), decided one day to get the Empress's choirboys to come and sing at his residence. He took a particular fancy to some of them because of the beauty of their voices and as he himself was a versifier he composed songs for the children to sing.

"An odious interpretation was put on this. It was known that no vice was more detested by the Empress. Beketov, in the innocence of his heart, used to stroll in the garden with the children. This was imputed to him as a crime. The Empress went to Tsarskoe Selo for a few days and . . . Colonel Beketov was ordered to remain there [where] he fell sick of a brain fever of which he almost died. . . . He recovered but remained in disgrace and retired into the background. Afterward he was transferred to the army, where he made no progress. . . ."

If more were needed than the examples of her mother-in-law, the Empress, to make Catherine examine the Ninth Commandment in a spirit of mordant realism, it was at hand in the examples of the Choglokovs, symbols of the ideal marriage she was supposed to attain with the Grand Duke.

"M. Choglokov, according to the Empress's orders"—again this is Catherine—"slept in the Grand Duke's antechamber: he occupied it after the Grand Duke had gone to sleep and rose when he was told that the Grand Duke was awake. . . . Mme. Choglokov was very fond of one of my ladies-in-waiting, Mlle. Koshelev, a large, stupid girl, very clumsy, but with a white skin which was her only merit. This girl spent all her time with Mme. Choglokov and the latter, though herself none too bright, found much amusement in her uncouth simple-mindedness. For the reason mentioned, M. Choglokov could only occasionally spend a night with his wife, so Mme. Choglokov used to have the girl stay with her, on a small bed alongside her own. M. Choglokov would come in his dressing gown to his wife's room and usually found her thus with Mlle. Koshelev. Opportunity makes the thief and gradually he came to desire the little ninny, which was not surprising as he was not much more intelligent than she."

Catherine was recovering from an illness, and "M. Choglokov

persuaded his wife that it was her duty to look after me [and] spend more time in my company." From another of her ladies-in-waiting Catherine learned the reason, no doubt with some amusement, but she wrote, "I looked upon the secret with a favorable eye, as it kept Choglokov occupied elsewhere and made him less ill-natured."

A few months later: "From the Summer Palace we went to Peterhof, which was then being rebuilt. . . . We occupied Peter I's old palace on the hill [and] saw from our windows, which looked across the garden and out to sea, that M. and Mme. Choglokov were constantly going to and fro between the Palace on the hill and that of Mon Plaisir, right on the sea, where the Empress was staying. This intrigued us as much as it did Mme. Krause. To find out what these comings and goings were all about, Mme. Krause went to her sister, the Empress's chief maid. She returned radiant with joy, having discovered that it had come to the ears of the Empress that Choglokov was having an affair with Mlle. Koshelev, and that she was pregnant. The Empress had summoned Mme. Choglokov . . . and told her—adding that she intended to dismiss Choglokov from his post and suggesting that Mme. Choglokov separate from him.

"Mme. Choglokov at first denied her husband's infatuation, maintaining it must be a calumny, but Her Imperial Majesty, while she was talking to the lady, had sent some one else to question Mlle. Koshelev. That young woman promptly admitted everything, which enraged Mme. Choglokov against her husband. She came home and breathed fire and fury on him; Choglokov fell upon his knees and begged forgiveness, using the power he had over her to calm her down."

After a week of domestic scenes and imperial audiences, the Choglokovs were reconciled with each other, and Choglokov was reinstated as Argus to the Grand Duke, while Mademoiselle Koshelev was sent home in disgrace. Madame Krause (Madame Choglokov having learned of her talebearing and complained of her to the Empress) was replaced by a pious Madame Vladislavov. None of this suited Catherine, but the sequel was much worse.

"I noticed that M. Choglokov became very mellow . . . where

I was concerned, I began to fear he . . . would pay court to me, which did not at all suit me; firstly he [was] a disagreeable toad; furthermore his wife's jealousy and ill-temper were something to avoid, particularly for me who had no other support in the world except myself and my reputation—if any. Therefore I avoided and escaped—very nimbly, I thought—M. Choglokov's pursuits without, however, ever failing to be polite to him. All this was noticed by his wife, who appreciated such behavior on my part and became a staunch friend partly because of this."

Yet, within a year or so, hardly more than a pregnancy—her eighth—later, Madame Choglokov herself, "so righteous and apparently devoted to her husband, had fallen madly in love with Prince Repnin and taken a dislike to her husband. She could not feel really happy without a confidante and . . . showed me all the letters she received from her lover, and I kept her secret very loyally, with scrupulous discretion."

And so, with these examples before her and with the state's urgent need for an heir, her own natural womanly desire for motherhood, and certainly not least the strong emotions that Serge Saltikov aroused in her, Grand Duchess Catherine entered into a liaison that the young Princess Sophia of Anhalt-Zerbst would have thought impossible, too shocking to contemplate. The affair began during the summer of 1752, quite possibly on an island at the mouth of the Neva that the Choglokovs owned and where they had built a chalet for hunting and other sports.

During an outing there, Saltikov "waited for the moment when the others were pursuing the hares to come up to me and start upon his favorite subject; I listened to him more patiently than usual"—in fact, for "about an hour and a half."

This was the first time they had been alone together long enough and with enough assurances of privacy to be able to speak and respond to each other as they liked. That evening, when the guests had reassembled at the chalet and were having supper, "a strong gale began to blow. The waves rose so high that they reached the steps of the house; the whole island was under several feet high. We were compelled to stay with the Choglokovs until the storm abated and the waves retreated, which was not until about two or three in the morning.

"In the meantime Serge Saltikov kept saying to me that Providence itself was on his side that day because it permitted him to enjoy the sight of me for a longer time, and many things of that kind. . . . I believed it possible to govern and influence both his heart and mine, but now realized that this was going to be a task difficult if not impossible."

In fact, Catherine soon was so deeply and passionately in love with Saltikov that her "thousand apprehensions" were lost in the single fear that because of the continual subterranean intrigues of court politics, something would happen to destroy the relationship. She had observed that "Choglokov and his wife had become as meek as lambs." This implied that they were being restrained by someone of high authority or influence but guaranteed nothing about the future. How could she get certain protection? How could she enlist the power she needed?

Until this point in her career, Catherine had carefully avoided involvement with any faction at court. Her own position, as she was constantly aware, was so delicate that her best protection was to cultivate friendships in all directions and to seem to be far above, and disinterested in, the fray. It was also important to dissolve her original "Prussian identity" by adopting enthusiastically and exhibiting conspicuously every trait that was characteristically Russian. Now, however, impelled by the urgency of her love for Saltikov, she took her first plunge into politics. This was a historical landmark in her life and in the affairs of Russia and of Europe generally. For as events were to show, she had a genius for politics and developed an appetite for them that fully matched her talent.

She had hated Bestuzhev. Now, she relates, "We decided that to reduce the number of [Saltikov's] enemies I would send a few words to Count Bestuzhev which would allow him to hope that I was less antagonistic to him than I had been before." The "we" of the sentence is not explained but almost certainly meant herself and Saltikov. There are good reasons to think that Saltikov had suggested the idea.

She entrusted her message to a man called Bremse, who was

known to be Bestuzhev's personal spy and agent in the affairs of the Grand Duke's Holstein homeland. "He accepted the mission with great alacrity and told me that the Chancellor was beside himself with joy. He asked Bremse to tell me that he was at my disposal whenever I wanted and begged that if he could be of any help to me I should indicate a safe channel through which we could communicate should we find it necessary. . . .

"I repeated all this to Serge Saltikov and he at once decided to visit the Chancellor . . . the old man received him warmly, took him aside, spoke to him of the ins and outs of our Court and of the Choglokovs' stupidity, saying among other things: 'I know that although you are a friend of theirs you can see through them as well as I do, as you are an intelligent man.' He then spoke of me and my position as though he had lived in my room. . . ."

The Chancellor talked about Catherine's ménage. The devout Madame Vladislavov, who had replaced Madame Krause, had herself been replaced. Said the Chancellor, according to Saltikov: " 'In gratitude for the good will the Grand Duchess has shown me, I will render her a small service, which she will appreciate, I hope: I will give her back Mme. Vladislavov, gentle as a lamb, and she will be able to do what she likes with her. She will see that I am not the treacherous wolf I am supposed to be.' Finally Serge Saltikov returned delighted with his mission and with the old man, who had given him some wise useful advice. All this laid the foundation for a friendship between him and us of which not a soul was aware. . . . We decided to forget the past. . . ."

The present was entrancing, and the future beckoned: The love affair was protected by the most powerful man in Russia. It was more than likely that Count Bestuzhev had in fact arranged it all from the start.

Twice Catherine had miscarriages. But at last, on September 20, 1754, she gave birth to a son, who was named Paul, and who —by the grace of God and of Empress Elizabeth, Bestuzhev, Saltikov, the Choglokovs, Madame Vladislavov, Catherine (of course), and numerous lesser others—would one day ascend the Russian throne as Czar Paul I.

The dynasty was preserved. But was it the Romanov dynasty? Almost surely it was not. By patronym Paul I and subsequent

Czars to the end of the line in 1917 should have been not Romanovs but Saltikovs. And yet, and yet. . . .

There remains a tantalizing possibility to the contrary, based on a mystery that Catherine deliberately left suspended in the void of paragraphs that she never wrote (or perhaps wrote and destroyed) in her memoirs. Perhaps, in fact, she herself could not be altogether certain of the answer. And so, before closing this saga of the adventures leading to Paul's birth, it is necessary to look briefly at the role played by the father of record, Grand Duke Peter, and the peculiar adventures that befell him.

Throughout the Saltikov episode Peter remained, as usual, preoccupied with his own interests: drilling and marching and uniforms, the affairs and grievances of Holstein, his violin, his hunting dogs, his infatuations (the newest at the time Catherine surrendered to Saltikov was one of Catherine's ladies-in-waiting, Mademoiselle Chafirov), his drinking, which was becoming progressively heavier and rendering him even more irresponsible and incompetent—and, a new pleasure, his friendship with Serge Saltikov. Truly this young man was a "prince of intrigue," as Catherine once called him. While wooing Catherine and ingratiating himself with the Choglokovs, he was making himself Peter's boon companion, partner in his drinking bouts and hunting parties, appreciative audience to his military games, and so congenial and attractive all in all that Peter (like Catherine) wanted to see him every day.

According to the memoirs of the Marquis de Castera, a French diplomat who was at court during this time and whose own talents as a *bon vivant* made him popular in the Young Court, one evening after the affair began the Grand Duke and his friend Saltikov were at a stag dinner where drinking and jollity and male braggadocio led to talk of sexual exploits. At the right moment, with Peter well drunk and Serge simulating drunken candor, the latter challenged him to join in these pleasures by submitting to corrective surgery—a mere trifle, perfectly easy for any physician or rabbi, yet which Peter because of fear and ignorance had avoided and which had prevented him from achieving consummation with a woman.

Peter drunkenly agreed, and the deed was done—that very night, according to one version of the same tale—and enabled him to be a man at last with women—including his wife. Saltikov's object, of course, was to be able to go on enjoying Catherine's favors while making the cuckolded Peter think he was the father of the child she had already conceived by Saltikov.

The story is worthy of the highest, or lowest, traditions of French bedroom farce, and one would dismiss it as impossible —except that, on sober consideration of everything else that had happened already (and more to come), it seems rash to declare anything impossible.

Catherine's memoirs contain not even a hint of any such physical defect in the Grand Duke, although they are altogether frank about his sexual incompetence up to this time. Following her description of the happenings on Choglokov's island, and in a context having to do with children and childbearing, she begins a story that adds both new mysteries and new illuminations. The Young Court had come down from Oranienbaum to Peterhof, she relates, and Elizabeth, deducing from her costume that she had been riding astride, began reprimanding Mme. Choglokov for allowing it because "riding in that way prevented us from having children and . . . my riding clothes were not suitable . . . when she herself rode in a trousered habit she changed her clothes afterward. Mme. Choglokov replied that there was no question about my having children; these, after all, could not appear without something being done about it and that although their Imperial Highnesses had been married since 1745—nothing *had* been done about it yet. Then Her Majesty scolded Mme. Choglokov and blamed her for not persuading the interested parties to do their duty; she showed much ill temper and said that Mme. Choglokov's husband was an ass who allowed himself to be led by the nose by mere dirty-nosed brats."

The "brats" evidently were Saltikov and his friend and confederate Leon Naryshkin, probably Catherine, and—even this could be—perhaps Grand Duke Peter. Elizabeth evidently knew there was a romance between Catherine and Saltikov. Why was she angry? Because she knew the affair had begun and wanted Catherine to have a child by Saltikov but could not admit this fully to herself and therefore lashed out at the Choglokovs? Because she was not sure the affair had begun and still actually clung to the hope that Peter could produce an heir? Because in either case, she wanted—for the important sake of the credibility and ostensible dynastic legitimacy of the birth after so many glaringly infertile years—to bring about in some way, almost any way, some evidence of potency in Peter and was demanding that the Choglokovs find the way.

Catherine continues the passage opaquely: "All this was repeated by the Choglokovs to their confidantes twenty-four hours later; the brats at this mention of themselves felt the cap fit and wiped their noses and at a special meeting held by them for this purpose it was decided and determined that following very precisely Her Majesty's intentions Serge Saltikov and Leon Naryshkin would . . . retire to their respective houses for three weeks or a month."

And then, after touching on some wholly irrelevant topics, and without further explanation: "M. Choglokov asked for and was granted permission to go to one of his country seats for a month. During his absence his spouse gave herself a lot of trouble to execute the Empress' wishes to the letter. She had many conferences with the Grand Duke's valet, Bressan, who in Oranienbaum had found the pretty widow of a painter, Mme. Groot. It took several days to persuade her, promising her I do not know what, and then to instruct her in what was expected of her and what she had to agree to do. Then it was left to Bressan to bring the Grand Duke together with the young and pretty widow. . . . At last, after many efforts, Mme. Choglokov obtained what she wanted, and when she was certain of her facts she informed the Empress that everything was going on according to her wishes."

With this carefully stilted exercise in obscurity, Catherine leaves the subject entirely and goes on in her usual lucid way to report on certain negotiations involving Holstein, Denmark, and Schleswig.

VIII

Lessons of the "Third Rome"

WHAT seems clear enough is that the Grand Duke Peter at long last, at the age of almost twenty-seven, was initiated into full manhood by the widow Groot. Thereafter he had numerous affairs and a succession of mistresses. He continued for a while, at least, to share Catherine's bed; and it was to her advantage to encourage him to act as a husband—at least often enough to confuse the issue. There is a possibility, therefore, that he could have been Paul's father. This is strengthened, again inferentially, by two factors: The child bore a certain physical resemblance to him, and the child grew up to be equally neurotic and incompetent.

But weighing against these, and far outweighing them, are other factors. Despite his subsequent liaisons and his mistresses, Peter did not produce a child; almost certainly—a result of his asthenic and sickly nature and successive severe illnesses—he was sterile. And Catherine, although most carefully never saying directly, clearly believed that the father of her firstborn was Saltikov. And she was exceedingly shrewd and wise, wise enough to know her own child.

What the Grand Duke himself thought is unknown. In an age

of memoirs, diaries and journals, and correspondence, he apparently never put any of his thoughts on any subject on paper. His behavior was no more eccentric and self-centered than was expectable under any circumstances. Awakened and told that Catherine was in labor, he came to her apartment—as protocol required—to be present at the birth of his royal heir. He had dressed himself in the full uniform of general of the Holstein Army, and when the baby was presented to him, he raised his sword in the air in formal salute. Then, with barely a word to Catherine, he went back to his room to receive the congratulations of his aides and servants and spend the rest of the day in drunken celebration with them.

The next day, Catherine relates, he "came to my room for a moment and then went away saying he had no time to stay." A few days later: "At last the Grand Duke, who was bored in the evenings without my ladies-in-waiting whom he liked courting, offered to spend an evening in my room. He was then courting the ugliest one, Princess Elizabeth Worontsov."

He showed no signs at all of thinking the child was not his. Neither did he show any interest in it. In fact, his emotions were stirred by only one matter: "On the day of the christening, the Empress came to my room after the ceremony and brought me on a golden plate an order of her cabinet to send me one hundred thousand gold rubles. . . . Four or five days after I received the money . . . her secretary of the cabinet came to beg me in God's name to lend it to the Empress's private funds. . . . The Grand Duke, upon hearing about the present, had flown into a horrible temper because she had given nothing to him. He spoke about it angrily to Shuvalov [who] repeated the conversation to the Empress." She ordered the same sum sent to the Grand Duke, but when she asked for the money, "there was none: her treasury was bare"—which is why "the money had to be borrowed from me." The incident holds another clue, perhaps, that Elizabeth believed that the child was not really Peter's.

Aside from this gift, which was given without any mark of affection, almost as if it were a payment for services rendered, Elizabeth acted as if she considered the child not really Catherine's. She acted as if it were her own. In effect, she kidnapped the child.

Among all the strange turns and grotesque situations that characterized the relationships in this extraordinary household of Elizabeth, Catherine, and Peter, this surely is among the strangest —and, at the same time, the most poignant.

There were omens even before the birth. On returning late that summer from Peterhof to the new Summer Palace to await the accouchement, "It was a deadly shock for me"—Catherine writes —"to learn that the rooms prepared for my labor adjoined the Empress's apartments, in fact were part of them." Elizabeth was present or nearby during all of Catherine's long, difficult labor but not, apparently, to give aid and consolation to the mother.

No sooner had the baby been born, baptized, and swaddled than "the Empress ordered the midwife to take the child and follow her." Catherine did not see the baby again, or the Empress, for well over a month. Then "the Empress came a second time to my room for the churching ceremony. I had got out of bed to welcome her but she found me looking so weak and worn that she made me sit down for the prayers read by her confessor. My son had been brought to the room, and this was the first time I had seen him since his birth. I found him beautiful and the sight of him made my heart rejoice, but the moment the prayers were over the Empress had him carried away and herself departed."

That was late in October. In the spring of the following year, after the Easter ceremonies, the Young Court went as usual to Oranienbaum, and "Before we left, the Empress allowed me to see my son for the third time since his birth. . . ."

This child, which had been so much needed for reasons of state, was the ward of the state, even in a large sense the property of the state. Thus, in this absolute monarchy, he was the ward and property of the Empress to safeguard and mold in the interests of the throne.

But however the facts were rationalized, it was not reason but emotion that accounted for it. All the love and nostalgia for family that haunted Elizabeth and contributed to so many of her actions, all the thwarted yearnings for motherhood and the maternal impulses that were in her female nature, coalesced and found an object in this infant. In her infinite capacity for self-deception she could ignore the tangled and fairly sordid circumstances that had brought it into the world and could treat the baby as if she fully believed it was the great-grandson of Peter the Great.

And with her capacity for role playing, she could enter into make-believe motherhood with utter conviction and devotion, lavishing love on the child. It was, of course, a kind of dementia. Catherine learned the Empress had taken the baby directly to her own room "and the moment he cried, she rushed and literally smothered it with her attentions." The room was kept "excessively hot," and the baby was "swaddled in flannel, laid in a cot lined with silver fox, covered with a satin, padded quilt over which was another counterpane of pink velvet lined with silver fox. Later on, I often saw him like that, bathed in sweat from head to foot. . . ."

The birth of the royal heir was, of course, a patriotic and religious event of greatest magnitude. Cannon boomed salutes from every fortress and warship, the palaces were draped with flags, bells rang praises from the golden and multicolored domed belfries, and in the churches the Russian people gathered for prayer and thanksgiving. Amid this panorama of national delight, while the Empress let others attend to the business of the throne while she tended the baby, and while the Grand Duke drank and drank and drilled his dogs and troops and swaggered and enjoyed his newfound prowess with Mademoiselle Worontsov and others, perhaps the saddest soul in Russia was Catherine.

This was the worst, cruelest, indeed the most devastating period of her whole life. During it she arrived at the edge of emotional collapse and perhaps even of lifelong emotional invalidism. She survived. And in surviving became a different person.

Her labor had been twelve hours of progressive agony, but with none of the emotional compensations before, during, or afterward that would ordinarily have made this acceptable. The man she loved and whose child almost surely she was bearing was necessarily absent at the time. But in any case she had for some months seen little of him, partly by circumstances but partly too, as she began to admit to herself, because he did not really want to see her. She still was very much in love with him, but every sign, including his own evasions and slackened ardor, filled her with a premonitory dread that their relationship was ending. In fact, she had never felt so alone and isolated as when she was approaching childbirth, for now even the Choglokovs were gone, swept away in the riptides of the intrigues of Elizabeth and Catherine with respective lovers.

As noted earlier, Choglokov had developed a passion for Catherine. To distract him, she and Saltikov had encouraged him in a new and even more incongruous infatuation for the Empress. As Catherine related: "He had been kindly received and all went well, but he spoiled everything with too much zeal. The Shuvalovs took umbrage . . . the glances thrown at Choglokov were too languorous." They set about destroying him, in ways that are unreported, and "Finally the Empress . . . addressed him publicly at table as a madman and a traitor which upset him so much that he developed jaundice." The doctor who treated him was "devoted to the Shuvalovs, and knowing Choglokov to be their enemy he may have believed he was doing them a service by contributing to Choglokov's death; anyway the doctors called in during his last days maintained that he had been treated like a man marked down for killing."

After his funeral Madame Choglokov set off to the Winter Palace to rejoin Catherine, but the Empress, watching from a window and seeing her crossing the long bridge over the Neva, "sent someone to meet her and tell her that she was relieved of her duties with us and should return home. Her Majesty considered that she was doing wrong to leave the house when she had been a widow such a short time."

Elizabeth appointed Alexander Shuvalov to the Choglokov post as Argus-guardian-adviser to the Grand Duke. Alexander was a brother of Elizabeth's lover, Ivan Shuvalov, and, as Catherine says, "was the terror of the Court, of the town, and of the whole Empire: because he was the head of the Secret Chancery, a select body charged with guarding the security of the Throne and State against traitors, foreign agents and potential plotters of coup d'état." As such he had at his disposal an apparatus of spies and secret police that rivaled that of Chancellor Bestuzhev—Catherine's newfound friend and, of course, the Shuvalov family's deadly enemy.

Alexander Shuvalov's attendance on the Grand Duke carried with it, for Catherine, the extra penalty that she was under almost continual surveillance by his wife, "the most tiresome minx God ever made."

As Catherine had advanced in pregnancy, she had declined correspondingly into melancholy. She felt smothered in an "uneasy and heavy atmosphere which gave rise to depression which I could no longer control . . . until at every moment and on every occasion I was ready to cry . . . a thousand preoccupations filled my mind. . . . I went for long walks, but all my troubles followed me relentlessly."

It was in this morbid state of mind that she came to the end of her term and went through her exhausting labor. As was the Russian custom, she lay on a heavy mattress on the floor by her bed and was attended not by a physician, but by a midwife. After Paul's birth it was the midwife, as we saw, who on command carried him to Elizabeth's bedroom. Although this was nearby, the woman did not return. Catherine remembered:

"I had sweated abundantly, and I begged Mme. Vladislavov to change my linen and put me back into my own bed; she said she dared not do that. She sent several times for the midwife but the latter did not come. I asked for water and got the same response. At last after three o'clock"—that is, more than three hours after the birth—"Countess Shuvalov arrived . . . dressed up for the occasion. When she saw me still lying on the labor bed . . . she cried out with indignation [and] left the room at once and I believe went to fetch the midwife . . . the latter arrived half an hour later and told us that the Empress had been so busy with the child that she would not let the midwife leave her for an instant.

"I had been in tears ever since the birth had taken place, particularly because I had been so cruelly abandoned. . . . Nobody worried about me. This neglect was not very flattering to me . . . at last I was carried into my bed and did not see a soul for the rest of the day nor did anyone come to ask after me.

"The next day I began to feel a dreadful rheumatic pain . . . along the hip and left leg; the pain prevented me from sleeping and gave me a high fever. I cried and moaned in my bed. There was only Mme. Vladislavov in my room: she was sorry for me, but could do nothing to help. Besides, I did not like being pitied, nor did I like to complain. I was too proud and the very idea of being miserable . . . of showing my misery . . . was repulsive to me. . . ."

Serge Saltikov did not visit her. In fact, this would have been altogether unseemly; their affair had been one of the staples of the court's gossip for two years. It was widely rumored that he was the father, but it was essential to avoid any slight gesture that might feed this talk. Actually, having fulfilled his important historic role, he had now, at this point, become something of a danger to the state. Just as Madame Choglokov had vanished into the wings at Elizabeth's cue, so now it was time for Saltikov to leave.

Little more than two weeks after the birth he was given a special mission. On behalf of Her Imperial Majesty and as her plenipotentiary, he was to travel to Sweden and notify the Swedish monarchs and court that Czarevich Paul Petrovich had been born. Perhaps this was calculated as a bluff so barefaced that it would succeed by sheer effrontery, but to the well-informed gossips of the Swedish court—and eventually all over Europe—it seemed hilarious, a masterpiece of wit that could have come only from that sly fox Chancellor Bestuzhev.

Catherine, learning of Saltikov's mission, felt only anguish. He was being sent away from her, perhaps for a long time. She wrote: "I buried myself even deeper in my bed, where I could sorrow in peace. . . . I could not and would not see anybody in my grief."

Although Catherine was well enough six weeks after the birth to follow Elizabeth from the Summer Palace to the Winter Palace, she did so "with the firm resolution that I would not leave my room until I felt enough strength to overcome my melancholy." Moreover, instead of occupying her bedroom at the Winter Palace "because it was very cold and also because of its proximity to the Grand Duke's apartments," she used a small, makeshift room that was more like a hall closet than bedroom, being only some six feet long and four feet wide and with wall space disarranged by two windows and three doors. It was a cave, a retreat, a hiding place.

"I remained the whole winter in this miserable little narrow room. . . . Thus began the year 1755. From Christmas to Lent there were many balls at Court and in town—they were celebrating the birth of my son. Everybody surpassed everyone else in the desire to give dinners, suppers, balls, masquerades, firework displays and illuminations, each more splendid than the last. I was present at none, pleading illness."

Throughout the drab, circumscribed, sterile, and pointless years with Peter she had been able to keep her mind alive with books. She turned to them now for solace and balm and for the lessons of the world that she could thus learn by living in it vicariously. Without this resource and this tie to life—or so at least her symptoms suggest—she might have slipped away slowly but finally from reality. Her books that winter included Voltaire's history of Germany and his history of the world. "After that I read all the Russian books I could get hold of . . . then I devoted myself to Montesquieu's *Spirit of the Law*; after that I read the *Annals* of Tacitus which produced a curious revolution in my mind, aided perhaps by the gloomy disposition of myself at the time. I began to see everything in black, and searched to find deeper and more intrinsic causes for the various events which presented themselves to my sight."

Catherine does not elaborate on the discoveries she made. Actually their nature is quite clear in the light of her subsequent actions, particularly if we remember that the events that had reduced her to such despair had occurred in the "Third Rome." Catherine undoubtedly was familiar with this concept,* which was deeply embedded in Russian mythology, and later in her life she based some of her own most ambitious ventures on it.

The "Third Rome" had proved to be a bruising and baffling place, a dangerous and mysterious place, and, as she had now begun to realize, especially dangerous for anyone, like herself, who arrived in it with preconceived notions of society which were out of phase with the premises that underlay this particular society. The events that had presented themselves to her sight, the attitudes and actions of the people around her were inexplicable until she understood these premises and the motives of these people.

In the annals of the First Rome, reading of the reigns of

---

* A concept going back to the reign of Ivan the Great (1440–1505) holding that Russia was the natural heir of ancient Rome and the Byzantine Empire centered on Constantinople.

Augustus, Caligula, Claudius, and Nero and of Roman palace politics with its crimes and deceits and boiling factionalism, of intricate sexual intrigues and depravities, of thefts and betrayals and bribery and brutality and a multitude of other sins and hypocrisies, she could not help being struck by the parallels in the court of Elizabeth—and by the evident fact that (despite Tacitus' strong disapproval) these things were somehow compatible with the grandeur that was Rome, with a society not only viable but mighty and that even contributed to the world a great deal that was good.

Life in the First Rome, thus encountered in the Third Rome by a leading participant and victim 1,500 years later, was a source of relief to Catherine. It enabled her to see her troubles in deep perspective and was a source of protection by demonstrating to her—Tacitus makes it a continual thesis—how often facts belie appearances, how often favors and friendship and love mask duplicity and self-interest. Roman pagan or Orthodox Christian, the affairs of men and empires seemed to be governed finally by two elementary premises and motives: survival and self-gratification. And survival and success depended on the free and, if necessary, ruthless use of opportunism.

Another, somewhat later student of Tacitus, British Foreign Secretary Lord Palmerston, expressed the principle in a famous aphorism: "We have no perpetual allies and we have no perpetual enemies. Our interests are perpetual."

But if these, or closely similar, inferences were drawn by Catherine from her reading, it seems to have required one final, extremely painful disillusionment as a catalyst to bring them together as a congruent philosophy for rational action. She was still in the grip of irrational emotion: her love for Serge Saltikov.

"Count Bestuzhev sent me all the news he got from him, as well as the dispatches of Count Panin, then Russian envoy in Sweden. These messages were passed on to me by way of Mme. Vladislavov, who received them from her son-in-law, the Grand Chancellor's assistant. I sent messages back in the same way." Correspondence through these channels, even if secret, was not conducive to intimacies, and if Saltikov's messages lacked ardor, it was easy for Catherine, reading with hope and love, to find more in them than the words said.

But in fact, Saltikov considered the affair over and himself lucky to be out of it. And his ardor was being spent in other directions. If he had felt any embarrassment at all from the incongruity of his mission, he lost it on finding himself a celebrity at the Swedish court. More than that, he was, as the lover of the Grand Duchess of Russia, the presumed father of the future heir to the Russian throne, an Important Personage.

Men were curious and somewhat awed. Women were fascinated. He was able to enjoy himself with many casual affairs. He showed his true lack of real feeling for Catherine and lack of decency by telling his Swedish friends and inamoratas about the affair. Almost surely Ambassador Panin was aware of Saltikov's behavior and almost surely reported or implied it in his dispatches to Bestuzhev, who almost surely would have passed this information on to Catherine. For Bestuzhev knew there could be no future in the liaison, and he tried to make the point to Catherine as plainly as possible by letting her know that when Saltikov returned from Sweden, he was to be sent away again, as minister to one of the German states.

But Catherine's state of mind and emotions allowed her to disregard all this simply as symptoms of an intrigue against him. And so "When Saltikov returned, he asked me through Leon Naryshkin to indicate some method whereby I could see him. . . . Mme. Vladislavov agreed to arrange a meeting. He was to go first to visit her, then me. I waited for him till three o'clock in the morning, but he did not come; I underwent agonies wondering what could have prevented him."

She learned next day that the Vice Chancellor, Count Worontsov, had invited him to a Masonic meeting and—his message to her was—he could not avoid going "without arousing suspicion."

"But I questioned and importuned Leon Naryshkin so much that it became clear as day to me that Saltikov had failed to come . . . [because] he was no longer eager to see me, and was blind to all I had suffered lately only out of attachment to him. . . . I wrote him a letter bitterly reproaching him." Saltikov then visited

The four Russian Empresses of the eighteenth century, reading clockwise from the top, Catherine I, Catherine II, Elizabeth, and Anna Ivanovna.

Empress Elizabeth's summer palace, the creation of Bartolomeo Rastrelli, the great Italian architect favored by Russian royalty.

(New York Public Library Picture Collection)

Peter the Great, Empress Elizabeth's father,
as a young man.

(The Bettmann Archive)

Catherine I, the camp follower who became wife
and Empress of Peter the Great.

(The Bettmann Archive)

Elizabeth, Empress of Russia, daughter of Peter the Great.

(The Bettmann Archive)

Catherine II, Catherine the Great of Russia.

(Radio Times Hulton Picture Library)

Gregory Potemkin,
Catherine the Great's lover.

(Culver Pictures, Inc.)

Alexis Orlov, Gregory's brother
and ringleader in the plot to de
pose Peter III in favor of Cath
erine.

*(The New York Public Library
Picture Collection)*

Gregory Orlov, Catherine's lover who, with his brothers,
engineered the coup that brought her to power.

(The New York Public Library Picture Collection)

Czar Paul I, Catherine's son.

(The New York Public Library Picture Collection)

Alexander I, Catherine the Great's grandson, eldest son of Paul I.

(The Bettmann Archive)

her, and with his fine talent for dissembling, "He did not find it hard to appease me, for I had a deep feeling for him."

She was appeased, but she was not convinced. In her heart she now knew the truth. He did not love her, and he would not. Everything was finished. And before long, stories came to her from Stockholm and then also from Dresden, his new post, that he had been "indiscreet" in his talk and that "In both countries he had also been frivolous with all the women he met." Although "At the beginning I did not want to believe this . . ." she finally had to confront the realization that she had been used, and misused, by a scoundrel.

The worst she could ever bring herself to say of him, however, was a mild reproof. It is contained in some lines she wrote while describing the beginning of their love affair. They show no bitterness, and they hold at least a hint of nostalgia: "He was a distinguished gentleman both by birth and other qualities; he knew how to conceal his faults, the greatest of which were his spirit of intrigue and his lack of principles; those were not very clear to me at the time."

Yet this essentially insignificant aristocratic adventurer had still another important function in his history, before disappearing into the shadows and oblivion. During his visit to her, it was he who "persuaded me to show myself in public. I took his advice and made my appearance on February 10th, the Grand Duke's birthday."

It had been eleven years to the day that Catherine had made her first public appearance in Russia. This occasion, too, was to be a debut, although of quite another order of magnitude. For, from all these trials and lessons there had been created the mature character of the woman who would be Catherine the Great.

In her own account of this public revelation of her new self, she gives instinctive priority to an item whose importance any woman would comprehend instantly, and which indicates that nothing of her own womanly nature had changed: "I had a superb dress made for the occasion, of blue velvet embroidered with gold."

And then: "Having reflected a great deal during my solitude, I had resolved to make those who had caused me so much grief realize that they could not hurt me with impunity or gain my affection and approval by graceless behavior." She would defend herself; she would retaliate. She would refuse to be afraid; she would instead make others fear her. She had been seeking affection and approval. Those who had taken advantage of her submissive attitude to disregard her feelings and who might expect her—"a humiliated and oppressed person"—to be diffident and uncertain were to be disconcerted. For, as she relates, "I drew myself up and, with head erect, stood as one bearing great responsibilities."

As her immediate target she chose the Shuvalovs. They had been instrumental in her humiliation and oppression. Moreover, they were so powerful at court, so much feared and so conspicuous that her attack could not fail to cause a sensation and serve as a general advertisement that she had become an adversary to avoid, placate, and cultivate. If it were seen that she had such confidence that she could challenge even the Shuvalovs, it would be thought that she must have good reasons for confidence, that her position must be very strong. This would bring her allies and make her as strong as she was pretending to be.

Accordingly: "I missed no opportunity to show the Shuvalovs how hostile I was to them . . . and wherever I went I dropped sarcastic remarks about them, which went the round of the town and made them the butt of all gossip. . . . As many people hated them, I found numerous disciples. . . ."

The Shuvalovs, in return, ingratiated themselves with the Grand Duke, "who was made to see that it was his duty . . . to bring his wife back to her senses.

"With this object in view, His Highness came to my room one day after dinner and declared that I had become insufferably proud and that he would soon bring me to see reason. When I asked him in what my pride consisted, he said that I held my head too high. I wanted to know if in order to please him I should bend to the ground as if I were a slave and he was God. He flew into a rage and repeated that he would soon pull me up short. I asked him how he would proceed to do so. At this, he stood with his back to the wall, half-drew out his sword, and showed it to me.

"I wanted to know what this signified, and whether he intended to challenge me to a duel, in which case I, too, ought to have a sword. He pushed it back into its sheath and told me that I had developed an evil temper.

"I asked in what way. He replied, stammering, 'Toward the Shuvalovs, of course.' I retorted that this was only retaliation and that he had better not speak about something of which he knew so little and understood less. . . . Then he started making such extravagant statements, devoid of all common sense, that . . . I suggested he should go to bed for I could see that he was under the influence of drink which had dulled his mental powers. He followed my advice and went off to bed."

The scene left the Grand Duke as disconcerted and perplexed as the Shuvalovs. There had never before been a confrontation of wills, for Catherine had made it her policy from the beginning to humor him, to listen to his childish schemes and tactless confidences, and thus to cultivate his friendship, hiding as best she could her exasperations and chronic boredom. Because of Catherine's illness and their mutual inclinations, they had seen little of each other since Paul's birth, and this visit in behalf of the Shuvalovs seems to have been the first of any personal nature since then. It is unlikely that Peter, occupied with himself, had noticed any change in Catherine prior to this meeting. The woman he now encountered—self-possessed, unyielding, scornful—was a stranger to him, confusing, unnerving, alarming.

There was no break between them because there really had been so little to break. There had been a *modus vivendi* from which now arose a new *modus vivendi* of a different kind, based on different terms. In everything personal, they led separate lives, sharing only in those matters that convenience and official duties and customs required. Peter continued with his mistresses. He even continued, from long habit, to tell Catherine about them, and—sign of how complete had been the destruction of any feeling that they were man and wife—he often asked her advice on how best to pursue them and entertain them.

For her part, Catherine began her own series of affairs, with no questions from Peter. It was not to the advantage of either, at this stage, to break this arrangement of coexistence. For Peter, Catherine still had her uses: She helped him in duties he found burdensome and did badly, and he was not in love with anyone else. For Catherine, Peter as Grand Duke still offered her the reasonable expectation that she, as Grand Duchess, would become Czarina when he became Czar.

But now, as she had come to realize fully and in all its potentialities, her position and destiny no longer depended on him. She was no longer an appendage but a personage: she, after all, was the mother of the heir and future Czar.

IX

Politics, War, and Love

ALL this while events in Russia and abroad were moving in majestic disharmony to create a general situation rich in opportunities (and risks, of course) for one who had decided it was better to sin than be sinned against and (a jotting to herself while reading Tacitus) that it was best to "steel oneself in good time against the calamities of the State." The Prussian war that Bestuzhev had so long expected loomed now as a virtual certainty. And when it came, it would be part of a general European war, because all the leading European powers had interests that had been or could be affected for better or worse by Frederick's rising military strength and ambitions.

In preparation for the war that all considered inevitable, all were maneuvering for positions that might offer maximum gains at minimum expense and hazard. During the fifteen months or so between Catherine's reappearance and the outbreak of war, the various courts were aswarm with embassies and "gentlemen travelers" on arcane missions for clients who in turn might be acting for concealed secondary or tertiary sponsors and with spies, provocateurs, and agents of confusion or persuasion recruited among influential courtiers and government officials.

Now King Louis XV and his ministers decided that the main threat to France's interest in Europe was not Hapsburg Austria, the ancient foe, but Hohenzollern Prussia, the continent's newly emerged great power and France's present ally. The French government therefore, with characteristic and famous French common sense, prepared to abandon its pledges to Prussia and seek an alliance with its own traditional (and Prussia's current) mortal enemy, Austria. When Frederick's efficient intelligence apparatus had informed him of this in advance, he made secret approaches to England and secured an English alliance. This—the Treaty of Westminster—was announced on January 5, 1756.

During the next few months all the other pieces fell into place: Austria and France formed an alliance against Prussia, England, and Hanover; Saxony, Sweden, and Poland joined Austria and France. In May, Russia formally renewed its pledge to Austria against Prussia, meantime having sent outraged protests to its ally, England, for allying itself with Russia's enemy, Prussia.

In brief, this was the celebrated Diplomatic Revolution of 1756, which inaugurated a vast, inchoate, but decisive struggle.

Once begun, this war soon developed into a world war, bitterly fought on three continents and involving many people other than Europeans. In Europe itself it became a melee in which friends and foes were ill-defined and each nation tended to concentrate on destroying its favorite enemy. For lack of a descriptive term that would encompass it even approximately, it became known in the general history of Europe as the Seven Years' War—since it was bounded roughly by the years from 1756 to 1763. But reflecting its actual diversity, in every area of major conflict it acquired a local name corresponding with local aims and enemies. Thus, for example, in North America in the Thirteen Colonies, it was (and in U.S. history books still is) known as the French and Indian War. During it, a strapping young Virginian named George Washington acquired battle and command experience and earned a lieutenant colonelcy and a reputation for sound leadership. In Russia—where Prussia was considered the only enemy—it was called the Prussian War or, as Catherine called it, the War Against the King of Prussia.

By whatever name, this war changed the world massively and

permanently. As one immediate result, France lost Canada, the West Indies, and the Northwest Territory (the present U.S. Midwest) to England, and its hold on the Louisiana Territory was jeopardized by British seapower. In Europe, there ensued in due course both the partition of Poland and the unification of Germany under the leadership—and militant traditions—of Prussia.

The convulsions of the personal and political aspirations loosed in the preliminaries to the war and during the war very nearly destroyed Catherine. These wild currents also, with the same unpredictability, produced two men who were to become successively her lovers, each to be the father of a child by her, each to have a memorable role in the history of Europe and Russia.

Our narrative can now profitably return to the year 1755 and to the arrival in St. Petersburg that spring of a new British ambassador, Sir Charles Hanbury-Williams, who was to have a great deal to do with the next major events in Catherine's life. Sir Charles Hanbury-Williams (who appears in Catherine's memoirs as "Sir Hanbury-Williams" or simply "Sir Hanbury") came to Russia with two special objectives: to negotiate a new Anglo-Russian trade treaty and to encourage Russia to attack Prussia. Russian trade was never more important to England than now because Russia and the eastern Baltic regions were the prime sources of strategic materials—ship masts, timbers, calking pitch, and others. These were needed by the British Navy, the indispensable instrument of British power and ambitions in the world.

Hanbury-Williams was a widely experienced and talented diplomat who had served all over Europe, most lately in Poland. A gentleman and amateur scholar, sophisticated, handsome, and charming, adept in every social grace and in every kind of suave deception, he was a flower of British diplomacy and an almost perfect instrument of the policy of aggressive self-interest that had long been building in the British Empire. Now in middle age, he could look back on a career filled with successes. And with every reasonable expectation he could look forward to new successes in Russia. Despite England's alliance with Prussia, England, Russia, and Austria were bound by common fears of Prussia, and their alliance was implicit, although not yet in treaty form.

Russian enmity against France was not so secure, for there was a strong pro-French "party" at court, led by the Shuvalovs. Yet

France had so often opposed Russian aims, both to check the rise of Russian power in Europe and by indirection to weaken Russia's ally, Austria, that a great store of anti-French feeling had accumulated. Grand Chancellor Bestuzhev was an out-and-out Francophobe; he regarded France and Prussia as Russia's "natural enemies." And he was an Anglophile.

With these convictions Bestuzhev was also certain to support a trade treaty with England—although, of course, with advantageous terms for Russia. From the very beginning of Russian relations with England, the Czars had exacted payment from the English for trade rights. Unofficially but effectively, so had various government ministers and courtiers. The combination of import tax and private extortion was summed up in the euphemism the British government gave to the successive treaties that had been negotiated: They were Subsidies Treaties. The amount that would be demanded for the imperial treasury could be guessed approximately and negotiated in a businesslike way with Bestuzhev. But even the Grand Chancellor could not act without the approval of the Empress, who in turn listened to the advice of her senior councillors and senators and courtiers, who in turn were supporting their own factions and "parties" and wished to spread the largess where it could do the most for themselves and their friends.

This involved Hanbury-Williams and his staff in diplomacy of considerable delicacy and intricacy: discerning those who were expecting to be bribed and deciding how much their influence actually was worth; discerning those others whose influence could be important and who in some circumstances and by tactful means might allow themselves to be "subsidized." These people could be enlisted only by cultivating a relationship in which valuable gifts, favors, honors, and attention could be given in an aura of personal friendship and social grace. And in this task, as Hanbury-Williams and his superiors at the Foreign Office were well aware, his strongest asset was himself.

Hanbury-Williams knew how to make himself liked and welcome in society. He was a bachelor and a gallant. He was extremely attractive to women, and at Elizabeth's court this had incalculable potentialities. Indeed it seems quite certain that Hanbury-Williams, for God and country, hoped that events might lead him to the Empress' bedchamber. It is altogether probable —Catherine's affair with Saltikov having marked her, in all the foreign chancelleries of Europe, as perhaps susceptible to attractive diplomats—that he had the same thoughts concerning her.

But rationally taking into account the fact that he was nearly twice Catherine's age and that she might prefer someone younger, he had brought along as a member of his staff, apparently with the same patriotic purpose in mind, a young, charming, and extraordinarily handsome Pole, Count Stanislaus Poniatowski.

Poniatowski was the scion of a great family whose power and fortunes were currently at low ebb. His father had been one of the foremost supporters and companion-at-arms of Sweden's King Charles XII in the latter's wars with Peter the Great (during which Poland was a principal battleground) and later a strong partisan of Stanislaus Leczinski, the French-backed King of Poland whom Peter deposed in favor of his ally Augustus of Saxony, who thus became king of both countries. In the aftermath the elder Poniatowski had been obliged to spend years in exile. Consequently his son had been raised and educated in Western Europe, mainly in France. With his good looks, good mind, and good family connections, he had been sponsored by such eminences as General Étienne de Choiseul (soon to be the Duc de Choiseul, France's Foreign Minister) and the most famous hostess of her time, Madame Geoffrin, at whose busy salon, on the rue St.-Honoré, Poniatowski met all the *encyclopédistes*, the other leading intellectuals, writers and artists of Paris, as well as such luminous visitors as Horace Walpole, son and heir of the great English Prime Minister and art collector.

Visiting England, Poniatowski met—among many others of status—Sir Charles Hanbury-Williams, who became a special friend and patron. In Poland, meanwhile, Poniatowski's father and his mother's family, the aristocratic Czartoryskis, now led the political faction favoring close ties to Russia. Hanbury-Williams of course had known the Poniatowskis and Czartoryskis during his time in Poland, so when he was appointed ambassador to Russia, it suited everyone that Stanislaus go along as a member of his staff.

Poniatowski was then twenty-five—two years younger than Catherine—by some reports "one of the best looking men of his time." He was not vain, however; he seems to have accepted his handsomeness, as he accepted the patronage of his elders and the general good fortune that attended him, with pleasure but without a trace of conceit. His nature was friendly, open and affectionate, with a certain sensitivity and shyness that only added to his likability and encouraged warm relationships. He called Madame Geoffrin *Maman*; Hanbury-Williams called him "son." He had a good mind, an excellent education, a wide knowledge of the world, and a sense of honor. In short, in most ways he was Serge Saltikov's opposite.

In his first dispatch to London, Hanbury-Williams reported: "The Empress's health is very bad; she suffers from a cough and from breathlessness, she has water on the knee and dropsy—but she danced a minuet with me." Elizabeth's health was indeed very bad now and worsening. Catherine, describing her as she was a few months later, wrote: "At first, nobody was certain what the trouble was; some people attributed her ailments to the change of life period." (Elizabeth was forty-five.) "The Shuvalovs were constantly looking mournful and afflicted and showered caresses upon the Grand Duke. There was a lot of whispering among courtiers about her Imperial Majesty's illness . . . some called it hysteria, others spoke of fainting fits, convulsions, or nervous disorder."

In later times it has been surmised that the fainting fits and convulsions were symptoms of a late-emerging diabetes and that the "nervous disorder"—a euphemism that covered a whole range of psychoneuroses and psychoses—reflected the fact that Elizabeth was at last declining into intermittent but increasingly overt madness.

Certainly there were enough signs of mental decline and distress. She spent hours at a time sitting (kneeling was too painful) in prayer and reverie before her favorite icon. Sometimes she spoke aloud to the holy figures about her problems, and they sometimes replied to her with good advice. She was drinking heavily too, now and then to the point of unconsciousness; then her ladies-in-waiting, after the great labor of getting her hoisted into her bed, had to cut her clothing and tight corsets from her to prepare her for sleep.

Elizabeth brooded about many things; her mind was filled with ghosts and dreams and fears. She feared death, which she felt was near, but almost worse was the anxiety she had about her own physical appearance. Tall and voluptuous as she had been —a true daughter of Peter the Great and Catherine I—she had been trim in legs and waist. For a long time as Empress she had given masquerade balls called Metamorphoses, in which the men wore women's clothes and the women wore men's, not because of Sapphic designs but, quite to the contrary, because her feminine attractions, ordinarily hidden under the billowing gowns and tentlike hoop skirts of the era, could best be displayed in the stockings, knee breeches, and general gear of male attire. Now her body was bloated with dropsy. There was no hope for it, and the best she could do was to hide it under grand gowns of sumptuous materials. Above it, her face was like a carefully preserved relic of famous beauty: ravaged, yet recognizable for what it once had been.

Elizabeth fought desperately to save what remained and restore what was gone. She tried every cream and nostrum and hired platoons of physicians and apothecaries, herbalists, chemists, and masseurs to find new preservatives and remedies. Hairdressing styles were tried, altered, tried again, altered again, and tried again until the Empress, staring in the mirror, believed that the ultimate possible effect had been achieved. When everything had been done and a day spent on it, she was majestic, the very image of an Empress, but as a woman she was unsure. At galas and balls and other occasions where she would be judged by gallants such as Hanbury-Williams and by other women, she came late, amid the flatteries of wine, music, and candlelight.

Next to Christmas and Easter the holiest and most joyful day of the calendar was St. Peter's Day, June 21, the patron saint's day and name day of Peter the Great and of his city of St. Petersburg. Actually it was a double holy day. It was St. Paul's Day too, a fact that had received less notice but now, with both a Peter and a Paul in line of succession, called for joint celebration. And this year especially, its being the first saint's day of the little Czarevich so long awaited and so beloved by Elizabeth, the court expected her to preside over a really extraordinary gala. Instead she ordered that the festivities be held at Oranienbaum, with Catherine as hostess. She did not appear there at all but stayed at Peterhof with the baby.

This was the first time that Catherine had performed as hostess for the whole court, let alone for the diplomatic corps and the senior officials of the government and military forces—all of whom, by custom, were invited to help celebrate the great patriotic day. She enjoyed herself and the party was a grand success. "We danced in the ballroom at the entrance to my garden; then we had supper. . . . I remember that Sir Hanbury-Williams, the British Ambassador, was my neighbor at table, and we had a pleasant and gay conversation. He was witty, well-informed and knew the whole of Europe, so that it was not difficult to converse with him. I learnt later that he had come away from the evening as well entertained as I had been and that he had talked of me with great admiration.

"When I encountered minds which harmonized with my own, admiration of this kind was never lacking," she added, and continued on in the spirit of the newly self-assured Catherine: "I had a reputation of being intelligent, and many people who knew me well honored me with their confidence, relied on me, asked for my advice, and usually profited from that which I gave them. The Grand Duke had long been calling me Madame la Ressource and though he was often angry with me and sulked whenever he was doubtful or miserable about anything, he would usually come running to me as fast as he could to get my advice—and once he had got it, would rush away again so fast as he had come.

"I remember also, at this feast of St. Peter's Day in Oranienbaum, while watching Count Poniatowski dance, that I spoke to Sir Hanbury of Poniatowski's father and the harm he had done to Peter the Great. The British Ambassador spoke very well of the son and confirmed what I already knew: that his father and his mother's family . . . formed the Russian party in Poland, and that they had sent their son to Russia and placed him in Sir Hanbury-Williams' care to bring him up with their own feelings for Russia, and hoped he would be successful there. . . ."

It is true, as she said, that Hanbury-Williams spoke of her with great admiration, and the more so to those who might hurry to tell Catherine. From his first encounter with the Empress and what he learned from the stories circulating about her health and state of mind, he knew that Elizabeth was too ill and too distracted for him to be able to do much with her directly. But Catherine was a glorious surprise and a godsent opportunity, stimulating in every way, vivacious, acutely intelligent, full of wit and wisdom, a striking beauty in her own special style, politically alert, clearly engaged in building her own party and seeking useful likeminded allies. The very next day he hurried to inform London: "The Grand Duchess is not only convinced that Frederick is the natural and most dangerous enemy of Russia; she also hates him personally."

Actually, Catherine had only the kindest and best personal memories of Frederick. In her heart, as she said in her memoirs and was to prove when she became Empress, she saw no reason why Russia and Prussia had to be enemies. The mutual admiration between ambassador and Grand Duchess was genuine: so, too, was the deceitful ambition of each to use the other for private ends.

It was Count Bestuzhev who introduced Catherine and Poniatowski. Bestuzhev had another candidate that he really preferred, a stalwart and handsome Baltic German, Count Lehndorff, who was under direct obligation to him and whom he was sure he could control. On the other hand, Poniatowski, as the protégé of Hanbury-Williams, was acceptable to the Grand Chancellor.

There was a reenactment of the earlier charade when Madame Choglokov had asked Catherine's preference between Serge Saltikov and Leon Naryshkin. One evening some of her friends who were also Bestuzhev's agents turned the conversation to the Balt and the Pole, and Catherine said that she felt that Poniatowski was easily the more attractive. Naryshkin was present. He had already made friends with Poniatowski, now carried this news to him, and thereafter was once again the chief accomplice in arranging the affair.

In her memoirs, Catherine's references to Count Poniatowski are few and reticent, strikingly so in comparison to the detailed narrative given of her relationship with Serge Saltikov. But Poniatowski wrote his own memoirs; from this source and from correspondence most of the story can be reconstructed.

X

High Jinks and
the Higher Intrigue

FOR Poniatowski there was nothing adventurist or opportunist in the relationship with Catherine. He was dazzled by her. In his memoirs he wrote of "her black hair, her skin fair but the liveliest coloring, her very eloquent big blue eyes and long dark lashes, her Grecian nose, her mouth which seemed to ask for kisses, her perfect arms and hands, her dignified and noble bearing, and a laugh as gay as her humor." It was not only love at first sight but a kind of paralysis. He was both idealistic and innocent enough —odd for one of his background—that he could not think of what to do about his feelings.

Finally the ever-inventive Leon Naryshkin smuggled him up a back staircase of the Winter Palace and into Catherine's apartment. Poniatowski was there alone, confused about the route by which he had arrived, not daring to leave by the normal entrance where someone would be sure to see him. Catherine, returning to her apartment and finding him in her boudoir, was altogether surprised, but she quickly recovered. Poniatowski wrote: "I cannot deny myself the pleasure of noting even the very clothes I found her in that day: a little gown of white satin with a light trimming of lace, threaded with pink ribbon for its only ornament."

This was the beginning, and then: "My whole life was devoted to her, much more sincerely than those who find themselves in such a situation can usually claim."

Toward the end of the summer of 1755, Catherine and Count Stanislaus were in a glow of new love. The third principal, Sir Charles Hanbury-Williams, with whom Poniatowski lived at the British embassy, suppressed his personal chagrin (for he had found himself so much attracted to Catherine that he was half in love with her himself) and enjoyed his professional successes.

His successes were indeed extraordinary. In only about three months' time he had discovered and surveyed the outer limits of Russian corruptibility, had found his targets and their prices, and was in the process of arranging his deals. In August he wrote to London that he would be able to settle the new Subsidies Treaty for an annual payment of 50,000 pounds sterling to the imperial treasury.

Elizabeth was in the midst of two grand architectural projects, both dear to her and both enormously expensive. She needed a great deal more money to finish them. Therefore, an additional subsidy payment to her royal purse, in admiration of her good and holy works and to be used as she thought best, would secure her private gratitude—which in the Russian autocracy could be worth everything, depending on her degree of gratitude.

King George II and his ministers understood this very well and authorized a private donation to Elizabeth. "In a word," Sir Charles had said in his advice, "all that has so far been given has served to buy the Russian troops; whatever may be further given will serve to buy the Empress." The price was commensurate with Elizabeth's style of life: 500,000 livres—that is, 500,000 pounds of silver.

At the end of September, 1755, Hanbury-Williams could inform London that the new Subsidies Treaty, with the secret codicil, had been agreed on and signed and a copy was on its way. Knowing that Elizabeth's years were numbered, knowing that Peter's pro-Prussianism was beyond the reach of reason or money, and doubting, in any case, that he would be allowed to reach the throne or actually to rule if he did, Hanbury-Williams found it clear that an investment in Catherine was the best insurance England could buy for the future.

He knew that her income was 30,000 rubles a year and that with her mother's debts, which she had assumed, and with her own extravagant tastes in clothing, her natural generosity to people she liked, and her calculated generosity to people whose support she wanted for her ambitions, she was bound to be in financial troubles. She needed money? Very well, why should she be poor when so many others so much less deserving—the Shuvalovs, for instance, waxing fat from their tobacco monopoly and with their hands in a hundred pockets—were becoming rich? And when the Empress herself, to gratify her private fancies, her inveterate building of convents and palaces, had seen fit to accept a vast donation from His Majesty's government?

Sir Charles must have put the matter to Catherine in some such light. So she too was bought—not by a "subsidy" or outright gift but, more politely, through British "loans." Hanbury-Williams arranged an unlimited line of credit for her with the British consul in Petersburg. Within the first year she drew 100,000 pounds sterling.

The new French ambassador, the Marquis de l'Hôpital, informed Paris that he had no hope of recruiting Catherine for France's interests because she was so thoroughly under the influence of Bestuzhev, Hanbury-Williams, and Poniatowski. He added dyspeptically that Hanbury-Williams had "left such a deep layer of English principles at the bottom of the Grand Duchess's heart as only time can erase" and that meanwhile she "is an incorruptible Englishwoman."

The Marquis exaggerated the case. So, in his own thinking and in his self-congratulatory reports to London, did Hanbury-Williams. In their own view of their relationships with Catherine, so did Bestuzhev and Poniatowski. The former believed that because he had put his power at her disposal, she would pledge her potential future power to his use. The latter supposed that because he was so unreservedly devoted to her, she must feel the same all-enveloping love for him.

The truth was that Serge Saltikov was the only man to whom Catherine ever surrendered herself completely. Afterward she never committed herself wholly to anyone or anything except her own ultimate interests.

Final ratification of the Subsidies Treaty on which Hanbury-Williams had lavished such care and talent was delayed by diplomatic formalities and then by bad winter weather that lengthened the long time it took for couriers to travel between London and Petersburg. The courier bearing the final corrected copy, signed by George II and his ministers, arrived in Petersburg after the arrival of news that England had made an alliance with Prussia via the Treaty of Westminster, as noted earlier.

Bestuzhev and Elizabeth naturally enough felt that the events had made the Anglo-Russian agreements meaningless and absurd. On behalf of the imperial treasury and the imperial private purse, they refused to accept any of the subsidies and benefactions.

This put Hanbury-Williams in an impossible position—or logically should have. Whereas his duty from June to January had been to encourage by every means a Russian attack on Prussia, his duty now became to discourage it by every means. It is a tribute to Hanbury-Williams' savoir-faire and a measure of his cynical belief in the essential gullibility and wickedness of mankind that he stayed on in Russia.

Catherine continued to respect him and learn from him. He had thoroughly compromised her through his Poniatowski, through his own constant avuncular attentions, and through his notorious "loans." While adding to her hardened knowledge of the world, her future character as a ruler, and her own diplomatic nerve and skill, he also was instrumental in bringing about the state of disgrace to which she fell and which she barely survived to become a great Empress.

In his reports to London, Hanbury-Williams as much as declared that he controlled Catherine and that in turn she had such influence with Bestuzhev and with General Apraxin, the commander of the army, and other high officials that she could, and would, prevent or delay a Russian invasion of Prussia. Failing that, Catherine would arrange that the invasion would be unsuccessful. Also, in earnest of his overnight conversion from Frederick's foe to friend, Sir Charles conveyed through London his cordial willingness to act in Russia as Frederick's unofficial "agent" and his confidential emissary to Catherine who now, it appeared, had Frederick and Prussia's interests much at heart.

Frederick was delighted and at least half-convinced. He considered Peter a fool not worth his attention, but he had always had fond hopes for his little protégée from Zerbst. Frederick caused the British ambassador in Berlin to write, via London to Hanbury-Williams in Petersburg, this analysis: "General Apraxin is entirely devoted to the Grand Duchess. He is completely unwarlike, and has a very bad opinion of his army—it can, therefore, be assumed that he does not wish to enter into open battle with the Prussians. Moreover, Apraxin is extravagant and perpetually in debt. The King of Prussia believes one might offer Apraxin a large sum of money and induce him to check the advance of the Russian army; a general can easily find a pretext. If the Grand Duchess is willing, she can be used as a go-between."

The Russian preparations for war continued. There is nothing in any existing correspondence to show whether Catherine accepted this role or whether Apraxin accepted the bribe. But later, via London, Frederick received from Hanbury-Williams a report on the invasion plan, which he said he had learned from Catherine, who had learned it from Apraxin.

Actually, when the invasion came, the plan turned out to be quite different. To the extent that Frederick acted on Hanbury-Williams' forecast he was not helped but hurt. The two facts together—that Apraxin did invade, that the purported plan was wrong—might be enough to show that Hanbury-Williams had deceived himself about Catherine or was being deceived by her. But there were events that came later from which equally sinister imputations about her could be drawn.

Could she actually have been a traitor? In the Russian court at that time—the temptation is to say in almost any European court at that time—almost anything was possible. There is no way to prove that she was not or that she was. The matter finally comes down to one of believability, to that intuitive logic that weighs a known character in a known situation and judges whether an alleged act fits in congruently.

Catherine's alleged betrayal of Russia to Frederick makes little or no sense. What does seem altogether consonant with her character and circumstances is that, engaged in perpetual pursuit of her perpetual interest, the throne of Russia, she was playing a multiple game. She was caught and compromised. She was still new to the higher intrigue. She played the game with more verve than skill. The pleasures of self-assertion, of acting instead of reacting to others—all this seems to have stimulated her to the point of recklessness. One evening at supper, she transfixed the French ambassador, whom she disliked, with a cold stare that he never forgot and declared to him and to all present, "There was never a woman bolder than I; I have an unbridled temerity."

Perhaps the only person who still awed her and whose favor she feared to lose was Elizabeth. But although the old rules laid down by the Empress and the Grand Chancellor still existed *pro forma*, Catherine broke the rules at her convenience. In one matter she remained circumspect. Elizabeth undoubtedly knew—and Catherine undoubtedly knew that she knew—about the affair with Poniatowski. Yet it was essential to both to pretend that it did not exist because of Elizabeth's sense of the proprieties and dignities of her court, because of their implicit mother-daughter relationship, because of the huge investment of the emotions of both in the fiction of her marriage with Peter. And possibly too, on the part of Catherine, because deception and intrigue added to the excitements and pleasures of love.

As she relates in the memoirs, it was again Leon Naryshkin who arranged that this affair would be not only a romance but an exhilarating game. "Before entering my room," Catherine says, "he used to miaow like a cat at my door, and when I answered he would come in. On December 17, 1755, between six and seven o'clock in the evening, he announced his arrival at my door in that way." (Such precision is almost unique in Catherine's memoirs and suggests that in some way she considered the next event a landmark, perhaps of her final emancipation.)

Leon had come to say that his sister-in-law Anna, who was one of Catherine's best friends, was indisposed and to suggest that she go with him that evening to visit her.

"I cannot go out without permission," Catherine reminded him.

" 'Oh,' he said, 'no one will know of it; we will take our precautions. . . . I will come and fetch you in an hour or so; the Grand Duke will be having supper. . . .' (For a long time I had taken to remaining in my room instead of joining the Grand Duke for supper.) 'He will stay at table for the greater part of the night, and not get up until he is tipsy and ready for bed.' Since my confinement he had almost always slept in his own room. 'To be on the safe side, dress up as a man and we will go together to Anna Naryshkin.' The adventure began to tempt me . . . and for the sake of a moment's entertainment and gaiety I agreed to do it.

"I called my Kalmuk hairdresser and told him to bring me one of the men's suits I had and everything that belonged with it." (She had men's suits presumably for use at Elizabeth's Metamorphoses.) "As soon as Mme. Vladislavov had put me to bed and retired, I got up and dressed as a man from head to foot, arranged my hair as best I could—I had learnt to do that a long time ago and was quite clever at it. At the appointed hour, Leon Naryshkin came . . . to miaow at my door. . . . We passed through a small antechamber out into the vestibule and got into his carriage without anyone seeing us, laughing madly at our escapade.

"When we arrived, Anna, who knew nothing about it, was there"—apparently in fine health. "We also found Count Poniatowski. Leon introduced me as one of his co-officers . . . and the whole evening went by in the maddest vein one could possibly imagine. . . .

"Next day—the Empress's birthday—at the Court ceremony in the morning and in the evening at the ball, all of us who had been in the secret could not look at each other without bursting with laughter at the folly of the night before. A few days later, Leon offered to arrange a reciprocal visit to my rooms, and in the same way brought his friends in so cleverly that no one was any the wiser.

"This was the beginning of 1756. We found peculiar pleasure in these secret meetings. Not a week passed without one, two, or even three—now in one house, now in another, and if anyone among our little group was ill, that was where we would foregather. Sometimes in the theater, without exchanging a word, through a series of signs, previously agreed upon, even if in different boxes and some of us in the stalls, we would know by a gesture where to go, and never make a mistake; except that on two occasions I had to walk home—which after all was only a walk."

Here truly was a metamorphosis: the good little Princess of Zerbst, the sad, dutiful, imprisoned little consort of the heir to Russia, walking home to the Winter Palace through the streets of St. Petersburg in the Baltic night, unattended, unashamed, unafraid, exhilarated.

As for Grand Duke Peter, he "preserved his instinctive confidence in me; he kept this almost to the last, in a singular manner, without at all realizing it himself.

"He had at that moment quarreled with Countess Worontsov and was in love with Mme. Teplov, the niece of the Razumovskys. When he felt the desire to see her in his apartments, he consulted me on how to decorate the room. Wanting to make the surroundings more pleasant for her, he had filled his room with rifles, grenadiers' caps, swords, and shoulder-straps so that it looked almost like an arsenal.

"I did not interfere with his scheme and left him to it; apart from her, he was philandering with a little German singer named Leonore. . . . The Grand Duke's love affair with Mme. Teplov lasted until we went to the country . . . when she insisted that he should write to her at least once or twice a week. In order to engage him in such a correspondence she started with a letter of four pages. When he got this he came to my room, his face livid, holding Mme. Teplov's letter in his hand, and said to me angrily and loudly: 'Can you imagine it—she writes me a letter of four full pages, wants me to read them and, what is more, reply. . . . I will break off all relations with her until the winter.' I told him that this was certainly the easiest way out."

It suited Catherine's purposes that Madame Teplov remain the Grand Duke's favorite, for this was a way of tying him to Catherine's own political faction. Madame Teplov's uncles, the Razumovskys, were Catherine's and Bestuzhev's allies, whereas Elizabeth Worontsov was the daughter of Count Roman Worontsov, the Vice Chancellor, an ally of the Shuvalovs and an enemy of Bestuzhev. That winter Catherine noticed that "The Grand Duke's love affair with Mme. Teplov had . . . sunk to a low ebb; one of the greatest difficulties about it was how to meet;

it had always to be on the sly" because the Shuvalovs naturally disapproved and would have reported him to the Empress, and "this annoyed the Grand Duke, who disliked all complications as much as he disliked letter writing."

At a ball, Catherine observed "that a lot of whispering was going on between His Highness and Countess Marie Worontsov, Count Roman's eldest daughter. . . . I did not welcome with any pleasure the return of young Elizabeth Worontsov to the fore; to hamper this I told the Grand Duke about [a] statement made by her father" that he could win the Grand Duke's affections anytime by giving him half a dozen bottles of English stout. Peter was enraged by this slur, and "For a time this created a break in his relations with the two daughters," as well as their father.

"But in order to clog the wheels even more, Leon Naryshkin [put up to it by Catherine] persuaded Marshal Razumovsky to invite the Grand Duke secretly once or twice a week in the evening to his house. It became almost a regular fixture: the Marshal, Marie Naryshkin, the Grand Duke, Mme. Teplov, and Leon Naryshkin were the only ones present. This . . . gave rise to another amusing idea. The Marshal lived in a . . . spacious house," and since he "had several times been among the small secret circle which gathered in my rooms, he wanted that circle to come to him, and with this in view placed at our disposal what he called his 'hermitage,' comprising two or three apartments on the ground floor. Everybody hid from everyone else, because we dared not go out, as I said before, without special permission: through this arrangement, there were three or four groups of people assembled in the house, and the Marshal went from one to the other; only my circle knew what was taking place in the house, and nobody else knew we were there."

In short, Catherine not only maneuvered her husband back into the arms of Madame Teplov and supplied a trysting place that was convenient for them and politically advantageous for her, but had arranged to deceive him, the Shuvalovs, and the Empress with her lover Poniatowski at the same time in the next apartment. It was an exercise in duplicity as well as a political game played for high stakes, for thrills, for her own sardonic pleasure.

Her temerity went further. In the summer of 1757 the Shuvalovs and Vice Chancellor Worontsov conspired to bring the Empress' disfavor down on Poniatowski and so make it necessary that he return to Poland. Catherine bluntly and adamantly refused to lose him. She brought such pressure to bear on Grand Chancellor Bestuzhev that he—reluctantly, and with considerable difficulties and risks to himself—coerced the Polish government into sending Poniatowski back again to Russia and to Catherine as its official ambassador. He returned that December, invested with all proper credentials as representative of Russia's valued ally, the King of Saxony and Poland, and thus impossible to expel without creating a major diplomatic problem. Catherine had become pregnant soon after their affair began but had miscarried. Within two or three months of his return she was again pregnant.

Again, there seems to have been a nominal possibility that the father was Grand Duke Peter.

In her memoirs, Catherine refers to her pregnancy only in an opaque and tangential way: "At the beginning of September [1758] the Empress was in Tsarskoe Selo, and on the eighth day of that month—the Day of the Nativity of the Blessed Virgin—she went on foot from the Palace to the parish church, only a few steps northward from the gate, to attend Mass. Divine service had scarcely started when the Empress, feeling indisposed," left to return to the palace, only to fall down "insensible on the grass, surrounded by the crowd of people who had come from the whole neighborhood to listen to the Virgin's mass. . . . The Empress was tall and powerful and the sudden fall alone must have done her great injury. Somebody covered her with a piece of white fabric. . . . At last a few screens and a sofa were brought from the Palace; she was placed on the sofa and, after administering many remedies, they succeeded in reviving her a little. But she . . . recognized nobody and asked almost unintelligibly where she was.

"All this lasted more than two hours, after which it was decided to carry her Majesty, upon the sofa, to the Palace. One can imagine the consternation. . . .

"The next morning I learnt of all these circumstances through a note sent to Oranienbaum by Count Poniatowski. I went at once to read it to the Grand Duke, who knew nothing, for everything was always carefully concealed from us—particularly anything personally concerning the Empress. . . ."

A fortnight or so later, the Young Court moved back from Oranienbaum to the Winter Palace. Elizabeth was still convalescent, and "As I had become very heavy in my pregnant condition, I did not appear in public"—which left the Grand Duke with the burden of representing the throne "at Court functions, balls and feasts," which he disliked intensely. "Therefore the Grand Duke began to resent my pregnancy and one day said, in the presence of Leon Naryshkin and a few others, 'Heaven alone knows how it is that my wife becomes pregnant. I have no idea whether this child is mine and whether I ought to recognize it as such.' Leon Naryshkin rushed to give me this news while it still was hot. I was naturally very much alarmed by such statements and said to Naryshkin: '. . . you must ask him to swear on his honor that he has not slept with his wife and tell him that if he is ready to give his oath you will immediately inform Alexander Shuvalov, the Great Inquisitor of the Empire.' Leon Naryshkin did go to His Highness and asked him to swear this oath, to which he got the reply: 'Go to hell. Do not talk to me any more about it.'

"The Grand Duke's words, uttered so imprudently, angered me very much. . . ."

Beyond reasonable doubt, Poniatowski was the father of the child, and Peter actually could not have been in the least mystified. For in his eccentric and perverse way he had become a good friend and frequent companion of Poniatowski (just as he had, earlier, of Serge Saltikov) and knew quite well what the relationship was. For his part Poniatowski, as much as he held Peter in contempt, developed a certain good-humored affection for him. In his own memoirs he wrote rather touchingly:

"Nature made him a mere poltroon, a guzzler, an individual so comic in all things that seeing him, one could not help thinking, 'Here is the very type of *Arlecchino finto principe* [Harlequin in the role of Prince].' In one of the outpourings of his heart with which he frequently honored me, he observed, 'See, though, how unhappy I am. If I had only entered into the service of the King of Prussia I would have served him to the best of my ability.

By this present time, I am confident, I should have had a regiment and the rank of major general, and perhaps even of lieutenant general. But far from it: instead they brought me here and made me Grand Duke of this damnable country.' And then he railed against the Russian nation in his customary ridiculous manner. . . . He was not stupid, but mad, and as he was fond of drink, this helped to addle his poor brains even further."

On the night of December 8, 1757, Catherine began to feel labor pains and, in accordance with protocol, sent messages to the Empress and the Grand Duke that a royal birth was imminent. "After a certain time, the Grand Duke came to my room, in his Holstein uniform, top boots and spurs, with a sash round his waist and a huge sword hanging at his side: he was dressed up in all his finery. It was close to half-past two in the morning.

"Surprised at his appearance, I asked him the reason for so elaborate a costume. He replied that it was only in times of distress that one recognized one's true friends, that in this attire he was ready to act according to his duties, that the duty of a Holsteinian officer was to protect, in accordance with his oath, the Ducal House against all its enemies and as I was feeling ill he had hastened to my help.

"One might have thought that he was joking, but not at all; he was in deadly earnest. I realized that he was tipsy, and advised him to go to bed, so that when the Empress came she would not be doubly displeased to see him drunk and armed from head to foot in the Holstein uniform, which I knew she disliked. I had a lot of trouble in getting him to go . . . he left at last. . . .

"I gave birth, on December 9th, between ten and eleven o'clock at night, to a girl, and begged the Empress to call her after Her Majesty; but she decided that the child should bear the name of her elder sister, the Duchess of Holstein, Anna Petrovna, the Grand Duke's mother."

And so, once again, Elizabeth's capacity for self-deception was large enough to accommodate her love and nostalgia for her family.

"The Grand Duke seemed pleased about the birth of this child: he organized great celebrations in his rooms and ordered that festivities should also be arranged in Holstein and accepted all the congratulations with every sign of satisfaction.

"On the sixth day the Empress had the child baptized, and brought me an order from the Cabinet for the sum of sixty thousand rubles." (A considerable discount from the 100,000 awarded her for the birth of Paul.) "She sent the same amount to the Grand Duke, which further increased his satisfaction. The celebrations began after the baptism.

"I was told that some of them were magnificent. I did not see any. I was lying in my bed all forlorn, without a soul to keep me company except Mme. Vladislavov, for as my confinement was over, not only did the Empress—just as she did the time before—take the child to her rooms, but also, on the pretext that I needed rest, I was abandoned like a miserable creature and no one set foot in my apartments, nor sent to ask how I was.

"As I had already suffered enough the first time from neglect, on this occasion I took all possible precautions . . . my bed was in the center of a rather long room . . . there was a private door leading into a kind of store room which also served as an antechamber. . . . From my bed to this door, I had placed an immense screen which concealed the prettiest alcove one could imagine, given the place and circumstances. It contained a sofa, mirrors, a few movable tables and some chairs. When the curtain of my bed was drawn—there was nothing to be seen; when it was pulled back, the alcove and those who were in it came into view. . . .

"On January 1, 1759, the Court celebrations ended with immense fireworks between the ball and the supper." (Elizabeth was honoring the tradition of Peter the Great, who was fascinated by fireworks and used them at all important celebrations.) "Count Peter Shuvalov came to bring me a plan of the display, a short time before it was set off: Mme. Vladislavov told him I was asleep, but that she would see if I would receive him.

"It was not true that I was asleep, but I was in bed, surrounded by my little group of friends [including] Count Poniatowski, who . . . often came to see me. . . . Mme. Vladislavov did not know for certain who was with me, but was shrewd enough to suspect that someone was there. . . . She gave me Peter Shuvalov's message and I said she could let him in. She went to fetch him while my guests behind the curtain were dying of laughter at the hilarious situation of my receiving Count Peter Shuvalov, who could swear later that he found me in bed, all alone, while only a curtain separated my merry little crowd from this pompous Court oracle, this eminent confidant of the Empress.

"He came in, bringing his plan of the fireworks—he was the Grand Master of Artillery. I began by apologizing for having kept him waiting. I had only just woken up, I said, rubbing my eyes and looking very sleepy . . . and then talked to him at some length until he seemed in a hurry to go in order not to keep the Empress waiting for the fireworks to start.

"I indicated that he could withdraw. He left the room and I then pulled the curtain apart. My friends had meanwhile laughed themselves hungry and thirsty. I told them: 'Of course you must eat and drink; it is only fair that you should not die of hunger and thirst while keeping me such pleasant company.' I again closed the curtain and rang the bell. Mme. Vladislavov came in and I told her to send me some supper, that I was ravenous and needed at least six portions.

"When the supper was ready and brought to my room, I . . . dismissed the servants. My friends came out from behind the screen and threw themselves like wild beasts upon the food. Their gaiety had increased their appetite. I must admit that the evening was one of the maddest and merriest that I had spent in my life. . . . I think the servants must have been slightly surprised by my appetite. . . . Count Poniatowski always put on a blond wig and a cloak before leaving my rooms and when the sentries asked him: 'Who goes there?' he replied: 'The Grand Duke's musician.' This wig made us laugh a lot that day."

It was the last good laugh that Catherine was to enjoy for a long while. Her brazen self-confidence and industrious politicking had exposed her to grave dangers which at that very moment, unrealized by her, were building rapidly to climax. Only a week later the unthinkable happened: Grand Chancellor Bestuzhev, her great ally and protector, was arrested on suspicion of treason.

As she relates: "Though Count Bestuzhev was arrested in the same palace"—the Winter Palace—"in which we occupied a wing and not far from our apartments, we heard nothing about it that evening, so careful was everybody to conceal from us all that was going on. The next day I received, through Leon Naryshkin, a note from Count Poniatowski . . . [which] began with these words: 'Man is never without resources. I use this means to warn you that last night Count Bestuzhev was arrested and relieved of all his charges and decorations. With him were arrested your jeweler Bernardi, Jelagine and Adadurov.' I was astounded. . . . After having read this note and pondered over it . . . my head was crowded with thoughts each more unpleasant and disturbing than the other."

XI

"Three Equally Dangerous Paths"

ELIZABETH'S physical decline and recurrent illnesses had made the royal succession a matter of continual preoccupation among the court factions. Catherine does not define the precise role she was planning for herself but implies that she expected Grand Duke Peter to become Czar and that because of his incompetence, disinterest in Russian and state affairs, and "instinctive confidence" he had kept in her "in a singular manner," she as Czarina would become the *de facto* ruler of the nation. Because of her vendetta with the Shuvalovs, they would do everything possible to prevent this. They hoped to control the throne, either by establishing their influence over Peter or perhaps by deposing him in favor of the little Czarevich Paul and installing themselves and their allies as a regency council. Catherine might find herself exiled, deported to Holstein with the Grand Duke.

Knowing how easy it had been for Elizabeth and her predecessors to take the throne by armed coup d'état, she looked for armed support. Naturally enough, and probably at Bestuzhev's specific suggestion, she turned to Field Marshal Apraxin, Bestuzhev's close friend and ally.

In the spring of 1756, Apraxin was preparing to leave Petersburg to take command of the troops assigned to the invasion of Prussia, and as Catherine relates: "His wife came . . . for a farewell visit. I spoke to her of my fears about the Empress's health and told her that I regretted her husband's departure at this moment, when I relied so little on the Shuvalovs whom I considered my personal enemies and who resented my preference for their enemies, the Counts Razumovsky and Bestuzhev. She repeated this to her husband, who was just as pleased with my feelings towards him as was Count Bestuzhev, who also did not like the Shuvalovs and was allied to the Razumovskys, his own son having married a niece of theirs."

As usual, boudoir politics were involved in the equation, for as Catherine goes on to explain: "Marshal Apraxin could be a useful intermediary among all the interested parties, owing to the intimate relations between his daughter and Count Peter Shuvalov; these relations were supposed to be known to her parents."

It was true, as Frederick had communicated to Hanbury-Williams, that Marshal Apraxin had "a very bad opinion of his army." He found it badly trained and equipped, and it took him a full year to convert it into a force capable of challenging Frederick's superb regiments. Further, although it was untrue that he was "completely unwarlike"—he was an extremely able commander—he undoubtedly had some heavy misgivings about committing his army unreservedly to this campaign, knowing that Elizabeth's death could make the whole effort worse than meaningless. The delay enabled Hanbury-Williams to report to London and thence to Frederick in Berlin that it was the fruit of his diplomacy, especially of his influence on Catherine and her influence on Apraxin.

Yet there is a letter from Catherine to Count Bestuzhev dated January 30, 1757, about midpoint in the delay and in her alleged efforts to restrain Apraxin, in which she wrote: "I have heard with pleasure that our army will soon put our Declaration [of war] into action—we should be covered with shame if it were not fulfilled—I beg you to urge our mutual friend [Apraxin] when he has beaten the King of Prussia, to force him back to his old frontiers, so that we may not have to be perpetually on the *qui vive*."

Bestuzhev forwarded this message, which Catherine had written at his request, so that Apraxin could be reassured that she favored the war against Prussia and that on Elizabeth's death, her influence would be on the side of continuing. And Bestuzhev meant for her to have very great influence indeed.

Catherine says: "He looked upon me personally as perhaps the only individual upon whom at that time the hopes of the people could be based when the Empress was no more." That same January Bestuzhev sent her—via Count Poniatowski—a draft of a manifesto he had prepared, "according to which, at the death of the Empress, the Grand Duke would be declared emperor by law and at the same time I would be declared as participating with the Grand Duke in the rule of the country. All the offices were to continue and he, Bestuzhev, would be made lieutenant-colonel of four guards regiments and the president of three Imperial Colleges [ministries]—those of Foreign Affairs, War and the Admiralty." Thus, with Catherine on the throne as co-ruler, with Bestuzhev in charge of the armed forces including the politically crucial Guards regiments, Peter would be a powerless nullity, a figurehead Emperor who could be put aside entirely later on if that proved desirable.

Catherine did not accept the scheme, partly because Bestuzhev's own "pretensions were, as one can see, excessive." She was not willing to pledge so much power to anyone, not even her closest ally, whose interests, after all, might someday diverge from her own. Nor did she like the idea of co-rule with Peter on the "participating" basis proposed because "I considered it noxious to the empire, which would have been torn apart by a domestic quarrel between me and my husband, who did not love me." In short, so she wrote, "To tell the truth, I looked upon this plan as drivel." Nevertheless, she did not reject it. Instead, "I had asked Count Poniatowski to reply verbally that I thanked Bestuzhev for his good intentions in regard to me, but that I considered the plan difficult to execute." She then took her copy of the draft "and corrected it with my own hand"—changing it in ways she does not relate—and put it away among her confidential papers.

In the summer of 1757, Field Marshal Apraxin finally moved against Prussia. In June he captured the important Baltic fortress of Memel. By mid-August his advance had carried him deep into the Prussian territory and to a massive confrontation with Frederick. On August 17, at the Battle of Grossjägerndorf, the Russians inflicted a stunning defeat on the Prussians. It was the worst setback Frederick had suffered since beginning his aggressions and a cause for great celebrations in Paris, Vienna, and Petersburg.

Grand Duke Peter was so nearly heartbroken at this defeat of his hero that he stayed in his rooms grieving and drinking. Catherine, to help cheer him up and to demonstrate her own Russian patriotism, gave a grand garden party at Oranienbaum following the *Te Deum* offered up in thanksgiving at the same hour at all the churches of the empire. And with that perceptive concern for, and instinctive understanding of, the feelings of common men that distinguish great politicians, she also "had an ox roasted that day for the laborers and masons of Oranienbaum."

The celebrations were premature. Only two weeks or so later "we learned that Marshal Apraxin, far from profiting by his successes . . . and making further headway, had withdrawn so precipitately that the retreat looked more like a flight. . . ." It seemed incredible. Apraxin "threw away or burned his ammunition and dismantled his guns" and put the countryside to the torch behind him as he retreated eastward to the fortress of Memel. "Nobody could understand these operations; even his friends . . . began to search for some hidden explanation."

Historians have been on the same search ever since, with modest success but with undiminished zeal, for it is a fine mystery. The elementary and more or less generally accepted fact of the matter is that the Russian military logistical apparatus had broken down. If so, it would seem to be far less Apraxin's fault than that of the high staff officers and ministerial bureaucrats back in Petersburg. By the standards of the time his army was very big, some 80,000 men and many thousands of horses. It was far too big a force to live off the land. Hence, supplying it was a complex problem, the more so as it moved farther from its bases and deeper into Prussia. Apraxin's great victory left his troops exhausted and his stores very low. In effect, because of inadequate planning and the familiar plague of corruption and inefficiency, the victory left him stranded in Prussia without the means even to feed his army, let alone make good his losses of war materials.

A fortnight after the glorious victory, the high war council in Petersburg faced up to the ignominious facts. It ordered Apraxin to break off the campaign for the time being and to bring his army back to the region of Memel, where it could be provisioned fairly easily by ship.

Frederick, misinformed by Sir Charles Hanbury-Williams, had not expected Apraxin even to attack, let alone with such strong forces and with such evident intention of winning.

This initial surprise was as nothing to his incredulity over the Russian withdrawal. This led him to think that perhaps his intrigues in Petersburg had succeeded after all and that in some peculiar way Apraxin had defeated him by mistake and now regretted it. Frederick quickly became aware, too, from captives and his far-flung intelligence operations, that Apraxin's supply troubles were dire.

In any case, Frederick wasted little time in bemusement. His army, although badly mauled, had by no means been destroyed, and the Russian failure to follow up the victory gave him a precious chance to reassemble his troops and reequip and reinforce them. By the time Apraxin's withdrawal eastward began, Frederick was strong enough to make this a miserable and dangerous undertaking.

He harassed the Russian rear and raided the flanks. He became convinced that if he could make the invaders stand and fight a second battle, he had a good chance of destroying them. Apraxin, following his orders and very likely his own inclinations, wanted at almost all costs to avoid battle and to get his troops to Memel reasonably intact. To impede the Prussian advance, he had his rear guard set fire to villages and farms as it quit them, and to put more distance between him and the impetuous Frederick, he imposed forced marches on his troops, ordering them to abandon or destroy whatever they could not carry. The two commanders reacted to each other—Frederick becoming bolder as Apraxin became warier. Soon what had begun as a disengagement and orderly retreat took on aspects of a rout.

Judged in this light, with knowledge of Apraxin's situation and his orders, the astonishing reversal of roles—the vanquished in hot pursuit of the victor—is explicable and in a certain sense reasonable.

But was there something more? The supply problems and the orders to Apraxin were secret. So there began a search for some hidden explanation—an inquisition much abetted by the Marquis de l'Hôpital, who immediately assumed (being a hardworking competitor of Hanbury-Williams in the black arts of diplomacy) that Apraxin had been bribed or somehow subverted.

But it is fairly unthinkable that Grand Chancellor Bestuzhev would be ignorant of any state secrets affecting Apraxin, and, according to Catherine, even he found the marshal's haste unseemly and peculiar: "Count Bestuzhev . . . asked me to write to the Marshal as his friend and to join with Bestuzhev in trying to persuade him to resume his march and halt the retreat, on which his enemies were putting such an odious and sinister interpretation. I did in fact write and warn him of the virulent Petersburg rumors: I explained that his friends found it difficult to justify the speed of his withdrawals and begged him to resume his advance and execute the Government's orders. Chancellor Bestuzhev sent this letter to him. Marshal Apraxin did not reply to me."

That Bestuzhev, who was intimately allied with Apraxin, should need Catherine's help in persuading the marshal seems wholly incongruous until Catherine supplies in a few demure passages a perfectly cogent, if not perfectly complete, revelation that it was for her sake that Apraxin acted as he did. A dozen years afterward, Catherine wrote: "I still think that [Apraxin] kept receiving . . . detailed reports on the Empress's health, which was deteriorating all this time. . . . Marshal Apraxin, believing the danger to be more imminent than it really was, did not think it opportune to penetrate deeper into Prussia, but preferred to retreat, drawing near to the Russian frontiers, on the pretext of lack of supplies, foreseeing that the war would come to an immediate end in the event of the Empress' death." That is, if Peter became Czar.

In the event of Elizabeth's death, Catherine continues, "he believed his presence to be necessary in Russia, as I said when I spoke of his departure." The clear implication is that he was hurrying back to prevent this and to put his influence and elite regiments at Catherine's disposal in a coup organized by Bestuzhev which would bring her at least equal, probably dominant, power as Empress or Regent.

However, the reports of Elizabeth's approaching death had been greatly exaggerated. Catherine's letter was to inform Apraxin of this implicitly and to warn that in his premature dash to her rescue he was destroying his very capacity to rescue her at a later time. Very likely he did not reply to her because by the time he realized his error any attempt to do so would have been both pointless and dangerous. Elizabeth, furious and filled with suspicions, had relieved him of command, imprisoned him, and prepared to court-martial him.

With these events, Catherine's situation suddenly became vulnerable. Her family affiliations with Prussia, the fact she was married to the notoriously pro-Prussian Grand Duke, her friendship with both Apraxin and his deputy commander, General Lieven, her close ties to Hanbury-Williams—all these could be grist for rumors that she was in secret partnership with Frederick. Her letters to Apraxin, anti-Prussian and patriotic though they appeared, could be interpreted otherwise. Besides, her writing to Apraxin at all was a violation of the rules she was still supposed to be living by.

The fact that she wrote to him while he was a commander in the field against an enemy who had been her girlhood sponsor, and moreover wrote secretly and on matters concerning the state, could easily imply that there were other letters besides these with far different, sinister content. In Elizabeth's court, where there were "as many spies as there were courtiers," secrets of any sort were hard to keep for long. Rumors, once set afloat, took on a life of their own, grew vastly and developed bizarre forms. The more fantastic and sensational the rumor, the more convincing.

Hanbury-Williams was declared *persona non grata* and sent packing to England. It was one of the more anomalous features of the disorderly, oddly fragmented war called the Seven Years' War that England and Russia, although members of opposite warring alliances, had remained officially and in all overt ways at peace with each other and in fact continued so to the end. The Anglo-Prussian alliance irked Elizabeth considerably, and she never did accept the 500,000 pounds sterling despite Hanbury-Williams' constant efforts to persuade her. To Bestuzhev and the pro-English faction in general, that alliance demonstrated not English perfidy, but the perfidy of France in reversing its policy.

Consequently, for a whole year after Russia declared war on Prussia, Hanbury-Williams had been able to continue as before, seeing Catherine often, spreading his charm and leaving a trail of intrigue and the sweet scent of money in most of the important salons of Petersburg. So his expulsion was a major event. It was more than a personal rejection: it was a rebuff to England and marked a major decline in English prestige.

When Hanbury-Williams was recalled, he came to Oranienbaum to say farewell to Catherine. We know little about that scene except that he broke down and sobbed. She spent the rest of the day in tears. And however he may have mismanaged other matters, he took away with him, to show his government, a trophy of his success with the Grand Duchess. It was a letter in her handwriting:

"I will use every conceivable opportunity of persuading Russia to enter into a friendly alliance with England, in which I see the real interests of my country. I will always put the interests of England first, where I consider this to be necessary to the welfare of Europe and particularly of Russia, against the common enemy, France, whose greatness is a disgrace to Russia."

When the ship that took Sir Charles back to England put in at Hamburg after encountering bad weather, he was so ill that he needed medical care. The doctors took very little time to decide he was insane. He was put under medical escort and sent on to England. There, a year later, he killed himself. In tribute to his services to his country he was buried in Westminster Abbey.

Whatever Catherine's involvements, foreign and domestic, may have been in the Apraxin affair, they were enough to put her nerves on edge. It was only a fortnight or so after Apraxin's arrest that Grand Duke Peter spoke "so imprudently" about Catherine's pregnancy. She was "alarmed" and "angered" because she realized that if he actually proceeded with his casual threat to deny his paternity, she could be ruined. Even for him to express such doubts in public could encourage her enemies to make troubles for her. The episode caused her to make one of the fundamental decisions of her life.

She wrote, "I then saw that three equally dangerous paths opened up before me: *primo*—to share His Highness' fate, whatever it might be; *secundo*—to be exposed at any moment to anything he might undertake for or against me; *tertio*—to take a route independent of any such eventuality. But to speak more plainly, it was a matter of either perishing with (or because of) him, or else of saving myself, the children, and perhaps the State from the wreckage to which the moral and physical qualities of this Prince were leading us."

With this decision, Peter was in effect doomed. And these words contain in a concise way Catherine's *apologia* to her son, the future Czar Paul, and her descendants and to history for the actions she took, as soon as she was able, to seize the throne for herself.

Although Catherine had now defined her goal—power for herself without Peter—in the actual event the route that took her to it turned out to be altogether different from the one she planned.

Her seemingly indispensable guide, accomplice, and colleague had been Grand Chancellor Bestuzhev. She was aware that he was having difficulties from many quarters and that these were compounded by the disgrace of Apraxin. But he seemed indestructible. After all, he had now been Elizabeth's chief minister for sixteen years, surviving innumerable intrigues and complications. When, in the same October that saw Hanbury-Williams' departure, Poniatowski was recalled by the Polish Prime Minister, Count Heinrich von Brühl, she wrote to Bestuzhev: "I know that Count Brühl would obey you even if you commanded him to give up his daily bread. If you will only act as I wish, no one will dare to oppose your will."

The Grand Chancellor was already annoyed and disturbed about the recall, for Brühl had neglected to consult him in advance. This had led him to "serious altercations," as Catherine says, with Brühl, who finally told him that the recall had been requested by Vice Chancellor Worontsov and Elizabeth's favorite, Ivan Shuvalov. By clear implication, they had been speaking for the Empress herself, who had chosen to bypass Bestuzhev—a very bad omen, one that gave Bestuzhev reason for pause and reflection.

He decided to risk the Empress' displeasure and do what he could for Catherine.

"Chancellor Bestuzhev had Count Poniatowski's recall orders passed on to him," Catherine relates, "and sent them back [to Brühl] on the pretext that certain formalities had not been complied with." This gave him time for maneuver, during which, living up to Catherine's finest expectations, he managed in unexplained ways to bring such pressure on Brühl that the latter withdrew the orders and moreover wrote, "They are so well satisfied with Count Poniatowski here that there is no question of his recall."

Truly it was a virtuoso performance and Bestuzhev's last one.

The French had been particularly eager to dispose of Poniatowski because they considered that Hanbury-Williams had infected him with a pro-English bias which in turn made Catherine even more "an incorrigible Englishwoman," as De l'Hôpital had called her.

Soon after Bestuzhev's success with Count Brühl, the French ambassador notified Vice Chancellor Worontsov that, on instructions from his government, he would henceforth deal only with Grand Chancellor Bestuzhev as being the only man in the Russian government with any real authority. As foreseen by De l'Hôpital and the Shuvalovs (who probably supplied the idea) the Vice Chancellor's ego was bruised so painfully that he went to the Empress. One complaint led to another, and one complainant to another: De l'Hôpital and other important enemies of Bestuzhev's had their turns with Elizabeth.

Finally, Elizabeth was convinced, despite all her inclinations to the contrary, that the man she had trusted so completely from the beginning of her reign had been betraying her with England and probably with Frederick and was now disregarding her wishes—as in the matter of Poniatowski—because he considered her as much as dead already and was intent on pleasing the Young Court.

Thus, while Catherine—with a degree of hubris guaranteed to tempt fate—was enjoying Poniatowski's company in his improbable blond wig and musician's disguise, entertaining her light-hearted friends and poking ridicule at the Shuvalovs, the latter and their allies were energetically preparing her ruin.

On the day that Catherine learned of Bestuzhev's arrest, her friend Leon Naryshkin was at last giving up his rapscallion bachelor's life to marry Mademoiselle Zakrevsky, one of the ladies-in-waiting. Count Buturline, son of one of Peter the Great's noted commanders, was marrying Marie Worontsov, daughter of the Vice Chancellor, who, overnight, had now become Grand Chancellor. The double wedding was to be followed by a gala feast and grand ball at the Winter Palace. In honor of the union of four such great families, this was certain to be a dazzling scene, a convocation of the highest aristocracy and most important personages of the realm. Considering her rank and her friendship with Naryshkin, it would be difficult for Catherine not to attend. Considering the morning's news, which had swept through Petersburg and occupied everyone's thoughts, it would even be more difficult for her to attend. Everyone knew that Bestuzhev had been her ally and protector, and the other three men arrested— Bernardi, Ivan P. Jelagine, and Basil Adadurov—were known to be closely associated with her.

Adadurov had been her Russian teacher "and had remained loyal to me. It was I who had recommended him to Count Bestuzhev" as a reliable and discreet assistant. Jelagine once had been aide-de-camp to Count Alexis Razumovsky. "He had become the friend of Count Poniatowski. . . . He had always shown marked zeal and devotion for me." As for Bernardi, he was "an Italian jeweler . . . whose profession secured him an entry into every house. . . . As he went to and fro all the time he was given messages to carry. . . . Thus the arrest of Bernardi upset the whole town, for everybody's messages were in his keeping, mine among them." What Catherine does not mention is that Bernardi had been acting as courier for delivery of the English "subsidy" Hanbury-Williams had arranged for her and that it was through him that she communicated her financial needs to the English embassy; these were some of the messages that "were in his keeping."

"With the iron in my soul, so to speak, I dressed and went to Mass," Catherine relates, "where it seemed to me that everyone had as long a face as mine. Nobody mentioned anything to me. . . . I, too, remained silent. The Grand Duke . . . seemed to me rather cheerful that day, though unostentatiously keeping at a distance from me. In the evening . . . I dressed and went to the blessing of the marriages . . . to the supper and the ball."

With a vivacity and coquetry she was far from feeling, she "went up to the best man, Prince Nikita Trubetskoy" (another of Peter the Great's companions-at-arms) and, on the pretext of examining the ribbons of his marshal's baton, whispered to him: "What are all these wonderful goings-on? Have you found more crimes than criminals, or more criminals than crime?" Prince Trubetskoy was known as an enemy of Bestuzhev, but he was perhaps too surprised to be less than frank. He replied, "We did what we were ordered to do, but as for the crimes, we are still searching for them. Up to now, we have not been very lucky in our searches."

"After talking with him, I went to speak to Marshal Buturline, who told me: 'Bestuzhev has been arrested, but we are trying to find out why.' This was the attitude of the two heads of the committee appointed by the Empress to examine the arrested man, together with Alexander Shuvalov." Catherine was somewhat relieved, but very far from comforted; the Grand Inquisitor could be counted on to apply himself devotedly to the search and to find any incriminating evidence that existed. It was not until the next day that she could begin to breathe more easily. Bestuzhev sent word that she should have no apprehensions because "he had had time to burn everything."

Catherine followed his example. "I summoned my valet Shkurine and told him to collect all my accounts and everything in the way of documents which were to be found among my belongings and bring them to me. He fulfilled my instructions with promptitude and precision. When he had brought everything . . . I threw all the papers into the fire." And it was indeed everything, a clean sweep of letters, diaries, records, and even philosophical jottings from the time she had come to Russia some fifteen years earlier. Through Madame Vladislavov and her son-in-law, the former Chancellor's chief clerk, she managed to get a note to Bestuzhev: "You have nothing to fear; everything has been burnt." This calmed him down, for since the Chancellor's arrest he must have been more dead than alive.

In the first crucial days after the arrest the accused men managed to communicate with one another and with Catherine through a network of friends and servitors, an odd assortment that included Poniatowski, Madame Vladislavov, and a man named Stambke, who as resident minister of Holstein was supposed to be Grand Duke Peter's executive officer in running the affairs of the dukedom, but who actually was Bestuzhev's creature. Also, Catherine's valet Shkurine, some of whose good friends, it turned out, had been assigned to guard the prisoners, and notably, one of the musicians who were allowed to come and play for Bestuzhev at his home, where he was being held under house arrest. Stambke, the Holsteiner, had been the one who brought Bestuzhev's reassuring message to Catherine. He told her also that he would be sending future messages "through the same channel. I asked Stambke what that channel was. He told me that it was the Count's hunting-horn player who had passed him the note [evidently smuggling it out in his instrument] and . . . that in future all communications would be deposited in a special spot among some bricks not far from Count Bestuzhev's house. I told Stambke to be careful lest this ticklish correspondence be detected. . . .

"After several days had passed, Stambke came to my room very early one morning, looking pale and upset. He said that his and Count Poniatowski's correspondence with Count Bestuzhev had been intercepted, the little horn player arrested, and it looked as if all their recent letters had fallen into the hands of Count Bestuzhev's guards. Stambke himself expected to be expelled, if not arrested, at any moment; he had come to see me and say good-bye.

"What he said did not serve to put me at my ease. . . ."

That very afternoon the Empress ordered Stambke expelled to Holstein. He left "immediately." Also, "The Government now

asked the King of Poland formally for the recall of Count Poniatowski," which meant that he, like Hanbury-Williams, was officially *persona non grata* and unquestionably would have to leave.
"Meanwhile, Count Bestuzhev's interrogation was taking its
course."

Catherine could feel the noose tightening.

"I was all alone, not seeing a soul. I refrained from asking anyone to come and visit me, for fear of exposing them to some unpleasantness or disaster." So far as possible she avoided appearing
in public, and when protocol required her attendance at court, she
was careful in approaching anyone, "afraid of being shunned."
In short, her new and immoderate appetite for intrigue, her new
and rash confidence that she could manipulate life entirely to her
liking, had left her far more isolated and threatened than she had
ever been as the obedient young bride. The "bad odor" of disgrace
surrounded her. ". . . rumors began to spread that I was to be
banished, or forbidden to appear at all in public, and who knows
what else." The "what else" included permanent "retirement" to a
convent, imprisonment in the fortress of Schlüsselburg, or con-
ceivably even death.

That extraordinary ego, firm and resilient, that had brought
her to Russia and enabled her to survive and prevail until this
point, now showed how tough and nearly impermeable it could
be. A more fragile woman—or man—might have waited numbly
for the worst to happen or perhaps in panic have lashed out in
irrational ways. Catherine went to the theater.

XII

Elizabeth and Catherine: The Great Confrontation

"A Russian play was to be performed in the Court Theater," Catherine relates. Poniatowski, whose recall was still being processed by the Russian and Polish official diplomatic apparatus, "asked me to go to it, because . . . every time I failed to appear at Court or at a spectacle everybody wondered what the reason could be," and the rumors, increasingly lurid, were becoming a grave danger in themselves.

Whatever her inner tensions, it was time for a display of bravado and insouciance. This was the last play of the carnival season before Lent, and the fact that it was a Russian play made it especially useful for Catherine's purpose. The dramatic arts were still in their infancy in Russia, and Elizabeth was doing her best to encourage them. Consequently, showing special interest in Russian theater had connotations of patriotism and of loyalty to the Empress, who almost always attended these productions. Catherine was in sore need of such advertising.

Moreover, from the attitude that Elizabeth showed toward her she could get clues to just how much trouble she was in. Possibly she would have a chance to speak directly with her and to declare herself innocent of wicked or disloyal intentions. For, as she wrote, "At the bottom of my heart I was . . . convinced that as far as the government was concerned, I had nothing with which to reproach myself." Still more, Poniatowski would be there, and although he could not be her escort, it would be worth a great deal even to be able to see him from a distance, to exchange loving glances. Thus her decision to attend, far from being in the least quixotic, was the product of a complex equation. And if difficulties stood in the way of her attending, they would be removed.

"I knew," she writes, "that the Russian theater was one of the things the Grand Duke liked least of all and that the mere talk of going to it gave him great displeasure, but this time another motive was added to his distaste." He had renewed his affair with Elizabeth Worontsov, who all this time had remained one of Catherine's ladies-in-waiting. "If I were to go to the theater, these ladies would have to accompany me and this would upset the plans of the Grand Duke. . . . Regardless of these circumstances . . . I sent word to Count Alexander Shuvalov to order my carriages. . . . Count Shuvalov came to tell me that my desire to see the Russian play found no favor with the Grand Duke.

"I replied that as the circle which surrounded the Grand Duke did not include me, it could not matter to him whether I was alone in my rooms or in a box at the theater. He went away, his eye twitching as it always did when he was upset about something.

"After a while, the Grand Duke arrived in my rooms; he was in a terrible rage and shouted like a trooper that I found pleasure in upsetting him, and had only planned to go to the theater because I knew he hated that type of show. I tried to make it clear to him that he was wrong in not liking it.

"He said he would countermand my carriages. I said that in that case I would walk.

"After we had both discussed the matter for a long time, at the tops of our voices, he went away as furious as ever and I remained determined to go to the theater.

"When it was nearly time . . . I sent to ask Count Shuvalov whether my carriages were ready and he came to say the Grand Duke had said they would not fetch me. Then I really lost my

temper and said I would walk to the theater and if my ladies-
and gentlemen-in-waiting were forbidden to follow me I would
go alone and would complain to the Empress about him and the
Grand Duke.

"He asked me, 'What exactly will you say to her?'

" 'I will tell her,' I said, 'how I am being treated; and how, so
that the Grand Duke can enjoy the company of my ladies-in-
waiting, you encourage him to prevent me from going to the theater where I may have the happiness of seeing the Empress. I will
also ask her to send me back to my mother because I have had
enough of the role I am made to play here, alone and neglected
in my room, detested by the Grand Duke and not really liked by
the Empress; all I wish is peace, I do not want to be a burden
to anyone any longer.

" 'I am going to write to Her Majesty this moment and we shall
see whether you can avoid taking that letter to her yourself!'

"The fellow was intimidated . . . he left the room and I began
to write in Russian to the Empress, in the most pathetic tones
I could summon.

"I began by thanking her for all the kindness and graciousness
she had shown me since my arrival in Russia, saying that, alas,
the present situation proved that I had not deserved it, as I had
only provoked the hatred of the Grand Duke and the marked
disfavor of Her Majesty; that since I was deprived of the most
innocent entertainments, I sat in my room in distress and solitude.

"I begged her to put an end to my misery and send me back to
my mother in whatever manner she found convenient and suitable. As I did not see my children, though I lived in the same
house with them, it did not matter to me whether I was in the
same place as they or hundreds of miles away. I knew she surrounded them with care that surpassed anything which my poor
capacities were able to give them; I begged her to continue with
this care and, in the confidence that she would do so, I would
spend the rest of my days in my home, praying to God for her, the
Grand Duke, and my children and for all those who have been
both kind and unkind to me. . . .

"Having written this, I summoned Count Shuvalov, who told
me as he came in that my carriages were ready.

"I said to him, as I handed him the letter to the Empress, that he could tell the ladies- and gentlemen-in-waiting who did not wish to accompany me to the theater that I dispensed with their company. Count Shuvalov took my letter, his eye twitching. . . . He also passed on my message . . . and it was the Grand Duke himself who decided who was to go with me and who was to remain with him.

"As I crossed the antechamber I saw him settling down with Countess Worontsov to play cards in a corner. He rose and so did she, as they saw me pass. Usually he remained sitting. I made a low curtsy in response to such ceremony and went on my way.

"I went to the theater, but the Empress did not make an appearance there that day. I believe it was my letter which prevented her."

Not only had it touched and disturbed the Empress, as Catherine intended, but evidently had succeeded too well: Elizabeth "was not at all inclined to such spectacular measures" as banishing or imprisoning a member of the royal family, for "She remembered the old troubles . . . and would by no means wish to see them repeated now." She had been led to think of repeating them, according to Catherine's version of events, only by the machinations of the Shuvalovs. Confronted suddenly by a petition in which Catherine turned everything upside down or right side up and undercut the whole problem of banishment by asking to be allowed to go home to Zerbst, the Empress naturally needed time to compose herself and to think. "I was convinced in my heart of hearts," Catherine says, "that . . . the steps I had taken would upset the Shuvalovs' plans."

After all, Catherine assured herself—and her future readers— "The only point against me was that I did not consider her august nephew the most amiable of men, just as I did not appear to him the most amiable of women." And as for that: ". . . the Empress shared my views and knew him so well that for many years she had been unable to spend a quarter of an hour with him without being filled with disgust, anger, or sadness. When talking about him privately in her own room, she either burst into bitter tears at the idea of having such an heir, or showed her contempt for him and used violent epithets at his expense which he well deserved."

In any case, "The day after the theater I feigned illness and did not leave the room, quietly awaiting Her Majesty's reply to my humble request. But in the first week of Lent I considered it opportune to perform my devotions, in order to show my attachment to the Orthodox Greek faith."

From Elizabeth, no reply. Strong as Catherine's nerves were, the strain was beginning to show, and then "I was dealt another, insupportable blow. One morning . . . Count Alexander Shuvalov had summoned Mme. Vladislavov. This seemed to me peculiar, and I waited anxiously [until] he came to tell me the Empress had considered it necessary to remove Mme. Vladislavov from her duties to me. I burst into tears and . . . begged him, conjured him, to solicit Her Majesty to put as quick an end as possible to this situation, which only created misery around me, by sending me back. . . . Count Shuvalov was on the verge of saying something, but seeing my tears he, too, began to cry." Through his tears, the Grand Inquisitor "said that the Empress would speak about all this to me herself. I begged him to speed up this interview and he promised he would do so. . . .

"In the evening of that day, after I had cried a lot and eaten little, I was walking up and down in my room, my body and soul deeply disturbed, when I saw one of my maids . . . enter my bedroom. . . . She told me, her face bathed in tears and with great affection: 'We are all afraid that you will succumb to the condition we see you in. Will you permit me to go to my uncle, who is the Empress' father confessor as well as your own? . . . I will give him any message you wish to send him and I promise that he will speak to the Empress.' . . . Seeing her good intentions I told her how things were, what I had written to the Empress, in fact, everything.

"She went to her uncle and . . . returned towards eleven o'clock to tell me that he advised me to declare myself ill during the night and ask for him as father confessor . . . between two and three in the morning I rang; one of my women came in and I told her I felt so ill that I wanted to confess. Instead of the priest, it was Alexander Shuvalov who came running and I repeated to him in a weak and halting voice my request for the priest. He sent for the doctors, I told them it was spiritual help I needed, that I was suffocating; one of them took my pulse and found it faint; I kept repeating that my soul was in danger and that my body had no need of doctors.

"At last the priest came and we were left alone. I made him sit by my bed and our conversation lasted for at least an hour and a half. I told him all about the past, the present . . . I found him infinitely well disposed towards me and much less stupid than he was supposed to be. . . . He ended the interview by undertaking to go at once to the Empress . . . and hasten the interview she promised me. . . . About half-past one [the next] morning Count Alexander Shuvalov came into my room and told me that the Empress was waiting for me.

"I got up and followed him through the empty antechambers." This was late March, still dead winter in Petersburg. The corridors were cold and dark, with only the candelabra carried by Shuvalov's footmen to cast a thin, flickering illumination and monstrous weaving shadows in the long halls and ornate chambers. As they passed, the gilded furnishings came to half-life, gleaming, then vanishing in blackness. There were no sounds but their own footfalls, no signs of life except, now and again, a glimpse of imperial guards, stiffly standing sentry, like statues. In this way Catherine went to her fate.

"Arriving at the door of the gallery I saw the Grand Duke passing through the door opposite, on his way, too, to the Empress. I had not seen him since the night of the theater; even when I had declared I was dying, he neither came nor sent for news of me. I learned later that on that very day he had promised Elizabeth Worontsov to marry her as soon as I was dead. . . .

"At last I reached Her Majesty's apartment . . . as soon as I saw her, I fell on my knees in front of her and begged her, sobbing, to send me back to my parents. The Empress made as if to help me to my feet but I remained kneeling. She seemed sad rather than angry, and with tears in her eyes she said: 'How can you speak of being sent away? Remember that you have children.'

"I said to her: 'My children are in your hands and could not be in better ones; I hope you will not abandon them.' Then she said, 'How would I explain such a thing to the people?' I replied, 'Your Majesty will, if she finds it opportune, enumerate all the reasons that brought me her disfavor, as well as the hatred of the Grand Duke. . . .'

"The Empress again told me to rise to my feet, which I did. . . . The room we occupied was long, with three windows, between which stood two tables and the Empress' golden toilet set. There were only she, the Grand Duke, Alexander Shuvalov and I in the apartment; opposite the windows stood a few high screens and, in front of them a sofa. I suspected that Ivan Shuvalov was hidden behind the screen . . . I stood beside the dressing table nearest to the door through which I had come, and noticed a tied-up packet of letters in the basin.

"The Empress suddenly came up to me and said: 'God is my witness to how I wept when you were so desperately ill on your arrival in Russia; if I had not loved you, I would not have kept you here.'

"I replied, thanking Her Majesty for all the graciousness and kindness she had shown me at that time and afterward. . . . She then came closer and said: 'You are excessively proud. Do you not remember how I came up to you one day at the Summer Palace and asked if your neck were painful, because I had noticed that you had hardly bowed to me . . . ?' I said to this: 'Good heavens, ma'am, how could you imagine that I should show pride in your regard? I swear to you it never crossed my mind. . . .' She went on: 'You fancy that no one is as intelligent as you are.' I replied: 'If I ever had such a fancy, nothing could be more likely to destroy it than my present situation. . . .'

"The Grand Duke was whispering with Count Alexander Shuvalov, while the Empress talked to me. She noticed this and moved toward them. . . . The Grand Duke raised his voice to say: 'She is terribly cruel and incredibly stubborn.' . . . Turning to the Grand Duke, I said: 'If it is about me that you are talking, I am glad to be able to say in the presence of Her Majesty that it is true I am cruel to the people who advise you to commit injustices and that I have become stubborn since I realized that my meekness has only brought about your hatred.'

"He then said to the Empress: 'Your Majesty can judge for herself, by what she is saying, how wicked she is.' But my words made a very different impression on the Empress. . . . I could see clearly as the conversation advanced that . . . her attitude gradually became softer, in spite of herself and her resolutions."

Then, however, ". . . by a brusque transition . . . the Empress came up to me and said: 'You interfere in many matters that do not concern you. I would never have dared to do so in the time of the Empress Anna. How could you venture, for instance, to send orders to Marshal Apraxin?'

"I exclaimed: 'I, send orders? It never entered my head to do that.' 'How can you deny it,' she said, 'when I have it in writing? Your letters are over there in the basin.' She pointed to them."

This was a crucial moment for Catherine. She had had no communication at all with Apraxin since his arrest and had no way of knowing whether, like Bestuzhev, he had had the wit to destroy her correspondence; whether, for that matter, he might have kept a personal journal or made notations which would link his retreat to Elizabeth's illness and Catherine's plans; or whether, under the severe interrogation that she assumed had been taking place, he had said or implied something that might incriminate her.

What had happened, in fact, was that Alexander Shuvalov had forced Apraxin to admit having received three letters from her and had extracted them from him; they were the ones in the basin. But Apraxin steadfastly had declared that Catherine had nothing to do with his retreat and had never asked him, directly or indirectly, to do anything that could compromise Russia's interest in the war.

Catherine did not know this, but she seized a clue in Elizabeth's next statement: "You know that you were forbidden to write." This was a relatively minor charge: that she had violated the code of behavior imposed on her by Elizabeth and Bestuzhev a long time ago.

"I replied: 'It is true that I transgressed this order and I beg Your Majesty's forgiveness, but if my three letters are here, they will prove to Your Majesty that I never sent him any orders; but in one of them I told him what was being said about his behavior.'

"She interrupted me: 'Why did you write him about that?' I

replied: 'Simply because I took an interest in the Marshal and liked him. I begged him to follow your instructions. Of the other letters, one contains congratulations on the birth of his son, and the other, New Year's greetings.' She went on: 'Bestuzhev says that there were many others.' I replied: 'If Bestuzhev says that, he is a liar.'

" 'Well,' she said, 'if he spreads lies about, I will put him to torture.' She thought to frighten me with this. I replied that she was a sovereign and at liberty to do as she liked. . . . She remained silent, and seemed to concentrate upon her thoughts.

"I report the most salient features of this conversation which have remained in my memory. . . . It lasted an hour and a half. The Empress walked up and down the room, now addressing me, now her august nephew and even more often Count Alexander Shuvalov. . . . I have already said that the Empress seemed to me more preoccupied than angry. As to the Grand Duke, he showed much malice, hostility and even fury against me in the course of the interview, but . . . the Empress' intuition and understanding inclined her to my side. She listened with particular attention and a kind of unwilling approval to my steady and balanced replies to my consort's exaggerated statements which showed as clear as day that all he wanted was to sweep me aside and put in my place, if possible, his mistress. . . . His behavior became so objectionable that the Empress came up to me and whispered: 'I have many more things to say to you, but I find it difficult at the moment. . . .' With a movement of the eyes and head she showed that it was because of the presence of the two others.

"Seeing this intimate and friendly demonstration to me at so critical a moment, I opened my heart to her and whispered back: 'I, too, find it difficult to speak now, in spite of the great desire I have to tell you all there is in my heart.' I could see that my words made a strong and favorable impression on her. Tears stood out in her eyes and to conceal how much she was moved, she dismissed us. . . ."

It was a superb drama. Catherine had played her part brilliantly. She sensed that she had very nearly won her case. But she could not be sure, and until she was sure, she would not jeopardize her gains.

That same night Alexander Shuvalov came to her apartment and "asked me to open the door, which I did. He told me to send away my women—they left the room. He said the Empress had . . . told him to present her compliments to me and ask me not to have too heavy a heart and to say that she would have a second conversation with me soon. I curtsied deeply to Count Shuvalov and told him to convey my deepest respects to Her Majesty. . . .

"I remained closeted in my apartment as before, under the pretext of ill-health. I remember I was reading then the first five volumes of *Histoire des Voyages*, with a map spread on the table and it was both interesting and instructive. When this wearied me I glanced through the first volumes of the *Encyclopaedia* and waited for the day when it would please Her Majesty to summon me to a second conversation. . . .

"I had to wait a long time. I remember that on April 21st, my birthday, I didn't leave my room. The Empress sent word by Alexander Shuvalov during her dinner that she was drinking my health; I sent word back to thank her for thinking of me . . . as to the Grand Duke . . . I only knew that he was impatiently waiting for me to be sent back and planned to marry Elizabeth Worontsov; she used to come to our apartments and was already playing hostess . . . when the Grand Duke heard that the Empress had sent me that message on that day, he decided to send me a similar message; when it arrived I rose from my chair and with a deep curtsy uttered my words of thanks.

"At last . . . Count Alexander Shuvalov came to tell me on behalf of the Empress that I was to ask that afternoon through him for permission to see my children and after that visit I was to have the second interview with the Empress, promised so long before. I did as I was told and in the presence of many people asked Count Shuvalov to beg the Empress's permission for me to see my children. He went away and came back to say that I could go and visit them at three o'clock.

"I was very punctual for my visit. I remained with my children until Count Alexander Shuvalov came to tell me that the Empress was ready to receive me. I went to her rooms, where I found her alone; there were not even any screens about, and therefore she and I could talk quite freely.

"I began by thanking her for allowing me to come, adding that the gracious promise alone of that visit had brought me back to life. She said to me after that: 'I insist that you tell me the truth about everything I am going to ask you.'

"I assured her that she would hear nothing but the exact truth from my mouth and that all I wanted was to open my heart to her entirely, without any restriction. She asked me then if I had really written only three letters to Apraxin. I swore to her that it was so, which indeed was the truth. Then she asked me for details about the life of the Grand Duke."

And with that, Catherine's memoirs stop.

XIII

The Death of Elizabeth

WHATEVER the content of this second meeting—and there is not a scrap of actual information in either Catherine's papers or Elizabeth's—it is a reasonable guess that Elizabeth did in effect ask "everything" and that Catherine did in effect "tell the truth." Not the whole truth, of course, for that would have meant, among other indiscretions, recriminations against Elizabeth. But she probably told the essential truth about Peter's incompetence and his unwillingness to make their marriage genuine; the Saltikov affair and the production of an illegitimate but viable heir in little Paul; the Poniatowski affair and the true paternity of baby Anna. Perhaps she even set forth her honest and, as Elizabeth could agree, well-justified doubts about Peter's competence to rule even his duchy of Holstein, let alone the empire, without her help and the delegation of substantial authority to her.

Both were passionate women; both were Russian patriots; both had at heart the interests of the dynasty; both had contempt for Peter. Once the barricades were down and they could talk together with candor, they could find themselves in substantial agreement about most of the things that most concerned them. It is clear that they did, no doubt after many tears were shed by both. From this time on, Elizabeth's remarks about Catherine, transmitted in the gossip that flowed incessantly along the court grapevine, were invariably friendly and free from the suspicious and critical tinge that had colored them for almost fifteen years. From this time on, too, Catherine was able to see her children, not at her own pleasure as to time and place, to be sure, but at any rate often enough to become acquainted with them and achieve some of the satisfactions of motherhood.

Until this second interview with the Empress, which took place at the end of April, she had had not even a glimpse of her daughter since the birth. By then the child was nearly five months old. The children were being brought up mainly at Peterhof. Catherine's official residence, the grand ducal property of Oranienbaum, was fourteen miles away, but she was allowed to make the journey every Sunday and spend the day with them.

Although Catherine was restored to imperial favor, the others involved in the Apraxin affair and its aftermath were not. Apraxin himself was kept under arrest and interrogation for a whole year. With the help of fellow officers, including General Count William of Fermor, his successor as commander of the forces against Frederick, he was able to show that his retreat was justified by lack of supplies. The court-martial convened anyway, but on the first day of trial, at the beginning of cross-examination, the marshal—much overweight and inclined to high blood pressure—had an apoplectic stroke and dropped dead. Count Bestuzhev's trial also took a year to prepare. Even so, nothing could be found to support the serious charges that had been made against him, and in this dilemma his judges convicted him of *lèse majesté*.

"The perfidious minister," they explained in their judgment, "has, in a blind effort to make himself important, endeavored to prejudice Her Majesty against her dear niece, the Grand Duchess." As punishment he was stripped of all his honors, barred from the government, and banished to one of his country estates. "Everybody in Petersburg, humble or great," Catherine had written, "was convinced that Count Bestuzhev was innocent and that there was no crime or misdeed with which he could be charged." The verdict against "the first gentleman of the Empire" thus "despoiled without reason" made Catherine indignant, but she was in no position to do anything about it—not yet.

The three other men arrested at the same time—Bernardi, Jelagine, and Adadurov—were all exiled from Petersburg to distant parts of the empire.

Count Poniatowski, although officially unwelcome and bound to go, managed through various excuses and subterfuges and pieces of luck to linger on for seven months, through the whole period of Catherine's disgrace and well into her official rehabilitation. During this latter time they even renewed their affair. At first this was done clandestinely and then—unbelievably—by the Grand Duke's insistence as well as arrangement.

How this bizarre turn of events came about is related by Poniatowski in his memoirs. He had gone to Oranienbaum to see Catherine and by chance was discovered by the Grand Duke and members of his party as he left her. He was taken to a pavilion to be interrogated: "the Grand Duke asked me, in no uncertain terms, whether I had . . . [sic] his wife. I said, 'No.'

"He: 'Tell me the truth and then everything will be arranged; if not, you will go through some bad moments.'

"I: 'I cannot say that I have done something I have not done.'

"After that he went into the next room to consult with his suite and then came back to say: 'Well, if you will not talk, you will stay here until further orders.' At that, he left . . . placing a guard on the door. After two hours . . . Count Shuvalov appeared. His arrival led me to understand that the Empress had been informed. He stammered something to the effect that he wanted an explanation.

"Instead of entering into details, I said: 'I am sure you will understand, Count, that it is in the interests of both your Court and myself, that all this should end as quickly as possible, and that you should get me promptly out of here.'"

And Shuvalov did.

Poniatowski continues: "I spent two anxious days. I could see that everyone knew of the adventure, but no one spoke of it. At last, the Grand Duchess managed to send me a note to say that she had succeeded in conciliating her husband's mistress. Next day . . . there was a ball in the evening, and as I danced a minuet with Elizabeth Worontsov, I said to her: 'It is in your power to make several people happy.' She replied: 'This is already almost done; come an hour after midnight, with Leon Naryshkin, to Mon Plaisir, where Their Highnesses are lodging, in the garden.' I shook her hand." And so Poniatowski was led to the Grand Duke, whom he found "very gay, welcoming me and giving me the 'thou.' 'How foolish not to have been frank with me,' he said. 'None of this mess would have happened then.'

"I readily agreed to accept this situation (as can easily be believed) and at once began to express my admiration for His Highness's military dispositions. He was so flattered by this, and made so happy that, after a quarter of an hour, he said: 'Now that we are such good friends, I find there is someone missing here.' He crossed over to his wife's room, dragged her out of bed, leaving her time only to put on her stockings and no shoes, and slip on a Batavia dress without an underskirt, and then brought her in, saying, as he pointed to me: 'Here he is! I hope I shall have satisfied everybody!' . . .

"We sat down . . . laughing and chattering and frolicking around a small fountain in the room, as though we had no care in the world, and separated at four in the morning.

"Mad as it may seem, this is the exact truth. . . .

"Next day, everyone's attitude towards me was quite different. The Grand Duke made me repeat my visit to Oranienbaum four times. I arrived in the evening, walked up a secret staircase to the Grand Duchess's room, where I found the Grand Duke and his mistress. We had supper together, after which he took his mistress away, saying to us: 'Well, my children, I do not think you need me any more,' and I remained as long as I liked.

". . . I gathered, nevertheless, that the situation was still uneasy and that I had better leave Petersburg. . . ."

And that, it turned out, was the end of that affair.

The affair with Poniatowski had begun, as will be recalled, because he had arrived in Petersburg at a painfully delicate time for Catherine, when she was still suffering the sorrows of bereft love over Serge Saltikov. By coincidence, Poniatowski departed within a few weeks of an event that was to bring a worthy successor to

Petersburg and to Catherine's notice while she was suffering from her new bereavement.

In August, a year after Marshal Apraxin's great victory and precipitate retreat, General Fermor engaged Frederick in a tremendous battle near the Prussian town of Zorndorf. Both sides claimed victory, but in fact they fought each other to a standstill, leaving the battle positions little changed, both sides incapable of further initiative and the battlefield a carnage. The casualties were fairly evenly divided: more than 10,000 dead on each side. The Russian dead included 1,200 officers, the Prussian only a few less. Many thousands more on both sides were wounded, and in the melee both sides took many prisoners of all ranks.

Among the eminent Prussian officers captured was Frederick's own adjutant, Count Schwerin, scion of one of the most aristocratic Prussian families. When he was sent off to Petersburg, protocol required that he travel in honor and comfort under escort by a Russian officer who would be as much his aide-de-camp as his security guard. The officer assigned to this duty was a twenty-five-year-old guardsman, Lieutenant Gregory Orlov, a strapping, handsome daredevil whose bravery and zeal at Zorndorf, where he led his troops in furious assaults even after he had been wounded three times, had made him one of the notable heroes of the fight. Escorting Count Schwerin was a practical reward for his gallantry. Orlov's duties, almost wholly honorific, would continue for some considerable time after they arrived in Petersburg, where the young hero could recuperate fully, live life on the comfortable level of a Count's equerry, and enjoy the plaudits of the city.

Grand Duke Peter saw to it that Count Schwerin was treated with the hospitality and honor that ordinarily would have been appropriate to a visiting royal ally. He was the man Peter would have adored being: the close personal assistant and companion of the great Frederick. Assuring him that "If I were Emperor you should not be a prisoner of war," Peter did everything to make amends. He secured a splendid palace for him near the Winter Palace and visited him there often for dinner and the evening. Count Schwerin was given the freedom of the city, to come and go as he liked, accompanied by his retinue—and by his Russian escort officer, Lieutenant Orlov. He was even presented to Elizabeth at court.

At some point, before or during the summer of 1759, at Oranienbaum, the Winter Palace, or one of the other royal residences, Catherine and Orlov saw each other. Apparently for both it was passion at first sight.

Catherine wrote a great deal about Serge Saltikov, little—and circumspectly—about Stanislaus Poniatowski. About Gregory Orlov she wrote almost nothing that would illuminate their relationship, and Orlov, for his part, wrote nothing at all. What is known and can be surmised comes from other sources—memoirs, diplomatic reports, and the like.

Catherine's love affair with Orlov turned out to be her direct avenue to the throne, as Empress and Sole Autocrat. The affair lasted nearly fourteen years and was one of the most consequential romances in history.

Gregory Orlov came from a family of professional soldiers. His extraordinary, perhaps slightly demented bravery was the result not only of training, but of family tradition as well. His grandfather had been a common soldier in the *streltsy*, had taken part in the mutiny against Peter the Great, and was among the many sentenced to death. When his turn came in the mass beheadings that Peter was carrying out, he strode unhesitatingly across the platform. Finding the freshly severed head of one of his comrades still on the block, he kicked it away, declaring: "I must make room for myself here!"

Peter was so impressed by this nonchalance that he pardoned him. And instead of exiling him, as he did with practically all the *streltsy* whose lives he spared, Peter put him in one of the new regiments for the war against Sweden, during which he distinguished himself and rose to a high rank. His son Gregory spent his life in the army, became a lieutenant colonel, and in turn begat five sons—Ivan, Gregory, Alexis, Feodor, and Vladimir—all of whom took up soldiering as a matter of course and became officers in the Imperial Guards. It was a close-knit family, all for one and one for all. All were handsome, hard-living, hard-fighting, robust, and ambitious, and each had special qualities.

Gregory was the handsomest, with "the head of an angel on

the body of an athlete," and the boldest not only in battle, but in love. One of his conquests, soon after Zorndorf and before returning with Count Schwerin to Petersburg, was the beautiful Princess Kurakine, Apraxin's daughter, who had resumed her affair with Count Peter Shuvalov. This rash invasion of the preserves of the mighty Shuvalovs could have put Orlov into trouble, but the fortuitous sudden death of Peter Shuvalov saved him. The news of this escapade, preceding him to Petersburg, added fascinating dimensions to the earlier news of his military heroism and made him a very glamorous figure indeed.

Catherine was nearing thirty, five years older than this unfettered male animal. The unnatural life of chastity and emotional deprivation she had led during the first nine years of her marriage had perhaps stored up such a reservoir of unsatisfied wants, physical as well as emotional, that once she had encountered the experiences of love she could not again do without them. She was still, she was certain, "in love" with Count Poniatowski, and she still hoped and schemed for his return. At about the time her affair with Orlov began, she was writing to the Russian ambassador in Warsaw—writing secretly, again breaking the rule that Elizabeth had reaffirmed—charging him to arrange this in some way:

"Count Poniatowski . . . is wrong if he believes that obstacles or other incidents can detach me from him. . . . I desire only the moment of our reunion. . . . Adversity shall not conquer me and if it is necessary to triumph, courage will not be lacking. I esteem and love Poniatowski above all. . . . He must be sure of that, and if I have good fortune events will prove it. . . ."

There is evidence enough that she truly believed this, for a good many years later, when Orlov had gone his way and Catherine was trying to explain herself to a jealous successor, she wrote of Poniatowski: "This one was both loving and loved from 1755 until 1761 including an absence of three years . . . until the repeated entreaties of [Orlov] changed my state of mind."

Yet, during the later and larger part of this same three-year period, Poniatowski was not there. She was drawn to Orlov, initially at least, by plain physical desire. These feelings, which were to drive her into the arms of a succession of lovers and to make her the scandal of Europe, never ceased really to bother her own conscience, which always remained a Lutheran conscience despite the elaborate disguises that at one time and another were layered onto it, ranging from ornate Russian Orthodox piety to Voltairian skeptical agnosticism. In some part of herself she was never-endingly shocked at herself, while at the same time always looking for perfectly logical reasons why she should forgive herself and be forgiven by her descendants and by her unknown judges in some future time.

In one aside in her memoirs she wrote: "If I may venture to be frank, I would say about myself that I was every inch a gentleman with a mind much more male than female; but together with this I was anything but masculine and combined, with the mind and temperament of a man, the attractions of a lovable woman. I pray to be forgiven for this description which is justified by its truthfulness and which my vanity admits without any pretense at false modesty.

"Besides, all that I have been writing should be sufficient proof of what I say about my brain, my heart and my temperament.

"I have just said that I was attractive. Consequently one-half of the road to temptation was already covered and it is only human in such situations that one should not stop half-way. For to tempt and be tempted are closely allied; and in spite of all the finest moral maxims buried in the mind, when emotion interferes, when feeling makes its appearance, one is already much further involved than one realizes, and I have still not learnt how to prevent its appearance.

"Perhaps escape is the only solution, but there are situations, circumstances, when escape is impossible, for how can one escape, be elusive, turn one's back, in the atmosphere of a Court? Such an act itself might give food for talk.

"And if you do not run away, nothing is more difficult, in my opinion, than to avoid something that fundamentally attracts you. Statements to the contrary could only be prudish and not inspired by a human heart. One cannot hold one's heart in one's hand, forcing it or releasing it, tightening or relaxing one's grasp at will."

Elizabeth had been greatly distressed by the Russian losses at the Battle of Zorndorf, and, Catherine says, there had been "consternation" in Petersburg "when the details of this day became known, on which many a family lost their sons, friends and acquaintances, or found they had been wounded or taken prisoner."

General Fermor was relieved of command and replaced by General Peter Saltikov, a member of the same aristocratic clan that supplied Catherine's first lover. General Saltikov proved to be an extremely able commander, and the course of the war began to take an encouraging turn. Yet it was a long and costly process: costly in lives, for the Prussians were fierce fighters who sold ground only for a price in blood; costly in money, which was even more difficult for Elizabeth to find than skilled soldiers. Her purse was thin even before the war began, but she would not be deflected. "I intend to continue the war and to remain faithful to my allies," she declared to the Austrian ambassador, in an audience on January 1, 1760, "even if I have to sell half my diamonds and my dresses." General Saltikov repaid her firmness with a string of victories. That summer the Russian Army captured and occupied Berlin.

Frederick still had forces enough to go on fighting. But with his capital and principal city gone, his whole military apparatus was crippled. His regiments, decimated, undersupplied, and greatly outnumbered, faced confident enemies on three frontiers: the armies of Russia, Austria, and France. His back was to the Baltic, which was controlled by the Russian fleet. He was surrounded and in all logic was doomed. No one knew better than he how desperate and nearly hopeless his situation was, but he fought on, persisting in the faint hope that he could salvage something from the situation. His plight grew steadily worse, however, through the rest of 1760 and 1761, until it seemed that only a miracle could save him.

The miracle occurred. On December 23, Elizabeth was seized by another of the massive convulsions with fainting spells and impaired thought and speech, to which she had been subject for several years and which had so often produced rumors that her death was imminent. Each time she recovered and renewed her firm control of events. During recent months, she had been so bloated with dropsy and in such a state of generalized physical decay that she never left her apartments. She barely had energy to maneuver her vast waterlogged and pain-ridden body from her own bed, to help a little as her ladies dressed her, and to navigate the distance to a nearby sofa or armchair from which she conducted the business of the empire. It was only her own vitality that sustained her. Now, however, the last of her sustaining energies trickled away.

Knowing that she was dying, she managed to reserve enough strength to make her confession, to recite with her confessor the prayer for the dying, and to say good-bye to those few persons who, at this ultimate time, she wanted to be with her: Count Alexis Razumovsky; his younger brother, Count Cyril Razumovsky, whom she loved as a brother; Peter; and Catherine. To each, as she said farewell, she asked to be forgiven her trespasses. And then, on the afternoon of Christmas Day, 1761, Elizabeth died.

XIV

The Reign of Peter III

THE Empress was dead.

Long live . . . long live who?

This was the moment so long anticipated by so many with such various emotions. Grand Duke Peter's incompetence was so evident and so widely realized that in 1757, a full five years before Elizabeth's death, the Marquis de l'Hôpital could predict categorically: "If the Empress should die we shall see some sudden revolution, for the Grand Duke will never be allowed to come to the Throne and will surely be prevented." There were different notions, depending on the personal interests to be served, as to how this ought to be done. There was broad agreement that it ought to be and would be done. Frederick of Prussia, much as he might wish the contrary, the more so as his plight became more and more desperate, took this for granted and wasted no thoughts on the Grand Duke. Instead he tried as best he could and as discreetly as possible (evidently without any effect) to win the sympathy or at least the tacit neutrality of Catherine.

To be sure, Catherine no longer had those sure and powerful resources—military, political, and financial—that a few years earlier could have almost guaranteed her a successful coup d'état. The chain reaction ensuing from the Apraxin debacle had smashed her party and taught her caution. Her own close brush with disaster and her still-recent emergence from disgrace to a state not yet of full grace inclined her to be discreet and inconspicuous. Decidedly this included her romance with Gregory Orlov; there were no backstairs palace visits or moonlit masquerades at Oranienbaum this time. No chances were taken. Their assignations were at a nondescript neighborhood on St. Basil's island.

On the other hand, the very nature of the situation and her official position were bound to attract new allies to her with very little overt effort on her part. Gregory Orlov confided to his four brothers, and they became confidential missionaries for Catherine among the Guards regiments. Count Nikita Panin, the former ambassador to Sweden, a Bestuzhev protégé who had survived his master's ruin, was tutor and majordomo for young Prince Paul, a position that gave him much prestige at court and put him in the thick of all the maneuverings about the succession. He was a natural ally of Catherine's, although his own cherished plan for the succession was that little Paul be installed as Emperor, with Catherine as Regent and himself as Grand Chancellor. There were other old and still influential friends she could rely on, such as the two Counts Razumovsky. The younger one, Cyril, was especially well situated: he commanded the Ismailov Regiment, which with the Preobrazhensky and Semenovsky, ranked as an elite group of the Imperial Guards, those makers and unmakers of royal destinies.

And there were new friends, friends of opportunity searching for the best odds in a risky game, eager to jettison past affiliations for future advantage. Among these, grotesquely, were the Shuvalovs, who presented themselves to Catherine wreathed in smiles and goodwill. Most grotesquely, Ivan Shuvalov, the "favorite," even attempted to strike up a romance with Catherine. His purpose was so plain that the French ambassador reported to Paris: "The favorite seems anxious to grace a twofold position, dangerous as this might appear."

Catherine was neither charmed nor deceived. Besides, she knew from Count Panin that Ivan Shuvalov had been to see him recently, soliciting his best practical opinion on the advantages of exiling Catherine along with Peter versus allowing her to stay in Russia in the honorific position of Dowager Mother to the Czar, in which case the real power would be shared by Panin and the Shuvalovs. Rejected on both these fronts, the Shuvalovs reinvested their hopes and affections in Grand Duke Peter—reluctantly, and only provisionally, in lieu of something better.

One of the main reasons they were so "very anxious about Her Majesty's approaching end and about their coming fate"—in Catherine's words—was that Peter was clearly determined to rid himself of Catherine and to make Elizabeth Worontsov his wife and Empress, which would make him the nephew by marriage of Grand Chancellor Worontsov. Family ties and political ties being inextricable, as the Shuvalovs had good reason to appreciate, this held the unbearable threat of raising the Worontsov family to the premier position, in Peter's reign, that the Shuvalovs had achieved at such effort and enjoyed so much in the later years of Elizabeth's reign. Worontsov, who had been their ally and co-conspirator against Bestuzhev, was now perceived to be an incipient deadly enemy. It was a bad dilemma, a situation filled with painful anxiety.

Among the numerous odd and implausible recruits who came forth for Catherine's cause, the most surprising of all and easily the most engaging was nineteen-year-old Princess Catherine Dashkov. She was the much younger sister of Elizabeth Worontsov and, besides being of almost another generation, seemed to be almost another manner of being.

Elizabeth Worontsov was a lumpish, homely woman who, in the description of one of Peter's Holsteiners—a friend of hers at that—"Stank, spit when she talked, and swore like a trooper." She had an earthy sense of humor and a raucous laugh. She liked to drink, dance, and carouse at parties, and she could hold her own in a fight with any female and not a few males. Also, she had a quick temper. Now and then she and Grand Duke Peter, both up late and far gone in drink, would fall into an argument which would develop into physical combat, and both would show up next day with bruises and contusions. This vulgar, goodhearted female roustabout, whose natural milieu might have been a sailor's café on the Petersburg waterfront, was consistent. Although she had been exposed to a fair amount of arts and learning, her interests remained wholly mundane, her intellectual life that of an experienced barmaid. Probably it was because of all this, not despite it, that Peter was so drawn to her, always returned to her despite their brawls, and finally wanted to marry her. She was as homely, as banal, as limited as he, and so he could be comfortable with her.

Catherine Worontsov, on the other hand, was pretty, slender, supple, well formed, with extraordinary vitality and enthusiasm for life and an equally extraordinary versatility as a woman and human being. She had married Prince Dashkov when she was fifteen. Now, at nineteen, she had two children and was her husband's good wife and enterprising hostess at a Petersburg palace and a splendid estate that lay on the Baltic coast between Peterhof and Oranienbaum. She had a quick mind, an eager curiosity, and an intellectual appetite that was not only precocious but, for her time and circumstances, prodigious.

Catherine, first meeting Dashkov when the latter was fifteen, was astounded and delighted to find this Russian girl, one who read history and philosophy and the classics; who already knew and relished the works of Voltaire and Montaigne; and who already was beginning to make invidious judgments on Russian life and to think of a better future based on moral and political philosophy. In many ways she was naïve and immature, but she was vividly full of promise. Undoubtedly many things about this Catherine reminded our Catherine of herself as a girl—including the naïveté, the innocence, the idealism, the high-principled morality.

The Dashkovs were often at court, both at Elizabeth's and at the Young Court. Catherine always paid special attention to the young Princess; later on, when the Empress allowed her the Sunday visits to her children at Peterhof, she often stopped at the Dashkovs' on the way home to Oranienbaum, and sometimes she invited the Princess to go back with her for a visit.

Princess Catherine had from the beginning been enchanted by Grand Duchess Catherine. In the course of time the Princess developed an admiration for her that was almost worshipful.

Princess Dashkov was not fond of her coarse-grained sister Elizabeth Worontsov. She felt a certain liking for Grand Duke Peter because he was her godfather, and in his oafish way he took some interest in her and tried to be pleasant to her. Seeing her admiration for the Grand Duchess, he once said to her: "My dear, remember it is safer to have to do with a fool like me than with those sublime intellects who squeeze all the juice out of a lemon and then throw it away." The remark has more wit, insight, and humility than anything else ever attributed to Peter and probably was polished in the retelling through the years before finally appearing in Princess Dashkov's memoirs, but the sense of it rings true.

Whether or not Peter really thought he was a fool, Princess Dashkov did. Only a fool, in her view, could prefer the company of her sister to that of the Grand Duchess. Learning that they were having an affair and that Elizabeth was assuming the role of mistress, the Princess was increasingly scandalized and indignant—scandalized because of her own principles and because a member of her own family was involved, indignant on behalf of Catherine. Learning finally that Peter was promising Elizabeth to displace Catherine and marry her instead, the Princess resolved to protect and defend her heroine in every possible way. One way was to appoint herself as a spy in the enemy camp.

One night late in December, 1761, she was with the Grand Duke and her sister when Peter, full of drink and less discreet even than usual, indicated that the time was almost at hand when Elizabeth would be his wife. Other remarks showed that he felt sure the Empress was in her last illness. Princess Dashkov excused herself as soon as she could and hurried to the Winter Palace. By then it was well past midnight and Catherine was asleep, but the Princess demanded that the maid awaken her. Then she burst in to tell her what she had heard.

"The Empress has only a few more days to live, perhaps only a few hours! What are you going to do? What are your plans? You are in danger! I will do anything you tell me to do!"

Catherine answered that she had no plans: "God is my only hope."

"Then if you have no plans your friends will have to act for you!" cried the Princess, aglow with excitement and high resolves.

"I have courage enough to inspire them all: I will make any sacrifice!"

Catherine implored her not to put herself in danger: "If anything happens to you on my account I would reproach myself the rest of my days." And besides, she went on to say firmly, "Believe me, there is nothing you can do."

"'I can promise only that I will do nothing that might expose *you* to danger,' declared the young heroine, 'even if my blind devotion brings me to the gallows. . . .'" Thereupon, she vanished back into the night. A few days later, as Catherine relates: "The Empress died . . . at three in the afternoon," and practically at once "Prince Dashkov sent word to me: 'You have only to give the order and we will enthrone you.' I sent back my reply: 'For God's sake do not start this chaos; what God wills will happen in any case, but your idea is both premature and immature!'"

This was categorical enough to stop any attempt at a coup. Further, instead of coming out of Elizabeth's bedroom to be seen by the throngs of court officials and courtiers and thus possibly set off some sort of demonstration for her, she stayed by the deathbed. Grand Duke Peter hurried off to the Council of State and soon "sent word ordering me to stay beside the body until I heard from him. I told his messenger . . . 'You can see that I am here and will obey the orders.' I gathered from the order that the party in power"—Peter, the Shuvalovs, and their faction—"feared my influence."

Catherine's behavior confused the Dashkovs and her other supporters, as well as those diplomats and statesmen all over Europe who had been predicting that Peter would never become Czar. It was a mystery that Catherine did nothing then or later to explain.

The answer was simple: She was pregnant. She had conceived in the late summer or early fall of that year. Her estrangement from Peter was complete, and there was not the faintest chance that he would pretend this time that the child was his. Catherine could not afford a new scandal. Consequently, as soon as she knew her condition, she decided that it must be kept secret and that if she carried the child full term, she would somehow contrive that it be born in secret.

By the time of Elizabeth's last illness keeping the secret already was requiring Catherine to stay in her own rooms as much as she could and to appear in public, when she had to, corseted and in ample skirts. By then, too, since she aborted easily and had trouble carrying children full term, she knew that at almost any time in the next hours, days or weeks, she might find herself prematurely in labor.

From almost every aspect, as she examined the situation, there were so many risks and unpleasant possibilities that the best course was to do nothing, hoping that Peter, lacking any publicly acceptable excuse to get rid of her at once, would bring her to the throne as Empress-consort. From that vantage point she would put her faith in God's will, as she told Prince Dashkov, and in her own guile, the machinations of her faithful friends, and, most of all, Peter's incompetence to rule.

This pregnancy, coinciding with the Empress' death and effectively immobilizing Catherine, was the second and essential element in the miracle that saved Frederick and turned his imminent defeat into victory. Grand Duke Peter became Czar Peter III. Almost his first official act was to order Russia's armies to stop all hostilities against Prussia. He notified the Austrian and French governments that Russia was withdrawing from the war and advised them to do the same. When they refused, he entered into a treaty of mutual assistance with Frederick, leaving the two allies with no real alternative but to negotiate for peace. Moreover, he insisted on returning to Frederick all the territorial gains that Russian arms had won at such vast cost, in blood and money, during four and a half years in the field.

Thus Frederick suddenly found that he had won the war. And thus Prussia, so nearly extinct, emerged instead as a great power, which was in due course to organize all the German states into one nation under the rule of Frederick's House of Hohenzollern, imbued with the traditions of Prussian militarism which helped bring about two world wars.

The reign of Czar Peter III lasted six months, during which time he managed to fulfill all the worst expectations of him and to add to them in ways no one had imagined. In an amazingly short time he committed major errors that were to cause trouble for Russia abroad and at home for many generations and to alienate so many of his subjects in such an ingenious variety of ways that he made his sudden end inevitable. He lost no time in giving offense, starting within an hour or so of Elizabeth's death.

"The body had hardly been laid out and placed on a bed," Catherine wrote in one of the fragments of her unfinished memoirs, "when the Marshal of the Court sent me word to say there would be a supper that evening in the gallery (three rooms away from the body) at which we were ordered to wear light-colored evening dresses." There was to be church service before supper. "When I arrived I found everyone gathered for the oath"—to Peter only, leaving both Catherine and little Czarevich Paul, now the new Grand Duke, conspicuously unmentioned—"after which, instead of a funeral service, a thanksgiving Te Deum was officiated. Then the Novgorod Metropolitan delivered a speech to the Emperor. The latter was beyond himself with joy and did not conceal it, behaving outrageously and playing the fool, uttering inane speeches . . . deporting himself more like an ineffectual clown than anything.

"On leaving the church I went to my room, where until supper I cried bitterly, mourning the dead Empress, who had shown me great kindness and in the last two years real love. . . . When supper was ready I found the table laid for 150 people or more and the gallery filled with spectators. . . . Ivan Shuvalov stood behind Peter III's chair joking and laughing with him. I sat beside the new Emperor; on my other side was Prince Trubetskoy who spoke of nothing but his joy at seeing the Emperor reign."

The next night Peter held another banquet in the same room— the ladies were ordered to "dress richly"—and the next night he went to a party to celebrate Christmas. So it went for weeks, with parties day and night in an atmosphere of carnival rather than mourning.

By custom, burial was scheduled six weeks after Elizabeth's death. During the interim her body lay in state at the Winter Palace, then at Kazan Cathedral on the Nevsky Prospect, then again at the palace. Catherine: "Ten days before the Empress's burial, her body was laid in the coffin and taken to the mortuary chamber, where the crowd was allowed to enter twice a day. The

Empress lay in silver robes with lace sleeves and with a golden crown on her head bearing the inscription: 'The Most Pious Autocrat, Her Imperial Majesty Elizabeth Petrovna, born on the 18th December, 1709, enthroned on the 25th November, 1741, died on the 25th December, 1761.'" The coffin stood on a dais under a canopy, with ermine furs hanging to the ground and a golden state crest on top of the canopy.

"On January 25th, 1762, the Empress's body was taken with great pomp from the Palace, across the river to the Peter and Paul Cathedral in the Fortress. First came the Emperor; then myself, then the Skavronskis, then the Naryshkins, and then all the others according to their rank, on foot from the Palace to the Cathedral."

Peter III outdid himself on this grand and solemn occasion with the proud regiments of the Imperial Guards—many of whose senior officers had been, as young men, among the guardsmen who had given Elizabeth the throne—escorting the catafalque and standing at attention along the route, with all the great figures of the realm in procession and with thousands of silent people looking on.

Elizabeth's foibles had been known little, if at all, beyond the court. The masses of her subjects knew only of her beauty, her patriotism, her piety and good works. To them she was the faithful daughter of the Great Czar Peter I, who in twenty years had come to occupy a place of reverence almost equal to Mother Russia.

"The Emperor was very gay that day," Catherine relates, "and during the sad ceremony invented a game for himself; he loitered behind the hearse, on purpose, allowing it to proceed at a distance of thirty feet, then he would run to catch up with it as fast as he could. The elder courtiers, who were carrying his black train"— Peter the Great's old captains, legendary heroes, chief among them Field Marshal Sheremetev, now in his eighties—"found themselves unable to keep up with him and had to let the train go. The wind blew it out and all this amused Peter III so much that he repeated the joke several times, so that I and everybody else remained far behind and had to send word to stop the ceremony until everybody had caught up with the hearse. Criticism of the Emperor's outrageous behavior spread rapidly. . . ."

Having already outraged the military by throwing away its victories and, in effect, declaring all the deaths and patriotic sacrifices to have been pointless, Peter added profound insult by deciding to make the Russian Army over in the image of the Prussian Army: tactics, formations, drill, uniforms, and all. With consummate tactlessness he began with the regiment with the proudest traditions, the Preobrazhensky Guards, Peter the Great's own first regiment, which also—a case of instinctive bad choice —was the regiment of the Orlov brothers.

Peter III then attacked the other pillar of the throne, the Orthodox Church. He had always held it in contempt, while paying some necessary lip service to it, and in his own feelings had remained a convinced Lutheran. He was now the official head of the church, and he decided that it, too, should be remade on the Prussian model. By his ukase, the priests were to be beardless and to put on somber short and simple vestments like those of the Lutheran pastors. All private chapels were to be closed. All sacred images except those of Jesus and Mary were banned from the churches—those innumerable icons of the saints that were so much part of Russian life, history, and art were to be removed. He decreed freedom of religion for Protestants and all sects and built a Lutheran chapel in the palace. Capping all this, he confiscated all the property of the church and made its priests civil servants paid by the state.

Whatever virtues there may have been in some of these policies, they were rash beyond belief. They came in such a sudden flood, mostly in the first few months of his reign, that the nation had no time to absorb one shock before being struck with another. Further, whatever was good in them was overcast by the increasingly wild, brutal, and demoniac behavior of the new Czar. All the pent-up furies and hatreds of the past seemed to be let loose. One day at Oranienbaum, during one of his large parties, it seemed to him that Leon Naryshkin, Ivan Shuvalov, his equerry, and his secretary were disrespectful and were in league against his plans. (In one way this was true, for all saw the dangers and were trying to influence him toward moderation.) He had the four flogged in the presence of the diplomatic corps and a hundred or so other guests. A diplomat who had been on close terms with Peter as

Grand Duke said to Countess Bruce, Catherine's principal lady-in-waiting, "Do you know that your Emperor must be mad as a hatter? No man could behave as he does otherwise."

Frederick, viewing and hearing from afar, was alarmed lest this miraculous disciple and savior destroy himself and deprive Prussia the shower of blessings he so frantically wanted to give. While writing a friend that "The young Russian Czar is a divine creature; altars should be set up to him," he wrote to Peter urging him not to attempt too many things at once, to slow the pace, to take care not to offend the Russian people, and in particular to cherish his intelligent wife and make use of her good advices. But Peter felt no need of anything at all from "Madame de la Ressource."

Late that March the new Winter Palace, a fabulous building that Elizabeth had begun, was finished at last, and the royal family and court moved from the "old" Winter Palace. In the new palace Peter III took the main wing. Elizabeth Worontsov had rooms next to his. Catherine was assigned an apartment far away at the other end of the palace—a location that, in her circumstances, could not have pleased her more. She had made only two appearances in public since the Empress' burial, and she wished to remain as little noticed as possible, particularly by Peter.

Here in her corner of the new Winter Palace, on April 11, she gave birth to a healthy son. She was attended only by a trusted and well-bribed midwife. During the actual delivery, to ensure that the attention of Peter and the courtiers would be diverted elsewhere, her faithful valet Shkurine, who had been so helpful to her when Count Bestuzhev was arrested, set fire to his own house, which was near the palace.

Directly after the child was born he was smuggled out of the palace in the care of Shkurine's wife. Catherine named him Alexis. In the Russian fashion, he had his father's first name as his middle name; he was Alexis Gregorevich, son of Gregory. Being illegitimate, he had no last name, but he acquired one in a strange way. Catherine had read Rousseau, whose ideal of the "natural man . . . the noble savage" was the American Indian. Among many Indian tribes a child was named for a significant creature, event, or object in evidence at the time of his birth—Running

Bear, Thunder Cloud, Broken Arrow. Catherine thought of Gregory Orlov in terms very similarly: a virile, unspoiled, but also unimproved natural hero. She once wrote of him that he "has the mind of an eagle . . . an honesty which is proof against any assault . . . his mind and character are the product of the extreme strength of his body and temperament; it is a pity that education has not improved his talents and qualities, which are indeed supreme." Perhaps this explains why his son, Alexis Gregorevich, who was swaddled in a soft beaverskin—a *bobrinsky*—against the April chill when he was taken away, was called Alexis Gregorevich Bobrinsky.

XV

Peter Deposed

THE BIRTH and existence of little Alexis Beaverskin were successfully kept secret. A little more than a week later, in blooming good health and fine figure, Catherine received dignitaries who came to pay their respects on her thirty-third birthday. She took the opportunity to inform the ambassador of the jilted ally, Austria, that she "heartily detested the new treaty with the sworn enemy"—Prussia. It was her reentry into politics.

Perhaps Peter noticed a new assertiveness in her attitude, for a few days later, at a state banquet celebrating the newly signed treaty with Prussia, he delivered a shocking public insult to her. He had proposed a toast "to the imperial family," to which all the guests rose. Catherine remained seated, and Peter sent his adjutant to ask her why. She sent word back that it would have been improper for her to rise since she herself was a member of the imperial family. Peter leaned forward in a rage and shouted at her, the length of the banquet table, "Fool!"

Peter now undertook to restore by military action the province of Schleswig to his dukedom of Holstein, which had lost it to Denmark in 1721. An army and a large fleet of warships and transports assembled at Reval in Estonia; Peter III's plan was to embark from there in the middle of June.

Frederick had pledged to help with Prussian troops if they were needed (it was the least he could do), but he regarded the whole enterprise as foolish and told his ambassador, Baron August von der Goltz, to try his best to dissuade Peter. Goltz finally wrote back: "No one in the world save Your Majesty can persuade the Emperor to abandon this fatal war."

Frederick then wrote to Peter, suggesting that during his planned absence, a coup might be undertaken on behalf of Ivan, the infant Czar Ivan VI, deposed by Elizabeth when he was only a year and a half old, in custody as a prisoner of state ever since and now twenty-two.

It is true that for years there had been talk of a coup for Ivan, increasing in Elizabeth's last years as people thought of all the possible ways to keep Peter from the throne, but it was altogether unlikely that this would be tried or could succeed. Frederick was far too shrewd at covering his tracks and leaving himself openings for the future to mention Catherine by name, but when he reminded Peter III that Peter I's own "sister plotted to overthrow him" and invited him to "think of a discontented person," assuredly it was not Peter III's third cousin Ivan that he had in mind but Peter III's wife. And, as he so often was, Frederick was right.

Official celebrations of the peace with Prussia and a tripartite alliance among Russia, Prussia, and England began on June 10. Peter III arranged a spectacular fireworks display with allegories and symbols of the allegiance, including, as a *pièce de résistance*, the flaming monumental sign, "Three times three," symbolizing the friendship of the three monarchs: Peter III of Russia, George III of England and Frederick of Prussia. It was pointed out to him that Frederick was Frederick II, but Peter liked his idea so well that he went ahead with it anyway. The celebrations lasted two days, after which he decided to go to Oranienbaum to pass the time until his fleet was ready. With him he took Elizabeth Worontsov and a number of friends. He sent specific orders to Catherine that she was not to be at Oranienbaum—which for twenty years now had been her country residence—but was to spend her summer at Peterhof.

This was a piece of good luck, for none of the court was there and she could receive visitors and send messages without being observed. With only a personal maid to see to her needs and keep her company, she settled cozily and peaceably enough in the little palace called Mon Plaisir, Peter the Great's first country home and his lifelong favorite residence. It was all very largely as he had left it, for Elizabeth had kept it that way in his memory. She, too, had loved the place and often stayed there. One of her pleasures was to putter about the kitchen, discharging some of her domestic instincts and preparing favorite dishes for herself. It seems a marvel of coincidence that Catherine's reign, which was to carry on Peter the Great's work and the best features of Elizabeth's, was launched from Mon Plaisir.

On June 21, Peter gave a great feast at Oranienbaum and ordered Catherine to attend. He wanted her there for no other reason, as it developed, than to revenge himself by inflicting another and especially meaningful public humiliation on her. The Order of St. Catherine, founded by Peter the Great to honor Catherine I, was awarded only to members and close relatives of the imperial family. Catherine had received hers, as we saw, from Elizabeth's hands at the time of her betrothal. Now, in a special ceremony during the banquet, Peter III presented the order to Elizabeth Worontsov and himself pinned it on her bodice—an open declaration that he intended to marry her. Catherine watched this with no outward signs of emotion. She continued through the evening to show such poise and apparent unconcern that Peter, drinking heavily, finally became enraged and ordered her arrested.

Fortunately Prince George of Holstein was there. He was Catherine's uncle, her mother's youngest brother. As a very young man, when she was a girl in Zerbst, he had shown such great affection that she realized later he had thought himself in love with her. He was also a second cousin of Peter III. Soon after becoming Emperor, Peter had brought him to Russia to command a regiment and to be generalissimo of the expedition against Denmark.

Prince George intervened in Catherine's behalf, managed to get Peter to countermand the order, and Catherine was able to leave safely and return to Peterhof.

It was a narrow escape, and she could not feel any confidence that Prince George could save her again. A few days later, June 29, would be the feast of St. Peter, the great national holiday which, of course, was Peter's name day. Peter was planning to keep the usual custom of celebrating it at Peterhof. He and his entourage would come from Oranienbaum that morning. The next day he would leave for the Danish invasion.

Was he also planning, perhaps, as a macabre feature of his personal celebration, to dispose of her on the eve of his departure? She would be entirely defenseless. She could be arrested, with Prince George and others entirely unaware, and taken away in the night to be immured in a convent or locked up in Schlüsselburg Fortress. Or perhaps worse. There is some evidence indicating that he meant her to have a fatal accident or be poisoned that day.

Catherine's conspirators had more or less decided not to do anything for the moment, but on June 28, St. Peter's Eve, they were forced to act. What happened was this: One of the Guards officers involved in the plot, a Captain Passek, excitable and the worse for alcohol, spoke out in the barracks against Peter III. He was overheard by a police informer and was arrested for "offensive and treasonable speeches against His Majesty the Emperor."

Gregory Orlov hurried to tell his co-conspirators. In a confused rump session of the main leaders—himself and his brother Alexis, Princess Dashkov and Count Panin—it was decided that what Captain Passek might reveal under interrogation (likely to include torture) could destroy them all, and Catherine too, by morning. The revolution would have to be lit that night.

Who would go to Catherine?

Princess Dashkov yearned to be the one, but to her chagrin she had nothing to wear that was suitable for a midnight ride to the country. The trousered outfit she had ordered as practical garb for a revolution and in which she could have disguised herself as a boy had not arrived from her dressmaker. It was decided that Alexis Orlov should go to Peterhof and fetch Catherine, while Gregory Orlov went to the barracks of the Ismailov Regiment to tell the commander, Count Cyril Razumovsky, to prepare for

Catherine's arrival. Quartered on the far outskirts of the city, the Ismailov would be the first Guards regiment she would come to along her way, and success there was crucial.

The brothers left on their missions shortly after midnight. In order to be as inconspicuous as possible on the journey, Alexis Orlov hired an ordinary, nondescript Petersburg street carriage. In this unlikely rig, with its pair of low-spirited horses, he set off in the luminous silvery twilight of the June night—a magical spring "white night"—on the road to Peterhof, seven miles away, where Catherine lay asleep.

It was past five o'clock in the morning of St. Peter's Day when Alexis stepped through the open French windows of her bedroom at Mon Plaisir—there were no guards or watchmen—and awakened her. Quickly he told her the plans. She and her maid dressed in a few minutes—Catherine in a simple black gown she had used during the time of mourning for Empress Elizabeth—and then they were on the road in Orlov's ramshackle hired hack, with Alexis sitting beside the driver, urging him on. They went careening through the now-golden dawn, Catherine with her nightcap on to keep the wind from blowing her hair, which she had put up with a few hairpins. The horses were soon in a lather, snorting and trembling from their exhausting effort. Along the way they encountered a peasant with a cart and team, and Alexis, with some money and a little explanation, exchanged the street horses for the farm horses.

A little farther along they met Catherine's hairdresser, on his way from the city to fix her coiffeur in the elegant manner proper to a high feast day. Catherine, perhaps with some slight regret, told him that she would not need him that day and sent him home. A mile or two later they found Gregory Orlov approaching in another ordinary street hack. Catherine transferred and rode the rest of the way with her lover.

Gregory had been delayed in his mission, it turned out, because he had barely arrived at the Ismailov barracks when he was confronted by the chilling figure of Guards Lieutenant Perfiliev who, as Orlov knew, was the chief of the secret police squad that for some time had been keeping track of his movements. Orlov had taken recourse to the only solution open to a Guards officer and gentleman. Counting on Perfiliev's conditioned response to their shared tradition, he suggested a game of cards and ordered wine. He lost heavily and ordered more wine. Finally, by four in the morning he had lost 3,000 rubles but had sent Perfiliev, happy and stupefied, reeling off to bed. Only then could he deliver the message to Count Cyril Razumovsky and other key conspirators, among whom was Father Alexis, the regimental chaplain.

The incongruous pair of Petersburg hacks drew up in front of the regimental headquarters shortly before eight in the morning. Gregory Orlov jumped from the carriage and entered the building. A minute or two later out came a drummer, one of only twelve Ismailovsky who knew that Catherine was on her way. He drummed roll call. Guardsmen and their officers, some in various stages of undress, began pouring out of doorways.

Catherine stepped from her carriage and advanced to face them, a lone woman in a sea of soldiers, small and fragile, her mourning dress streaked with the yellow dust of the road and her black hair loose around her face, her blue eyes beseeching them.

The men knew her by sight as the Grand Duchess or as the Empress, but never like this. A good many of them had received gifts of money from her, dispensed through the Orlovs with remarks about her generosity, her appreciation for the brave work of the Guards, her special affection for them. They had known her as a benefactress, but never as one who herself needed help.

She spoke: "I have come to you for protection. The Emperor has given orders to arrest me. I fear he intends to kill me."

She said no more.

"The soldiers rushed to kiss my hands, my feet, the hem of my dress, calling me their savior," she wrote to Poniatowski. "Two of them brought a priest"—the chaplain, Father Alexis—"with a cross and started to take the oath." In a contagion of emotion the others joined in. While the voice of the regiment was raised in a mighty shout of loyalty, Count Cyril Razumovsky, the commander, who was held in extraordinary admiration by his men, appeared.

He made his way to Catherine and knelt at her feet.

Catherine had met the Ismailovsky and they were hers. From that moment, really, so was Russia.

She wrote: "After that I resumed my seat in the carriage, the priest with the cross walked in front of us, and we went on to the Semenovsky. They came to meet us, shouting 'Vivat!' Now the procession, swollen by two regiments of the Guards, went with drums and Vivats!" Thus she was borne into Petersburg, and down the Nevsky Prospect. There "I alighted at Kazan Cathedral. Then the Preobrazhensky regiment arrived, also shouting 'Vivat!' and saying: 'Forgive us for being the last to come, some of our officers tried to arrest us, but here are four of them, whom we arrested to show you our zeal. We want what our brothers want.' The Horse Guards then came, led by their officers, in such a frenzy of joy as I have never seen before, weeping and shouting that the country was free at last."

Word had spread fast through the city, and the streets and walks were jammed with excited crowds. She found the church already filled and the clergy, headed by the Metropolitan of Petersburg, awaiting her. In her dusty black dress, following at a respectful distance—so that now again she seemed alone, a fragile but dauntless woman in a vast space, enveloped in a nimbus of her own dignity and courage—she walked in measured pace down the long aisle to the altar. There the Metropolitan held a gold crown above her head and blessed her, and she took the oath as Empress and Sole Autocrat.

It was somewhat after nine o'clock. Her transformation from refugee to ruler had taken four hours. The Metropolitan blessed her reign and added blessings to "the heir to the throne, Paul Petrovich."

The cathedral bells rang, and soon all the bells of Petersburg filled the air with a vast clangor of rejoicing. To this wild, stirring sound, with the Metropolitan and cathedral priests in their rich vestments now in the vanguard and with the regiments and populace streaming behind, Catherine—still in her shabby carriage—proceeded to the new Winter Palace, where the members of the Senate and the Synod had assembled and were waiting to give her their oath.

As she arrived at the palace steps, there was an extra commotion in the great crowd that pressed around her. Catherine saw with astonishment the lively figure of Princess Dashkov levitated above the human sea and, propelled by multitudes of hands, bouncing rapidly toward her like a cork on the crest of a wave. The Princess had been at home, in a terrible state of worry and impatience, until she learned of Catherine's arrival in the city, then had started out in a carriage to join her, but had been forced to abandon the carriage because of the crowds. She had managed to squirm her way on foot to Palace Square and into the middle of the throng. There some friends in the Guards recognized her. They lifted her above their heads and started her on her way. She landed at Catherine's feet, rosy and breathless but ecstatic, and crying, "Heaven be praised!" embraced her.

Catherine took her along into the Winter Palace, where she found another of her chief conspirators, Count Panin, waiting with Paul Petrovich. Panin, although he showed proper pleasure in seeing her, was in fact feeling rather glum. Through the whole course of the conspiracy, he had maintained that the proper object of the coup was to put his pupil, Grand Duke Paul, on the throne with Catherine as Empress Mother and Regent, and he felt that he had been somewhat hoodwinked. However, now that Catherine had taken the oath as Empress and Autocrat there was nothing to do but submit gracefully.

After the ceremony with the Senate and Synod, Catherine took Paul with her to the central balcony that overlooks Palace Square. At the sight of them, mother and son, lovely Empress and handsome little Czarevich, the crowd went wild with joy. Looking about during this ovation, Catherine suddenly realized that she was seeing the Preobrazhensky Regiment in an old, yet new, light. The men had used the interval to rush off to their storerooms, divest themselves of the Prussian-style uniforms they hated, and dress once more in the uniforms that had been designed for them by Peter the Great.

XVI

"The Death of the Monster"

CATHERINE and her advisers were acutely aware that the coup was not secure until and unless Peter III abdicated. In theory at least, he had enough military power with the big force at Reval, the fleet units still at Kronstadt, and his own Holsteiner troops at Oranienbaum to defeat the Guards regiments if it came to civil war. Peter III would have to be located, captured, and made to sign papers of abdication. Then, for a while, until the military situation was clearly secure, he would have to be held under arrest. And then? The rest could wait, but Catherine knew that for him the happiest solution by far would be to send him home to Holstein, the mythical dukedom of his dreams.

Where was Peter? At this hour, still only early in the afternoon of St. Peter's Day, he was presumably on his way to Peterhof. It was decided that a Guards' force should be sent to Peterhof, a force big enough to deal with the Holsteiners in case he returned to Oranienbaum. With this decided, Catherine made a decision of her own. She would lead her troops personally, as Elizabeth had done.

"Having expedited our messengers and taken all necessary precautions," she wrote, "I put on the Guards' uniform"—the Preo-brazhensky—"having had myself proclaimed Colonel with great jubilations." She sent a message to the Senate: "Gentlemen and Senators: I go now with the army to secure and safeguard the Throne, and leave, in the fullest confidence, the Fatherland, the People, and my Son in your protection as my highest governing authority. Catherine."

At eleven that night, with green oak leaves in a wreath around her guardsman's cap and her black hair flowing loose to her shoulders (in the Elizabethan manner) and accompanied by Princess Dashkov similarly suited and handsomely mounted, she led 14,-000 men through the white night to Peterhof.

No news had reached Peter III at Oranienbaum. He and his entourage had set off after lunch for Peterhof, arriving there in mid-afternoon. He was astounded that Catherine had not given instructions for his reception and that she could not be found. He went to Mon Plaisir and looked everywhere for her, even in closets and under her bed. Finally, from a Holsteiner who had managed to come from Petersburg, he learned of the revolt.

The men with him—among them Grand Chancellor Woront-sov, Ivan Shuvalov, General Trubetskoy, General Burhard von Münnich, and Prussian Ambassador Goltz—were all ready with advice: He should go to Petersburg with picked troops and fight the rebels; he should go to Kronstadt; to Reval; to Holstein. Peter was paralyzed with indecision. He wrote ukases and sent them off to the city by messengers and members of his party; but no news came back, nor did the men.

Catherine explains what happened to the men: "Chancellor Worontsov arrived loaded with reproaches. He was taken to the church to swear the oath. Then came Prince Trubetskoi and Count Shuvalov with the object of securing the regiments and killing me; they were also taken without resistance and made to swear the oath."

At last, at eleven that evening, Peter set sail with the remainder of his party—including Elizabeth Worontsov and twenty young ladies of the court—for Kronstadt. But meanwhile Catherine's delegate, Admiral Talysin, had arrived there and secured the loyalty of the base for her. When Peter's yacht came to the harbor entrance, he found it closed, and when he called out, "It is the Emperor!" shouts came back from sentry posts and gun stations: "There is no Emperor; there is an Empress!" and "Move off or we fire!" Peter fell sobbing into Elizabeth Worontsov's arms.

From then on, his only thought was to reach Oranienbaum and from there try to make terms with Catherine. A letter from him, offering to share the imperial power with her, reached her while she was still on the road. She ignored it and marched ahead to Peterhof.

"Then came a letter brought by General Ismailov, who, throwing himself on his knees, asked me: 'Do you consider me an honest man?' I replied that I did. 'Well,' he said, 'it is a relief to be among intelligent people. The Emperor offers to abdicate. I will bring him to you and avoid a civil war for my country.' I agreed to this and Peter III abdicated in perfect freedom. . . .'"

With Elizabeth Worontsov and a few others he was brought to Peterhof. Catherine, perhaps for fear of weakening in her own resolution, did not see him but dealt with him through intermediaries. One was Count Panin. Peter, wholly distraught, groveled, wept, and tried to kiss his hand. Years afterward Panin wrote, "I regard it as the greatest misfortune of my life that I was forced to see Peter on this day." Peter was told to choose where he should be detained during the next days—"while respectable and comfortable rooms were being prepared for him in Schlüsselburg"—and he asked for Ropsha, a small estate 15 miles from Petersburg. "Peter asked me for his mistress, his dog, his Negro and his violin," Catherine wrote, "but in order to avoid a scandal and prevent increasing the excitement of his guards, I sent him only the last three."

At five in the afternoon of June 29, Peter left Peterhof for Ropsha in a closed and curtained carriage guarded by grenadiers and accompanied by Alexis Orlov and three other Guards officers, his custodians.

He was allowed to write to Catherine, and in the next days he sent her three notes:

"I beg Your Majesty to have confidence in me and to have the sentries removed from the second room, as the one I occupy is so small that I can hardly move in it. As Your Majesty knows I always stride about the room and my legs swell if I cannot do so. Also I beg you to order that no officers should remain in the same room with me, as I have needs that I cannot possibly indulge in front of them. I beg Your Majesty not to treat me as a criminal as I have never offended Your Majesty. I recommend myself to Your Majesty's magnanimity and beg to be reunited with the indicated persons in Germany as soon as possible. God will repay Your Majesty.

"Your very humble servant,
"Peter"

"P.S. Your Majesty may be sure that I will not undertake anything against her person or her reign."

The second note:

"Your Majesty,

"If you do not wish to kill a man already sufficiently miserable, have pity on me and give me my only consolation which is Elizabeth Romanovna. It would be the greatest act of charity of your reign. If Your Majesty would grant me also the right to see Your Majesty for a moment I would be highly gratified.

"Your humble servant,
"Peter"

The third note:

"Your Majesty:

"Once again I beg you to let me, since I have followed your wishes in everything, leave for Germany with the persons for whom I have already asked Your Majesty to grant permission to accompany me. I hope your magnanimity will not permit my request to be in vain.

"Your humble servant,
"Peter"

From Alexis Orlov, Peter's chief custodian at Ropsha, she also had three letters:

"Your Majesty, we wish you many years of health. We and the whole detachment are all very well, only our Monster is gravely ill, with an unexpected colic. I fear he might die tonight, but even more I fear that he might live. The first fear is caused by the fact that he talks nonsense the whole time which amuses us, and the second that he is really a danger to us all and behaves as though nothing had happened.

"I have, according to Your Majesty's wish, distributed money to the soldiers for six months, also the subalterns. . . . The soldiers speak with tears of Your Majesty's kindness and say that they have not done enough to deserve this. . . .

"I write this on Tuesday at 9:30. Your true slave unto death."

The second letter:

"Your Majesty, I do not know where to begin, fearing Your Majesty's wrath or that you should think that we were the cause of the death of the Monster, Monster to you and all Russia: now his valet Maslov has also fallen sick and the Monster himself so ill that I do not think he will live till the night. He lost consciousness and we, as well as the whole detachment, pray God that he should rid us of him and Maslov can report to Your Majesty in what a state he is, if Your Majesty does not believe me.

"Your faithful slave,"

And the last letter:

"Little Mother, Gracious Empress! How shall I explain what has happened? You will not believe your devoted servant, but I myself do not know how the misfortune came about. We are lost if you have no mercy for us. Little Mother! He no longer lives in this world. But no one thought that, and how should we have come to the idea to raise our hands against the Czar? But, Empress, the misfortune had happened! He quarreled with Prince Feodor at table; we could not separate them, and already he was no more! We ourselves cannot remember what we did, but we are all guilty to the last man and deserve death. Have mercy upon us, if only for my brother's sake! I have made my confession and there is nothing more to investigate. Pardon me, or make an end of me quickly. I no longer wish to see the light of day: we have angered you and our souls are doomed to eternal destruction."

Peter was murdered on July 5, 1762, strangled probably by Alexis Orlov or certainly with his assistance and connivance; perhaps in a drunken brawl, as this letter suggests.

Catherine did not punish Alexis Orlov, and her sense of expediency went so far that she deceived the public in an official statement that "on the seventh day of Our reign we received the information to Our great sorrow and affliction that it was God's will to end the life of the former Czar Peter III by a severe attack of hemorrhoidal colic. We have ordered his mortal remains to be transported to the Alexander Nevsky Cloister, to be interred there. We conjure all our faithful subjects to bid farewell to his earthly remains without rancor, and to offer up pious prayers for the salvation of his soul.

"I had him opened up—but his stomach showed no traces of ill health. The cause of death was established as inflammation of the bowels and apoplexy. He had an inordinately small heart, quite withered."

She was cold as ice, unrelenting, unforgiving—or so she makes herself sound, so she may seem, and so she may have tried to be. She had received the last two letters at the same time from Orlov's messenger. She read them, with what first emotions are unknown, then locked them away in a secret drawer of her desk. An hour later she went to a reception in one of the splendid halls of the Winter Palace. Her manner was perfectly normal; she chatted, moved among the guests, and did her best to charm.

The next day, in the privacy of her own rooms, with no one there but her young friend Princess Catherine Dashkov—one person, at least, whose understanding she trusted and from whom she need not hide her feelings—she suddenly broke down. Sobbing, she put her head on young Catherine's shoulder and said, "My horror at this death is inexpressible. . . ."

And that would seem to have been true. She suffered an agony of the spirit, a sorrow so profound, so complex, so deeply rooted that there were no words to utter it.

XVII

Petro Primo, Catharina Secunda

"STUDY mankind, learn to use men without surrendering to them unreservedly. Search for true merit, be it at the other end of the world, for usually it is modest and retiring. Virtue does not shine through a crowd. . . .

"Have confidence in those who have the courage to contradict you if necessary and who place more value on your reputation than on your favor.

"Be gentle, humane, accessible, compassionate and liberal-minded: do not let your grandeur prevent you from condescending with kindness toward the small and putting yourself in their place. . . . Behave so that the kind love you, the evil fear you, and all respect you.

"Preserve in yourself those qualities of the spirit which form the character of the honest man, the great man and the hero; reject all artificiality, do not . . . lose the ancient principles of honor and virtue. Great men do not know duplicity, they despise it.

"I swear by Providence to stamp these words in my heart and in the hearts of those who will read them after me."

These lines, which Catherine wrote at or near the beginning of her reign, were addressed to herself. They were her credo, the moral ideal with which she approached the great task of ruling Russia. The credo was found tucked in a volume of Fénelon's *Télémaque*, which would imply that Catherine considered that her principles had a close relationship to Fénelon's and helps us to see her in the role in which she saw herself. For Fénelon, a French theologian, educator, and political philosopher in the generation of Peter the Great, was a radical and utopian visionary who condemned despotism, upheld the natural rights of man against entrenched wealth and aristocracy, and defined the proper goal of rulers as the creation of a brotherhood of man in the spirit of the Gospels. *Télémaque*, a political allegory in which he put these views most forcefully, was one of the seminal and most influential sources of the ideas that in Catherine's time bloomed in France as the Enlightenment.

Many of Catherine's aphorisms and reminders-to-herself are in the Enlightened spirit of the credo and can be regarded as codicils or further thoughts on main themes. For instance:

"Liberty, the core of everything, without you there would be no life! I want the laws to be obeyed, but I want no slaves. My general aim is to create happiness, without all the whimsicality, eccentricity and tyranny which destroy it."

"To allow one's hands to be tied as much as possible in order to prevent one from doing harm, but to be left enough elbow room to do what is good—that is what every sensible person should aspire to."

"Sovereigns acquire greatness in the measure in which . . . all those who approach them feel more at their ease from the point of view of riches. . . . I want the country and all its subjects to be rich; this is a point of departure. With the help of a wise economy we should be able to achieve this."

"It is not surprising that Russia had many tyrants among her sovereigns. The nation is naturally restless, ungrateful and filled with informers and men who under the pretext of zeal try to turn everything in their path to their own profit. One must be knowledgeable and enlightened to distinguish real zeal from false, and good intentions in words from those in deeds. . . ."

"Only education and knowledge of mankind supply the golden

mean. . . . Domestic education is still a muddy stream. When, oh when, will it become a torrent?"

"Peace is necessary to this vast empire; we need population, not devastation. . . . As to foreign policy, peace gives us greater equilibrium than the hazards of war, which are always ruinous."

"Helvidius . . . joined the sect of philosophers who maintain that nothing is good except what is honest, nor bad except what is shameful. . . . He was reproached for being a little too fond of glory: this passion is the last to die, even with wise men."

"All I hope, all that I wish is that this country in which God had cast me should prosper. God is my witness to that. The glory of this country is my glory. This is my principle, a fine and happy one."

"Power without a nation's confidence is nil."

"When you have truth and reason on your side, they should be exposed to the view of the people. . . . If necessity is based on reason, one can be sure that the majority will then accept it. It is truth that induces compliance, not ceremonious language."

It was with this collection of humane, wise, and enlightened and "fine and happy" principles that Catherine embarked on her reign, which was to last for thirty-four and a half years, one of the longest reigns in Russian history. During her last year or so as Grand Duchess she had already begun a correspondence with Voltaire, her intellectual hero and the most influential figure of the Enlightenment. The sentiments conveyed to him in her letters were passed on by him among his fellow *philosophes*. At home, Princess Dashkov and Count Panin—who had absorbed the principles of the Enlightenment during his dozen years in Stockholm —and many others among the educated elite saw in her triumph the triumph of Reason and the arrival, in their still partly barbaric country, of the Age of Reason.

There is no doubt at all that Catherine was sincere in the ideals she professed. For that matter, it seems likely that she believed in them, or at least thought she did, all the rest of her life—as ideals. She was an efficient executive, a demon for work, often spending fifteen hours a day at her duties, which included vast amounts of paper work. She had a great feeling for logic, order, and tidiness. The mere fact that these memorandums to herself survived among her private papers would be enough to show that she valued them. It is a fair assumption that she looked at them from time to time, mused over them, and kept them as principles to be cherished and, when possible, observed. She began her reign full of zeal and as if she meant to observe them fully and consistently.

History, however, has distinguished her "good intentions in words from those in deeds." By the end of her reign she had compromised most of these principles, sometimes flagrantly, and in some cases had acted in ways that completely contradicted them.

The reasons were of course complicated. Among these reasons one would have to put a calloused conscience. The events of twenty years had taught her, in the course of learning self-protection, the jungle laws of self-interest and the devices of expediency. Her ends could remain worthy and, in the case of her credo, entirely admirable—the more easily to justify the means. Another reason, powerfully joined to this, could be summed up in Carlyle's statement that "history is the essence of innumerable biographies." Catherine, navigating in the full stream of history, could choose a course but was no more a free and independent agent than any other mortal. When she took the throne, she confronted a nation that was the product of innumerable biographies stretching in geography from Byzantium and Kiev and Moscow to Petersburg, bearing the fresh imprints of the biographies of Peter I, Elizabeth II, and Peter III, and consisting at that moment of some 19,000,000 living, ongoing biographies. This nation, moreover, was merely one member of a European community, all with "perpetual interests" to assert.

She herself was the product of her own biography and of all the sentiments and loyalties and obligations and enmities and expectations that had accumulated in her thirty-three years. She had no legitimate claim to the throne; she has usurped it from Peter III, the legal heir named by Empress Elizabeth, and in effect had usurped it also from her son Paul, who in normal procedure would have been the next heir. She was widely suspected of having arranged or connived in Peter III's death. An authentic Romanov heir, the deposed Ivan VI, was still alive and could become the center of a coup by her numerous enemies. Her obligations were many: "Not a guardsman sees me," she wrote, "but that he says to himself, 'This the work of my hands.'" She measured the situation and began to pay debts, to compromise, to "know duplicity," to seek to consolidate her power. She became a despot. And ultimately, by spreading serfdom in order to bind the nobles and the gentry class to her, she grievously reduced that liberty—"the core of everything"—she had once so passionately avowed as her aim for all.

Yet she became Catherine "the Great." And within the largest frame of Russia's interest—political, economic, and cultural—there is no real doubt, despite her sins and contradictions, that she deserved that title. An eminent English historian, G. P. Gooch, has called her "the only woman ruler who has surpassed Queen Elizabeth [of England] in ability and equaled her in the enduring significance of her work."

The Empress Elizabeth, as much as she had idolized her father, for some reason had never put up a monument to him. Soon after coming to Peter's throne, Catherine set about providing one. She instructed her ambassador to Paris, Prince Dmitri Golitsyn, to secure some leading sculptor in that center of arts to cast an equestrian statue in bronze. She offered to pay 300,000 livres. After protracted negotiations, Étienne Maurice Falconet was chosen and agreed to do the work in Petersburg. It took him the better part of twelve years, but the result was one of the greatest equestrian figures of the world and one of the great landmarks of Petersburg. The mounted figure of Peter stands on a rising wave carved from an enormous block of granite. On the base Catherine had these words engraved:

PETRO PRIMO
CATHARINA SECUNDA

Thus she reminded Petersburg for all time of its founder and the founder of the new Russia, paid her tribute to him, associated herself and her reign with him, and yet, by this subordinate position of her name, near his but below, acknowledged his primacy and his tutelage. At least these meanings can be and often have been read into this deliberately enigmatic inscription. Catherine herself explained innocently that it was meant to prevent possible, and natural, misapprehension in later ages that the statue had been erected to Peter by his wife, Catherine I.

At the time she commissioned the statue she was deeply absorbed in domestic matters, especially in the preparation of her "Instruction." This was a basic statement of aims and principles for the guidance of the Legislative Commission that she was about to summon. The purpose was to reform and simplify the cumbersome, inconsistent, and often oppressive apparatus of Russian law, tax collection, and government administration. In effect the aim was to supply the nation with a constitution.

This was a project dear to her. With Montesquieu's *Spirit of the Laws* as her "prayer book," she was adapting, with much labor and thought, the principles of the Enlightenment to the special conditions of Russia. It was part of the general obligation she had taken on herself to push forward and implement Peter I's revolution. To her, as it had been to Peter I, this meant a primary concern for the advancement of knowledge and all those matters —science, humanities, the arts—summed up in the term "culture."

Peter's emphasis had been on science and above all on technology, both because of his native inclinations and because this was Russia's primary and urgent need at the time. Catherine did not neglect science and industry any more than Peter I had neglected the arts and humanities, but to her, the primary function of education and the spread of knowledge was to correct the intellectual poverty of most Russians.

Accordingly, Catherine saw it as her historic mission to civilize the Russians. Instead of importing technicians and engineers, astrolabes and milling machines, she would import philosophers and scholars and teachers. And it was this that led her to become the founder of the Hermitage, itself to become one of the world's foremost collections of art. So we must briefly leave the main course of the narrative at this point to relate the story of Catherine the art collector, who influenced the course of history almost as much as did Catherine the Great.

Catherine's direct concerns intellectually were mainly literary and philosophical, as well as political. Her memoirs, although containing numerous references to books she read, with titles, authors, and dates, mention only one painting, the portrait of herself as child which made her look "excessively ugly." As Grand Duchess she lived so far beyond her means that at Elizabeth's death her debts amounted to "the terrible sum of 657,000 rubles. . . ." But there is no evidence that she had spent any money at all on paintings.

This is not to say that she was deficient in visual esthetic sense. She spent great sums on objets d'art, jewelry, her personal wardrobe, furniture and decorations for her apartments. At Oranienbaum she had made her first venture into landscape gardening and architecture, employing the Italian architect Antonio Rinaldi to design a formal garden and a garden pavilion for her outdoor entertainments.

As Empress and Sole Autocrat, Catherine found herself sole proprietress of the new Winter Palace that Elizabeth had commissioned. It was as elegant as any royal palace in Europe, as majestic as any, and bigger than all: 1,050 rooms, 1,786 windows, 117 staircases, and miles of corridors.

Heedless of costs in so many things, Elizabeth always had been peculiarly tightfisted about spending money on household goods; all her palaces had only the scantiest furnishings—except when she was in residence. As she moved about from one to another, she was accompanied by a wagon train loaded with furniture and even linens and kitchen utensils; during the annual moves to Moscow and back to Petersburg, the train had hundreds of vehicles and stretched for miles.

The Old Winter Palace was a mere fourth the size of the new, and besides, some of its furnishings were too worn or inappropriate for the new. So the largely unfurnished new Winter Palace was a challenge to Catherine, a problem not only of chairs and tables and other objects that could bring these 1,050 rooms with their 4,200 walls, not to mention the miles of corridor walls, to life and make this vast monument livable. Naturally she thought of paintings.

Peter I had begun a collection of paintings. In the years since his death, the imperial collection had grown little in size and less in merit. Most of it was scattered here and there in the various palaces and pavilions. There still were first-rate pictures at Peterhof, particularly Peter I's own favorites at Mon Plaisir. But it was unthinkable to disturb these.

And so Catherine's thoughts—as would the thoughts of any woman in such a quandary—turned to shopping: to the art dealers and markets of Europe.

A Polish art dealer living in Berlin had as his most important client Frederick of Prussia and for some while had been accumulating paintings for Frederick's account and country pleasure palace, Sans Souci. However, because of the massive devastation of Prussia in the Seven Years' War, Frederick needed every pfennig for reconstruction. He could not afford the paintings. The dealer was left with a large investment. He needed a customer and was willing to bargain. Catherine, in 1763—her reign less than a year old—took the whole lot, 225 paintings.

What were her emotions and thoughts? She never described them. Did she remember herself as a shy and uncertain fourteenyear-old, a princess who was not pretty, had an insignificant title and no money, by some strange conjunction of circumstances traveling toward an unknown land to marry a boy she hardly knew and stopping in Berlin to visit the great Frederick II?

Now, twenty tangled years later, after blood spilled and trouble spent in more directions than one could have imagined, she carried off a whole collection meant for him because she was rich and he was poor. The fact that the paintings were chosen to suit the taste of Frederick, a connoisseur, made her trust their quality sight unseen.

So began one of the greatest collections ever seen.

Catherine had her purchase delivered to her by sea, across the Baltic to the Neva in Petersburg, and direct to the Winter Palace quay, where the ship tied up literally across the street from the Neva-side delivery entrance, a matter of some 50 feet. It was to be a scene often repeated: ships from France, from Holland, from here and there, lying close in by the quay, unloading dozens and scores and hundreds of boxes and crates—boxes of Rembrandts and Rubenses and Ruisdaels, crates of Caravaggios and Canalettos and Carpaccios, shiploads of masterpieces.

This would apply as literal fact at various times in the future—

but not, one must hasten to say, in the case of this first acquisition. Of the 225 paintings, the majority were competent, pleasant, and undistinguished. There were some others of high merit, though not high enough for greatness. But there was a small brilliant complement of masterpieces. There were Frans Hals' "Man with a Glove" and Rubens' "Head of an Old Man." There was Jan Steen's "The Loafers"; there was Snyders' "Cock at a Table with Dead Game." And there were three Rembrandts: "Incredulity of Thomas," "Potipar's Wife," and "Portrait of a Turk."

Catherine watched the unloading of her 225 surprise packages, watched some of them emerge from their wrappings. She passed among them all, when they had been readied for inspection and propped up against various walls, studying them with great interest and the unclouded eye of the complete amateur. She decided that she was pleased. In fact, she found herself experiencing not only pleasure, but proprietary pride and more than a little excitement. And so, quite soon, she sent instructions to her ambassadors and agents—as Peter the Great had done—to be alert to other prospective or potential offerings of good collections or single items and to keep her informed.

She had not yet, at this stage, decided to conquer the world, but she was setting up her art intelligence network for encounters with many foes on many fronts—for even an amateur in art knew that entering into the art markets was entering into a state of permanent, undeclared, but remorseless diplomatic warfare with most of the other monarchs in Europe and most of their richest and noblest subjects.

In Paris, which since Louis XIV had been the most important center of the arts, Catherine luckily had as her ambassador Prince Dmitri Golitsyn, a polished product of the Enlightenment, personal friend of Voltaire, Diderot, and leading artists and writers, and one of the favored foreigners incorporated by Madame Geoffrin into the charming circle of her salon. Madame Geoffrin's was, among other things, a kind of informal information center for art. The habitués were often the first to know that Comte X was thinking of sharing out his celebrated collection among his four children, one of whom did not care much for art but wanted money to invest in Louisiana, and that the Marquis de Y was feeling ennui with his eighteen scenes of Dutch country life by David Teniers, Paulus Potter, and Adraen van Ostade.

Thus it was very likely at this intelligence post that Golitsyn learned of the possible availability of a superb Rembrandt, "The Return of the Prodigal Son." The painting was owned by a M. d'Amezune, who let it be known to someone connected with the Geoffrin circle that he could be persuaded to sell it for quick and good profit—which Golitsyn supplied. Catherine's campaign could not have got off to a better or more propitious start.

It was from Madame Geoffrin herself that Golitsyn learned, and immediately sent on to Catherine, another piece of intelligence that was of great interest to her and that she turned to great advantage, not only in her art campaigns but in her whole long-range, lifelong objective of enlightening her realm. Golitsyn's news was that Denis Diderot, through various misfortunes and some follies of his own, was so desperately in need of money that he was thinking of selling his library—the library that he had accumulated, with such an amount of searching and careful selectivity over so many years, to write his *Encyclopédie*. The *Encyclopédie* was to the Enlightenment much what Aristotle had been to the Middle Ages and Plato to the Renaissance: both the source of understanding and the iconographic symbol of it, a kind of bible of the age. Although many of the Enlightened managed to keep their reason and their faith separate and fairly well intact—accepting with Blaise Pascal that "the heart has reasons which reason cannot understand"—a great many others became agnostics, professedly or privately, and some, like Voltaire, became atheists. Consequently, there was a strong tendency to make Reason itself —with its trinity of natural law, education, and progress—a kind of surrogate deity and the object of a substitute religion.

Thus there was, so to speak, a confrontation of rival religions —as usual engaging strong emotions and producing bigotry, repressions, sacrifices, and martyrdom. In the Rationalist religion, the *Encyclopédie* had something of the status and meaning of the Gospels: It was "revealed truth."

The tensions implied in the rationalist-religious conflict, which was a general one throughout Europe, were important in a number of ways in the long reign of Catherine, a Rationalist Empress of an intensely religious empire. The special tensions surrounding the *Encyclopédie* and her own special relationship to them through Diderot and Voltaire explain why she made such a sensation by coming to Diderot's rescue.

No sooner had the first volume of the *Encyclopédie* appeared in 1751 than the denunciations began, led by the Jesuits. The government appointed a Jesuit board of censorship to supervise the next volumes, which were supposed to appear at the rate of one a year. The Jesuit censors, however, being intellectuals themselves and infected with the spirit of Reason, passed materials that inflamed other churchmen.

In response to the outcry that greeted Volume II, Louis XV's Council of State ordered both volumes suppressed and all manuscripts seized. But the government's own director of publications, Chrétien Lamoignon de Malesherbes, was a secret convert and warned Diderot in time for him to escape the police with all the manuscripts. Malesherbes then took the sacred writings to his own home for safe hiding. The suppression, naturally, became a *cause célèbre*. Weighing the protests, which came not only from within France, but from friends of Enlightenment and disappointed subscribers in other countries and colonial regions overseas, the government perceived that the *Encyclopédie* contributed to the honor and glory of France. The ban was lifted.

Volume III appeared in 1753, some months late, with an explanation written by the mathematician Jean Le Rond d'Alembert, a co-founder and Diderot's co-editor in charge of mathematical subjects. The next three volumes were published amid admiration and outrage. Volume VII, carrying the inventory of human knowledge through the letter G, contained an article on Geneva by D'Alembert, who, in the spirit of the Renaissance and the Enlightenment, did not like to be bound by his specialty. Jean Jacques Rousseau, who had been writing on musical matters for the *Encyclopédie*, took umbrage at D'Alembert's theory that lack of any theater helped make Genevans dull, dour, and intellectually deficient and, declaring that since theater was artifice, it could only corrupt nature's blessings, took the opportunity to denounce not only D'Alembert but Diderot's editorship of the *Encyclopédie*.

In the developing uproar D'Alembert resigned, and the next year —in February, 1759—the Council of State, finding the honor and glory of France affected adversely, banned future volumes.

It was a black time for Diderot. He stood to lose everything, not only the very core of his life's work, the grand design that consumed his thoughts and ambitions, but in all possibility his liberty. There was enough political tension in France, and he had made himself obnoxious enough to the Establishment and had acquired enemies enough in high places, that the chances were he would go to prison. Had he been less emotionally dedicated to his goal and more rationally prudent, he would have left the country, as many of his friends begged him to do.

Among Catherine's earliest acts as Empress was to invite Diderot and D'Alembert to move to Petersburg and resume publication of the series there, under her protection. She also offered D'Alembert the job of tutor and guide to little Grand Duke Paul in place of Count Panin, whom she had loaded with other responsibilities. Meanwhile, however, Diderot had found a way to keep the project alive and in Paris until, he hoped, the council would change its mind again. He persuaded his publisher to persuade the government to allow publication of the volumes of illustrations—portraits, diagrams, maps, scenes, and so forth—that were originally supposed to come at the end of the series. The first of these was ready in 1762, the same year Catherine came to the throne and made him her offer.

While preparing the volumes of illustrations, Diderot was at the same time working on the remaining ten volumes of text, which were even then going off to be printed and bound—and held in storage. It was a perilous scheme, politically and financially, but by 1765 all ten text volumes were finished, and several sets had been smuggled out of the country to ensure that, whatever happened, this scripture of Reason would not be lost to future generations.

It had been a triumph of faith, determination, and subterfuge —in more than one way, for Diderot, while readying the last volume, discovered that the publisher and even the printer had been censoring him behind his back. They were deleting material they thought might offend the authorities and jeopardize their own

investment. Their censorship and another shift in political sentiment allowed the ten volumes to pass government inspection
and be distributed in 1766. The deletions were not big and perhaps were not very important—they seem innocuous enough now
—but they were numerous, and naturally Diderot was outraged.
There was little he could do at that point except to berate the
guilty pair and, according to his daughter's memoirs, force them
in penance to print a set for him with all the deletions restored.
(If they did, the set has been lost.)

But in the year 1765, at the age of fifty-two, Diderot found himself with his great (if somewhat bowdlerized) work done to the
last Z but still in storage. He was unemployed except for super-
vising the remaining plate volumes and warring with his publisher. He was in debt, without savings and an income too meager
and unreliable to support his family. Hence, as a desperate resort,
he would sell his precious library. This word Prince Golitsyn
relayed to Catherine.

In no more time than it took a courier to travel the round trip
between Paris and Petersburg—posthaste, a matter of about two
weeks—her answer arrived. Golitsyn was to tell Diderot, from
Catherine, that the library was worth more to her than the sum he
asked. Moreover, she would like him to keep the books with him
in Paris until she needed them in Petersburg—in the indefinite
future, by implication until his death. Meanwhile, she would be
honored if Diderot would serve as her librarian and custodian,
with an annual salary from her. For the sake of convenience she
would like to pay him now, in a lump sum, fifty years' salary in
advance. In all, Diderot found himself with a fortune of 41,000
livres. He had saved his library and been relieved of financial worries for the rest of his life.

The news was sensational at Madame Geoffrin's, among Diderot's fellow *encyclopédistes* and *philosophes*, in all the intellectual,
artistic purlieus of Paris, France, Europe. Catherine was a heroine
or, in the religious imagery that Voltaire, the atheist, often used,
a saint. He wrote to Catherine: "Diderot and I are lay missionaries
who preach the cult of Saint Catherine, and we can boast that
our church is almost universal."

She replied, with becoming modesty: "I should never have believed that the purchase of a library would earn so many compliments."

Diderot and his friends were eager to lay offerings at the feet of their patron St. Catherine. One way they could honor her, a way as congenial to them as it was useful to her, was to help in building her collection of paintings and, in general, serve as her volunteer scouts and agents in such artistic enterprises as she might develop.

Within a few months of Catherine's magnificent benefaction, Diderot had an opportunity to show his gratitude, for it was he who persuaded his sculptor friend Falconet to accept the commission to do the equestrian statue of Peter the Great.

Despite her newfound fascination with art and art collecting, Catherine by no means neglected affairs of state. The year 1766, when Falconet took up residence in Petersburg, was also the year that she issued her imperial manifesto for the Legislative Committee which was supposed to remake the Russian legal and administrative system, and at least in some substantial measure the whole Russian social system, in the spirit of the Enlightenment. Early the next year delegates from all classes and regions of the empire assembled in Moscow—not Petersburg, the seat of all that was new and modern and as such still mistrusted by a good share of the empire's population. Catherine, with her acute feeling for the importance of psychological intangibles, wanted fundamental changes and wanted them to emerge from the very citadel of conservative tradition. She opened the session herself. During the next months she was present at nearly all its meetings, sitting behind a screen so that she could see, hear, send and receive messages, while remaining officially invisible. The delegates knew she was there but were relieved of the elaborate protocol of the Empress' presence, and she hoped they would tend to forget her and speak freely.

So she was busy and preoccupied during a good part of 1766–67, and in the same years the Paris art market, though it was never less than frantic, was only routinely so; none of the really major collections came up for private or public sale. Even so, Prince Golitsyn managed to pick up some remarkable prizes. At the end of this period—late 1767 or early '68—he changed posts, becoming ambassador to Holland, where he could keep personal watch over the Dutch scene, with its numerous private collections of Dutch masters and the busy art markets centered in Amsterdam and The Hague and the Flemish market centered in Brussels. He kept in touch with the Paris market too, by correspondence and visits, but the functions of resident scout and buyer devolved on Diderot.

For the next half dozen years or so, well along into the 1770's and thus spanning the period of Catherine's most active interest in the art markets, the foundation of her enterprise rested on this triangle: Golitsyn in The Hague, Diderot in Paris, Falconet in Petersburg.

XVIII

Building the Hermitage and
a Palace for Orlov

NOW Catherine needed to build a house of her own, a "hermitage," for essentially the same set of reasons that Peter wanted his. Like an art collection, it was a mark of status and culture. Also, it would give her privacy when she wanted it, which was often. It would be small enough to discourage unwanted visitors, but large enough to accommodate those few choice objects—furnishings, mementos, books, and works of art—and those special persons with whom for one reason or another one might wish to share one's privacy. Although her nature was sociable, it was also contemplative, and she needed time by herself to read, write, and think and simply to recharge her social energies.

Moreover, her love affair with Gregory Orlov was settling into a relationship of quasi-marriage, much like Elizabeth's earlier and durable relationship with Alexis Razumovsky. Elizabeth, with the self-centeredness of the consummate actress she was, had seemed oblivious to the salacious gossip and smirks that attended the Night Emperor and the open secret of his place in her life. Catherine had been among those who observed and made jokes. She was resolved not to put herself and Orlov in this same undignified position; her Hermitage was thus a necessity for the quasi-respectability that she cherished in her quasi-marital life.

She commissioned the building in 1764. Architecturally it is altogether different from the style of the Winter Palace to which it is joined. The "Russian Baroque" of Rastrelli's Winter Palace and many other buildings designed for Elizabeth was not to Catherine's taste. From the time of her accession, Rastrelli never received another royal commission. Thus she ended the public career of this great architect, whose works were so closely associated with Elizabeth.

Catherine's attitude toward Elizabeth was full of ambiguity. During the fortnight the dead Empress lay in state at Kazan Cathedral, Catherine had spent hours there every day, clad in full mourning, kneeling in prayer, sometimes weeping, sometimes prostrating herself. Her grief was genuine, and so were her tears. Yet her public vigil was also a way of showing the Russian people that she, a German princess, was as Russian and Orthodox as anyone. Elizabeth's towering shadow had blotted her out and oppressed her, but as she showed even at the time of Elizabeth's death, she knew how to find shelter under the shadow and how to evoke that Elizabethan image when it suited her—and to use it for her own ends. This was especially useful when her goals were in actual contradiction to the policies and wishes of Elizabeth. Thus, for instance, the march on Peterhof: Instantly evoking Elizabeth's image, it also disposed of Elizabeth's chosen heir.

And, as it happened, the year 1764, when she began building her Hermitage, was especially rich in examples of her method of associating herself with Elizabeth while implementing policies diametrically opposed to those of her predecessor. She became skilled in the art of what we might term "illusionism."

Elizabeth's demonstrated piety by her pilgrimages to holy places and the creation of a new holy establishment, Smolny Convent. Catherine adapted Elizabeth's demonstrations to her pragmatic purposes. Peter III, as we saw, had nationalized the properties of the Orthodox Church. On coming to power, Catherine had immediately revoked this edict. However, since she in fact regarded the church's wealth as a scandal and believed it should be put to the uses of the state, she soon appointed an "independent" commission to look into the question and recommend what should be done.

Then she made a pilgrimage to Holy Trinity Convent.

As suspicions rose among the clergy that her commission intended to reinstate Peter III's edict, Archbishop Arsenius of Rostov took the lead in trying to rally the church against "despoilment." He sent a petition to the Synod and in his own cathedral pronounced and posted an anathema on "enemies of the Church who stretch out their hands to snatch what has been consecrated to God." Catherine haled the rebellious archbishops before the Synod for ecclesiastical trial. She herself presided as head of the church. Arsenius was stripped of his office, his name was changed to "Andrei the Liar," and he was exiled to an obscure monastery in Siberia, where he was forbidden to write anything at all and given the lowest tasks to perform.

A month later Catherine summoned the Synod to hear her views on the question of church property: "You are the successors to the Apostles who were commanded by God to teach mankind to despise riches, and who were themselves poor men. Their kingdom was not of this world. Do you understand me? I have frequently heard these truths from your own lips. How can you presume, without offending against your own consciences, to own such riches, such vast estates? . . . If you wish to obey the laws of your own Order, if you wish to be my most faithful subjects, you will not hesitate to return to the State that which you unjustly possess."

The Synod submitted without objection. That day the Senate passed a law, immediately approved by Catherine, expropriating church property and making all ecclesiastics the paid servants of the state. The next day she began a pilgrimage—on foot, in the hallowed manner of the Empress Elizabeth—to Rostov, where, as head of the Orthodox Church, she personally consecrated the Shrine of St. Dmitri, causing countless Russian hearts to rejoice that their new Empress was as pious and devoted to the church as their previous one.

Secularization of church properties made it easier for Catherine later that year to accomplish another feat of illusionism with Smolny Convent. She had been especially disturbed by the poor-

to-mediocre education of Russian women, even those of the nobles and the gentry class. The exceptions were so few that young
Princess Dashkov had once said, with some complacency but probably also with accuracy, that no other two women in all Russia
could have had the intellectual conversations she and Catherine
enjoyed. To make a start on what she perceived to be a massive
need, Catherine decided to create a state school for daughters of
the gentry, using as a basic model the famous academy at St. Cyr,
which graduated educated Frenchwomen who often became wives
of the young officers being trained at the equally famous national
military academy in the same town.

St. Cyr was staffed and operated by nuns. This presented a
delicate problem. Russian women were only two generations away
from the seclusion of the Terem. Even among the gentry there
remained a deep-rooted feeling that girls should be reared in an
atmosphere and educated in ways primarily calculated to instill
lifelong morality and piety, and little else.

Among Catherine's papers, there was found this memorandum
to herself:

"Establishment of St. Cyr. The way to initiate it with both
purposefulness and facility would be to invite one of the teachers and obtain the statutes and journals of that house from the
French Court itself. . . . And to prevent the ignoramuses from
protesting against a French nun and her heresy, one could have,
at the beginning, to put one or two orphans in her care, on the
pretext of giving them a special education and these would serve
eventually as teachers in the school; thus, after a number of years,
one would cease to need the cooperation of the Frenchwoman,
having educated our own nationals to be instructors in the
school. . . ."

How to house this project? Smolny was Elizabeth's. Catherine proceeded to ease the resident nuns and novices to other quarters, and Smolny Convent became Smolny Institute. She paid a
great deal of attention to it, and a few years later wrote to Voltaire:

"You know, for nothing escapes you, that five hundred young
ladies are being educated in a house which was formerly designed
for three hundred brides of heaven. The young ladies I confess

far surpass our expectations. They make astonishing progress and everyone admits that they are as lovable as they are knowledgeable. Their conduct is justly regarded as blameless without having at the same time that strict and stern manner of the cloister. . . ."

Not as much could be said for the conduct of the guardsmen. "They watched every term of dismissal," an English diplomat in Petersburg wrote later, "to ensnare the prettiest." On the other hand, many of those ensnared and many who passed virtuously onward to graduation snared the Guards officers as husbands. Eventually the barracks next to Smolny were leveled, and on the site a large elegant new building was put up to house the lecture halls and main classrooms of the expanded institute, with the original Smolny cloisters serving mostly as dormitories.

As architect for the first Hermitage—the Little Hermitage as it is called now—Catherine chose Jean Baptiste Vallin de la Mothe, a Frenchman who had been brought to Petersburg to build an Academy of Fine Arts. Working in the general form and richness of the Baroque but with elements of the classicism that was the rising mode in Europe, Mothe created a structure that reflected Catherine's character as the Winter Palace reflected Elizabeth's. And different as they were, they proved compatible enough. The Hermitage was completed in 1767, and Catherine was able to occupy it late that year.

The Hermitage was a large house, or small palace, of three stories, with spacious reception and dining rooms and all the comforts that might be expected by a rich Parisian. Its general aspect was much that of the "town house" seen in a thousand versions in the best neighborhoods of major cities all over Europe and later in the Americas. With its upper stories carrying pilasters on all four sides, and the front, or Neva side, a columned portico as well, the exterior conveyed dignity and quiet elegance. On entering, one confronted a high and spacious foyer and a very broad staircase rising to the second floor and main rooms.

Catherine's family consisted officially, and so far as the general public knew, solely of her son and heir, Grand Duke Paul. Her daughter, Anna, Poniatowski's child, had died when little more than a year old. Paul was a pretty little boy, with blond, curly hair and big, limpid brown eyes, rather shy, yet with an engaging look of serenity and quiet confidence about him. There was very little of Catherine in his appearance; nothing of Peter III; something of Serge Saltikov. He had been a delicate infant and grew into a frail child, often ill. Catherine attributed his frailty to the smothering overattentions of Elizabeth and her "old women." During the last two years of Elizabeth's reign, Catherine had visited him every Sunday—as often as she was allowed—and had established a warm relationship with him. In the hectic times of the coup and the busy turmoil of the year or two afterward she had not been able to spend much time with him. Even so, she made it a point to go every day, even if briefly, to see him at his apartment.

In his tenth year he suffered a severe illness which undermined his frail health still more and left him susceptible to nervous "fits." The attack seems also to have affected his biological mechanism and upset his physical and emotional development. For his little-boy prettiness now began changing to a wizened quality, a certain stunting and distortion. As he grew older, his resemblance to the handsome Serge Saltikov vanished entirely. He became ugly. Most peculiarly he began to resemble Peter III. At the same time, there were signs of emotional malformation; this also was progressive.

The uncertain health and competence of Grand Duke Paul, the heir whose creation had cost such vast and complex efforts, now caused the whole problem of the succession to arise again. Would he be fit to rule? Would he survive to rule and to marry and beget? If not, what then? The only sure safety lay in numbers: There should be at least a second alternate, preferably a third, since child mortality was high. As a result, there was a rising sentiment that Catherine should remarry. But to whom? To whom but Gregory Orlov, to whom she was already married in all but name; whom she loved and who loved her; with whom, moreover, she had already had a healthy son, little "Beaverskin."

The existence of this child was still unknown to the general public but was well known at court. While he was still a toddler, she had retrieved him from her valet and his wife and brought him back to his birthplace, the Winter Palace, to live in his own suite with his own staff in the "children's quarters." This was an area containing Grand Duke Paul's apartment, facilities for children of resident officials of the court, and small protégés who for one reason or another were taken under Catherine's wing to be reared and educated in the palace.

She took a great interest in Bobrinsky, tried to see him every day, supervised his education, indulged and spoiled him considerably, and when he was five (the year her Hermitage was finished) made him a Count—Count Alexis Bobrinsky. Officially, he had no other identity. But the disguise was perfectly transparent, for he was treated as a son and was as much in evidence in Catherine's household as any child of a busy Empress could be—just as Count Gregory Orlov (his title dated from the first day after the coup), who officially was not her husband and officially not the father of Bobrinsky, was as much in evidence as any prince consort.

All that was required was a marriage ceremony to legitimize the positions of both father and son, making the one Prince Consort and the other an heir in line for the throne. (There would be some awkwardness about date of birth and other niceties, but not impossible to overcome.) As a matter of fact, by the time the concern about Paul's health and succession became chronic there was already extant a potential second alternate, for in 1763 Catherine had another son by Orlov—like Bobrinsky, carried full term in secret under corsets and ample gowns, born in secret, his existence a secret until he was introduced at a manageable age into the children's quarters as another of the Empress' protégés.

Orlov wanted this marriage not only for the obvious advantages to himself and his family, but also, and for him a reason that actually seems to have been more important, because loving Catherine, he nevertheless felt demeaned and uncomfortable in the position of "favorite." Through historical precedents, the position had acquired a status that was almost official and almost respectable. Its perquisites included great wealth, public honors, almost unlimited potentialities for influence and power, with no responsibilities except to please the sovereign. No wonder its occupant was envied and lived in jeopardy from would-be rivals standing ready to offer lusty competition. Even so, with all that could be said for it, the position remained unnatural and visibly ludicrous.

Elizabeth's Emperor of the Night apparently had no qualms about accepting these drawbacks as a small price for the large advantages. But Gregory Orlov was a very different kind of man: a natural daredevil full of self-assertiveness and male pride; a predatory, rough-and-ready man's man to whom it would be altogether unnatural and impossible to be a woman's man—any woman's. Not that he was a brute. He was capable of love, sentiment, tenderness, and even constancy. But it was an intrinsic part of this masculine love that he be the possessor, protector, and giver, not the possessed, protected, and receiver. Before and during the coup he had filled a role that entirely suited him, a man working and taking risks on behalf of the woman he loved. But in helping to make her Empress, he had made himself her subject, no longer her bold, possessing lover but her imperial "favorite."

Catherine did everything to show him her love, gratitude—and respect. She made him her adjutant general, consulted him on all important matters—and sometimes even took his advice. She awarded him the orders of St. Andrew and St. Alexander Nevsky and, to wear with these, a special decoration that blazoned their relationship: a miniature portrait of herself set in diamonds. She settled on him an income of 150,000 rubles a year and gave him a sumptuous apartment at the Winter Palace adjoining her own. She also ennobled, decorated, and enriched Alexis Orlov and the other brothers. But all this was not enough. Gregory, always gallant before, began to be irritable and quarrelsome; he enjoyed his honors, in fact flaunted them, but would not be at ease until she made him an honest man.

Catherine wanted to marry him. But there were problems. Initially, there was the problem of dynastic legitimacy. There was deep feeling about this in the country, especially of course among the nobles.

The Romanov dynasty could trace its descent all the way back to the very founder of Holy Russia, Grand Duke Vladimir—St. Vladimir—of Kiev. Dubious as this chain was in historical fact, it was universally believed in and valued because it supplied a precious sense of continuity in the life of the nation.

Catherine had added the next link to the mystical chain by giving birth to Grand Duke Paul; even though his legitimacy might be doubted, it could not be disputed. But she herself was a German, without a drop of Russian, let alone Russian dynastic, blood in her. And Orlov had been a common soldier with no connection to the dynasty or any of the nobility. Marriage to him and the legitimization of their children would mean, if Paul died, the end of the chain, the start of a new dynasty. Still alive in Schlüsselburg Fortress was Ivan, deposed, invisible, silent—an accusatory presence.

In this delicate situation, it would have helped considerably if Catherine could have found a respected historical precedent. And so, once again, she sought to wrap herself in the mantle of the revered Empress Elizabeth. For many years it had been rumored that Elizabeth had been secretly married to Alexis Razumovsky—a Ukrainian peasant, a mere shepherd, even lower than Orlov in origin.

Count Michael Worontsov, whom she had kept on as acting Grand Chancellor, was of the same generation as Razumovsky. He had been one of Elizabeth's early sponsors for the throne and a ringleader of the coup that put her there. He and the former favorite had been close friends and colleagues and also had gone through times of political enmity. But now they were both old men. The issues that divided them had vanished. And so, one day, Grand Chancellor Worontsov came to call on Razumovsky. On behalf of Catherine he raised a question in a circumspect way: If Count Razumovsky had been Elizabeth's husband and could furnish some kind of documentary evidence of it for the sake of the official formalities involved, then as the widower of the late Empress he would be entitled to a large pension and to all the honors due a member of the royal family.

Razumovsky, although a simple man, was not at all a simpleton. He knew and disliked Gregory Orlov, knew and deeply distrusted the Orlov brothers and their motives, knew the reports, widely current, that Alexis Orlov had murdered Peter III so that the way would be open for Gregory to marry Catherine.

Thereupon, according to a story handed down through Worontsov's descendants, Count Alexis Razumovsky went to a cabinet and took out a yellowed parchment rolled up and tied with a pink ribbon. He walked to the fireplace and put the parchment in the open fire without a word of explanation—and they sat there together, two old men, watching it burn. . . .

Among the nobles and the gentry, Gregory and the other Orlovs were disdained as uncouth parvenus, swaggerers, bad influences. Among the new intelligentsia, Catherine's fellow spirits of the Enlightenment, they were regretted as living fossils of a barbaric past. Catherine had seen the look of shock and incredulity on Princess Dashkov's face when, at Peterhof, with the abdication and coup's success only hours old, it dawned on her (belatedly) that this tough, unlettered, handsome roustabout was actually the lover of her idolized, idealized Catherine. Count Panin regarded Orlov as a hotheaded ignoramus and therefore an obstacle to the rational progress of Russia. He also considered him so unscrupulous, and his brother Alexis unspeakably more so, that in Panin's view, a marriage and consequent legitimization of Count Bobrinsky and other offspring would be the death warrant for Grand Duke Paul.

But then there were the Guards. In every case from the death of Peter I and accession of Catherine I to the accession of Catherine II, the issue had been decided by the intervention of the Guards. Catherine knew very well that her basic debt was to the Imperial Guards, particularly to those forty or so crucially placed officers and, above all, to Gregory and Alexis Orlov. They had acted for her at acute risk to themselves: Russian history was full of violent efforts to seize power that failed and produced bloody reprisals.

However, the very qualities that had given the Orlovs success— the energy, bravado, cunning, and ruthlessness that made them great field officers—were drawbacks when the battle was transferred to the palaces and ministries of Petersburg.

There Alexis Orlov, with his shrewdness and ambition, began to be seen as a Machiavellian hero-villain, the perfectly evil man who would stop at nothing to get what he wanted. He had been the mastermind of the coup—so the general opinion went—and all along had calculated it as an instrument for Orlov aggrandizement, without any real concern about Catherine or the country.

Yesterday the murder of Peter III; tomorrow the marriage of

his brother Gregory to Empress Catherine. And next? Gregory Orlov as Emperor? And Alexis his Grand Chancellor?

Gregory himself was full of vanity and arrogance. On the evening before Catherine's coronation, he declared in front of some members of the coronation party—loudly enough for her to hear—that if he were so minded he could repeat the coup and dethrone her within "one or two months."

Catherine's old friend and admirer Count Cyril Razumovsky, colonel of the Ismailov Regiment, was one of those present, and he replied: "Possibly. Very possibly, young man. But a fortnight before then we would have hanged you."

Orlov's remarks had been sheer brag, of course, but before many months he had emptied it of all meaning by alienating most of his old friends in the Guards. And soon Gregory Orlov confronted a shattering moment of truth. There was a new conspiracy in the Guards, but this time it was aimed against him and his brothers. Its members were all from the same group of forty key men that he and Alexis had organized. The ringleader, a young officer named Khitrovo, had been one of Peter III's guards at Ropsha and was now a Gentleman of the Bedchamber at the court of Catherine II.

Brought to secret trial, Khitrovo said plainly that he considered the Orlov brothers a plague on the country and that he would be quite willing to kill them all. Alexis first, because he was the worst and the cleverest. But his main object was to prevent a marriage between Catherine and Gregory Orlov because he and his group felt that would be a national disaster. They were in favor of Catherine's being married again, but not to Gregory Orlov.

Catherine followed this trial closely. Khitrovo's candor and his resolute defense of his plans for patriotic murder made a guilty verdict inevitable. However, Catherine saw to it that he was given light punishment, merely being deprived of his military rank and banished to his family's country estate. She had read the omens, and sad as they were for her hopes, she seemed not greatly surprised.

She did not tell Orlov that marriage was out of the question because she did not want to lose him. Instead, she equivocated, never saying no but always saying that the time was not yet ripe. Because of the Khitrovo conspiracy and other evidence so plain that even he could not misunderstand, Orlov grudgingly agreed. But he was not happy, and he vented his frustration and humiliation by being disagreeable, quick-tempered, and aggressively independent. Worst of all for Catherine, he flaunted his official bachelorhood by paying court to any attractive woman who took his fancy, including some of her own ladies-in-waiting. From 1764 on he was unfaithful to her, as she knew, for he made no effort to hide his philanderings. They were his way of punishing her.

She was jealous and unhappy when these episodes happened, yet so busy with so many matters of state and many other interests that she could not find time to worry much about them. She knew that she wanted to keep him. She forgave him. She wanted him to be happy—and not having time to devote to him, she resorted to the traditional devices of the busy executive placating the resentful, demanding wife or mistress. Instead of time, she gave him money, jewels, estates. His numerous estates, strewn here and there around the country, totaled many thousands of acres. Diamonds pleased him; therefore, he had a suit covered with diamonds worth 1,000,000 rubles. His estates brought him a princely income—and Catherine did, in due course, make him a Prince—but in addition, she spent about half a million rubles a year on him.

To this peculiar situation, the Hermitage, the city that was Petersburg, and its countryside owe some of their most remarkable treasures of art and architecture. In the mid-1760's, while her Hermitage was being finished, Catherine was overtaken by the same guilty feelings about Orlov that Elizabeth had had about Alexis Razumovsky when she was building her Summer Palace. In Elizabeth's case the guilt led to a grand palace for Razumovsky. Perhaps because Orlov was easily twice as difficult a man as Razumovsky, Catherine decided to give him two new palaces of his own, one in the country and the other in the city. Both were designed by the Italian architect Antonio Rinaldi, who had come to Russia in the early 1750's to work for Count Cyril Razumovsky, but then, like so many other talented foreign architects, had found himself in such demand and with such opportunities to express himself imaginatively on a grand scale that he had stayed on.

He had been Catherine's first architect, her guide to the heady, habit-forming pleasures of structural design when she built her entertainment pavilion and formal garden at Oranienbaum. Thereafter Catherine had kept him busy for several years adding pleasure facilities to the big park at Petersburg. There was a theater. There was a "Chinese Palace" in the *chinoiserie* style in great vogue in Europe at the time (and which was no more Chinese than rococo was Italian). Catherine and Rinaldi's palace was a low, single-storied central structure with a wing and pavilion on each side, all quite soberly Occidental-looking until one went inside, where all the walls were covered with frescoes rococo in style, make-believe Chinese in subject, painted by Italian artists.

Another divertisement was a "Sliding Hill" or chute-the-chute, an artificial hill some hundred feet or so high with a smooth stone course down which, in wintertime, one coasted on sleds, in summertime in small wheeled carts. These had steering gear and brakes—and needed them—for they went like the wind; a daredevil could swoop down the course at 30 miles an hour. At the base, as a staging area and pleasure room, there was a large pavilion in Classical-Baroque style, quite calm and dignified.

The versatile Rinaldi seemed to have a special talent for creating dignified structures which lent themselves to informality and pleasure, a combination that must have seemed to Catherine ideally suitable for Orlov. The country palace, Gatchina, begun in 1766, was almost sternly classical below, with much use of Doric and Ionic pilasters, but the upper floors of the projecting side galleries were open loggias: dignity below, delight above, all set in a vast park conveniently near the city.

The city palace, begun two years later, was a large, rectangular, mainly Neoclassic, dignified, and handsome building. It was set in large garden grounds overlooking the Neva, a short stroll up the river from Catherine's Hermitage. It was a source of amazement in its time and remains one of the most noted and admired buildings of the city, for its exterior walls consist of alternating bands of pink marble from Finland and blue marble from Siberia, harmonious since the tones are soft, creating an effect of great elegance and richness. Such precious materials had never before been used in Petersburg. As a result, the building, almost from its completion, was known to awestruck Petersburgers not as the Orlov Palace but as the Marble Palace. Usage fixed the name; it was and is the Marble Palace.

These two landmark structures were finished the same year, 1772, but various main rooms were completed and inhabited before then, enabling Catherine to begin furnishing them with such symbols of her love that Orlov could not fail to be flattered, honored, impressed—even, perhaps, staggered. He would, of course, be entertaining often and would want something for the banquet table; so Catherine gave him a many-thousand-piece set of Sèvres china made to her order and from her design, each piece an individually crafted and signed work of art. It is one of Gregory Orlov's secure claims on immortality, for the fabulous Orlov Service is on display at the Hermitage.

So is the Orlov Silver Service, an imposing array of items of table service, tea service, covered dishes, wineglasses, pitchers, trays, bowls, and everything else useful and decorative that could plausibly be made of solid silver and fit appropriately into the richest imaginable life in the richest imaginable environment.

So are grand jewels of all sorts, jeweled and enameled objects from snuffboxes to sword hilts and intricate watches and Easter eggs—and other priceless memorabilia beyond mention: the gifts of Catherine and Orlov to each other. Mostly they were hers to him, although he could not be called niggardly. He gave her a diamond that is one of the world's largest gems. This was the Orlov Diamond, and Catherine had it set into the Imperial Crown.

XIX

Toward the Restoration of Kievan Russia

THE notes and memorandums that Catherine wrote to herself were not all solemn. There were ideas for parties, small anecdotes about people she knew, and now and then items that she must have written for her own amusement and perhaps to show a few close friends whose sense of humor she could count on. (She could also wiggle her ears, and did, but only for reliable friends.) One of these items she titled "Characterizations of Certain Courtiers; Forecasting the manner of their deaths." She listed twenty-five names in a row, and opposite each, her forecast. Thus:

Countess Rumiantsev	While shuffling cards.
Mme. Palensky	Regret.
M. d'Osterwald	As if he were in a hurry.
Count Panin	Abstinence.
and . . . Myself	Complacency.

From internal evidence, the paper seems to have been written fairly early in her reign and probably at about the time—1767–68 —discussed in the passages above. One can see why she might well have felt some "complacency" at this particular juncture. She had survived on her precarious throne for some five years, long enough to prove her competence to rule and assert her authority by rewards and punishments, long enough that her subjects were growing accustomed to her.

Not everything had gone as she had hoped, of course. She had reasons for disappointment and disillusionment in both personal and political matters. One disappointment was the peculiar refusal of her art collection to thrive even under the most loving and expert care.

It had been five years now since her Gotskowski purchase. Since then her collection had increased by only a dozen or so paintings—all of fine quality, to be sure. When she furnished her Hermitage, it is reasonable to suppose that she took at least some of these acquisitions and some personal favorites from the Gotskowski set and installed them there.

The fact that the combination of Diderot, the most prestigious and most widely informed art critic of France, sponsored by the Empress of Russia, the richest and most powerful woman in the world, should have difficulties finding and buying good paintings in Paris is a measure of how competitive the art traffic had become. Diderot had especially strong hopes of making a private purchase of the very large and excellent collection of Gaignat, late secretary of Louis XV. He alerted Falconet and Catherine that this was a prime possibility. In the end, despite all his planning and plotting, the Gaignat heirs put the collection up for public sale. Diderot was outbid and finessed by the Duc de Choiseul, whose own financial agent had assured Diderot the Duc was not interested. Choiseul bagged nearly the whole collection, leaving Diderot and Catherine with one Murillo and three Dous.

This was a special aggravation because, as it so happened, it added mortification to insult. After her coronation, Catherine had sent a general notice to the other courts of Europe that the proper form of salutation in addressing messages to her was "Your Imperial Majesty"—not the simple "Your Majesty" that most had used in addressing Elizabeth. It was one detail within her general campaign to make Russia respected abroad.

The only objection came from France, where it was felt that

French grandeur would suffer if the King, who contented himself with the title "His Most Christian Majesty" were to address the Russian monarch as an "Imperial Majesty." As Louis XV's Chief of Cabinet and Foreign Minister, the Duc de Choiseul conveyed regrets to Count Panin, Catherine's Foreign Minister, on the grounds that Czar and Emperor actually did not mean the same thing and that to be a Czar or Czarina did not, therefore, carry with it the right to be titled Emperor or Empress; hence, the term "Imperial" would be improper.

Catherine sent word back to him that familiar and ancient usage made the meanings the same for practical purposes. Choiseul continued nevertheless to address her as "Your Majesty." When, through Panin, she demanded an explanation, Choiseul replied that the distinction could be glossed over in other languages but not in French; the designation "Imperial" did not fit the circumstances of the Russian throne according to the canons of the French Academy, which was charged with defending the purity of the French language and whose judgment Louis XV and he, as the King's First Minister, had the sacred duty to uphold.

Catherine refused to accept messages until they were correctly addressed. Choiseul refused to yield. Officially, correspondence between the French and Russian thrones ceased—although it did continue unofficially and by the use of various circumlocutions.

There was more to the matter than these semantic exercises, as Catherine knew very well. She was mistrusted and disliked by Louis XV's court, where her Anglophile and anti-French sentiments had been known since the days of Hanbury-Williams. She admired French culture, but what she most admired in it were the Rationalist elements—represented by Voltaire, Diderot *et al.*— whom the court of France considered most subversive. To Louis and Choiseul, she herself was a dangerous radical. One of Louis' ambassadors to Petersburg had reported that while she was Grand Duchess, a book had only to be banned in France to make her reading list. The "Instructions" that as Empress she issued to her Legislative Commission were considered so inflammatory that publication of them was banned in France.

Rumors that she had conspired in the death of Peter III, for the safety of her usurped throne and so she could marry Gregory

Orlov, had already been circulating in Paris. Now they were taken up and given semi-official status by the Duchesse de Choiseul, who in wifely anger at the inconvenience Catherine's attitude was causing her husband, went about denouncing her as a brazen scarlet woman, probable regicide, and, in all, a "monster."

The Duchesse was a formidable enemy. Before marrying Choiseul she had been Louise Honorine Crozat, descendant of one of France's richest men and owner of its largest, finest, and most celebrated art collection—Pierre Crozat. This Crozat was known as Crozat the Poor because he had a brother who was even richer. As part of her dowry she had brought a number of paintings, the foundation of the Choiseul collection, which had grown and become famous also. She had also brought a great deal of money and political influence, which had been instrumental in her husband's rapid rise. He had been a professional soldier and at the time of their marriage in 1750 had achieved the rank of lieutenant general. In eight years he had risen in the nobility from the fairly commonplace level of Marquis to the exalted one of Duke of the Realm and from an inconsequential place in politics to that of Foreign Minister. His Duchesse did not propose to have this brilliant performance tarnished by an upstart German Princess who was unfriendly to French interest.

For Catherine there was some balm for the loss of the Gaignat collection. In Brussels that same year, Prince Golitsyn managed a major coup. Learning that Count Philipp Cobentzl, long one of the most important diplomats of Empress Maria Theresa of Austria and at that time her plenipotentiary in the Netherlands, was planning to dispose of his collection, he opened diplomatic negotiations and secured the collection practically intact. There were forty-six paintings, including five by Rubens, three by Van Dyck, two by Dou, and choice items by Van Ostade, Wouwerman, and other masters. Even more significant was the huge collection of drawings, 6,000 of them, including many by Rubens.

The year before this, at the Jean de Julienne sale, Golitsyn had acquired 850 drawings by the great French draftsman, Jacques Callot. A year afterward, in the Brühl purchase described a bit later on, Catherine got many additional hundreds of items from many other masters. As a result of these three acquisitions, all in three years, she found herself with some 8,000 drawings and engravings and prints, the foremost collection in Europe, the first of the Hermitage's list of "firsts."

Today the collection has grown to the incredible number of 600,000 and includes the work of practically all important artists in all the leading centers of European art in all periods from early Renaissance to the early twentieth century.

These were times when the incredible and incalculable were happening often, presaging a time when the impossible would become the normal mode as the Age of Reason turned into an age of social cataclysm. Throughout Europe and the Western world, which Russia had rejoined to its great benefit and great hazard, states and statesmen were increasingly at the mercy of events which often seemed to appear from nowhere and suddenly overwhelmed the scene. It was, for instance, in these same years of the 1760's, coinciding with the early years of Catherine's reign, that Choiseul made it one of the main aims of his policy to build up the strength of the French fleet after its disasters in the Seven Years' War. Within a decade his success enabled France to avenge itself against England by helping the rebellious English colonists in North America (France's own chronic enemies until then) in their Revolutionary War. In 1768, Choiseul managed the cession by Genoa to France of the island of Corsica. A child born in Corsica the very next year was Napoleon Bonaparte, who might have risen to a generalship in the Corsican militia or in the inconsequential army of Genoa, but since he was born a French citizen, he received his higher education in France.

Similarly, through the unforeseen, seemingly fortuitous conjunction of haphazard circumstances in 1768, Catherine found the opportunities that enabled her to fulfill the imperial designs of Ivan the Great and Peter the Great and to bring to full cycle, in full triumph for Russia, the saga that had begun 500 years earlier with the Tatar invasion and destruction of Kievan Russia.

This achievement confirms what has been said earlier in the narrative of Catherine's life: that the major historical events of her reign are inseparable from her love affairs. To understand these culminating events, we must look back a few years to her relationship with Count Stanislaus Poniatowski. He had left Russia, in effect had been ejected from Russia, as will be recalled, in 1758, in the aftermath of the Apraxin scandal. Catherine and Poniatowski corresponded regularly in the years between his departure and her coup. Their letters were full of mutual expressions of affection, yearning, and love. Then, after the coup, as noted before, Catherine wrote, giving him a vivid account of how it had happened. Her first hurried note, written on July 2 after the drama of June 28–29, is brief and worth quoting in full:

"I beg you most urgently not to hasten to come here, as your arrival in the present circumstances would be dangerous for you and do me much harm. The revolution which has just taken place in my favor is miraculous. Its unanimity is unbelievable. I am deeply engaged in work and would be unable to devote myself to you. All my life I will serve and revere your family but at the moment it is important not to arouse criticism. I have not slept for three nights and have eaten twice in four days. Good-bye, keep well. Catherine."

Though the letter showed loving-kindness on Catherine's part to have taken time even for this scribble under the hectic circumstances, it conveyed a premonitory note of disengagement. Her next letter, a month later, a 2,500-word account of the coup and its aftermath in Peter III's death—which Poniatowski had every reason to suppose would enable him to rejoin Catherine as her lover and future husband—began with these lines: "I am sending at once Count Kayserling as Ambassador to Poland to declare you King after the death of the present monarch." (This was Augustus III, King of both Saxony and Poland.) "All minds here are still in a state of ferment. I beg you not to come here now, for fear of increasing it." And she ended with this:

"I received your letter. A regular correspondence would be subject to a thousand inconveniences, I have twenty thousand precautions to take and have no time for harmful little love-letters.

"I feel very embarrassed. . . . I cannot tell you what it is about, but it is true.

"I will do everything for you and your family, rest assured of it.

"I have thousands of proprieties and discretions to consider and also to bear the burden of government.

"You must know that everything was carried out on the principle of hatred of the foreigner; Peter III counted as such.

"Good-bye, the world is full of strange situations."

She did not tell him about Gregory Orlov in so many words; she did, however, say: "The ins and outs of the secret were in the hands of the brothers Orlov . . . [who] shone by their art of leadership, their prudent daring, by the care introduced in small details, by their presence of mind and authority. . . . Enthusiastically patriotic and honest, passionately attached to me and my friends among one another . . . there are five of them in all . . . the eldest of whom . . . used to follow me everywhere and committed innumerable follies. His passion for me was openly acknowledged and that is why he undertook what he did. . . . I have great obligations in regard to them, all Petersburg is witness to it."

It is difficult to know how obtuse Poniatowski was—or to put the matter more accurately, how obtuse love had made him. A fully rational man reading Catherine's letter could have seen that Catherine was breaking their unofficial engagement for reasons of evident self-interest, including an attachment to the unnamed heroic and passionately devoted elder Orlov, and that she was giving Poniatowski the Polish crown as consolation. This seems to have been Poniatowski's first reaction, for he wrote back to her:

"Do not make me a king! Only call me back to you! . . . That any other woman could have changed I would believe, but you, never! What is left for me? Emptiness and a frightful weariness of heart. Sophie, Sophie, you make me suffer terribly . . . I would a thousand times rather be an ambassador close to you than a king here. . . ."

A bit later on, however, with no discernible encouragement from Catherine, he seems to have persuaded himself that Catherine wanted him to have the Polish crown so that he, a King, would be a fully eligible bridegroom for her, an Empress.

How was it possible for Catherine to make her ex-lover the King of Poland? The tangled history of Poland is much, much more than we have room for here. Suffice it to say that at this time it was a country with a population divided into many antagonistic groups—by religious differences, national origin, class, political affiliations, domestic, and foreign, and economic interests. Politically it was an anomaly, an elective monarchy. Upon the death of a reigning king, the Sejm, or Diet, voted to elect a successor. Through the use of a practice known as *liberum veto*, a single negative vote dissolved the Diet, which then had to start all over again on its deliberations. Eventually it came to pass that all of the nobles constituted the elective body, and any one of them could cast the *liberum veto*.

Though Poland had long since declined from its days of greatness, when it was an empire that extended from Lithuania in the north well into Central Europe, its situation and potential power for troublemaking were enough to lead the rulers of its neighboring countries—all of whom coveted its territory—to interest themselves deeply in the selection of the Polish King. That is to say, all of them bribed various factions in an effort to swing the election to someone who would then be beholden to the successful briber.

At the time we are talking about, the reigning monarch was Augustus III, who was also King of Saxony. And he was ill. In fact, it was generally believed that he was dying. So his throne would soon be vacant, and Catherine intended Poniatowski to ascend it.

But Augustus III confounded everyone by remaining alive. His supposed mortal illness had brought Catherine's Ambassador Count Kayserling rushing to Warsaw, with her authorization to distribute bribes in Poniatowski's cause "and if it is not possible for less, to go up to a hundred thousand ducats." She also sent 80,000 Russian troops across the Polish border to make Russia's interest in the outcome quite clear. In addition, she opened negotiations with Frederick of Prussia, Poland's neighbor to the west, to enlist his support for Poniatowski.

Augustus III revived from his deathbed, sickened again, revived again. Finally, in September, 1763, a year after the first alarm, he died unexpectedly. "Do not laugh at me," Catherine wrote to Count Panin, "when I say that I leapt from my chair at this news; the King of Prussia leapt up from table when he heard it"—as indeed he had, giving utterance to one of his more famous remarks, "I hate those people who always do things at the wrong time!"

In the election that Augustus' death made necessary, there was

one other candidate besides Poniatowski: the son and heir of
Augustus, like his father the King of Saxony. His candidacy was
supported by Austria and France. His election would therefore
cause a serious dilution of Russian influence in Poland. By this
fact Poniatowski was doomed to become King of Poland.

Catherine did not want to impose him by Russian power alone,
for that would be certain to cause anti-Russian cabals and
alliances. Thus, her natural ally in her plan was Frederick of
Prussia, who astutely realized this quite as well as she did. That
was why both jumped to their feet at the news of Augustus III's
death.

Catherine had already tried some soundings with Frederick, in-
conclusively. She immediately renewed them, and Frederick
replied that he would cooperate in return for a general Russian-
Prussian alliance. Having come to power so recently on the wave
of resentment against this very thing, the alliance made by Peter
III, Catherine was taken aback by the idea. She did not reply at
all for a while, but meantime, knowing that Frederick liked good
food but was too stingy to buy delicacies, she sent him a shipment
of fine watermelons from Astrakhan.

Frederick replied: "There is a vast gulf between melons from
Astrakhan and the assembly of the deputies in Poland, but everything comes within the scope of your activity. The same hand that
gives away fruit can distribute crowns and guarantee the peace of
Europe, for which I, and all those who are interested in the affairs
of Poland, shall eternally bless you."

Catherine proceeded circumspectly, promising nothing. She
sent Frederick some lovely grapes from the Ukraine, and then
some caviar, and then some young sturgeon, and some choice skins
of black fox and marten. Her long years of apprenticeship in the
Russian court had made her expert in the arts of flattering and
seducing egos and corroding judgments and binding loyalties by
gift giving. However, none of these kindnesses made Frederick a
whit less vigilant. The upshot of the negotiations was that he secured the alliance he wanted, but in a context that made it acceptable to Catherine and Russian opinion: a "Northern Accord"
or so-called "Nordic System" linking England, Denmark, Prussia

and Russia in close mutual alliance against the southern powers—Austria, France, and Spain.

Within this system, Catherine and Frederick quietly made a Russian-Prussian mutual-defense treaty containing, as a secret clause, their pledge to cooperate in all matters concerning Poland. In the first instance this meant their joint support for the candidacy of Poniatowski, and as a corollary their joint resolve "to leave no stone unturned, and to resort, if need be, even to force of arms, should anyone attempt to prevent the free election of the king in Poland or to meddle with the existing constitution in this republic."

The Russian-Prussian understanding in favor of Poniatowski was of course soon known in the courts of all the other countries concerned. The two that felt most concerned were France and Turkey. The Duc de Choiseul had a strong suspicion—just as Poniatowski himself had a strong hope—that Catherine wanted to make him King the better to marry him. This would not suit French interests at all: Besides enabling Russia to dominate Poland, it would again expose Catherine to the nefarious Anglophile and Francophobe influences that Hanbury-Williams, even from the grave, would exercise through his protégé and disciple Poniatowski. However, since Choiseul did not want to add to the unpleasantness already existing between himself and Catherine, he maintained an air of disinterest in the election, while at the same time planting morbid anxieties in the minds of the Turks.

To that point in history, there have been scores of wars between Russia and Turkey. The Sultan's Grand Vizier now sent a diplomatic note to all the interested powers to object to Poniatowski's candidacy on the grounds that "He is too young, too inexperienced and unmarried." And directly to that point, "A marriage taking place after his election might serve as a means of increasing the power of the king to the detriment of the neighboring states." This note carried the implied threat of war, a war that almost inevitably would spread into a general European war.

Poniatowski's friends and relatives understood the problem and saw the solution: He should marry at once, preferably a girl whose prime characteristic should be her political innocuousness. Poniatowski refused. Many pressures were brought to bear on him, but he was unmoved until finally he received official advice from the Russian Foreign Office that he should marry or select a bride before the election. He realized that the message must in fact be from Catherine. Even so he refused to give up all hope; he neither married nor became engaged, but he did sign a formal declaration that he would not marry anyone but a Roman Catholic and only with the approval of the Polish Diet.

And so, on September 7, 1764, Stanislaus Poniatowski was elected King of Poland as Stanislaus II Augustus.

Poniatowski had been in his unwanted and thankless job for only a little more than two years when Catherine and Frederick, after consultations, presented their first bill for having given it to him. Their demand, delivered by Catherine's ambassador, Prince Nicholas Repnin, was for religious toleration and equal political rights for the Orthodox believers and the Protestants, at that time about 10 percent of the Polish population. The idea was not, per se, inimical to Polish traditions or interests. But the Catholics of the country were among the world's most stiff-necked and intolerant. "The last orders given by Prince Repnin to introduce legislation for the dissidents," King Stanislaus II Augustus wrote to his ambassador in Petersburg, "is a real thunderbolt for the country and for me personally. If it is still humanly possible, try to make the Empress see that the crown which she procured for me will become for me a shirt of Nessus. I shall be burnt alive and my end will be frightful."

Catherine did not see. Instead she gave Prince Repnin carte blanche, which he used—even to the extent of stationing Russian troops in the chamber of the Diet to ensure that members voted according to his instructions—to repeal all the legislation that had been adopted against the Orthodox and Protestant minorities. This led to a Roman Catholic revolutionary movement, the Confederation of Bar, which produced a widespread uprising in 1768. Catherine and Frederick both sent troops to suppress it. In subduing the rebels in southeastern Poland, Russian troops pursued them over the border into areas that anciently were Russian but were now possessed by the Turks. This caused new consternation in Constantinople. On Choiseul's instructions, the

French ambassador there did everything to nourish Turkish anxieties.

The result was a triumph of incongruity, a historical triangulation that almost defies the imagination. On the grounds that Polish Roman Catholicism was endangered by aggressive Russian Orthodoxy, the Moslem Turks declared war on Russia.

Catherine was surprised by this development. But, as in earlier surprising turns, she quickly appreciated the opportunities that the peculiar convolution of history had given her. She had, of course, thought long and often of the need for regaining Russia's ancient access to the Black Sea. In one of her notes to herself she had written:

"To join the Caspian Sea with the Black Sea and link both of these with the Baltic Sea, to allow commerce from China and Oriental India to pass through Tartary would mean elevating the Empire to a greatness far above Asiatic and European Empires. What could resist [such] unlimited power . . . ?"

And with the Turkish declaration of war, she wrote: "Now the sleeping cat has been roused, and it will not rest until it has eaten up the mouse."

Within two years after the Turkish declaration, a Russian fleet—commanded by Alexis Orlov—sailed from the Baltic around Europe and into the Mediterranean and there met and utterly destroyed the main Turkish fleet. Another, newly built Russian fleet had been launched in the Black Sea; in a series of engagements this fleet defeated and largely destroyed Turkey's Black Sea forces. On land, a new generation of Russian commanders defeated large Turkish armies and were driving ahead into the Balkans and the Crimea. Alexis Orlov went on to take the Greek islands from the Turks and landed troops on the mainland to aid a Greek uprising against Turkish rule, while the army was advancing through Bessarabia and the Balkans toward Greece.

All these successes caused general dismay in Europe. Catherine and Russia's power was growing far too great for anyone's comfort. In France, in part because of this disastrous failure of his Russian policy, the Duc de Choiseul fell from power in 1770 and was exiled to one of his country estates. Voltaire was enchanted with "his" Catherine in the role of conqueror-liberator and compared her with Hannibal.

Frederick of Prussia, whose collaboration with Catherine in Poland had helped start this chain reaction, was as discomfited as anyone. At best, alliance with the superpower that Russia was becoming would make Prussia a subordinate; at worst, to have such a strong near neighbor could turn out to be fatal. Accordingly, he urged Catherine to make peace with the Turks soon and on liberal terms and emphasized to her the danger of intervention by other powers—Austria, for instance.

Along with this friendly cautionary advice, however, Frederick had a congenial suggestion, a proposal that would bring mutual benefits to Russia, Austria, and Prussia and would—he did not quite say but clearly hoped—assuage Catherine's appetite for territory. All three nations had interests in Poland, founded on numerous ethnic, religious, and historical relationships. If they now cooperated in a friendly, mutually helpful spirit of aggrandizement, instead of checkmating one another as in the past, each could take the Polish territories it wanted, for no one could resist such a combination of united power, least of all the Poles. Frederick's diplomatic representatives had already been in discussions about this at the Austrian court.

In fact, the initiative may well have come from Austria, for in 1769 Maria Theresa had sent troops across the Hungarian-Polish border to occupy the county known to the Poles as Spix and the Austrians as Zips. The Austrian Foreign Office afterward explained to the other powers that actually this was a simple and innocent matter of reoccupancy, the county having been "hypothecated" —in effect, lent—by Hungary to Poland 358 years earlier, and the Poles had never returned it.

Prince Henry of Prussia, Frederick's younger brother, was visiting Catherine when this news arrived at the Winter Palace. Being an intelligently well-informed man, he knew that relations between Catherine and Maria Theresa were spiteful and that the Austrian Empress disapproved thoroughly of Catherine and spoke of her as "that woman"; the Russian Empress, entirely unrepentant of her sins, considered Maria Theresa a sanctimonious old busybody and customarily referred to her as "Lady Prayerful."

Any venture in international affairs on Maria Theresa's part was thus likely to be viewed by Catherine with suspicion.

Prince Henry expected that the Austrian seizure of even a little bit of Poland would have made Catherine quite angry. But she appeared to take the news rather calmly. The worst she said of it in Prince Henry's hearing was a bit of double-edged sarcasm: "It seems that in this Poland one has only to stop and help one's self." Prince Henry lost no time reporting to Frederick. "Although this was only a chance pleasantry," he wrote, "it is certain that it was not said for nothing and I do not doubt that it will be very possible for you to profit by this occasion." Not long afterward Frederick presented his congenial proposal for a tripartite carving of "the Polish cake."

Because Russia acquired the biggest piece, and because Catherine had put Poniatowski on the throne and her plenipotentiary Prince Repnin had made the demand for religious toleration, it always has been commonly supposed that it was she who initiated the Partition of Poland, a supposition that has added measurably to her image as a cold-blooded, calculating Machiavellian. She had, of course, entertained some such thought, but so had most of Europe's political leaders. In any case, Catherine was at first prudently hesitant. Then, however, as in the case of the Turkish declaration of war, she made the utmost of the opportunity.

The three partitioners had to negotiate their portions among themselves while also suppressing the Polish rebellion—or rather, the rebellions, for in this tinderbox one outbreak led to another —and it took another two years to compose all the elements. Thus, 1772 was the date of the famous First Partition of Poland, an act of political cannibalism by three major states on a fourth, performed as it were in broad daylight in the sight of the world and with the victim fully conscious but immobilized, hypnotized, cataleptic.

When it was all over and officially ratified the next year by the Polish Diet and King Stanislaus II Augustus, Poland had lost a third of its territory and half of its population.

Austria's portion was the most populous, with some 2,700,000. Prussia's was the smallest in area and population (some 400,-

ooo) but the richest in resources—and the richest also in political troubles for future times. It united Prussia with the large Baltic enclave that adjoined Courland and that had been acquired by Frederick's grandfather, so-called East Prussia, and in the process left the main Polish port, Danzig, still Polish but isolated from the rest of the country. A century and a half later, when Poland was re-created in the peace settlements after World War I, this anomaly was replaced by another one, the Polish Corridor, which played a part in bringing on World War II.

Russia's portion took in 1,800,000 people and all the lands east of the Dnieper River that had remained in Polish hands. The populations acquired by Austria and Prussia, though mixed, were largely Polish and most of the lands had been Polish since early times. But the people living in the Russian portion were mainly Belorussian ("White Russian") and Ukrainian, somewhat hybridized, yet with Russian traditions and essential Russian identity; the lands themselves were integral parts of old Kievan Russia.

With her reign only ten years old, Catherine had brought Russia's borders all the way back to the Dnieper, the historic water route and life-giving artery of Kievan Russia, the perpetual interest and aim of Russian ambition since the Tatar debacle. But the route was a dead end as long as the Turks controlled the land to the south, where the river empties into the Black Sea. And the Turks, despite all their defeats, were living up to their reputation as stubborn fighters. The Russo-Turkish War went on for still another two years. Finally, the Turkish government, profiting, as we shall see, by internal Russian troubles to get peace terms that would be less than completely disastrous, signed a treaty in 1774.

Russia gave back its Aegean and Balkan conquests but achieved all its most important aims in the Black Sea. The southern lands of the Dnieper route and the mouth of the river itself became Russian again. In addition, Russia redeemed most of the northern coast and steppe lands of the Black Sea, the natal place of Russian history, the lands of the early Greeks and the Scythians.

The exception was the Crimean peninsula, where the residue of the Golden Horde had survived and thrived as a Tatar khanate, latterly under Turkish hegemony and protection. Now this khanate of Crimea was made fully independent of Turkey, and by natural processes it came under strong Russian influence; Catherine was to complete the process nine years later by annexing it outright.

Meanwhile, as part of the 1774 peace settlement, she went so far in reincarnating Kievan Russia's role and rights in the Black Sea region as to secure complete freedom of trade and navigation for Russian ships plying Turkish waters, including unlimited use of the Straits to the Mediterranean, and special privileges for Russian traders in Constantinople.

Thus, save for certain final amendments at the end of her reign, enlarging and solidifying these gains from Poland and Turkey, Catherine had retrieved Russia's position in the world and fulfilled the dream of her important predecessors on the throne.

XX

The Pugachev Rebellion

THE late King Augustus of Saxony and Poland had been one of the foremost art collectors of his time. Like other royal collectors, he had made use of the national treasury and the nation's diplomatic, political, and commercial associations abroad. And in this too, as in the administration of Poland and so much else, he relied greatly on his Prime Minister and Foreign Minister, Count von Brühl—the selfsame Von Brühl who, at Catherine's plea via Bestuzhev, had sent Poniatowski back to her in the protective guise of Polish ambassador to Russia.

Von Brühl was a connoisseur. He had a superb collection of his own. While managing King Augustus' acquisitions, he did not neglect his personal interests. Finally, his collection became one of the largest, finest, and most famous in all Europe, rivaling even that of the King. This led to a rising suspicion that he was using not only the same Saxon-Polish governmental apparatus in his endeavors as a collector, to which there could be no very serious objection, but also the government's money.

Consequently, at Brühl's death in 1763 (the year also of Augustus' death) his whole estate was impounded, pending an official investigation of his finances. His heirs had been contending ever since, in the courts and at court, to have it released. In this they had the good wishes of all the important art collectors of Europe, who anticipated that at least part of the great Brühl collection would then be for sale.

Catherine had chosen her ambassador to Saxony, Prince Alexander Bieloselsky, with this in the forefront of her mind, for he was a collector and connoisseur, as well as a skilled diplomat, a man much on the order of Prince Golitsyn. In 1796, she received an urgent message from him: The estate was about to be released; the heirs would sell the collection intact; he had negotiated the price and now needed only her approval. Though Catherine at that moment was beset with the complications of the Polish uprising and the outbreak of the Turkish war, she responded positively, and the collection was bought.

Soon afterward the collection arrived at the Neva quayside and was debarked into the Winter Palace and the Hermitage. It was indeed fabulous: 600 paintings, including 4 Rembrandts, 2 Rubenses, 4 Ruisdaels, 21 Wouwermans, and multitudes of other works by nearly all the other leading Dutch and Flemish masters; splendid works by such Italian masters as Bellotto, Crespi, Reni, and Albani and by such Frenchmen as Watteau and Poussin. Now Catherine had a collection worthy of an Empress. But as she remarked of herself and her appetite for works of art, "It is not love, it is voracity. I am not a lover—I am a glutton."

Hardly a year passed before she heard from Diderot of a potential feast that would surpass the Brühl collection. The fabulous Crozat collection founded by Pierre Crozat—Crozat the Poor— was for sale.

Pierre the Poor had made his enormous fortune as a banker and as royal treasurer to Louis XIV. In the latter role he controlled a large part of the French national income and, following the more or less normal standards of public service of his time, had kept a good portion of it for himself. In emulation of his sovereign, he built a palace for himself and began filling it with works of art until finally, as a contemporary wrote, "In his magnificent mansion was concentrated the greatest number of treasures of painting and various antiques which had been collected by a private person." He was not only a collector, but a patron of the arts. Fashionable Paris came to the weekly musical fetes held in his palace and, in good weather, in its beautiful garden.

Crozat the Poor died in 1740. Having no surviving direct heirs, he willed the main part of his collection to his favorite nephew Louis François Crozat, Marquis du Châtel, son of his brother Crozat the Rich. The Marquis died in 1750, leaving part of the collection as dowry for daughter Louise Honorine, who that year married Lieutenant General Choiseul—the future Duc de Choiseul. The rest of it he willed to his two brothers Joseph and Louis, respectively the Marquis de Tigny and Baron Thiers. They sold the gems, drawings, and other miscellany but kept the paintings.

At Joseph's death, Louis, Baron Thiers, bought in all the most choice items from his brother's heirs and thus reunited the main part of the collection in his mansion on the Place Vendôme, a short stroll from the celebrated salon of his friend Madame Geoffrin on the St.-Honoré. It was there, very likely, that Diderot first learned that Baron Thiers, growing old and without sons to carry on the family name and famous position in the world of art, had decided to liquidate the collection. For sentiment's sake, he preferred to sell it, or at any rate the greater part of it, to a single buyer, so that it would pass on as an entity rather than being dispersed among many collections in whose catalogues it would be reduced to a collection of footnotes.

Diderot had, of course, notified Catherine at once; she, of course, at once gave her approval to proceed with utmost speed. Voltaire's friend François Tronchin came from Switzerland to help appraise the paintings and to weed out any of questionable merit; Prince Golitsyn joined them from Amsterdam. Then, at this early stage of the projected coup, Baron Thiers died. The disposal of his property became a public question and, perforce, a question of national policy. Would the French government allow such a collection, so famous throughout Europe, such an adornment to French culture, prestige, and *gloire*, actually to leave France?

Conshin, the eminent engraver, became a key man in this exquisitely delicate diplomacy. Catherine had already been in correspondence with him about various commissions she had in mind.

Falconet, expert-in-residence on the political and social geography of the Parisian artistic scene, advised Catherine to nourish this relationship with sedulous and patient care, for "His wide reputation as a friend of M. de Marigny"—whose position as Director of Buildings made him in effect Louis XV's Commissioner of Fine Arts—"can make or mar the success of M. Diderot's negotiations."

Sooner or later, it seemed, half the leading artists, writers, and intellectuals of the French Enlightenment—moved by respect for Diderot and admiration for his remote, magnificent benefactress —helped in some way in what amounted to a conspiracy of the intellectual elite on Catherine's behalf. The coup was actually accomplished by the spring of 1771 and was legitimatized early the next year with a notarized bill of sale for some 400 superb paintings. Diderot, Tronchin, Golitsyn, *et al.* had eliminated another 150-odd; thus this was a distillation of the best of a marvelous collection. There were half a dozen other Van Dycks. And five Rubenses. And no less than eight Rembrandts. And works by most of the other great Dutch and Flemish painters. And many works by the great artists of Italy and France. Now came Raphael's "Virgin and Child with St. Joseph," one of the few Raphaels then outside Italy. And four Veroneses. And a Giorgione, and a Tintoretto, and two Annibale Carraccis; and works by Guercino, Reni, Tibaldi, and Domenico Fetti and others. As for the French: three Watteaus, five Roussins, three Bourdons, works by Chardin, Lorrain, Lancret, Le Nain, to mention only some of the most important names.

The news that these treasures were leaving France caused widespread dismay and indignation; it was a lucky chance indeed that Catherine's conspirators had, in Madame du Barry, a friend and tacit accomplice at court. Diderot wrote to Catherine: "The collectors, the artists and the rich are all up in arms." He added: "I am taking absolutely no notice." And: "So much the worse for France if we must sell our pictures in time of peace, whereas Catherine can buy them in the middle of a war. Science, art, taste, and wisdom are traveling northward. . . ." To have such a declaration from a man of Diderot's status and influence—in so many ways the epitome of the most advanced European culture, revered as seer and oracle by the Enlightened throughout the Western world—was a victory for Catherine's policies, her broadest aims for Russia, that properly could be ranked with any of her greatest victories over the Turks.

Packed in seventeen massive wooden crates and carted from the Place Vendôme to the Seine and loaded on a long barge, the 400 masterpieces began their long water journey to Petersburg—and then progressed not another inch toward it for three months. Politics and public outcry had nothing to do with this: The barge captain was waiting for more cargo to arrive; there was one delay after another; winter turned to spring, the snows melted, and the rains and the river rose in flood and slowly receded—and Diderot, in an agony of worry about what might be happening to the paintings, came every day to urge the barge captain to hasten, to set a date, to be off and away. The captain was courteous but immovable. The prophet of the Age of Reason confronted a riverman to whom it would be unreasonable to leave without a full, nicely profitable bargeload of cargo. And so the Crozat collection, arriving at the Seine late in January, at last began floating seaward early in May.

At Rouen the ship that had been engaged for the sea journey had long since left. Finally, another vessel in the Baltic trade, *L'Hirondelle*, was found. It left Rouen in July and made its way here and there, loading and discharging other, less exotic cargoes, as summer turned to autumn and early winter and the season of heavy storms, while Diderot—and many others from Paris and Petersburg—worried, and for good reason. Only a year before a number of paintings bought by Prince Golitsyn in Holland had been lost when the ship carrying them foundered in a storm off Finland. (Catherine's only recorded remark, on hearing the news, lends itself equally to proving that she was a philistine or a philosopher. "Well," she said, "there goes 60,000 *ecus!*")

But this voyage had a happy ending. The *L'Hirondelle* arrived in the Neva and at the quay of the Winter Palace and its adjunct, Catherine's Hermitage, in November. The Crozat collection had been in transit for close to a year, but when the seventeen packing cases were opened, the 400 masterpieces were found undamaged. With a few exceptions that in later times were sold or sent elsewhere, they have survived the varied and often not less hazardous storms of almost two centuries of Russian history and are still in place where they landed, in 1772, in the Hermitage.

The fall of the Duc de Choiseul from power, as related earlier, obviously suited Catherine for political and personal reasons. Its sequel gave her unexpected satisfaction as an art collector. With his removal from office and the rich perquisites that went with it, he was in financial trouble, for he and his wife had lived on a scale of such splendor and extravagance—keeping open house in their Paris mansion, where the table was customarily set for eighty— that not even their enormous income sufficed. He left office saddled with debt. In the spring of 1772 the Choiseul collection was auctioned.

Diderot had of course notified Catherine in advance. This time it was not a question of buying the collection en bloc or even the greater part of it, for although it was on the whole excellent and contained a number of extraordinary things, it was not considered one of the truly great collections of the time. But Catherine wanted the best of it.

Catherine's emissaries did not get everything they would have liked, but they bid successfully on eleven paintings, including works by Rembrandt, Rubens, Tenier, Steen, and Murillo. There were more than 150 paintings in the Choiseul sale. Catherine's 11 accounted for a fourth of the total proceeds. These figures suffice to show how the emphasis in Catherine's strategy in the art wars had changed. By now her taste had become selective and critical. Wanting only the best, she had learned that it came at high prices and that success required concentration of financial forces on objectives.

Catherine's eleven paintings left Rouen in their packing case on the next ship for Petersburg after the *L'Hirondelle* and arrived at the Neva quayside while the pictures from the Crozat collection were still being unpacked and hung in the Winter Palace and Hermitage. Several of them had been in the dowry of Louise Honorine Crozat. Thus, twenty-two years after their separation from the original Crozat collection, they were reunited with it— in Petersburg.

Now Catherine found herself running out of space for her art. She had something like 2,000 paintings (the first actual catalogue in 1774 listed 2,080), along with thousands of drawings and numerous pieces of sculpture and miscellaneous objets d'art—enough to overflow the fairly modest dimensions of the Hermitage and the Winter Palace's galleries. A few years earlier, when the collection was small and she was just beginning to furnish the walls of her Hermitage with paintings, she had written to Diderot, "Only the mice and I can enjoy all this." With a few paintings, even with a houseful, she could feel that they were entirely her own, for her private pleasure. But it had become implicit in the quantity and quality and celebrity of her acquisitions that they be exhibited for others to see. Therefore, she commissioned another building adjacent to the Hermitage, a structure designed specifically to be an art gallery. This gallery annex—built with the same roof line as the latter and in a similar but plainer style—was so far larger than its parent, with some sixty rooms, loggias, and halls, stretching along the Neva embankment with more than three times as much front footage, that the Hermitage finally began to fit its name, for it seemed only a small and easily overlooked interval between the bulk of the gallery and the greater bulk of the Winter Palace.

The year following the arrival of the Crozat collection and the Choiseul selections, Diderot himself arrived in Petersburg. For nearly a decade now, ever since Catherine had made the grand gesture of purchasing his library, he had wanted to visit her. For her part, she had sent many invitations, informally conveyed through her diplomats and correspondents. With the Crozat coup the time seemed especially suitable. He had at last finished his monumental labors on the *Encyclopédie*. The whole enterprise, twenty-eight volumes of text and plates, had taken twenty-one years of his life; now, in good conscience, he could take time for the journey.

This prospect fascinated him and yet caused him considerable apprehension. He was sixty. He had come to Paris as a boy of thirteen, and he had rarely been far from the city, had never traveled beyond the borders of France. He was of ordinary birth; his father was a cutler. Diderot lived frugally, at first by necessity and later by habit and choice. His working place, his library-study, was a Paris attic. His wardrobe was a plain, rather threadbare black suit or perhaps two black suits—his appearance was always the same, whether at Madame Geoffrin's, mingling with nobility and notables, or at the print shop reading proofs and consorting with ink-stained press workers. He knew of court life by report but not by direct experience.

Diderot arrived in Petersburg in October, 1773, and was met by his old friend Falconet. The Empress had arranged literally palatial quarters for him: in the palace of Leon Naryshkin, the jackanapes companion of her earlier years, whom she had made chamberlain of her court. This palace (later known as the Miatlev Palace) still stands, and it is easy to see why Catherine chose it for Diderot, for it commands one of the loveliest and most spacious views of any site in the city.

After resting from his trip, Diderot, a gray-haired, wizened figure in his black suit, went to his meeting with Catherine. She received him at her Hermitage; his first sight on entering was Giorgione's "Judith and Holofernes," Rembrandt's "Danaë," and other masterpieces he had secured for her. Then Catherine came to greet him. No sooner had he made an awkward attempt at a formal bow than she said, "Monsieur Diderot, did you notice the door through which you entered? It will be open for you every day from three to five in the afternoon." And she made it clear that this would be so as long as he stayed in Petersburg and that she hoped that that would be a long time. Her manner was warm, friendly, and informal. She led him to her favorite sitting place by a window overlooking the Neva and asked him to sit in an easy chair facing her own chair. Diderot's last trace of nervousness drained away.

They settled down together for a long, companionable chat, and each was highly pleased with the other. Diderot, at the end of the session, paid her this gallantry: "You have the soul of a Brutus and the charms of a Cleopatra." Repeated in correspondence, this soon became a famous remark all over Europe. It must have pleased Catherine very much, for it could not have more aptly summed up what she felt about herself.

But she was finding the role of Brutus, foe of tyranny and devotee of republicanism, uncomfortable, for now she was being accused of tyranny and made the object of insurrection by the freest and most liberty-loving of her subjects, the Cossacks of the lower Don River basin. This was more than a local insurrection. It spread and became a major rebellion in the very months that Diderot was her guest. Adding to the incongruity and her own discomfiture, its generalissimo, whose real name was Emelyan Pugachev, pretended to be—and convinced hordes of illiterate followers that he was—Peter III, her unlamented husband dead now almost a dozen years. According to this pseudo-Peter's version he, Czar Peter III, had eluded the assassination plot of his wife, the usurper Empress Catherine. The man murdered and buried was only someone who looked like him, while he had fled in disguise and joined the Cossacks. Now he revealed himself in order to regain his rightful place on the throne, protect the rights of succession of his beloved son Paul, punish plotters and the exploiters of the Russian people, and save the Russian nation.

The fact that Pugachev did not in the least resemble Peter III physically, mentally, or emotionally was no impediment to him, for the Russian masses had no way of knowing what Peter had looked like or been like. Gross illiteracy and gross superstition, primitive means of communication in a vast land, lack of participation or any influence in the affairs of their own government by the Russian people made the ground fertile for the production of that peculiarly Russian phenomenon, the Risen Savior.

There had been many Risen Saviors in the past. In the years between Peter III's death and the Pugachev "reincarnation" there had already been some half dozen "false Peters." So when Pugachev began to be heard of in Petersburg in the summer of 1773, this news of still another pretender caused no particular surprise or alarm. But by the time Diderot arrived for his visit with Catherine the "Pugachev uprising" was developing to a different order of magnitude. One reason was that Pugachev, an illiterate ruffian, was a virile natural leader of considerable intelligence, much guile, and a great amount of charisma. The other was that he offered the Russian masses a program which combined, in one incendiary package, answers to their deepest needs and discontents.

In part he was a counterrevolutionary. The revolution begun by Peter the Great and continued by Catherine against the suffocating power and archaic social influence of the Orthodox Church had succeeded on the surface but not deeply. In one of his manifestos Pugachev declared, "We make them a gift of their ancient prayers, of the long hair and the beard." But he was also a social revolutionary who aimed at wiping out by radical and bloody measures the economic and political inequities that Catherine herself, in the spirit of Enlightenment and Reason, had wanted to correct and in principle still did. A great part of Pugachev's success was due to the failure of her efforts to achieve substantial reforms by means of her Legislative Commission.

Her "Instructions" to the commission were radical, indeed revolutionary. Improvements in conditions for serfs and eventual abolition of serfdom were proposed by an enlightened noble at Catherine's special request but were drowned in objections and rhetoric. The few liberals were vilified and even threatened with murder by extremist members of the conservative majority. Catherine later wrote: "What had I not to suffer from the voice of an irrational and cruel public opinion when this question was considered in the Legislative Commission. The mob of nobles . . . began to suspect that these discussions might bring about an improvement in the position of the peasants. . . . I believe that there were not twenty human beings who reflected on the subject at that time with humanity, really like human beings!"

After five months of oratory and acrimony, during which almost no concrete progress had been made on any of the topics of her "Instructions," Catherine decided to end this session of the congress in Moscow and to reconvene it in Petersburg at the Winter Palace. It was early December. The ground was frozen, and the first heavy snowstorms of the long Russian winter had come, dressing in white the birch and pine forests, the endless plains, and the towns and villages with their curlicue wooden houses and onion domes and tented steeples in a blanket of pure white. The people, nobles and serfs and townsmen all alike, each according to means, were preparing the rituals and happy festivities of the Russian Christmas season.

In this evocative scene of beauty and peace and goodwill, Catherine, in her room-size imperial sleigh drawn by six horses, set off for Petersburg, followed by scores of members of her court in their own large ornate sleighs and by some 450 members of the commission. The nobles and wealthy townsmen were in their own grand sleighs; delegates of the lower classes rode in omnibus sleighs.

The "all-Russian ethnographic exhibition," as it has been termed, proved as divisive and cantankerous in Petersburg as it had in the Kremlin. Christmas and a two-month recess neither lifted hearts nor softened deeply rooted mutual suspicions and animosities. It was not just "the mob of nobles" with their selfishness and inhumanity toward the serfs and peasants; the merchant representatives fought to prevent the landowners—the "gentry"—from securing rights to enter commerce and industry. Representatives of the Cossacks, ethnic, religious, and other minority groups, and the peasantry of various regions carried written mandates or lists of complaints and demands from their constituencies, and each seemed to want to press his case as the primary concern of the gathering. There were more than a thousand such lists. The sessions went on and on, spawning committees and subcommittees, piling futility upon futility.

The outbreak of war with Turkey gave Catherine a good excuse to dissolve the sanguinely titled Great Commission, and at the end of the year she did so, with relief.

In eighteen months of life and more than 200 sessions its only important accomplishment had been to acquaint Catherine with the true extent and variety and intensity of the antagonisms that filled her realm—thereby confirming and deepening her conviction that the viability of Russia as a nation depended on the strength of the throne, the possession by herself as Empress of ultimate and absolute power for use as necessary.

As the Turkish War went on and on and taxes and special levies rose to pay its enormous costs, and as the overburdened agrarian masses and disaffected special groups gradually realized that no meaningful reforms had come from the commission's work and none was ever likely to, the old discontents began festering. Thus, Emelyan Pugachev, the right man for a revolutionary role—angry, unscrupulous, robust, magnetic—emerged at the right time. With shrewdness and a manifestly genuine understanding of the emotions and needs of the Russian masses, he offered the right set of appeals, beginning with his bizarre claim to being the legitimate Czar, Peter III, miraculously survived to become the savior of his people.

In the national mythology it was never the Czar who was at fault, but those around him: the crowds of selfish, deceitful, grasping nobles and officials and, above all, the big landowners. Pugachev's manifesto declared, "You, such as you are, I enfranchise you and give eternal freedom to your children and grandchildren. . . . You will no longer work for a lord and you will no longer pay taxes. . . . We grant all those who have hitherto been peasants and serfs of landowners the privilege of being the most faithful slaves to our own crown. . . . When we have destroyed . . . the guilty nobles, each man will be able to enjoy a life of peace and tranquillity which shall endure for hundreds of years."

What began late in 1772 as a negligible disturbance in an obscure Cossack settlement in the Urals and took until the summer of 1773 even to be noticed in Petersburg had developed by that winter into a true and massive social revolution—the largest uprising ever seen in Russia to that time. By December Pugachev's army—a motley of Cossacks, peasants, freed serfs, miners and factory workers, religious dissenters, ethnic minorities—was only 120 miles from Moscow. Ultimately a third of Russia was "liberated" and, in the process, devastated by Pugachev.

The Turks made good use of the situation. They counterattacked. Thrown back again and routed, their main army captured, they began negotiating for peace terms but dragged the talks out interminably while, with their remaining forces, they fought delaying actions and thus prevented the withdrawal of any substantial part of the Russian army to deal with Pugachev. Catherine decided to seek peace.

In the spring of 1774, toward the end of Diderot's visit to Russia, preliminary terms were reached. The final treaty was signed that summer. In the interval, troops released from the

Turkish front shattered Pugachev's forces. Soon he himself was captured—betrayed and delivered by some of his own lieutenants for the 100,000-ruble reward Catherine offered. Soon afterward she wrote to Voltaire, who had become very curious about this strange, bloodthirsty man (said to have cut off 30,000 heads with his own sword) and this massive venting of hatred and revenge, so unexpected under the enlightened rule of his good "St. Catherine": "He was an extremely bold and determined man. . . . He hopes for clemency because of his courage. If he had offended only myself . . . I should pardon him, but this cause is the Empire's and that has its own laws. . . . No one since Tamerlane had done more harm than he had. . . ." He was tried and executed. By Catherine's ukase it was forbidden to speak his name.

XXI

End of the Enlightenment
in Russia

THE Pugachev revolution had profound and far-reaching effects, foreign and domestic. Without this domestic crisis, Russia's military forces would in all likelihood have expelled the Turks from Europe, would have maintained Russian hegemony in Greece and the Aegean and strong Russian influence in the Mediterranean, and have extended Russian rule or dominance over most of the Black Sea regions. Possibly they would have crushed Turkey and dismantled the Turkish Empire, occupied Constantinople, and restored that ancient citadel of Greco-Roman-Byzantine civilization to an important position in the life of the West.

As for the internal effects, along with the great loss of lives and property, there was the gravest kind of damage to Russia's social fabric. Rebel terrorism provoked counterterrorism and ruthless repression by the authorities. Class animosities and resentments solidified into class hatreds and deep, intractable mutual mistrust. And though Catherine never ceased to regard herself as a champion of liberty and the natural rights of mankind, she was shocked and disenchanted to learn that so many of the common people

were so gullible, so easily roused to fury, so wantonly bloodthirsty
and destructive when released from the established bonds of authority. She could hardly believe that these were "her people." Her
letters refer to them as "rabble." Yet she could not really believe
that either; there were too many of them from too many groups
and regions; they were too evidently filled with the dreadful courage of fanatical belief in some aim far larger than individual gain;
they had the strength to take fortresses and fortified cities and a
mystique that overawed the defenders and caused many to desert
their posts and join this "rabble."

They had the strength, in fact, to put her own position as Empress in jeopardy. At the height of the disorders, she discovered,
some of the leading nobles and members of her government and
the court—among them even Count Panin and Princess Dashkov
—were thinking of deposing her and putting Grand Duke Paul
(who was now nineteen) on the throne, thus depriving Pugachev
of at least one of his strongest appeals.

She concluded that the Russian masses could not be enfran-
chised or given any considerable control over their own affairs
until they had been educated, a process that would inevitably take
generations. Meantime, for the preservation of the state and her
own position, her only recourse was to rally the present possessors
of power, the nobles, support them in their role in Russian society
and gain their support for hers.

She gave the army carte blanche in exterminating the rebels,
and she gave the nobles Draconian powers to punish dissidents
and rebels in their own lands and regions. Every village in Russia,
it was said, had its gallows, and many were kept busy for a year or
more after Pugachev's execution. Declaring herself the "first
landowner of Russia," Catherine made common cause with the
gentry. In the Statute of Provincial Administration issued in 1775,
she put local government and the courts in the hands of the landowners and embedded their special class privileges in law. Ultimately she extended serfdom to the Ukraine and the newly won
lands and gave landowners even more power over their serfs than
they had had before. The latter part of Catherine's reign became
known in history as "the golden age of the gentry."

It is another of the great ironies of Russian history that the need for social reforms was never so vividly illuminated as it was by the Pugachev revolution. Its actual result, in the view of many historians, was to prevent significant reforms for half a century. And these things occurred in the regime of Catherine, who of all Russian rulers up to her time and of those for the next generations to come was—by personal conviction—the most liberal.

Diderot's visit lasted from October, 1773, to March, 1774, when this grave crisis in the life of Russia and Catherine's life and reign was in mid-passage. He, of course, knew only at second and third hand and in a most fragmentary way what was happening in the country. Certainly there was nothing in Catherine's manner that would indicate concern. Her savoir-faire was remarkable, and her energy not less than amazing. Rising every day at dawn, fortified at breakfast by five cups of strong black coffee (distillate of a whole pound of coffee beans) and through the day by large quantities of snuff, she attended to her vast correspondence and all important matters of state.

In practical effect she was her own Minister of War, of Foreign Affairs, of Home Affairs, and of Finance. She closely followed and freely advised on the operations of her commanders against the Turks and the rebels. She dealt with the volatile circumstances of her family and personal life. She founded the School of Mining Engineering in Petersburg as a national necessity and, as a special tribute to Peter the Great, continued to give financial and moral encouragement, as well as items written by herself (under a fairly transparent nom de plume), to the first satirical journal ever published in Russia, founded a few years earlier at her instigation. She continued also with her fine needlework and jewelry design (even to the cutting and polishing and setting of the gems) which were her most personal means of esthetic expression.

At the same time she remained Diderot's attentive hostess, friend, and intellectual companion. The door of her sitting room in her Hermitage was always open to him, as she had promised, from three to five in the afternoon. Although Diderot in his preoccupied absentminded way often was late in arriving for appointments with the Empress of Russia, apparently Catherine always was punctual for her appointments with the great *encyclopédiste*. With him, as with Voltaire and her other friendly correspondents in Europe, her attitude was that the revolt was merely another incident in the early adolescent progress of her people.

She saw Diderot some sixty times during his five-month visit, and their conversations often lasted for hours. Since Diderot's interests were literally encyclopedic and Catherine's not much less so, they discussed—besides art—a great range of topics, but naturally much talk bore one way or another on Russia. Diderot was full of curiosity about this vast, raw land, its culture, laws, religions, economics, and social strata, and the more he learned, the more his imagination took fire.

A contemporary diarist recorded that Diderot "always remains true to himself no matter where we may happen to meet him—at the Hermitage of the Empress's Palace . . . or in his modest flat somewhere under the very roof of an old Parisian house. . . . In this conversationalist who dresses with a democratic simplicity and ignores the rules of etiquette of the salons could always be detected the workman, native of some backwoods, who was hardened in Paris during his struggle against abject poverty, his struggle for existence. . . ."

He was self-made; so was Catherine. They shared much in outlook and in sheer unconquerable determination; they were two giant egos. But whereas Catherine had learned circumspection, Diderot was an uninhibited enthusiast who spoke his mind and was carried along on the flood of his ideas. Catherine, "republican in spirit" though she was, was somewhat disconcerted when her distinguished, excitable friend pounded her on the knee for emphasis or clapped her on the back in approval. Her tactful solution was to have a small table placed between them in front of Diderot's chair; on this, whenever the great man came to call, was a brimming glass of his favorite beverage, milk.

With their incongruously different temperaments and circumstances, these two pillars of Enlightenment and social progress— one a headlong idealist and revolutionary, the other a careful pragmatist with a revolution on her hands—got along wonderfully well. When the time came to part, Catherine urged him not to say good-bye, for that would be too sad, but only au revoir—until another visit. For his return to Paris she supplied a splendid coach, a caravan big enough for sleeping, eating and light housekeeping, so big in fact that at Mittau in Courland thirty men were needed to load it onto a ferry and at Riga, assaying a crossing of the still-frozen Dvina River, it nearly plunged through the ice.

"I had lengthy and frequent conversations with him, but . . . with little profit. If I followed his advice I would have had to turn everything in my empire upside down: laws, administration, politics, finances. I would have had to do away with what existed and substitute castles in the air. For all that, since I listened to him more than I talked, anybody observing us could take him for a strict teacher and myself for his obedient pupil. In all probability he thought the same, for after a certain time had gone by and he noticed that none of the great changes he had been advocating had taken place in my reign, he expressed amazement and mortification. Then I told him frankly:

"'Monsieur Diderot! I have listened with great pleasure to everything you have told me, with admiration for your brilliant mind. Yet with all your great principles—which I understand only too well—it is a good thing to write books but it can be a bad thing to put them into practice. In your plans for reforms, you forget the difference in our situations. You philosophers are fortunate: you write only on paper, which is smooth, obedient to your commands and does not raise any obstacles to your imagination—while I, poor Empress, have to write on the ticklish and easily irritated skins of human beings.'

"I believe that from then on he began regarding me with pity, deciding that I was a simple and narrow woman. From that time he conversed with me only about literature. Politics disappeared from our talks."

There was no real falling-out between them, nothing remotely resembling a rupture; they continued a cordial correspondence and by all overt signs continued to hold each other in great regard. Thereafter, however, although Diderot was always available for advice about purchases of art, he seldom volunteered it. Instead it was Baron Frederick Melchior von Grimm who increasingly, and soon steadily, acted as Catherine's principal scout and adviser in the art markets of France.

Grimm had made his own pilgrimage to Petersburg a few months before Diderot and stayed on so that their visits overlapped, and he had taken part in a number of the conversations—

most helpfully, for not only was he a man of wit and knowledge, but as Diderot's close friend and colleague, he usually could bring out the best in him and smooth over the worst, the quick temper and general excitability. Catherine had long held Grimm in great esteem because of his literary *Journal*, because of the good judgment and wide acquaintanceship that made him the prime literary catalyst of the Enlightenment and because of the personal correspondence with him that began when she was Grand Duchess. She took a pronounced liking to him when at last they met in person. He lacked the depth, intensity, and diverse genius of Diderot; but he had human warmth and understanding that invited her personal affection and, to an extraordinary and sometimes quite astonishing degree, her trust.

After this visit Catherine and Grimm never saw each other again, but for the rest of her long life they corresponded regularly and at length—a massive literary flow that finally amounted to more than 1,500 letters and more than 1,000,000 words, providing a record of Catherine's thoughts and actions that invaluably supplement her memoirs. She discussed all manner of things with him, often in the most candid way, and she entrusted him with all sorts of delicate missions, one of these being to dissuade Voltaire from coming to Petersburg to visit her. She had invited Voltaire many times during the years, but when at last in 1778 he actually began making plans for the trip, he was in his eighties. Catherine, almost fifty, was becoming steadily stouter of figure and more conservative in her social views. The visit of Diderot had tarnished one treasured relationship; she did not want to risk another. She wrote to Grimm: "For the love of heaven, advise the octogenarian to stay in Paris! Tell him that Catherine is only worth seeing from a distance."

So perhaps for the best, these two incongruously situated mutual admirers never met and retained their enchantment with each other to the last. Voltaire died that year. Catherine wanted to bring his body to Russia and to erect a splendid memorial to him in the park at Tsarskoe Selo. This, as she envisioned it, would be both a mausoleum and an art gallery, museum, library, and archive celebrating his genius and encompassing his life and works. Again Grimm was immersed in delicate negotiations, the most delicate being to secure removal of the body. In this, finally, he failed. But meantime he succeeded in persuading Madame Denis, Voltaire's niece and heir, to sell Catherine the great philosopher's entire library of some 7,000 volumes, most of them with notes and comments in the margins by Voltaire.

Along with the library came the enormous file of Voltaire's correspondence—including, as Catherine had Grimm take particular care to ascertain, all her own letters. Madame Denis received a fortune, a collection of Russian furs, and a diamond-studded gold box in which were a portrait of Catherine and a note inscribed: "To Madame Denis, niece of a great man who loved me."

When news of this transaction spread in Paris, there was an uproar that matched the one stirred by the Crozat sale. Gadfly though he had been, almost always in or on the edge of official disgrace, sometimes imprisoned, forced to spend most of his years in exile, Voltaire was nevertheless considered even by most of his enemies to be a major cultural monument. His books, letters and memorabilia accordingly belonged to *la gloire* of France. The French ambassador to Petersburg even called to deliver a protest. Catherine paid not the slightest heed to any of this. The Voltaire books and papers were delivered to her at her Hermitage, where they remained for several decades; then they were transferred to the National Library on the Nevsky Prospect, the construction of which she had begun in 1796, the year of her death.

After Diderot's death (1784) and the delivery of his library and papers to Petersburg and her Hermitage, this other greatest literary treasure of the Enlightenment also was taken to the same library. Both collections have remained there ever since—the two most important intellectual legacies of eighteenth-century France —monuments to Catherine's intellectual energy and ambitions for the intellectual development of Russia.

And so one product of Catherine's admiration for the words of Diderot and Voltaire—and of her capacities for imagination and bold, unabashed initiative—was to compel future students of the French Enlightenment and its leaders to come to Russia for source materials.

In these same years she made the same pilgrimage a near necessity for specialists in the art of Raphael and for that matter for all scholars interested in the evolution of style, attitudes, and themes in art during the Italian High Renaissance. In 1778—the year before Voltaire's death—while looking through the vast collection of engravings she had acquired, she came across a set that showed general views and many of the specific details of the Vatican Loggia that Raphael had designed for the first Medici Pope, Leo X. She knew of the Loggia, of course, and may have seen a number of its components as recorded in etchings, engravings, or prints. But now, apparently, in this full set, for the first time she was able to get a clear idea of its grand scale and its amazing diversity of richness. She was fascinated. She wanted to own it. Manifestly it was neither purchasable nor movable. Accordingly she decided to have it duplicated, whole and intact, architecture and all.

The audacity of the idea cannot be measured, but at least some indication of the size of the project can be had from facts and figures. The Loggia is just under 230 feet long, about 16½ feet wide, and is constructed as a series of thirteen bays on pilasters, each section rising to form a vaulted dome 31 feet high—a tremendous surface area of walls, pilasters, and ceilings—all decorated.

From the parquetry floor to the carved doors and marble lintels and gilded moldings, the whole construction comprises a single, enormous work of art, a triumphant unity achieved from utmost variety. The walls are an intricate, fanciful pattern of ornamental grotesques—twining foliage, imaginary creatures, medallions, flowers, cupids, birds, lyres, a medley of odd and charming surprises all interwoven. The fantasies continue in lunettes, architraves, groins, and arches, and even into the ceiling, where one dome contains startling *trompe l'oeil* illusions of soaring columns and classical architectural ensembles that are (apparently) roofless and open to the sky. Framed and accented, as it were, by these pagan splendors and illusionist and manneristic jocularities, fifty-two curves, squares, rectangles, and hexagons in the domes contain frescoes of Biblical characters and scenes. These form a narrative of the Creation, the Fall, and the Redemption, a history of Old and New Testament canons of belief so encompassing that the series—and, incongruously, finally the Loggia—came to be known as Raphael's Bible.

It was simply all this immense intricacy that Catherine wanted duplicated, the parts in exact dimension so that, like an incredible gargantuan jigsaw puzzle, they would all fit with precision when assembled in Petersburg. And, of course, the parts were to be perfect counterparts of the originals in materials, colors, and qualities —above all else, the paintings to be so adept in technique, as "painterly" as the work of Raphael and the greatly gifted assistants, such as Giulio Romano, who actually did most of the brushwork. It was a perfectly eccentric, altogether implausible, and perhaps impossible project. But, as usual, Catherine had not initiated it without very good reason to think it would succeed.

Her ambassador to Rome, Count Reiffenstein, was a man much on the pattern of Prince Golitsyn: a skilled diplomat, a connoisseur of the arts and an art collector on his own account, an intuitive and energetic treasure-hunter, a tireless negotiator, a man of dignity, bearing, and firmness and of circumspection, social adaptability, and charm. She had sent him to Rome several years earlier as ambassador to the Papal States and Holy See, but also —and more to her interests—as head of the Russian Academy there and as her purchasing agent. Over the years he had acquired associations and knowledge which—when added to the power of his client as a ruler and patroness of the arts and letters and to the practically unlimited funds she was willing to supply—opened the ways and found the means to make this preposterous undertaking possible.

The Vatican's permission to copy the Loggia was not difficult to get. Reiffenstein then engaged a leading classicist and painter named Unterberger, noted for his uncanny skill in reproducing paintings of the masters of the Renaissance. Soon Unterberger commanded a small army of expert copyists, artisans, craftsmen, color blenders, and other technicians. This was really a reproduction of a Renaissance *botteghe*—studio, school, workshop, manufactory of arts teeming with assistants and apprentices—such as Raphael himself had used for the Loggia and for most of the actual execution of nearly all his other large subjects. (In fact, members of "the School of Raphael" were both so numerous and so faithful to his style that it is not certain where his own brushwork appears, if at all, in the Loggia; what is certain is that the general design was his and that he supervised the whole work, which was completed the year before his death in 1520.)

Reiffenstein, for his part, became a kind of surrogate Renaissance "Supervisor of the Fabric," supplying funds, expediting, scrutinizing and keeping the remote purchaser, Catherine, informed of problems and progress. The frescoes and other painted parts of the Loggia were copied on canvas; the pieces of canvas —ultimately hundreds of them—were put on keyed and numbered rollers, like scenic wallpaper, and shipped off to Petersburg in batches as they were completed. The last rolls left Rome in 1785. The Unterberger-Reiffenstein *botteghe* closed shop. The work had taken nearly eight years.

Meanwhile, in Petersburg, the structure of the Loggia—the body on which this skin was to be grafted—was also being reproduced: necessarily in exquisite concordance with the original so that the pieces of the puzzle would fit with lapidary precision and appear to the eye to be indivisible.

The Raphael Loggia adjoins the living apartments of the Popes and overlooks the Vatican gardens. Leo X, lavish patron of the arts and intemperate lover of beauty in nature and design, whose most famous (purported) remark was, "Since God has given us the Papacy, let us enjoy it," delighted in strolling the long arcade, surrounded by—literally enveloped by—beauty that lavished his senses and nourished his soul. It was Catherine's fancy (touched, probably, with some private amusement, since as head of the Orthodox Church she was at least tangentially the Pope's counterpart) to install her reproduction of the Loggia in a place that would also, so far as circumstances allowed, reproduce the original's setting and use.

She could not join it directly to her existing private apartments, for these were in her Hermitage, which nestled closely between the Winter Palace and the big art gallery. So she put her fantastic, magnificent trophy along the canal. And here, when finally it was all fitted together, late in her reign, she liked to take her winter morning constitutionals, refreshing herself in the brisk air under the "Raphael Bible," amid the imaginations, sprites, sphinxes, flora, fauna, arcane symbols of Nero's Golden Room and Herculaneum.

Despite all the emphasis on exact replication, there are two differences between the Loggia of the Vatican and the Loggia of the Hermitage. Above the central doorway from the Loggia to the papal apartments, a large lunette displays the Medici family coat of arms and the special insignia of Leo X, in which a Medici crest is surmounted by a display of his symbols of office: orb, scepter, and towering Papal crown. Manifestly it would have been inappropriate, to say the least, for Catherine as the supreme head of Orthodoxy to live with these assertions of Papal authority and display of the Medici escutcheon. The solution to this second difficulty was to replace the Medici arms with those of Raphael's family: a reasonable change and beneficial to Catherine's reputation as a friend of the arts. Catherine's personal emblem replaced that of Leo X. And instead of the Papal symbols—the Russian double eagle.

If Catherine profaned a great work of art by changing part of it to suit herself, she more than made up for this by the second change she made. The Vatican Loggia was open to the weather for years before the arches were filled in with the present protective windows. By then the frescoes had eroded. Now and again they were touched up, and at intervals some were given major restoration, only to fade, crack, flake, peel, and fall away again eventually. And so it went for centuries, with serious and now long since irreversible damage to the original.

Catherine enclosed the Hermitage Loggia from the beginning, as elementary common sense demanded in the Petersburg climate—both to protect the paintings and decorations and to keep the room usable and enjoyable during bad weather.

The Hermitage Loggia is not, of course, a precise rendering of the Raphael original, since by the time the Reiffenstein-Unterberger *botteghe* was set up, the Loggia had existed for more than 250 years. By then more changes had occurred than could be discovered and corrected by scholarly research. However, while the Hermitage Loggia was safe from the vagaries of weather, of touch-up crews and restorers, the Vatican Loggia suffered these perils for still another two centuries—two more centuries for Raphael's designs to blur and lines and colors to go steadily off his intention. The Hermitage Loggia is beyond any doubt much closer to the Vatican original than the Vatican Loggia as now seen.

And so it came about that Catherine made it necessary for those who wish to study Raphael's Vatican Loggia to travel not to Rome and the Vatican, but to Petersburg and the Hermitage.

XXII

The Bamboo Kingdom

IN the year she commissioned the reproduction of the Vatican Loggia, Catherine learned from her ambassador in London, Count Musin-Pushkin, that the heirs of Sir Robert Walpole, the great Whig leader who had been Prime Minister for twenty years in the early part of the century, were in financial trouble and had decided to sell his art collection. It was the finest, deservedly most famous collection in England, among the finest in the world, with a rich diversity of French, English, Italian, Spanish, German, and Dutch works by leading masters. There were some 200 paintings, including no less than 12 Van Dycks and 13 Rubenses. Catherine sent back word at once that she wanted the whole collection. After negotiations lasting two months, Musin-Pushkin got the lot for 36,000 pounds.

The public indignation in England at the news matched that in France at the time of the Crozat purchase. The outcry was sharpened by the fact that Catherine had been taking a lively interest in North America. Wanting to preserve and encourage the trade that Russian merchantmen had been developing there, her government had denounced Britain's naval blockade of its thirteen rebellious colonies and declared Russia's right to send its ships to American ports at will. This declaration of the right of neutrals to trade with belligerents was endorsed by other nations, and ultimately it became a fixed doctrine of international law. At the time it was helping the American rebels and causing rancor in Anglo-Russian relations.

That Catherine would now boldly buy up and carry away a British national treasure was deemed intolerable. There were questions in Parliament. Samuel Johnson launched a campaign to raise enough money from public contributions to redeem the pictures. Musin-Pushkin reported to Catherine that "a large number of the nobility here have concern and regret" about the sale. She was unperturbed. In fact, she felt quite pleased at having consternated the British aristocracy. Writing to Grimm, she declared with satisfaction, "The Walpole pictures are no longer to be had, for the simple reason that your humble servant had already got her claws on them, and will no more let them go than a cat would a mouse."

So once again a treasure ship arrived at the palace quayside and disembarked a fabulous cargo.

The Walpole purchase, the grandest of the whole series of grand coups, reconfirmed her reputation as Europe's greatest collector and as the prime prospective customer for all owners with major collections to liquidate. Within a few months Baron von Grimm sent word that "one of the best and most famous collections in Paris," that of Comte de Baudouin, soon would be available and the comte offered her first choice. Earlier, such news would surely have brought an instant bid from Catherine, for this was indeed an extraordinary prize: a collection of 119 pictures including 2 Rubenses, 4 Van Dycks, and 9 superlative Rembrandts. But Catherine's appetite had been sated for the moment. She expressed only a polite interest.

This caused a peculiar reaction in Baudouin. His willingness to sell to her on favored terms became eagerness, almost insistence. Grimm reported: "The Comte de Baudouin leaves it to your Majesty to decide conditions, timing and all other considerations." Catherine reflected on this a while, then finally wrote back: "It would indeed be discourteous to refuse such a generous offer."

She authorized the purchase, but took Monsieur le Comte at his word and offered a miserable low price. He suggested something more generous. Her reaction was cold. The negotiations went on in a desultory, long-drawn way, kept alive by Grimm, whose vanity was involved, and perhaps not less by Baudouin's intransigence. As the months, then the years, passed, Catherine admitted that she found herself increasingly tempted but that, unfortunately, she was poverty-stricken. Her position was quite pitiable; she was "poor as a church mouse." At last in 1784, five years after the first proffer from Baudouin, she wrote to Grimm:

"The world is a strange place, and the number of happy people very small. I can see that Monsieur le Comte de Baudouin is not going to be happy unless he sells his collection and it appears that I am the one destined to make him happy." The deal was made.

When, a few months later, the new cargo of treasures arrived at the palace quay and Catherine saw what she had acquired, she wrote at once to Grimm: "We are prodigiously delighted. . . ." And two days later she wrote again, in fine humor and with great satisfaction: ". . . the great and important news of the purchase of the Baudouin pictures has made many collectors green with envy."

According to an inventory of the Hermitage collection made the next year, 1785, Catherine now owned 2,658 paintings, all of them at least worthy and good and a great many of them masterpieces of the first rank. The collection was undoubtedly among the largest and best anywhere in Europe. Not since the Augustan Age of Imperial Rome—if then—had there been such an ingathering of the art treasures of foreign lands. As an early historian of Catherine's era, Stassov, remarked with pardonable chauvinistic pride: "The English, the French, the Germans . . . Lord Walpole in London, Crozat in Paris, Count Brühl in Dresden . . . they all imagined that they were collecting only for themselves and their countries, that none of their books or pictures would ever leave their native shores, but . . . something happened which none could predict—their collections lingered for only a short while . . . and then they all were carried into the far north and were landed in such places and became the property of such people as they never could have conjured up in their wildest imagination as the

future possessors . . . magnificent collections, carloads, moving
to St. Petersburg."

Catherine already had two theaters at her disposal: the two
"opera halls," Great and Small, that were included in the vast
reaches of the Winter Palace. But, being part of the palace, they
were part of the official grandeur, dignity, and paraphernalia of
the throne and of the official person, Empress Catherine II. She
wanted a new theater, a Hermitage Theater, as "a refuge for the
. . . pleasures and exercises" of the private, or semiprivate, person
who coexisted with the Empress—the redoubtable individual, the
informal, delighted and delightful hostess who was Catherine.

In every respect the theater was a gemlike success: 500 seats in
the form of a Greek amphitheater. As the architect, Giacomo
Quarenghi, explained: "This theater was built for the private use
of Her Imperial Majesty and the Imperial Court. . . . I selected
the semi-circular form because it gives everyone a good view of the
stage—all the seats are equally distinguished and anyone can sit
wherever he may like. And also, from his seat, no matter where,
every person can see everyone else which, in a full house, creates
a very pleasant effect."

There was nothing resembling a royal box. The only vestigial
sign of one, the only concession Catherine made to her own status,
was that a few seats front and center were set slightly apart. Ordinarily she sat there with her attendants and perhaps some special guests. But this was hardly more than any hostess of the time
might do at a theater party. And these events of hers were, in every
sense, theater parties, as lively and sociable as could be, with the
audience part of the performance. Indeed, fairly often members
of the audience were onstage, displaying their own talents as
amateur actors, dancers, monologuists, musicians.

It was Catherine herself who set the example, not as a per-
former, but as a playwright. She wrote dozens of theater pieces:
skits and novelty bits, parables, monologues, dialogues, and even
a few full-scale plays. Most were topical comedies or satires, and
sometimes she used her fine sense of the absurd and skill in caricature to make political points. But she was a storyteller, too. Her
theatricals, like her memoirs and letters, show her gifts for nar-

ration and character development and the valuable perspectives acquired during the long years when books were her refuge and the salvation of her sanity.

Her appetite for history and her fascination with Russia led her at one point to begin writing a history of Russia, a monumental enterprise that she never managed to carry beyond a few chapters, but from which come the idea and materials for her magnum opus as a playwright. This was a dramatic "history," in Shakespearean style and length, of the Varangian chieftain Oleg, prince of the House of Rurik, who left Novgorod and settled in Kiev, whence he expanded his power all the way from the Baltic to the gates of Constantinople. In short, it was the saga of "the founding of Russia." One could not ask for a more patriotic, romantic, and heroic theme. Catherine's treatment of it was at least as good as most surrogate Shakespeare, and whatever it lacked in dramatic felicities it made up for in audience appeal. A success from opening night, it was still being revived and receiving good notices more than a century later.

But homemade entertainments, even by Catherine, were the exception at the Hermitage Theater. To it she invited leading European performers, ensembles, and directors in a variety of theatrical arts—drama, opera, orchestra, ballet, music hall, and circus. She also used Russia's own theatrical resources, such as they were, and made particular efforts to encourage and develop them. Eventually the theater had its own, largely Russian repertory group, its own opera company, corps de ballet, and orchestra. (Catherine herself was so tone-deaf that music meant little to her and she could not even carry a tune. She and Princess Dashkov, who had the same problem, sometimes entertained friends at more intimate Hermitage gatherings—not in the theater—with caterwauling duets.)

Catherine once described herself as "an aristocrat by profession." She had favorites; she could be persuaded; she could hesitate and seem equivocal. But sooner or later she knew her own mind and imposed her will. In her memorandums to herself, she wrote vignettes of her senior officials and advisers, crediting each for his merits but invariably balancing these with a "but." Thus of Alexander Suvorov, her Inspector General, a hard-driving professional soldier and a military genius, she said: "Suvorov is very loyal to me and has great integrity . . . [but] his rigidity must be curbed in order that he should not go beyond the limits I have prescribed." Others proposed; she disposed.

With her upright carriage, her calm, blue-eyed, level gaze, her poise, and her intelligence, Catherine looked every inch an Empress. So it was all the more striking that within the precincts of her Hermitage she took off her crown and ermine, so to speak, put away her scepter like a commuter stowing an umbrella in the foyer, and insisted on being, and being treated as, a mortal human among other mortals.

At the entrance to the main salon, Pavilion Hall, there was a placard written in her own hand:

> Please be seated wherever you wish.
> Your hostess hates all ceremonies.
> Every guest in her house
> Is free to do as he pleases.

Nearby she posted the "Ten Commandments," also written out in her own hand, governing the behavior of "everybody stepping over the threshold of this door":

1.

Leave your rank outside, the way you leave your hat and especially your sword.

2.

Your Order of Precedence and your arrogance and any other such qualities, whatever they may be—leave them outside the door too.

3.

Be gay—without, however, breaking or spoiling anything.

4.

Sit down, stand up, walk about as you please, regardless of who else is present.

5.

Speak in a moderate voice, not too loudly, so that other people near you will not get headaches.

6.

Discuss anything, argue anything, but without bitterness or hot temper.

7.

Do not groan because of problems, do not yawn or cause yawns, do not inflict boredom or impose burdens on anybody else.

8.

Innocent pranks should be met in the same spirit—what one person starts, others should join in and continue.

9.

Eat well and with pleasure, but drink with moderation so that everyone, on going out the door, will be able to find his own feet.

10.

Do not carry gossip from this room: what enters one ear should go out the other before it can go out through the door.

At the bottom of these Ten Commandments, Catherine wrote the penalties for infractions:

"If anyone should behave contrary to the above rules, then, on the deposition of two witnesses, for each transgression each guilty person will drink a glass of cold water, the ladies not excepted, and read aloud a page of *The Adventures of Telemaque, Son of Ulysses*. Anyone found guilty of these transgressions will learn by heart six lines of the same book.

"And those who are found guilty of ten transgressions will never again be allowed inside the door."

All of Catherine's Petersburg entertainments came to be known as Hermitages regardless of the localities where they took place within the ever-expanding Winter Palace-Hermitage complex. The most formal occasions of state, with many hundreds or even thousands or more dignitaries—the diplomatic corps, senior officials, the great and noble of the realm—were held in the palace. First an opera, usually Italian, in the Great Opera Hall; then, in the State Dining Room, a supper with copious wine and vodka; then, in the Grand Ballroom, dancing, which Catherine opened with a minuet; finally, in the gardens, the Palace Square or perhaps the Neva embankment, spectacular fireworks—glorious and noisy enough to have pleased Peter the Great.

Peter the Great's Universal Joking and Drinking Society, with its travesty of ranks in a make-believe kingdom, had its counterpart in Catherine's Bamboo Kingdom, a nonsense land where the worst crime was to fail to be amusing and amused and the highest rewards were given for the most absurd feats. A hero of the Bamboo court was the German ambassador, Baron von Jourat, whose scalp was astonishingly flexible. It is recorded that the Baron could make his hair move almost down to his eyebrows and thus "also was able to wriggle it, like a wig, to right and left. For this ability he was awarded the rank of captain." Catherine's ability to wriggle her ears and move them up and down was also noted: ". . . the right ear down to the neck . . . but for this she ranked herself only as a lieutenant." Denis Fonvizin, the playwright, was a fine mimic and convulsed everyone with his imitation of Field Marshal Razumovsky and Prince Golitsyn falling into an argument during a game of whist, only to have the game and argument continually interrupted by General Betsky with news and opinions about such state enterprises as schools, the foundling hospital, and pawnshops. Catherine rewarded Fonvizin, too, with a captaincy.

Catherine had complained about the endless cardplaying at Elizabeth's court and maintained she was forced by circumstances to join in and gamble, but in fact she had long since become an avid player. Whist was the usual game at the Hermitage, and a version of it called Boston, a recent import from America, was the fashionable game around the late 1770's. A decade earlier a British ambassador, Lord Cathcart, had explained to his Foreign Office superiors, "Never having been a card player, and having long since ceased to be a dancer, I was obliged to decline the honour proposed to me of making the Empress' party. . . ." He was soon withdrawn. His successor, Sir James Harris (1777–83), a stalwart, younger, and livelier man, handsome and confident, with a thick thatch of prematurely white hair that caused him to be nicknamed the Lion, in 1799 wrote his father a letter worth quoting here on several counts:

"I have the good fortune to have made myself not disagreeable to the Empress. She notices me much more than any of my colleagues; more, indeed, I believe, than any stranger is used to. She admits me to all her parties of cards . . . and a few days ago carried me with only two of her courtiers to a country palace, where she has placed the portraits of all the crowned heads of Europe. We discoursed much on their several merits. . . .

"She calls this place *La Grenouilliere** and it was for it that Wedgwood made, some years ago, a very remarkable service of his ware, on which a green frog was painted. It represented the different country houses and gardens in England. This also we were shown; and this led us to a conversation on English gardening, in which the Empress is a great adept. From this we got to Blackstone, where she soon led me out of my depth; as I believe she would many . . . being most perfectly mistress of our Laws and Constitution. This distinction from the Sovereign insures me the good-will and civilities of her subjects; and, indeed . . . they carry these civilities to a degree of troublesome excess."

Cards, conversation, contortions, charades, fortune-telling, "mind reading," games (even, shades of Catherine's girlhood, blindman's buff), recitals, concerts, plays, recitations, declamations, imitations; also dancing, often the Russian national dances which Catherine adored (at these intimate gatherings she often wore traditional Russian dress); masquerades in the pre-Lenten carnival season and, during the Christmas season, impromptu part singing of carols (Catherine and Dashkov presumably *sotto voce*) and the special fairy tale; small ceremonials and colorful decorations of the Russian Christmas—all these were pleasures of the Bamboo Kingdom, with Catherine as the liveliest and most pleased participant of all.

She would have been the center of attention in any case because of her position (which, rules or no, nobody forgot), but she would have earned not much less, perhaps, on her own merits as a hostess. She was tactful, attentive, unobtrusive, and she had great spontaneity and wit. Baron von Grimm, who of all people was in a position to judge, considered her even more accomplished as a conversationalist than as a correspondent. She had always known how to charm, and years of necessity and experience had taught her how to calculate her effects. In this milieu of her own creation, and over which she exercised exquisitely restrained but

* The Froggery. The site had been marshy and locally known as the frog pond.

complete control, she could be, when it suited her to be, very
nearly irresistible.

And like her Hermitage art galleries and her Hermitage theater,
her delightful Bamboo Kingdom also served other ends than pleasure. History, in many dimensions, was made there.

All the "Hermitages" were a bourse for political news and views,
gossip, malice, intrigues, self-serving (or even, sometimes, selfless)
ambitions, schemes, trades, and deals, innuendoes and subtle invitations, leads and deceptions, understandings and nicely calculated apertures for potential future claims of misunderstandings.
In his six-year tenure as British envoy, Sir James Harris encountered at various Hermitages a great number of scenes and personalities beyond description. His dispatches are laced with such
terms as "incredible," "improper," "imperfect," "supineness,"
"insufficiency," "incompatible," "confusion," "anarchy," and "astonishment"—all of which in fact appear in the first 170 words
of a dispatch dated June 4, 1779, a rate of one confoundment every
seventeen words. His "astonishment" was that the officials of the
Russian government "do not fail in everything they undertake.
That they have not, is evidently the work of chance; a fortuitous
concurrence . . . and, if I may venture to say, a kind of preordina-
tion of good-luck which attends every operation of this Court,
has not only saved it from the most imminent dangers, but raised
it to a degree of greatness and power beyond that which even the
ambition of its Sovereign could ever expect to attain."

As for that ambitious sovereign, Harris plainly was more smitten with her than any ambassador should have allowed himself
to be—or at least to reveal in dispatches. She was a woman of "very
fine parts" who "long before she took the reins of the Empire into
her hands, had prepared her mind to govern," had "then governed systematically, judiciously and with dignity," making "the
seven or eight first years of her reign one of the most brilliant
periods of Russian history." Then, however, she had fallen victim
to bad advisers who had confused her judgment, corrupted her
morals, corroded her dignity, and led her astray into such "connections and impolitic measures" that "there is no hope of her
being reclaimed; unless," he added, "a miraculous gleam of light
breaks in upon her."

XXIII

Potemkin

CATHERINE'S gluttony for art was only one aspect of her gluttony for life. She combined abnormal vital energy with an apparently measureless capacity to be curious, to participate and lead, to enjoy—and to remain dissatisfied. Despite her own prediction that finally she would die "of complacency" she was insatiable. Life was never too much for her; the problem, rather, was time—time to devour it all. She was a grandchild of the Renaissance and inherited its ideal of universality; two centuries earlier she would have been termed a humanist. Two centuries later she might be thought of as an existentialist, for her response to the inexorable passage of moments leading to nonexistence was to be continually and entirely involved. And, since chance and these same qualities had put the resources of a great nation at her personal disposal, her engagement with life continued to be spectacular to the end of her life.

She never stopped collecting: works of art of all sorts and sizes; palaces, pavilions, garden parks; regions, rivers, mountains, nations.

She also collected people. She needed a great many of them

to serve her multitude of needs as Empress and egoist; these formed the bulk of the collection. But she was always searching for those who could give her the human intimacies and love that she craved almost as much as power and glory. Therein, indeed, lay one of the few fissures in a generally seamless, successfully pragmatic personality. The love of power and the power to love and attract love are difficult to reconcile; in the attempt, Catherine fairly often zigzagged unevenly back and forth, in the process creating some of those convolutions that caused Sir James Harris such astonishment.

Yet even the aberrations made sense and served purposes within the general structure of her life, a structure not intact but amazingly strong. Its parts were inseparable—national and international affairs, art, intellect, friendship, love—competing, yet mutually supporting, inextricable except at the expense of the whole and essentially meaningless except in relation to the whole.

Gregory Orlov's reign as her lover lasted about fourteen years (1759–72). In all probability, during the whole time she was faithful to him—a point perhaps not remarkable in itself but decidedly so in view of later developments. During those years she was adamantly and, in a way, rather pathetically proud of him, seldom missing a chance to tell her correspondents of the latest demonstration of his fine qualities or to reward him with new honors for his services to the state. This was an extravagant image which he sometimes even fulfilled. Although his defects of character included selfishness, conceit, and indolence, he had the animal intelligence and the raw courage that made him a hero and had brought him to Catherine's view in the first place. His finest hours came a year before the end.

In 1771 a smallpox epidemic in Moscow brought such scenes of terror, superstitious savagery, and violence that much of the population seemed to have gone berserk. Orlov took command there and restored sanity, less by force of arms—for his troops were hardly less superstitious or less fearful of the plague than the Muscovites—than by the force of his own will, which grew with danger. For his return to Petersburg, Catherine put up a triumphal arch on the Nevsky Prospect blazoned with "To Him Who Saved Moscow from the Plague" and had a medal struck with his portrait and the same legend. In that same year, she gave birth to her third child by Orlov, again having disguised her condition under corsets and full skirts, bearing the infant in secret and turning it over to a wet nurse for care. It was another boy. With three sons, a fresh triumph, and a "wife" who had adored and endured him for thirteen years, Orlov had every reason to think himself a permanent and indispensable partner of the throne.

In 1772, however, Catherine learned that he had been having an affair with his thirteen-year-old cousin, Catherine's own namesake, Catherine Zinovieva, and had seduced her. She had managed to tolerate his other infidelities, but this one sickened her. The day before learning of it she had sent him off to help negotiate peace with the Turks, though with such sweet sorrow as can be read in her letter to a friend in Hamburg: "He must appear to the Turks," she wrote, "as an angel of peace in all his great beauty." To the contrary, as she would hear, he appeared as a vainglorious popinjay in his diamond-studded attire, and his self-importance, arrogance, tactless and interminable demands so offended the proud Turks that he became a major hindrance to the peace treaty, delaying and endangering Catherine's triumph. Thus, he managed almost simultaneously to outrage Catherine's two most essential needs, for power and for love.

This was too much. For the first time he was fully vulnerable to his enemies at court. Rising to the opportunity, Count Nikita Panin gave strong advice, ably assisted by Princess Dashkov and others. They persuaded Catherine to break with him completely and to help her make this break endurable and irrevocable, they encouraged her affection for a strapping young guardsman, Alexander Vasilchikov, who in turn was willing and able. Vasilchikov suddenly was lifted out of his ordinary status and prospects and installed in Orlov's apartment at the Winter Palace (joined to Catherine's, in her small Hermitage, by a secret passageway), given Orlov's official position as adjutant general, and endowed with 100,000 rubles in cash and a salary of 12,000 rubles a month. He also received the wardrobe, jewels, orders, servants, allowances, obeisance, and other sumptuous perquisites of his exalted station.

When news of this reached Orlov, he abandoned the peace conference and rushed back to Petersburg to expel the upstart and bring Catherine to her senses, only to be intercepted as he neared the city and escorted to his fine new summer palace, Gatchina, literally in quarantine. As Catherine explained in the note he was handed, there was an outbreak of smallpox in the south, and for the public good she could not risk his bringing the contagion to Petersburg—a double irony and transparent excuse in view of his recent Moscow performance and the fact that he had been vaccinated.

It was not the public safety but her own, and that of persons near to her, that she was concerned about. "You don't know him!" she told friends. "He is capable of killing me, and of killing the Grand Duke." (Orlov and young Paul disliked each other heartily; also, Paul's death might open the way to the throne for Orlov's son, little Count "Beaverskin" Bobrinsky.) She put Gatchina under heavy military guard. She also took the precautions of posting extra guards at the small Hermitage, where Paul as well as she had private apartments, and at the Winter Palace and of having all the locks changed; for Vasilchikov's apartment she installed double locks. Even so, knowing Orlov's rashness and resourcefulness, she was so nervous that during one masked ball, when a rumor spread that he had arrived in disguise, she ran from the ballroom and took shelter in Count Panin's office.

Meanwhile, courtiers went back and forth between Gatchina and the Hermitage from day to day, sometimes hour to hour, as Orlov strove to reach her for a personal confrontation and Catherine strove to prevent it. Orlov's messages ran a gamut from righteous indignation to tender pledges, from pleading to threats. Catherine's were marked by dignity and restraint along with solicitude and rather motherly—if no longer wifely—affection: She sent him clean socks and linens. She also sent him appeals to reason, and, in mingled order and emphasis, threats (even exile to Ropsha, of all places, where her legal husband, Peter III, had been sent to his doom under Alexis Orlov), flattery, goodwill gifts, accusations, urgings, and demands. (When she asked for the diamond-framed miniature of herself, that unique insignia of his position, he refused to part with the portrait but disdainfully returned the diamonds.) She sent offers of honors and riches if he would promise to stay away from her and from the court entirely for a year. She suggested he travel for his health. He declined with hauteur.

Finally, however, after almost a month of these exchanges, some sort of *modus vivendi* was reached, apparently by oral messages relayed by intermediaries. (Nothing survives in writing.) The quarantine was lifted, the guards left, and Orlov returned to Petersburg and moreover began appearing at court functions. Outwardly composed, Catherine was discomfited and nervous, as he recognized. He responded with sardonic amusement, and he affected not to notice at all that Vasilchikov was attending to the official and unofficial functions that had been his for so many years. He even added tacit insult to Catherine and their former relationship by making friends with Vasilchikov and praising him to other courtiers. This was a grotesque reprise of Peter III's behavior with Poniatowski, though it would be hard to say whether this was a conscious taunt or simply another of the unpremeditated ironies festooning the cyclical patterns of Russian history.

During this initial period, Catherine gave, and Orlov consented to accept, such gifts as few men can have received. She raised him in rank from Count to the rare title of Prince, gave him vast estates from the crown lands and 6,000 serfs to see to them, a cash gift of 100,000 rubles and an annual cash allowance of 150,000 rubles, plus all the extravagantly costly furnishings of the apartments that had been maintained for him as undeclared consort at the Kremlin and other palaces. And since it was just at this time that the Marble Palace was finished, it was then that she gave him 200 paintings. And she ordered (delivery took another six years) the fabulous service of Sèvres porcelain known as the Cameo Service—each item adorned with an antique cameo—which even then cost 250,000 rubles and is of course beyond any price today.

No doubt there was some blackmail involved in all this generosity. The Orlovs, Gregory and Alexis, had not occupied their high positions for the decade since the coup d'état without forming their own party at court, and Catherine had to consider most gravely the stability of the empire and her throne. But far more important, as indicated earlier, when she was in a state of emotional crisis, lavishing emotional symbols in the form of gifts was a way of ventilating and relieving it. She still loved Orlov, and her fear of seeing him had included the fear that she would weaken in the resolution she had made to break with him for good.

Whatever the actual qualities of his replacement, Vasilchikov, they were bound to be diminished by the fact that he was cast by circumstance as an emotional expedient to tide her over what was, after all, the equivalent of a divorce after a long marriage that had been based initially on passionate love and been fulfilled in children and the excitements of uncertainty and challenge. It would seem that within the limits of her nature, she was ridden with feelings of despair and of guilt, with Orlov the beneficiary and Vasilchikov, if not altogether an innocent victim, still a victim.

"It was a random choice," she would write of Vasilchikov later, "made out of desperation. I was more heartbroken at this time than I can say." He was attentive, dutiful, decorative, competent, well meaning, and in general a worthy young man. She found him increasingly, at last unendurably, boring. After two years he was retired with large rewards for his services and good intentions: the rewards included a fortune in cash, paintings, and many objets d'art and a great country estate with a palace built for him, and to this he was, in effect, exiled.

Vasilchikov was the first but not the last to be sent off to pasture in this way. His own views of his situation while with Catherine are worth recording: "I was nothing more to her," he wrote, "than a kind of male cocotte, and I was treated as such. If I made a request for myself or anyone else, she did not reply, but the next day I found a banknote for several thousand rubles in my pocket. She never condescended to discuss with me any matters that lay close to my heart."

> From 'ere first I saw thee
> I thought of thee alone.
> Thy lovely eyes enthralled me
> I trembled to be gone:
> Knowing thy charms have such sweet powers
> To chain all hearts with garland flowers.
>
> Ah Heaven! what torment to love thee
> Silently
> Knowing bliss can never be.

Cruel Gods!
Why did you give her such charms
And then exalt her so high?
So far beyond reach of my arms
Why give me this destiny?
To love her, and her alone.
Her whose sacred name ne'er my lips will part;
Whose sacred image ne'er will leave my heart.
—Lyrics of a song by Gregory Potemkin,
addressed to Catherine.

"My Cossack, heart of my heart, my golden pheasant . . . my peacock, dearest pigeon, wolf-bird, tiger, lion of the jungle . . . my little heart, darling, dear, dearest doll, dear toy . . . my beauty, my marble beauty . . . my darling like no king on earth . . . I love you as I love my soul . . . I belong to you in every possible way" are some of the endearments in Catherine's letters to Potemkin.

As the hapless Vasilchikov exited, laden with rubles and confusions, simultaneously Gregory Potemkin entered like a demigod exuding natural force and trailing clouds of destiny. The simile is not so far-fetched, for in many ways Potemkin was a man beyond normal human measures. His appetite for life was, if possible, even more gluttonous than Catherine's. He gorged himself on the pleasures and challenges of the world. At the same time he was a mystic, a visionary who had the power found in the greatest saints and sinners of making his visions seem true to others and thus, fairly often, even become true. He was troubadour, satyr, warrior, organizer, statesman, spoiled priest, a man overburdened with talents and eccentric charm. He was the kind of man who leaves legends.

As the endearments addressed to him quoted above may suggest, Catherine was thoroughly and somewhat giddily in love with him. Further, she honored and respected him, being convinced with good reason that his mind, judgment, and general capacities were equal to her own. For many years, during most of the latter half of her reign, he was her close adviser and, in effect, her collaborator, sharing in the rule of Russia. Loving and honoring, she was even known on occasion to obey him. All this was unprecedented. His status was different from that of any of her other lovers. And indeed it is more than probable that she was secretly married to him.

Potemkin was born in a little town near Smolensk in 1739. Smolensk was one of the oldest of Russian cities and in the time of Old Russia had been one of the richest. It lies on the upper course of the Dnieper River, on high, defensible cliffs, a natural junction point on the great trade route from the Baltic Sea to the Black Sea. Potemkin's forebears and relatives were ardently Russian and ardently Orthodox, which led the males to careers in the military and the church. Gregory's father was an army captain; an uncle rose to colonel, retired, and became a monk.

In all this lay seminal elements of Potemkin's strong-willed, restless, mystical, impulsive, voracious, romantic, visionary, contradictory character. In boyhood, he decided to be a monk and at the age of about twelve entered a monastery, where he spent two years in studies. Then he went to the University of Moscow as one of its first students, only to be expelled after two more years for "systematic failure to attend lectures." He joined the Horse Guards, a unit of the Imperial Guards. Thus he came to Petersburg, where in due course he became a friend of the Orlov brothers and an early recruit in their conspiracy to depose Peter III and put Catherine on the throne.

He and Catherine first met face to face on that first evening of the coup as she prepared to lead the Guards to Peterhof. She was in a borrowed uniform and was having trouble with the knotted sash that held her sword and scabbard in place. Waiting nearby and seeing this, Potemkin impulsively rode to her side and gave her his own sword knot. He remained close to her during the ride through the June white night, and it was amid all the beauty, drama, risk, and excitement of this scene that he fell in love with her. Though Catherine's mind was filled with many things, and though she was in love with Gregory Orlov, Potemkin's peculiar magnetism had already begun to work, and his image stayed in her memory.

He was then twenty-three, ten years younger than she—very tall, big of frame and heavily muscled. He had black curly hair that framed his face in ringlets, flashing dark eyes, a somewhat aquiline nose, wide cheekbones, a sensuous mouth, and a dark complexion, so that his countenance suggested an intermingling of Europe and Asia. In the letter Catherine wrote to Poniatowski about the coup, it is notable that among the scores of Guards officers involved the only ones she singled out for special praise, besides the Orlov brothers en masse, were Lieutenant Khitrov, the man who would later lead the conspiracy that prevented her from marrying Gregory Orlov, and Sergeant Potemkin. Both, she wrote, had "displayed discernment, courage, and action."

Afterward Potemkin was among the guardsmen assigned to Ropsha, Peter III's way-station prison, and again in an oddly prescient way he figured in correspondence. Alexis Orlov's first letter to Catherine, besides telling her that the captive Czar—"The Monster"—was well, said that a special bonus had been distributed to all the custodians "except Sergeant Potemkin, who wants to serve without pay." (It should be noted that Potemkin apparently had nothing to do with Peter III's death in Ropsha.)

When Catherine was crowned six months later in Moscow and distributed honors to her supporters, there was again special notice for Potemkin. She gave him 10,000 rubles, an estate with 400 serfs, and a double advancement in rank. Most of the guardsmen in the conspiracy were raised one grade. When Potemkin's promotion order came to her for signature, it raised him from sergeant to ensign; the order still survives and shows that she personally crossed out "ensign" and wrote in "lieutenant."

She heard about him often from Gregory and Alexis Orlov, who considered him a fully kindred spirit, a drinking, gambling, wenching, robust, reckless figure of a young guardsman, and were delighted by his ready wit and humorous antics. He said and did surprising things. He was a wonderful mimic, with the effrontery, timing, intuition, and presence of a born actor. One evening they brought him along to one of Catherine's small Hermitage parties. She asked him to do one of his imitations. On impulse, and with supreme impertinence, he imitated Catherine's own voice speaking Russian with her German accent. Catherine was startled; then she laughed; she was enchanted. Lieutenant Potemkin henceforth was among the most frequent guests at her intimate Hermitage gatherings.

As Catherine's fondness and admiration for him increased, the Orlov brothers became jealous. According to one story they invited him to Alexis' palace, provoked a quarrel, and, well prepared, beat him so badly that he had to be carried away and was left permanently blind in his right eye. Another version is that during a game of billiards at the Hermitage, Alexis found a pretext to become enraged and lanced a cue at him, striking him in the eye. (Still another version, equally plausible, is that the damage was done by a neglected abscess.) In any case, the eye was lost, and in court repartee, abetted by the now venomously hostile Orlovs, Potemkin was nicknamed the Cyclops.

The misfortune crushed him. Under his amusing talents there were deep streaks of pessimism and melancholy. If his enthusiasms were boundless, so were his despairs. His mystical asceticism now, for the first of several times in his adulthood, drove him to renounce the world and revert to his boyhood dream of becoming a monk. He left Petersburg and entered a monastery. And there he might very well have stayed except for Catherine, who wrote him friendly notes and let her interest in his welfare be known. He decided after a year and a half to return to the court. Catherine gave him jobs that suited his interests and, at the same time, seemed designed to wean him progressively from heavenly to earthly preoccupations: Successively he was an official of the Holy Synod, member of the Commission on Civil and Religious Affairs, "Protector"—more accurately, supervisor—of the Tatar regions and other Asian nations and remnants that had been enfolded in the Russian Empire, and finally chamberlain, or executive manager, of the court. With the Turkish War, the metamorphosis, or restoration, was completed; he became a soldier again.

With a letter from Catherine to her chief commander, General Peter Rumiantsev, to smooth the way, but also by his conspicuous bravery (although the sound of gunfire made him tremble and sweat) and fiery qualities of leadership, he rose rapidly. Within four years he was a lieutenant general. By then it was 1773: Gregory Orlov had been deposed and replaced by the stopgap Vasilchikov, and Catherine, desperately bored, was wondering what measures to take. She and Potemkin had been in correspondence during all his time away. Now she wrote a letter so filled with compliments that he could hardly fail to see that she felt more than friendly toward him. She ended it with: "As I desire to keep men about who are zealous, brave, intelligent and discriminating, I beg you do not waste time wondering to what end this has been written. I can answer you that it is to give you some confirmation of my regard for you, since I am, as always, your well-wisher, Catherine."

Potemkin lost no time in getting to Petersburg. Unaccountably, he seemed completely unaware that it was not his mortal enemy Gregory Orlov that he had a chance to replace but Vasilchikov. When he saw the latter in all his shining, simple-minded handsomeness and realized that *this* was Catherine's adjutant, he fell into black despair. Again he forsook the world and entered a monastery.

Catherine was perplexed but, as usual, undaunted and not lacking in resources. She very soon learned his whereabouts and sent her chief lady-in-waiting and close confidante, Countess Bruce, to make certain, first, that Potemkin wanted to be invited from the cloister, and second, to make it delicately but unmistakably clear that everything he wanted, she wanted also. The air was cleared. Vasilchikov was sent away; Potemkin came to stay.

He was thirty-five by then, and the years since that white night in June had not served him well. Soldiering in the field had roughened him; drinking and gluttony had blotched his skin and filled out his big frame to massiveness. To the disfigurement of his blind eye, the turmoil of his character had added a spasmodic facial tic. He hated being stared at and was acutely aware of seeming strange to others. His tremendous physical energy was still impervious to debauchery. He still had his restlessness, obsessive and visionary ambition, ferocity as well as gentleness of manner, a quick and violent temper. When one adds to this list his general dishevelment, disregard for amenities, undisciplined carnality, admiration for learning and for the arts, a capacity for contrition and idealism, a great leaning toward sentiment, and a great need to be loved, the total image is in many ways reminiscent of Peter the Great.

And knowing Catherine's feelings about Peter—how much she felt herself to be his true successor, how much she revered him, how much, indeed, she would have liked to be like him had she been a man—one may find insights into her devotion to Potemkin, her earnest efforts to please and, as it sometimes seemed, to be worthy of him. Undoubtedly he adored her, but for that reason he was possessive, jealous of her attentions, jealous of the men in her past. As in the cases of Peter I and Elizabeth, her love affairs had been metamorphosed in folk sayings and in the court gossip of Europe; she was blamed, or credited, according to preference, as a wanton who had entertained galleries of men. It is evident that Potemkin heard some of these stories and was tortured by them. Having in effect seduced him, Catherine now found it essential to reassure him that this was not her custom. Sometime during 1774 she wrote him what she called "A Frank Confession":

"Maria Choglokova could see that there was nothing more between us [her and Grand Duke Peter] than there had been before our marriage. But as she was often being scolded by the Empress Elizabeth for doing nothing about the situation, she found nothing better than to offer both parties a choice, according to their wish, among the persons she had in mind. On the one hand, the widow Groot was chosen, who is now married to Artillery Lieutenant-General Miller, and on the other S.S. [Serge Saltikov]; the latter because of his obvious inclination and the advice of Maman [Empress Elizabeth], driven to this by dire necessity. Two years later S.S. was sent away as Ambassador, having behaved indiscreetly, and Choglokova was unable to keep him at the big Court. A year passed in great grief and then came the present King of P. [Stanislaus Poniatowski]. We took no notice of him to begin with, but other kind people, with their puerile gossip, forced us to take into account that he existed, that his eyes were of unparalleled beauty, and that he turned them (though they were so myopic that they could not see further than his nose) more often in one direction than in another. This one was both loving and loved from 1755 till 1761 including an absence of three years, that is from 1758, and then the repeated entreaties of Prince G.O. [Gregory Orlov] whom kind people again brought to our attention, changed my state of mind.

"This one would have remained forever had he not been the

first to tire; I learnt this on the day of his departure to the Congress [the peace conference with the Turks] from Tsarskoe Selo and simply decided that I could no longer trust him, a thought that hurt me cruelly and forced me, from desperation, to take a step which I deplore to this day more than I can say, *especially at the moments when other people usually feel happy.* All caresses provoke nothing in me but tears, so that I believe I have never cried since my birth as I have in these eighteen months [her time with Vasilchikov]. I thought at first that I would get accustomed to the situation but things grew worse and worse; on the other side, they sulked sometimes for three months and to tell the truth I was never happier than when they got angry and left me in peace, as the caresses only made me cry. . . .

"Now, Sir Hero, after this confession, may I hope that I will receive absolution for my sins; as you will be pleased to see, there is no question of fifteen but only of one-third of that figure of which the first occurred unwillingly and the fourth in despair, which cannot be counted as indulgence; as to the other three, God is my witness that it was not through wantonness, for which I have no leanings, and had I been destined as a young woman to get a husband whom I could have loved, I would have never changed towards him. The trouble is that my heart is loath to remain even one hour without love; it is said that human vices are often concealed under the cloak of kindness and it is possible that such a disposition of the heart is more of a vice than a virtue, but I ought not to write this to you, for you might stop loving me or refuse to go to the Army fearing I should forget you, but I do not think I could do anything so foolish, and if you wish to keep me forever, show me as much friendship as affection, and continue to love me and to tell me the truth."

The "Frank Confession," even if not wholly frank nor a whole confession, manifestly was a painful thing for Catherine to write. One almost feels her wincing as she tries to find the words to indicate what she does not like to believe has happened and wants Potemkin to forget. Certainly there is no trace of the Empress in it; this was a woman writing an apology and a plea—an almost humble plea for love, affection, friendship, and trust.

Potemkin accepted it with dignity and tenderness, sending in reply this short note, which Catherine charmingly and lovingly "annotated." Her comments are printed in italics:

"Allow me, my dearest, to say these last words to end our 'row.' Do not be surprised that I am so anxious about our love. Apart from the innumerable gifts you have bestowed on me, you have given me your heart.

I allow.
The sooner the better.
Do not be anxious.
When you wash your hands one rubs the other.

"I wish to be preferred to all the former ones, to make you understand that no one has ever loved you as much as I, and as I am the work of your hands, I wish that my repose should also be the work of your hands; that you should find joy in being kind to me, that you should try everything for my consolation and find consolation in me for the great work you have to accomplish, because of your high calling."

You are and will be this forever.
I can see it and do believe it. My heart is happy.
My primary joy.

It will come of its own accord.
Let the mind rest in order that the feelings should be free, they are all love, they themselves will find the best path.
The end of our quarrel.
Amen.

Not long afterward, in the fall or early winter of 1774, they were (almost certainly) married secretly in Petersburg in the Church of St. Samson.

XXIV

The Greek Project

IN July of that same year, 1774, there was a new peace conference with the Turks, at a town on the Danube deep in Turkish territory called Kuchuk Kainarji. It was Potemkin who now spoke for Russia as Catherine's personal representative.

It was his first appearance in an arena of international politics. There could not have been a more important or a more auspicious debut, for he proved to have an extraordinary talent for psychological warfare and a shrewd gambler's feel for the main chance. He got the peace treaty quickly. Even though the terms required some painful concessions, the treaty on the whole awarded a spectacular triumph to Catherine, and it symbolized a great landmark for Russia—the restoration of the Dnieper trade route. It was a diplomatic victory comparable to the greatest military victories, and Catherine was more than ready to applaud Potemkin's performance. "Ah," she wrote to her friend Baron von Grimm, "what a good head the man has! He has had a greater share in this peace than any other man, and this intelligent creature," she added fondly, "is as amusing as the devil!"

She hung Potemkin's barrel chest with decorations, put him on her Council of State, made him Minister of War and soon, as Count Panin's health began to fail, made him acting Foreign Minister—and gave him far more leeway than she had ever given Panin. Thus, in a very short time Gregory Potemkin—Catherine's "Grisha," "my little dove, my golden pheasant, heart of my heart" —had become the most powerful man and the second most powerful person in all the Russias.

Potemkin extracted from this situation everything it had to offer. He had a luxurious wardrobe and many uniforms. Sometimes he wore all his medals and went about as marvelous as a rainbow. More often he roamed the Hermitage and Winter Palace, received visitors, visited Catherine, reclined in indolent ease among the Hermitage Rubenses and Rembrandts and Aubussons clad in a dressing gown or a loose, monkish khalat, often rather dirty, his hair tousled and his feet sandaled or bare, his form vast and unkempt, disdaining not only the formalities of court life, but the opinions of ambassadors, palace servants, and, for that matter, his immaculate, punctual, abstemious, adoring, and disconcerted royal mistress-wife.

He worshiped her. Sometimes he literally knelt before her as she sat, framing her face in his hands, staring at her, stroking her cheeks, touching her hair, telling her in words poetic and sacerdotal—or without speaking, by touch and manner—how much he loved her. He sent her poems, entertained her and made her laugh beyond control, twitted her, defended her, and gave her presents—nothing like an "Orlov Diamond" that anyone sufficiently rich (by her bounty) could have bought, but unexpected and delightful things, surprises that could only have been thought of by loving observation and the intuitions of love: a basket of ripe cherries at the New Year; a whole fresh green-leaved heavy-laden vine of sweet Crimean grapes; a dancer brought from Paris to perform for her; a hamperful of Italian roses in midwinter. He accepted presents from her—ultimately worth many millions of rubles in cash or kind—in the same spirit, with the greatest pleasure and appreciation, while always remaining master of her house.

Catherine was continually amazed by him. She had understood the other men in her life—Peter III, "S.S.," "the present King of P.," "Prince G.O.," and of course the recent Vasilchikov—well enough and finally all too well, but Potemkin was a fascinating, exasperating, and endlessly challenging riddle. After the first ecstasies they began to have disagreements. Catherine, who had trained herself so well to keep her outer composure that the French ambassador, her admirer, the Comte Louis Philippe de Ségur, nicknamed her the Imperturbable, fairly often wept into her pillow. Where there were serious arguments, Potemkin punished her in the worst way—by ignoring her.

He would have died for her as Empress, but when in his opinion she behaved inappropriately toward him as a woman, he was capable of locking the door to his apartment and keeping it locked until she made amends. One time when she wrote him a peace-seeking note, his reply was a blank piece of paper. To that she answered: "It is not the first of April, that you should send me a blank page. Perhaps you had a bad dream, or perhaps you wish to make sure you do not spoil me too utterly. But since I do not understand your moods, I do not understand the meaning of your silence. Yet I am full of tenderness for you, you Muscovite, Cossack, Pugachev, tomcat, peacock, raging lion!" And later on, understanding that she never would understand him, she wrote: "You simply like quarreling. You preach to me that we should live in perfect harmony and have no secrets from one another, and in the same breath you find some new bone of contention, for tranquillity is a condition unacceptable to your nature."

They continued to love each other anyway and, moreover, were the dearest and most devoted and the most understanding and forgiving of friends. Their marriage certainly was not made in heaven, but they did seem made for each other. And this was so in one particular above all: Both had the same obsessive vision— one so big that they could lose their disagreements in it, their lovers' jealousies, and even in a sense their monumental egos. This was the "Grand Design" for Russia or, as they began to call it, the Greek Project.

The "Project" was to be achieved in two closely connected phases. The first aimed at gathering into Russia all the northern Black Sea coast and all lands along and above it, from the Caucasus to the mouth of the Danube. Thus there would be reclaimed the outermost boundaries of the territories that once had been under the hegemony of Kievan Russia. The Tatar invasion would at last be entirely undone. From this economic and military base, the second phase would aim at expelling the Turks from the rest of the Black Sea regions and from Europe and reincarnating the Byzantine Empire. Its capital would be at Constantinople as before. History would be replayed in reverse: Byzantium had brought Christian civilization to Russia; Russia would return Christian civilization to the reborn Byzantium.

Implicit was a third phase, undefined but with possibilities nearly limitless. The Russian Empire and a reborn Byzantine Empire would together have resources so strategic and advantageous that they would be able to dominate southern Europe and perhaps the routes through Asia to India and China. This would greatly enhance Russian prosperity, Russian power, and Russian prestige in the world. Ultimately the territorial expansion of Russia to the East would be expedited. Indeed, it was easy to imagine that someday Russia could secure a dominant position in all Eurasia and, by logical extension, in the Americas as well. Thus, Russia would become a world empire comparable to, but far vaster, richer, stronger than Alexandrine Greece and the Imperial Rome of Augustus and the Byzantium of Constantine.

Both Catherine and Potemkin had been nursing these ideas in one preliminary form or another for a long time.

Potemkin's boyhood in Smolensk made the great Dnieper River and its legends of Old Russia a vital part of his life. His early and abiding reverence for the Orthodox Church led him to desire to extend its Byzantine heritage. His years in the Turkish War, where the landscapes and artifacts and military maps spoke to his receptive mind of Greeks, Scythians, Kievan Russians, Byzantines, Tatars, and the endless to-and-fro of peoples and tides of history, and finally, his personal confrontation at Kuchuk Kainarji with the Turks, the last incumbent conquerors, imbued in him a sense of their encroaching decadence and essential vulnerability.

As for Catherine, she had applied herself to the history of Russia ever since she came as a fourteen-year-old to marry the royal heir. Further, she had helped fill the dead years as Grand Duchess by immersing herself in Greco-Roman and world history, in political philosophy and the arts and crafts of political maneuver. Most important, there was her reverence for Peter the Great, who had begun his career by fighting the Turks for access to the Black Sea. The Petrine legacy is found succinctly in one of Catherine's little private memorandums to herself: "To join the Caspian Sea with the Black Sea and link both of these with the North Sea." The latter point implied Russian domination of the Baltic and of Scandinavia. "To allow commerce from China and Oriental India to pass through Tartary would mean elevating the Empire to a greatness far above other Asiatic and European empires. What could resist the unlimited power of an autocratic prince ruling a bellicose people?"

So in the autumn of 1774 it appeared that Potemkin's special and largest role would be that of viceroy of the southern lands—the lower Ukraine and all the territories newly reclaimed from the Turks.

To this ancient region, where the prehistory of Russia had been developing for 1,000 years or more before the emergence even of Old Russia, it pleased Catherine and Potemkin to apply the term "New Russia." The analogy was to those Western European colonial aggregates—"New England," "New France," "New Spain," "New Holland"—which Russia had come to the world scene too late to acquire in the Americas or the Indies. It was actually a reasonable comparison. These lands of "New Russia," potentially very rich, were essentially still virgin, the perennial habitat of primitive nomads except for a few places such as the Greek and Byzantine settlements along the seacoast and those of the Kievan Russians along the rivers. New Russia presented many of the same challenges, opportunities, and excitements as the colonial regions, and the same implicit inspiring visions of a fresh start that could lead to a new and far better society.

Potemkin was appointed military governor and governor-general, with practically unlimited powers to pacify the New Russia and make it bloom as a new Eden, while at the same time, in an unannounced but vital ancillary move, to subvert the recent treaty and prepare ways and means for gathering in the rest of the Black Sea northern littoral. First this meant the Crimea.

This large peninsula—about the size of modern Belgium or the state of Maryland in the United States—dominates all the central and northern reaches of the Black Sea and all the important river mouths by reason of its geography. It had been a natural target for countless invaders, but it had a formidable natural defense against land armies in being joined to the mainland by an isthmus so narrow—only 5 to 10 miles wide—that militarily it was almost a causeway that could readily be blocked to entrap a foe. Cimmerians, Scythians, Goths, and Byzantines had controlled the Crimean redoubt in their times. Then it became part of Kievan Russia, then passed to the Tatars. In 1475, the Crimean khanate yielded suzerainty to Turkey and thereby became even more meddlesome in relations with Russia. But now, by the treaty terms, the Tatar Crimea was detached from Turkish suzerainty and made an independent state.

This state, without the shelter of Turkish power, exposed to the enveloping pressures of Russian power, would sooner or later predictably wither away and become a Russian appendage. In Catherine and Potemkin's design, this process would be too slow. Their aim was the destruction of the khanate and outright annexation of the Crimea—soon. An overt move, such as military invasion and occupation, would provoke the Turks to renew the war. Hence the plan—which Potemkin proposed, and which he would execute —called for the erosion of the khanate by bribery, infiltration of spies and *agents provocateurs*, the nurturing of factionalism and rivalries—all the while cultivating the Khan's friendship so that in despair and gratitude he would call on Russia to intervene in his tattered domain. Russian troops and authorities would arrive not as invaders but as saviors.

It was an extremely promising plan—and, of course, it had been an effective one from the times of Tacitus. But to Catherine and Potemkin it presented a serious penalty. Catherine and Potemkin would be separated by long distances and for long periods of time: she bound to be mainly at the Petersburg seat of government, he mainly in the Black Sea region a thousand or so road miles away, a hard fortnight's journey in the best weather, often much longer, sometimes impossible. He could visit Petersburg perhaps once or twice a year.

They were devoted to each other. They were also devoted to the Greek Project. Potemkin had already shown how tormented he could be by jealousy. She had already said in her "Frank Confession": "The trouble is that my heart is loath to remain even an hour without love." Could there be any answer to such a compound dilemma?

Evidently there could be. In the latter part of 1775, before Potemkin had gone south but while he was deep in preparations, Catherine acquired a new adjutant general, Peter Zavadovsky. He had been one of her private secretaries. He was twenty years old, a personable and charming young man with a good mind (in later years he served Catherine's grandson, Alexander I, as Minister of Education) and a fine physique.

The court and the diplomatic corps were stunned by Potemkin's sudden fall from favor. Then they were bewildered; for except in one or two particulars, such as that young Zavadovsky now escorted Catherine to her private apartment at the end of Hermitage evenings, nothing seemed to have changed. Potemkin went on living in his rooms in the Winter Palace and was as much present and in the middle of things at the Hermitage. He and Catherine were no less affectionate, and she was no less respectful of his opinions or less interested in securing his advice in matters of state. There was no strain, no sign of jealousy. In fact, Potemkin's attitude toward Peter Zavadovsky was fond, cheerful, and companionable, like that of a pleased uncle toward a worthy nephew.

Early in 1776, Potemkin went south to take up his active viceroyalty of New Russia. He was gone for a year, during which he and Catherine were in constant correspondence. Their letters are full of warmth and affection and exhibit the candor of mutual respect and understanding. Peter Zavadovsky's name crops up now and then but only casually. Several times Catherine mentions that he had asked to be remembered to Potemkin and sends his greetings.

Soon after Potemkin's return, however, he found something objectionable in Zavadovsky's attitude and complained about him to Catherine. Before long the young man was retired with honors and riches. The new adjutant general, Simon Zorich, was about the same age and had in general the same set of qualifications: he was tall, handsome, and well formed; he was polite, pleasant, and literate (later on he founded a boys' school); and Potemkin had a fond and easy relationship with him. Again Potemkin returned to his duties in the far south and was gone for the better part of a year.

Zorich's tenure was as insecure at Zavadovsky's. He was replaced —suitably rewarded—in 1777 by an exceptionally handsome sergeant of the Household Guards, Ivan Rimsky-Korsakov, whose term lasted two years. He was succeeded by a young officer of the Horse Guards, Alexander Lanskoy, who remained in office until he died four years later. His successor was named Ermolov, also a Guards officer. He proved to be vain and foolish, behaving toward Potemkin as if he considered himself the equal of anyone. Potemkin denounced him publicly to Catherine, with the result that he was sacked at once and the job given to another Guards officer, Alexander Dmitriev-Mamanov.

Until this bizarre Changing of the Guards began, Catherine's reputation, if far from stainless, had seemed to the aristocratic and intellectual society of Europe more exotic than sinful. Her affairs with Serge Saltikov *et seq.*, and even her reputed consent to the murder of Peter III, could be discounted or justified or even turned to her account, as Voltaire had done by his witty rejoinders on her behalf. The very size of her achievements made her errors easy to overlook. Moreover, as Sir James Harris remarked, "Her Court [was] conducted with the greatest dignity and exterior decorum," and the eighteenth century tolerated private sin so long as public amenities were preserved. But with the all-too-transparent successive appointments of handsome, stalwart, young *vremeinchick* ("the man of the moment") even her hardiest admirers were unsettled. Rumor had it that her ladies-in-waiting acted as "testers"—*les éprouveuses*—of these young men's virility before Catherine accepted them.

Catherine—the "Imperturbable"—never indicated by a flicker of an eye that she considered the arrangements unusual or that others had any reason to think so. In public, the adjutant general of the moment behaved and was treated as an equerry. He was someone to accompany her, alertly and respectfully attentive to her wishes, as she proceeded through her rigorous days, his strong right arm always ready to escort her at court and into carriages and to dinner and to her chair at the Hermitage Theater. In short, he was the kind of functionary any widowed, middle-aged, and very busy Empress would need near at hand. In her correspondence with friends abroad, such as Baron von Grimm, her position was that these young men were so fine and fair and altogether extraordinary that she, as a benevolent ruler moved by patriotism and humanity, as an older woman interested in the education of the young, as a mother with a maternal interest in young men of her own son's generation, as a philosopher with a neo-Platonist's reverence for the Ideal and its approximations wherever by good fortune found and apprehended—she, in all these capacities was bound in good conscience and by natural affection to give them opportunity to advance, to develop as her protégés.

Of Rimsky-Korsakov, for instance, she wrote Grimm: "You ask me whether I am in love with him? What a word to use when speaking of 'Pyrrhus, the King of Epirus'! Wonder and exaltation are called forth by this masterpiece of creation. He is the despair of painters, the unrealized dreams of sculptors. He makes no gesture, no movement, that is not graceful and noble. He sends out warmth like the sun; he is radiant; he delights in all sounds of harmony; he is the personification of every precious gift with which nature in an orgy of prodigality had endowed a single human being. . . ."

At the death of Rimsky-Korsakov's successor, Alexander Lanskoy, she wrote to Grimm: "A deep affliction has overwhelmed me, and my whole happiness has fled. I thought that I should die after the irreparable loss of my best friend. I educated this young man; he was gentle, tractable, grateful, and I hoped he would be the support of my old age. . . . I have become a desperate, monosyllabic creature. . . . I drag myself about, like a shadow. . . . I cannot set eyes on a human face without the tears choking my words."

Still, after a period of mourning for Lanskoy, lasting almost a year, there was young Yermolov, followed soon by young Dmietriev-Mamanov. Of the latter—in the manner of an understanding *babushka* describing a sweet, manly child—she wrote to Grimm: "We are as clever as the very devil . . . we adore music . . . we hide our fondness for poetry as though it were a crime."

Surely there was more in these relationships than mere "wantonness, for which I have no leanings"—her phrase in the "Frank

Confession." But in presenting herself to Grimm and others in the worthy role of kindly benefactress, it would seem that Catherine, the great actress, playwright of her own drama, propagandist for her own wishes, managed finally to deceive even herself, enough, at any rate, that in her own mind she could play the role successfully most of the time and live in uneasy peace with her own conscience. There is something precognitive in those words of her "Frank Confession": "It is said that human vices are often concealed under the cloak of kindness. . . ."

Nevertheless, she deceived few at Petersburg and few, if any, in other courts. The scandal grew. And as the years passed and Catherine herself grew older while the adjutants general always stayed young (their average age at appointment was twenty-three) a quality of unnaturalness, then depravity, and finally the grotesque colored the scandal. It was during these years that she began to be known by such terms as "the Messalina of the North" which were to fix her name in history as an archetype of licentiousness.

Through all this she was, in her fashion, faithful to Potemkin, while he, with numerous liaisons, remained devoted to her. She had written in 1774: ". . . if you wish to keep me forever, show me as much friendship as affection, and continue to love me. . . ." By mid-1779—that is, when Zavadovsky, Zorich, and Rimsky-Korsakov had come and gone and Lanskoy was adjutant—Sir James Harris reported to London: "Prince Potemkin rules her with an absolute sway; thoroughly acquainted with her weaknesses, her desires, and her passions, he operates on them, and makes them operate as he pleases." That, of course, was hyperbole and misconstrued the situation, but it is a measure of Potemkin's visible status that to an able diplomatic observer he seemed to rule the Empress.

Harris continued in the same report: "Prince Potemkin pays little regard to the politics on the West of Russia; his mind is continually occupied with the idea of raising an Empire in the East: he has so far infected the Empress with these sentiments that . . . the present reigning idea (and it carries away all others) is the establishing of [this] Empire. . . . The Empress discoursed a long while with me the other day on the ancient Greeks; of their alacrity and the superiority of their genius, and of the same character still being extant in the modern ones; and of the possibility of their again becoming the first people, if properly assisted and seconded. . . ."

By mid-1782 the plans for the Greek Project, carefully nurtured by Potemkin, were far advanced; it was almost time to occupy the Crimea and accordingly time to secure the benevolent neutrality of such great powers as England, which might otherwise be alarmed by this new expansion of Russian power and support the inevitable protests of the Turks. Harris had been trying, without success, to negotiate a new Anglo-Russian treaty, with a principal aim of undoing the League of Armed Neutrality which was impeding England's efforts to subdue the stubborn American colonies. He had cultivated Potemkin's friendship, and Catherine's, and had received such oscillating signs of encouragement and discouragement from both that he had written to Lord Stormont, the Foreign Secretary: "I never believe anything here till it has actually taken place . . . it is not to be wondered that [Russian foreign policy] operations and conduct are so incomprehensible to your Lordship, when I, who am on the spot, and whose attention is turned on that single object, am in a perpetual puzzle. . . ."

Now, however, after fresh oscillations and puzzlements beyond telling, he reported some marvelous news. Potemkin had come back to Petersburg from a trip to the south (where, as Harris could not know, he had been making final arrangements for the subversion and occupation of the Crimea) "and immediately wrote me, in his own hand, the following concise, but expressive, note: 'Long live Great Britain. . . . I have arrived, my dear friend Harris; write me at once and tell me when I may see you.' I was with him in an instant, and, after hearing from him the most friendly and cordial assurances . . . I entered with him on business. . . . I succeeded beyond my expectations; he entered warmly into my ideas, joined issue in all I said, and promised me immediate and effectual support. I passed the greatest part of that night and yesterday in his company, during which he frequently went up to the Empress, and ever returned in high spirits; he constantly made me fresh reports of her regard for England, of her esteem and approbation of its Ministers; and though our conversation naturally wandered, in so many hours, from one subject to another, yet he ever brought it back to our successes, on which he spoke with an enthusiastic satisfaction that, till now, I thought none but an Englishman could feel.

". . . Circumstances leave me no doubt of his sincerity. If you ask me, why this sudden change? . . . it must be sought for in the character of this very extraordinary man, who every day affords me new matter of amazement and surprise. Our conversation took place immediately on his coming off a journey of three thousand *versts* [about 2,000 miles], which he had performed in sixteen days, during which period he had slept only three times; and besides visiting several estates, and every church he came near, he had been exposed to all the delays and tedious ceremonies of the military and civil honours, which the Empress had ordered should be bestowed on him wherever he passed, yet he did not bear the smallest appearance of fatigue, either in body or mind, and on our separating I was certainly the more exhausted of the two."

Some months later, in 1783, with England and none of the other interested major powers having been satisfied but all having been sufficiently bamboozled and played off against one another, Catherine and Potemkin's Crimean scheme came to fruition. The Tatar Khan, Shangagarei, abdicated in favor of Catherine and retired to live in Russia on a pension of 100,000 rubles a year. The Crimea was annexed with no more serious consequences than a protest from Turkey and some disorders among distant Tatar factions, which Potemkin quickly suppressed. He became military and civil governor of the new province, to which he and Catherine restored its ancient Greek name, Tauris. Catherine promoted him to the rank of field marshal in the army; and then, shortly after, made him inspector general of all Russia's armed forces, commander in chief subordinate only to herself as Supreme Autocrat.

Moreover—although he did not lack for palaces and estates— she began building a Petersburg palace for him commensurate in scale and splendor to his power and glory. The name she gave it—and which it retains—memorialized the Crimean conquest and the Greek Project: the Tauride Palace.

While the Tauride Palace was rising above the banks of the

Fontanka in Petersburg, Potemkin was working feverishly to develop the reborn Tauris and the rest of New Russia as a staging area for the next and larger phase of the Greek Project and to make it at the same time a paradisiacal gift to Catherine. He built arsenals, harbors, fleets. By bribery, guile, charm, and enthusiasm he won the loyalty of the Tatar chiefs and raised and trained scores of Tatar regiments. He built villages, towns, and whole cities. He secured laborers by edict and worked them mercilessly. According to one reputable (but not necessarily reliable) source, Emperor Joseph II of Austria, "The lord commands; hordes of slaves obey . . . 50,000 persons were destroyed in these new provinces by the toil and the emanations from the morasses." Potemkin sent agents east and west, into Asia and Europe, to recruit workers: Georgians, Kalmuks, Circassians, Moldavians, Serbs, Albanians, Greeks, Germans in hundreds of thousands.

On the lower Dnieper he built a new city for her called Ekaterinoslav, literally "Catherine's Glory," and equipped it with a royal palace, a silk factory, vegetable gardens, houses and streets and a population. He planned it to have a great university, a cathedral bigger than St. Peter's, theaters, academies of the arts, every necessity and amenity of high civilization. Thus, it would become the southern equivalent of Petersburg—a monument, as Petersburg was to Peter the Great, to the reign of Catherine the Great.

In his unbroken correspondence with Catherine, and in person during his hurried trips to Petersburg, he kept her informed of everything that was and that was to be. She yearned to see it. And in 1787—three years after the Taurian coup—she made the trip, a six-month expedition, the echoes of which resound to this day.

XXV

To the Mother of Russian Cities

IT was more than a famous journey: it was a historical drama, with Potemkin as impresario, writer-director, scene designer, and stage manager—and so it was great spectacle, too. In fact, it was one of the most stunningly lavish dramatic spectacles ever seen.

The Greek Project, while certainly a "romantic idea," as Harris had called it, was not necessarily a chimera, as he also called it. Success depended on such earthly, practical matters as Russian military power, which was already demonstrably able to defeat Turkey if not destroy it, and on enlisting the help of one or two strong powers on Russia's side. Catherine's ally of choice was Austria. She had arranged to meet Emperor Joseph II during the trip to impress and beguile him into a military alliance. To persuade the rest of the world of the invincibility of this combination and the folly of intervention in aid of the Turks, she and Potemkin decided she should travel with the full court, including the foreign diplomatic corps. The ambassadors, properly honored, flattered, caressed, impressed, would become her champions and agents to their own governments.

The expedition left Petersburg in the mellow aftermath of the

Russian Christmas festivities, at the height of the bitter cold, glistening Russian winter. This was a climate that two generations earlier had weakened fatally the best army in Europe, that of Charles XII of Sweden, and destroyed many invaders (as it would do again). But for Catherine and her courtiers and guests—if not for the thousands of troops posted as guards along the way or the servitors and hostlers and animals contributing to effect—it supplied the setting for a winter carnival.

Catherine's sleigh, a miniature palace on runners, had been built especially for this trip. It contained a drawing room, a library-study, a bedroom, and the usual amenities. It was wide enough that eight people could pass abreast; it had six windows for the view, heavy draperies for privacy, and porcelain stoves for cozy warmth. It was driven by thirty horses managed by mounted hostlers and accompanied by outriders and by troops of the Horse Guards. Catherine shared it with Madame Protasova, her chief lady-in-waiting and confidante (Countess Bruce, occupant of the position for many years, had at last disgraced herself by falling violently in love and having an affair with Rimsky-Korsakov while he was still adjutant general) and with her current favorite young guardsman, Alexander Dmitriev-Mamanov. The court, the government ministers, and the diplomatic corps occupied 14 similar but less grand sleighs and 184 smaller ones; an additional 40 followed in reserve. Members of the party received as gifts sable hats, muffs, and lap robes.

Every evening at dusk the roads were illuminated, and the air was warmed by huge bonfires spaced closely along the way. Every night the travelers arrived at comfortable quarters: a town refurbished or if necessary rebuilt to receive them and where they had fine food and drink, dancing and cards, and the accustomed social pleasures of Petersburg life. At each stop there were 500 fresh horses for the morning. At each stop there was also a suitable palace for Catherine, its exterior lit by lanterns and 500 pans of tallow, enough to make the sky glow and the snowscapes sparkle far around. In twenty-one days the sleighing party arrived at Kiev and was greeted by the lord of the south, Prince Potemkin, who had preceded them to be sure that everything was to his taste.

Catherine had been there once before, as the fifteen-year-old bride-elect of Grand Duke Peter. Now—in January, 1787—it was nearly forty-three years later and she was nearly fifty-eight: gray, benign, and stout enough to fit the revered image of "Little Mother of all the Russians" as she visited "The Mother of Russian Cities."

They were to stay at Kiev for some three months, until the spring thaw cleared the ice from the Dnieper. In May, as the princes and merchants of Kievan Russia had always done, they were to assemble in a caravan of boats and glide down the great river to the Black Sea.

Meanwhile, Kiev was reconstituted as the capital of Russia and saw such activity, luxury, and pageantry as it had never seen in the greatest days of its glory. Catherine set up her court in the largest palace, received delegations from her subjects and allies, and gave banquets and entertainments. Each of the ambassadors was given his own palace and staff. There were balls, galas, card parties, theatricals. There was congenial fellowship and good conversation, both led by Catherine, insisting that no one talk politics lest it interfere with friendship and that everyone address everyone else in the familiar form—the "thee, thy, and thou" reserved for relatives and close friends. But the political talk did not stop, of course. The main arena soon became the Kievan palace occupied by the Austrian ambassador, Count Ludwig Cobenzl, a famously charming and intelligent man and a particular friend of Catherine's.

Potemkin had lodged them all in the High Town, the ancient city-citadel on the towering bluffs of the west bank of the Dnieper. The site, the view, the old structures lovingly restored after the city was reclaimed for Russia by Alexis I, Peter the Great's father —all these were enough to remind these intelligent people how natural were Russian ties to the Black Sea and Byzantium and how inevitable was the fulfillment of Russia's manifest destiny there.

Potemkin himself avoided the High Town as if it were filled with Tatar despoilers. He stayed at the headquarters he established at Pechersky Lavra, the Monastery of the Caves, built on and in a hill, downstream south of the citadel. The apotheosis of Holy Russia, Pechersky caused in Potemkin a startling reversion to otherworldliness. Melancholy and distracted, he made it plain that he preferred the company of the Pechersky monks—in devotions, conversation, chess, and gambling at cards—to that of the courtiers and diplomats. The French ambassador, the Comte de Ségur, described him as "most usually dressed in a gown, open at the neck, his legs half bare . . . lounging on a wide divan . . . nearly always pretending to be too busy playing a game of chess to notice the Russians or the foreigners who were arriving in his salon."

By May, when the ice left the Dnieper and the plum trees blossomed, Potemkin was ready to be his other luxuriant self, witty, exuberant, filled with energy and ideas, attuned to every mood and wish of his guests. The party left Kiev in a procession such as perhaps only he could have imagined. In place of the hundred carriage-sleighs that had brought them, they embarked now on the wide, swift, spring-swollen river in some eighty ships, all carved and decorated, gilded and painted with Byzantine decorations. The first seven were full-scale galleys that would have been suitable for Caesars and consuls. They were gold, "the color of desire," with trim of red, "the color of power." The living quarters were upholstered in fine brocade. The servants wore gold-braided liveries and served from gold plates, to the sound of music, for each galley had its own orchestra. Catherine's galley, emblazoned with the Russian-Byzantine imperial double eagle, led the line, followed by the galleys of the ambassadors of great powers and galleys shared by chief ministers and dignitaries of the court and ambassadors of lesser powers. Potemkin had chosen for his own galley the position fourth in line, behind Catherine and the ambassadors of the great powers but within hailing distance of his Empress.

He had personally seen to everything that could please and comfort her, even her bed, which lay against a large mirrored wall panel. At the touch of a button the panel slid away to reveal the adjoining bed of her handsome guardsman in the next stateroom. His own galley Potemkin had fitted out in an exotic mixture of Scythian-Greek-Byzantine-Tatar-Russian opulence. Here, sybarite monk, ascetic gourmand, melancholy humorist, cynical romantic, attended by his five pretty young nieces, he lolled about, drank and ate and joked and controlled the whole extravaganza.

The Dnieper was now referred to by the voyagers as the Borysthenes, for Catherine and Potemkin had restored the old Greek name. Floating along to the sea, the voyagers, citizens of a magical city—some 3,000 of them counting the oarsmen and sailors and servants and other supporting members—passed through pastoral landscapes that would have rejoiced the heart of Pindar or Ovid.

The riverbanks, the low hills, and the plains stretching away were covered in the lush tapestry of new spring growth and wild flowers. Sturdy youths and rosy maidens came to the riverbanks to stare and wave at the royal parade and sometimes to sing and dance for the Little Mother, the Empress. In their brightly colored skirts and blouses they were as pretty as the daisies and buttercups. The herds in the meadows were fine and sleek. Now and again troops that Potemkin had recruited in the countryside could be seen marching or riding in drill formation, splendid in colorful, clean, new uniforms. The villages reposed in the sunshine (and there was sunshine every day of the trip), models of neatness and enterprise, the roads tidy, the houses and the churches with steeples gleaming with the whitewash and fanciful warm colors of the south.

Catherine, viewing it all from her galley under a silken awning, was enchanted. "Is not my little household prettily furnished?" she said one day to the Comte de Ségur. "Do you not find it well and agreeably run?"

Ségur agreed. He was charmed and impressed. And so, indeed, were nearly all the guests, save a few who decided it was all simply too good to be true or who, for reasons of politics or personal pique, chose to disbelieve. Soon Prince Charles Joseph de Ligne, personal representative of Emperor Joseph II on this voyage, was reporting to Vienna: "They have already spread a ridiculous report that villages of cardboard have been distributed along our route at intervals of a hundred leagues, that paintings of vessels and cannon and cavalry without horses are displayed. . . ."

The chief dispenser of this report was G.A.W. von Helbig, the Saxon ambassador, who disliked Potemkin and entertained himself and the Saxon court by presenting him in dispatches as a barbarian, gross sinner, and charlatan. It was he who invented the term

"Potemkin villages"—*Potemkinsche Dörfer*—which soon became a German vernacular term for sham and spread from there to other languages. Thus, to the average person outside Russia (and perhaps Germany), "Potemkin village" is all that has survived of Potemkin: a consummate illusionist.

In fact, the villages, vessels, cavalry, and all the rest were real, as modern scholars have ascertained. Potemkin had done what any political showman of his time or any time would try to do: He had made the parade route as attractive and impressive as possible. Through local leaders, the villages were ordered to neaten their streets and paint their houses, the troops to spruce up in clean uniforms and smarten up in drill maneuvers. The peasants and villagers were told to wear their holiday clothes and come to the shore at the proper time to see their loving Little Mother as she passed by and to please her with their smiles and songs. Meanwhile, the infirm, the village idiots, the raggle-taggle were to be kept out of sight.

The countryside was naturally rich with the famous "black earth" of what later would become one of the world's most bountiful agricultural areas. The carnival spirit was natural, and reverence for the Empress—for any occupant of the Russian throne—was as deep as reverence for God and akin to it.

Potemkin's misfortune, historically speaking, was that he organized these resources too well. The evident serenity of the landscapes and the prosperity of the inhabitants were a challenge not only to Helvig—a third-rate man who fed his vanity by maligning his betters—but for all of those who for various reasons were happier thinking that Helvig was right. The "cardboard villages" canard must have satisfied a need of some sort in a great many people, for the attempts of Ségur and other witnesses to right the record were overlooked or mistrusted. Potemkin, acknowledged now in all serious works of history as one of the most gifted and effective statesmen of his time in Europe, has remained fixed in legend as one of the world's great montebanks.

The first stop of the voyage was Kanev. Otherwise unsung in history before or since, Kanev was the scene of a memorable meeting or at any rate a meeting full of memories.

Poland was one of the countries that could be helpful to Russia in a renewed war with Turkey. Despite the First Partition a decade before, it was still a considerable country, with 7,000,000 inhabitants, an area about the size of modern France, much natural wealth, and a long military tradition. It was still more or less independent; although Russian influence was predominant, it was limited by the interests of the other powers on Poland's borders, Prussia, Austria, and Turkey. Thus, in a precarious way and depending on their skill in playing off the powers against one another, the Poles had some genuine freedom of action. Accordingly, a number of influential Polish nobles had visited Kiev, and some were along in the flotilla. Now, at Kanev, there was to be a royal meeting between the Empress of Russia and the Polish monarch, Stanislaus II Augustus.

Once—a long time ago—the two rulers had known each other well. For King Stanislaus was, of course, none other than Stanislaus Poniatowski, Catherine's lover in her later years as Grand Duchess, father of her second child; a member, with Count Bestuzhev, General Apraxin, Hanbury-Williams *et al.*, of the premature and nearly fatal plot to put Catherine on the throne. Afterward, a refugee from Empress Elizabeth's wrath, he waited in Warsaw for the next attempt to succeed and for Catherine's message that he should return to her arms to share her glory. For reasons that we saw, the main one being, in Catherine's words in her "Frank Confession," that Gregory Orlov "changed my state of mind," the message had been instead that he should stay where he was. To make certain he did so, she had soon afterward bludgeoned the Polish electors into putting him on the throne of Poland. At the same time, in a message ostensibly from her Foreign Ministry, she had advised him to marry. Later on she had joined Frederick the Great and Maria Theresa in partitioning Poland, slicing off many square miles and nearly 2,000,000 subjects as her share of Poniatowski's realm.

On the face of things it would seem that Catherine had done more than enough to cool her discarded lover's ardor. But his was truly a love that passed understanding. Adamantly misconstruing everything, he freely forgave all. The fact that Catherine, continuing to feel a sentimental affection for him because of what he had once meant to her, had kept up a friendly correspondence with him and wrote nicely of him to mutual friends, such as Madame Geoffrin, apparently was the wisp of straw he needed to keep his hopes afloat.

He had had many mistresses. He had taken his first one after two celibate years in Warsaw waiting for Empress Elizabeth to die and for Catherine to send for him. Knowing that gossip travels, he had written at once to tell Catherine and explain that it was a mere liaison of convenience, a physiological expedient until he could return to her. Inasmuch as that time never had come, he had continued from one beautiful expedient to another through the years, treating them almost as generously as Catherine treated her lovers and choosing them in the same eclectic, democratic spirit.

Finally, he met a woman whom he admired and liked well enough to marry. This was the beautiful, intelligent, charming and famous Countess Grabowska. But it was a secret morganatic marriage—like Catherine's to Potemkin—and thus could be dissolved, or ignored, perfectly easily if King Stanislaus married a woman of royal rank suitable to his station. Countess Grabowska, with all her merits, remained like her predecessors, an expedient.

It has been said that Poles have an irresistible fatal attraction toward romantic lost causes, and if there is any truth in the idea, then surely King Stanislaus II Augustus was its archetype. After thirty-five years he was still in love with Catherine and approached their meeting at Kanev with the palpitations of a young lover. He hoped and apparently even half believed that after thirty years apart they would come together at Kanev and live happily forever after. To Catherine no idea could have been more preposterous. Realizing or sensing Stanislaus' state of mind, she deliberately delayed the arrival of the royal flotilla so that he and his court had to wait in the meager comforts of Kanev.

At their rendezvous it was evident that the years had been a good deal kinder to him than to Catherine. At fifty-five, he was a remarkably handsome man with at least an approximation of the fine, graceful figure that had held Catherine's eye the first day they met. The meeting which Stanislaus had imagined might be the climax of his life became instead a painful anticlimax. Catherine's manner was friendly, gracious, smiling—and quite impersonal. This was how she might have received almost any visiting foreign dignitary. Stanislaus was admiring, attentive, and clearly moved. She, with signs of increasing impatience, made it evident that she regarded this as a business meeting and that, as a busy person with many other responsibilities, she would like to get on to the matters at hand. Could she count on Poland's entire support in a new war with Turkey?

Stanislaus, prompted by his ministers, rejoined by asking whether she in turn would respect the integrity and existing borders of Poland. She answered—"half contemptuously"—that she would. With that, her professional courtesy turned to curtness, and the meeting was adjourned.

Stanislaus had prepared an elaborate and costly gala in her honor for the next evening. She sent her official regrets. That morning, without even the favor of a farewell audience to the man of whom she once had written, "I esteem and love Poniatowski above all the rest of the human race," she embarked on her imperial galleon and led her flotilla down the river.

Potemkin was furious with her. Polish support could be important to the success of the Greek Project, he reminded her. She replied that the King of Poland bored her.

XXVI

The Drama of Sevastopol

SHE was not bored by the Emperor of Austria-Hungary and the Holy Roman Empire, Joseph II, with whom she met at the next stop, a city called Kaidak. In an age of anomalies and contradictions, he was one of the most contradictory of characters. A moral rationalist and political cynic, he believed so passionately in the natural goodness of man that he was at the same time prepared as Emperor to make it prevail by the most arbitrary methods, if necessary. A friend, defender, and protector of all humankind, he was genuinely convinced that humanity's best interests could be best served by the aggrandizement and general dominion of his empire, not because it was Holy or Roman but because it was secular and rational, or at any rate would be, once his intentions were fulfilled. His philosophy was the child of a miscegenation between Rousseau and Voltaire; he was a mystical rationalist or a rational mystic, an enthroned revolutionary who was more devout in his social mission and more sanctimonious in his convictions than his mother, the Empress Maria Theresa, whom Catherine called "Lady Prayerful."

Maria Theresa—who despite Catherine's feline remark was a

successful ruler and a wise woman, herself a product and adornment of the early Enlightenment—was often disconcerted by
Joseph, but she loved him and hoped for the best. She was also
sometimes disconcerted by his younger sister and carefree opposite, Marie Antoinette, whom she managed to marry, to her imperial satisfaction, to the future King Louis XVI of France. While
allowing Joseph to become Emperor at the age of twenty-four
after the death of his father in 1765, and while sometimes giving
him his way, she kept final authority firmly in her own hands as
Dowager Empress and Co-Regent. This situation lasted until
Maria Theresa's death in 1780. If it had not quite made a misog-
ynist of Joseph, this long frustration had at least made him wary
and suspicious of opinionated older women (Catherine was twelve
years older) and inclined to disagree with them, especially if they
were empresses.

Thus, for Catherine, he was an object of great attraction:
kindred child of the Enlightenment, friend of her old friends
Voltaire, Diderot, and the *encyclopédistes*, enthusiast and devotee
of education as the ultimate cure for all evils, patron of culture,
benevolent absolutist, pragmatic sanctioner of the Partition of
Poland; fervent, truculent, suspicious, enigmatic; master now of
immense power which, at the very least, would have to be placated
and, she hoped, turned to account.

Austria had been at war against the Turks off and on for
centuries. The perpetual interest of the empire Joseph II had inherited was to expel Turkey from southeast Europe and acquire
that region for itself. It would be out of the question for him or
any other Austrian monarch to tolerate the replacement of Turkish rule there simply by another aggressive foreign nation, Christian or not. Consequently, Catherine could not prudently send
her armies toward Constantinople without a clear agreement
with him, in advance, that Russia's aims were limited and that
Austria's traditional interests would be satisfied. Obviously it
would be expedient to entice Joseph into a full military alliance.
Russian and Austrian power together ought certainly to be
enough to demolish the Turkish Empire, producing such a wealth
of loose debris that she and Joseph could divide it and both be
satisfied.

This plan, as it happened, was similar to one that Peter the Great had once spent several months in Vienna trying vainly to sell Emperor Leopold I.

After ceremonial greetings at Kaidak, which lies above the Dnieper rapids, the two monarchs—leaving to the courtiers and diplomats the dubious pleasures of shooting the rapids in the fleet —traveled together by carriage to the place where the river calms again and where Potemkin had established Catherine's new city, Ekaterinoslav. There, on the highest hill above the river, they laid a pair of cornerstones for the cathedral that Potemkin planned to be the largest in the world. Joseph wrote home dyspeptically to Vienna to his senior general, Field Marshal Peter Lascy: "I performed a great deed today. The empress laid the first stone of a new church, and I laid—the last."

In fact, the cathedral never was finished. But the city had a brighter future than Joseph could imagine; it is the present Dnepropetrovsk, southern Russia's most important industrial and commercial center. Nearby is a modern monument bigger even than the projected cathedral, the half-mile-long, 200-foot-high Dneprostroi Dam, the largest hydroelectric installation in Europe.

At Kherson, the next and last stop on the river, Joseph was more impressed and at the beginning, perhaps, of becoming amused. For this city, standing at the gullet of the river mouth, 25 miles from the Black Sea coast, was a thriving new city with port facilities and a busy shipyard on a deepwater harbor. From this yard, only four years earlier, Potemkin had launched the first ship of the new Black Sea fleet, a formidable 66-gun frigate, *Glory of Catherine*. Now the harbor held flotillas of warships and merchant vessels. For the edification of Catherine, Joseph, and her other 3,000 guests, three more warships were launched. On their way to the ceremonies the noble tourists saw a signpost freshly painted in Greek letters: "This is the way to Byzantium."

Here in the deep south, Potemkin was in his element. The closer the party approached to the sea, and then to the Crimea— his principality of Tauris—the more energetic and high-spirited he became, the more sumptuously his personality unfolded, and the more extravagant were the fruits of his imagination. "At the frontiers of Tauris," wrote Gina Kaus, one of the best of Catherine's chroniclers, "the empress was greeted by a delegation of *mirzas* [nobles]; Caucasian princes, beautiful as the dreams of Greek sculptors, rode to meet her armed with bows and arrows; Circassian troops in silver robes riding bareback on milk-white horses bore down upon her like a white dazzling cloud. At last the minarets of Bashtasarai rose on the horizon, and a few hours later they were . . . surrounded by men in long, gold-embroidered robes and women closely veiled. They were led to the palace, where cool fountains played in marble recesses, and there Catherine mounted the throne of the Great Khan."

The Prince de Ligne, Joseph's special emissary, was amazed by Potemkin, and so also in degree, it may be assumed, was Joseph. De Ligne wrote: "He is colossal, like Russia . . . and like Russia he has both wastes and gold mines. He looks idle yet he works unceasingly; he is always lying on his couch yet never sleeps; he craves amusement and is sad in the midst of his pleasures; he is a sublime politician, yet unreliable and capricious as a child." He was so full of wit and unexpectedness, De Ligne wrote, that "We often thought we should die laughing, the prince was so merry."

Catherine was very merry, too, not only because she was delighted with everything Potemkin showed her but because she was never so jolly, so seemingly unbusinesslike, as when she was aiming to persuade someone on a matter of great importance to her. Accordingly, with Joseph she was charmingly offhand, a friendly hostess and interesting travel companion. Her conversations with him, ranging far and wide, never touched directly on the question that both knew was foremost in their minds, the military treaty. She and Potemkin judged the moment finally ripe for this topic when they reached Sevastopol.

This was another of the new cities and the geographical culmination of the trip, a fortress on the far southwest coast of the Crimean peninsula. It was the well-constructed product of an English military engineer, Samuel Bentham, brother of the famous economist Jeremy Bentham (Father of Utilitarianism), one of Catherine's most admired and admiring friends among the

leaders of the English Enlightenment. The name Catherine
and Potemkin had devised for the city was Greek, an elision of
sevaste (august) and *polis* (city).

A grand banquet was held on the evening of their arrival in a
new palace overlooking the bay. For 80 guests there was an orchestra of 180, and all the rest was in scale. Here Catherine got
to the point. Joseph had been waiting for it, and he expressed his
doubts. Catherine rejoined that Russia now had such strength
that alone, if necessary, she could defeat Turkey. Potemkin declared, "A hundred thousand men are waiting for me to say 'Go!' "

On that cue the draperies parted, and the windows opened wide
to reveal uncountable forces of Potemkin's new Tatar regiments
massed all the way to the bay, and beyond them—anchored in
review formation—the whole new Black Sea fleet. From the sea-
men and troops a vast shout rose and enveloped the palace:
"Long live the Empress of the Black Sea!"

That night Joseph wrote to Field Marshal Lascy: "If I were
as close to Berlin, and if the Prussians were as stupid as the Turks
—I hardly think I should be able to resist the temptation of destroying them."

A fortnight later the tour came to its grand finale with a re-
creation of the Battle of Poltava, where Peter the Great defeated
Sweden to ensure a Baltic outlet for Russia and the survival of
Petersburg. Potemkin put two of his armies on the battleground in authentic costume, in the positions recorded in the
military archives, with scripts of the action, episode by episode,
and reenacted the whole fierce drama. The rounds were blanks,
but the smoke, noise, and turmoil were those of battle. The effect
was stupendous.

The next day Joseph signed the treaty that had been so long
delayed and was so essential to Catherine. Austria and Russia
together would fight the Turks and divide their empire. Joseph
would have Serbia, Bosnia, Herzegovina, and other Balkan lands,
the major portion of Turkish Europe (comprising most of present Yugoslavia). Catherine would have the whole of the northern
Black Sea coast, Constantinople, the Straits, the Black Sea coasts
of Asia Minor, and have hegemony over Greece and the Greek
Islands.

On this sanguine note, amid the greatest optimism and good-will—only moderately tinged with mutual suspicions—the conference ended.

The Turks inconsiderately did not wait to be attacked at the Russians' convenience. Catherine had hardly returned to the Hermitage when the Sultan sent an ultimatum demanding, among other unacceptable conditions, that Russia vacate the Crimea. When this was rejected, the Sublime Porte declared war and attacked. Potemkin had been counting on about another year to make ready, and he could not bestir himself to make a defense, let alone a counterattack. He seemed to be in the grip of emotional paralysis. The Turks fought with all their famous ferocity. Their early victories plunged Potemkin into such a state of depression that he was ready to abandon Crimea-Tauris, the pride of his life. As his despair deepened, he seemed ready to abandon everything that he had so recently gloried in, give up the world and its vanities, and retire to a monastery.

Catherine sent him letters full of advice and encouragement, reassurance, loving entreaties, and faith. She wrote twice or more a week; sometimes weeks passed before she heard from him. "Being so long without news of you, I die a thousand deaths. I receive news each week from every province of the kingdom save only the one which occupies all my thoughts and hopes. For God's sake and mine, take care of yourself! Nothing makes me more wretched than the fear that you may be ill. . . ."

A storm wrecked part of the new Black Sea fleet, and there was insurrection in the Crimean countryside. Potemkin wanted to give up Sevastapol, and Catherine wrote: "Your letter no doubt was written in a moment of agitation . . . how shall we voluntarily relinquish the great advantages we have won in war and peace? For heaven's sake, think no more of this. . . . Abandon this harmful policy of defense and proceed against Ochakov. . . ."

Ochakov was the naval base and fortress on the northwest Black Sea coast, the geographical hinge that everyone agreed had to be taken before the Russian and Austrian armies could meet and move together. Again, when Potemkin wrote her asking to be relieved of his command, she replied: "Do not rob me and the country of our most indispensable, capable, and faithful subject, and remember that a courageous mind can overcome temporary misfortune. You are my friend, my dearest pupil, you often give me better counsel than I can myself provide. But you are impatient as a five-year-old child, while the business entrusted to you demands patience, infinite and unshakable patience." And later: "Do you think any power in the world can lessen my confidence in you. . . . There are no tender endearments I do not say to you."

Finally, after a year of unhopeful preparation, Potemkin did take the offensive, did assault Ochakov, and, at enormous cost, did capture it. Catherine wrote: "I take you by both ears and kiss you in my thoughts, Grishenka, dear friend of my bosom!"

But the battle was not the war. Joseph II had been waiting with almost as much impatience as Catherine for Potemkin to move. When at last he did, Joseph committed the Austrian Army to a simultaneous campaign in the Balkans, under his own field command. He was a poor general, and the result was catastrophic. By the time Ochakov fell he was back in Vienna, his army fractured and in retreat, his own health ruined. Uprisings broke out in various parts of his empire as a resentful reaction to his arbitrary attempts to reform backward local customs. With his troops committed to the Turkish War, there was little he could do to enforce his so-called Rules of Reason. As his health grew worse, he lost control of the apparatus of his autocracy. His Prime Minister, Prince Wenzel von Kaunitz, not only ignored his orders but even refused to visit him in his sickroom at Schönbrunn Palace. Joseph was too ill, and too sad, to replace him.

But the military situation improved. Austrian troops had victories, even managing to capture Belgrade, "the key to the Balkans." This only aggravated the jealousies of the major non-belligerent powers, Prussia, England, and France. Austria's arch-rival for leadership among the German states, Prussia, allied itself with Turkey and prepared to invade Austria's northern frontiers.

At the beginning of 1790, only two and a half years after his grand soiree with Catherine and Potemkin down the Dnieper through Crimea-Tauris and to Poltava, Joseph formally retracted the major part of the Enlightened directives that had made him the foremost reformer among the famous trio of eighteenth-century Benevolent Despots—Frederick II, Catherine II, Joseph II. A few weeks later he died.

His younger brother and successor, Leopold II, took over a realm so sorely beset by internal and external threats that he needed peace at almost any price. He gave Belgrade and practically all the other gains back to the Turks and removed Austria from the war. Meanwhile, to Catherine's surprise and discomfort, Sweden came into the war and attacked Petersburg. King Gustavus III dispatched a fleet across the Baltic and landed troops on the Livonian shore without notifying his own ministers, let alone Catherine.

Gustavus and Catherine had a great deal in common. Both were German by origin. He was the nephew of Frederick the Great, son of Frederick's sister Louise Ulrica (in whose borrowed dress Catherine, poor little Princess of Anhalt-Zerbst, had dinner with Frederick on her way to Russia) and of Adolphus Frederick. Adolphus was the son of the selfsame Christian Augustus, sometime Bishop of Lübeck, sometime guardian of the future Peter III and administrator of Holstein-Gottorp, who rather inadvertently became King of Sweden. His sister, the Princess Johanna Elizabeth, was Catherine's mother—making Gustavus and Catherine, in short, second cousins. Both, too, despite their ethnic roots and national thrones, were primarily French in outlook, both enthusiasts of the French Enlightenment, both intellectually brilliant, ravenously interested in and responsive to life, and almost overburdened with multiple talents.

Gustavus fostered and lavishly supported the arts and sciences in Sweden. He founded the Swedish Academy (whose members would later be the world's arbiters of achievement in the arts, sciences, and humanities in awarding the Nobel Prizes). He was himself a prose stylist of merit and a distinguished playwright and librettist, and by his example and support he, like Catherine, brought about a flowering of literary and dramatic arts in his own nation. And, like Catherine, "he early began to exercise that charm of manner which later made him so fascinating and so dangerous."

Seventeen years younger than Catherine, Gustavus was young enough to have been the son she had wanted, but also old enough so that in other circumstances he might have been an eligible lover. Naturally, when he visited Petersburg and the Hermitage as Crown Prince, they found each other interesting, and thereafter for many years they were in frequent, friendly, personal correspondence. But there was still one more way in which they were alike.

Gustavus was a Swedish patriot as devoted to Sweden as Catherine was to Russia. Just as she wanted to fulfill the work of Peter the Great, he wanted to rehabilitate the Swedish position in the world that Charles XII had lost at Poltava. Perhaps the reenactment of that battle by Potemkin for Catherine's pleasure and the lesson suggested to friends and foes, had something to do with it; that reenactment, after all, had made a pageant of Sweden's humiliation. In any case, seeing Russia's main forces gathered in the south for the Turkish War, Gustavus thought he saw a historically decisive moment and sent his fleet and regiments to storm the capital city of his much-admired and admiring friend and cousin, Catherine.

Petersburg's defenses were almost as thin as he had hoped, and he had the advantage of surprise. The Swedish fleet actually penetrated the estuary and archipelago of the Neva all the way to cannon-shot of the heart of the city. For the first time (but not the last) the Winter Palace and Hermitage were brought under bombardment. Catherine took the elementary precaution of removing her most valued works of art but made no personal concession to danger. She lived at the Hermitage as if nothing were happening and began a note to her friend and fellow traveler, the Prince de Ligne, who was serving at Potemkin's headquarters, "Amidst the roar of cannon which shakes her windows your Imperturbable writes to you. . . ."

Among a good many reputations damaged during the early years of this war was that of the American naval hero, John Paul Jones. After the American Revolution he had come to Europe to work out conflicting naval-prize claims, particularly between the United States and French governments. By the time of the outbreak of the Turkish-Russian hostilities, he was on the verge of being unemployed. Thomas Jefferson, who was then American ambassador to France, wrote to Catherine (his letter was seconded by one from Benjamin Franklin) suggesting that she offer him service in her fleet.

Catherine admired Jefferson and Franklin and knew Jones' record of initiative and boldness, qualities she was feeling in sore need of. She brought Jones to Petersburg, made him a rear admiral in the Russian Navy, and sent him south with the promise that he would be commander of the whole Black Sea fleet. However, she was hiring at the same time other foreign soldiers of fortune (a young Corsican French lieutenant of artillery, Napoleon Bonaparte, almost joined her service, but was detained by the French Revolution), and among them were a number of British naval officers, several of high rank. Their resentment of Jones made the situation so complex that he was not given command. The operations he did conduct were not very effective, and the battles he won were credited to others. He returned to Petersburg to complain to Catherine and while there became the center of a noisy scandal in which he was accused (falsely) of raping a young girl. Catherine decided that this accumulation of troubles had destroyed his usefulness and gave him indefinite leave of absence. He returned to Paris, ruined in health and spirit, and soon died there.

Finally, on both seas, the fortunes of war turned in Catherine's favor. In the Black Sea, armies led by Marshals Rumiantsev and Suvorov stormed a series of important Turkish fortresses. In 1790 Suvorov took the key fortress of Izmail on the Danube. (The final charge was led by a young officer named Michael Kutuzov, later the famous Marshal Kutuzov, Alexander I's field commander, whose strategies defeated Napoleon in 1812.)

In the Baltic, faced with the prospect of an eventual Russian victory in the south that would permit the full weight of Russia's power to be brought against him in the north, King Gustavus III circumspectly (and under heavy pressure from the Swedish aristocracy, many of them bribed by Catherine's agents) recalled his forces. The undeclared war trailed off and ended in 1790 with no gains for Sweden.

The war had proved enormously expensive in every way; in money, in blood—20,000 Russians had died in the storming of

Izmail—and not least in the heavy strains it put on Catherine's own energies and emotions. Voltaire had once addressed her (to encourage her in her troubles during the First Turkish War) as "That great man whose name is Catherine." But the need to be a "great man" was bound to conflict at a deep level with another essential need, which was to be a woman and be loved by men. At this time, when this feminine part of her nature was unusually vulnerable, she suffered a bad blow.

Her handsome adjutant Dmitriev-Mamanov, companion of her days and nights during the grand expedition to Kiev and Crimea and ever since, had fallen in love with one of her pretty young ladies-in-waiting and wanted to marry her. Catherine had dismissed a goodly throng of favorites in her life; for the first time she found herself in effect being dismissed. Not all the wealth and glory of the throne could compete with a fresh young face and lovely young figure. Suddenly she was confronted with herself not as an Empress but as a woman and was demoralized by the shock of self-recognition.

She was sixty years old. Age had cruelly bloated those charms it had not withered. She had become immensely stout, in part because of the "dropsy" that had begun to fill her body with excess water and to swell her legs so ponderously that already she was having trouble standing for long or walking far. The long, black, lustrous hair of which she had been so proud was now completely gray. Like Empress Elizabeth in her later years (Catherine had remarked on this vanity of Elizabeth's in her memoirs, with some scorn), she had begun using a vast array of skin lotions and cosmetics, with results more garish than effective. Nothing really could disguise the crow's-feet, the creases, the developing dewlap, or the fact that, like most people of her age (at a time when no one yet knew about preventing cavities or filling teeth) she had lost her own teeth and wore dental plates. Her eyes—those candid, friendly, humorous, wise, amazingly deep-blue eyes that men from Poniatowski to Potemkin had praised—were her one remaining notable asset. Even they were now much weakened because of her prodigious labors of reading, writing, and paper work—and her refusal to wear spectacles because she thought them unbecoming. They were, however, good enough that when she looked at herself in the mirror and drew logical conclusions with her un-impaired rational faculties, she knew that the time she had dreaded had come. And that as for "love," she would be lucky, even as Empress, to provoke even some surrogate, dutiful desire in any robust, attractive young man.

As it happened, there was a robust, attractive young man who had been waiting for the moment when he might have a chance to take Dmitriev-Mamanov's place as adjutant. This was Platon Zubov, a darkly handsome, ferociously ambitious twenty-two-year-old Horse Guards officer who had the vigor of youth and the hardened guile and ruthlessness of an old courtier. He had come to court in early adolescence as a page and had had years in which to learn the names and ways and means of successful intriguers and to observe with fascination and mounting avarice the duties and rewards of the adjutants.

Thus, when Catherine faced the feminine crisis of Dmitriev-Mamanov's defection and was perhaps more vulnerable than ever before in her life, Platon Zubov was conspicuously ready, with all his dark and virile charms, to comfort her. Catherine had decided that she must not, ever again, involve her heart and her dignity in any new relationship. And for some months she kept her sensible promise to herself—meanwhile, however, struggling not only with conscience and logic but with a growing despond-ency. Finally she abandoned her rational resolutions and ap-pointed Zubov her adjutant with all the familiar duties and rewards. He proved to be a formidable success.

She wrote to Potemkin about her new adjutant, detailing his fine and lovable qualities, his talents and intelligent remarks, in the usual open and innocent—or cynical and shameless, if one prefers—way she had of telling everything to her partner, her hus-band, her best and most loved friend. She wrote: "I returned to life like a fly that has been frozen by the cold."

The departed Dmitriev-Mamanov had been Potemkin's protégé and admirer and therefore a reliable custodian. Though he had not chosen this adjutant (and thereby placed him in some similar position of debt, collectable as needed), Potemkin knew young Zubov—and had never much liked him—as a protégé or friend of several courtiers who at times had opposed him or had even been his enemies. His reply to Catherine has not survived, but evidently it was chilly and raised the matter of Zubov's allegiances. Catherine was long since reconciled to Potemkin's unpredictable moods. Fondly, indulgently, she assured him that "the little black boy sends his love." Later, when Potemkin persisted in his doubts, "The child thinks that you are infinitely more intelligent, amusing and charming than all your friends put together."

This was not in the least satisfying. Potemkin's "friends" were also his party and thus the apparatus by which he, nearly as much as Catherine, ruled Russia. He knew Catherine better than anyone ever had known her, and these signs of emotional commitment, of an infatuation which he was not present to supervise, began causing him intense discomfort. Finally, late in 1791, his worries became intolerable.

The war against the Turks was in a climactic phase. Suvorov was deep into the Balkans, and the Turks clearly were weakening. Somewhere not too far beyond the horizon, certainly this side of imagination, lay Constantinople. The Greek Project might well be, after all, an attainable dream. Nevertheless, at this time Potemkin left his headquarters at Jassy, in Moldavia, where he had been holding his own secondary court "in more than Oriental pomp," and returned posthaste to Petersburg—much as Gregory Orlov, at a crucial time in the First Turkish War, had done for the same reason.

In Russian the name Zubov is also the word for "tooth." Writing to Catherine, Potemkin trusted her to understand that the purpose of his visit was "to extract a painful tooth."

Catherine ignored the pun, accepted his untimely departure from Jassy, and greeted him with every reassuring honor and tribute she could think of, treating him (with not much mention of Suvorov, Rumiantsev, and others) as the nonpareil military hero of Russian history. And Potemkin (though he may have bitten his nails to the quick in private) with consummate authority played the role that circumstances—and he and Catherine both, as co-dramatists—had arranged. Catherine wrote to Grimm: "He glows in the splendor of his victory, bright as the day, he is as merry as a chaffinch, as brilliant as a constellation of stars, and wittier than ever."

Nevertheless, when he demanded that she discard Platon Zubov, she would not yield. It was the first time that she had refused in such a matter. And Zubov, knowing quite well that Potemkin was against him, pressed this victory. He began suggesting, then soon demanding, that she send Potemkin away.

Potemkin's finest hours had come during the triumphal expedition to Kiev and the Crimea. Catherine, loving and admiring, had never been so dazzled by him, and perhaps it was to evoke those memories and those feelings that he made his stay in Petersburg a fabulous entertainment in Catherine's honor. Night after night the Tauride Palace was a festival scene of banquets, masquerades, fireworks, pageants, balls—the latter in the magnificent pillared ballroom that Potemkin had named the Catherine Hall. All told, he spent a million rubles.

After the most sumptuous ball, as Potemkin escorted Catherine from the Tauride Palace to her carriage, and after he had kissed her hand good-night, she thanked him and said she would regard this as a farewell ball since she knew he was needed at Jassy to finish the war and arrange the peace terms and must therefore be eager to return there. Potemkin bowed, then for a few moments stood watching the royal carriage, with its clattering outriders, drive away in the night to the Hermitage. He had lost.

The next morning he left Petersburg. By the time he reached Jassy he was in the grip of suicidal depression. Soon after, during a trip to Ochakov, according to one account, after a great bout of overeating and drinking, he was stricken and died at the side of a country road.

Catherine fainted when the news reached her and had to be put to bed under care of her physicians. Even in bed she fainted and was in and out of coma. She was ill for days and stayed in almost complete isolation for weeks. When she had regained some composure, she wrote to Grimm: "My pupil, my friend, my idol I must say, Prince Potemkin of Tauride has died. . . . His most beautiful characteristic was to me the greatness of his heart, his mind and his soul. Because of that we were always able to understand each other and ignore those who could not do so. . . . Whom can I rely on now . . . ?"

XXVII

"In the Time of Monsieur Alexander"

CATHERINE herself had only a few years left.

Most of her old friends, mentors, protégés, favorites, agents, allies, and enemies (the roles were interchangeable) were gone.

"Fifty years ago today," she wrote to Grimm, on February 20, 1794, "I arrived in Moscow with my mother. I do not believe there are ten people here who remember that day. . . ." She had Platon Zubov, "the child"—remarkable child, young savage, gambler, confidence trickster, and, above all, emotional blackmailer—and, with him, his eager party of friends, sycophants, and family. And she was afraid to lose him. In this, after the defection of Dmitriev-Mamanov, her nerve was gone. "Wouldn't it be wonderful," she wrote Grimm, "if an empress could always be fifteen?"

As her "dropsy" (or Bright's disease) worsened, her weight became too cumbersome for her muscles to manage, and the varicose veins in her swollen legs made walking or entering or dismounting a carriage not only difficult, but often quite painful. For her morning promenades in the Raphael Loggia at the Hermitage or in the Cameron Gallery at Tsarskoe Selo, she now preferred a wheelchair. It was now, too, that she had a long, easy incline built at Tsarskoe Selo enabling her to be wheeled, or on her better days slowly to walk, between the Cameron Gallery and her beloved English Garden. For her convenience the proprietors of other palaces in the Petersburg area—friends such as Princess Dashkov on whom she might occasionally call—had similar inclines built. It was always Zubov who wheeled her or Zubov's strong arm that supported her as she made her stately way: still resolutely erect in posture, the same eyes and the same familiar smile, gracious, benign, impervious, refusing absolutely to acknowledge her condition. Of her handsome young escort, it has been said that "she wore him like a decoration."

She heaped honors and titles and imperial offices and palaces and perquisites and estates and incalculable wealth on him, honored and enriched his brothers, Valerian and Michael, opened her government and her treasury to his party, placated his endless greed and flattered his boundless vanity, and seemed sometimes actually to believe that he was as brilliant as he thought and as she hoped. ("I know of no one who showed greater talents at your age." Nevertheless, she kept all final authority in her own hands. Her plaint, "Whom can I rely on now . . . ?" had an answer implicit in her nature: In important matters—as she had substantially since age fifteen—she relied on herself. And, thanks to the sophisticated military and ministerial services that Peter the Great had begun and that she had done so much to encourage and bring to maturity, she did not lack competent servants.

While Potemkin had been away from the war, engaged in his fatal efforts in Petersburg, his generals had marched ahead against the Turks. By the spring of 1792 Marshal Suvorov was deep in the Balkans with Constantinople itself his next and militarily feasible destination. Turkey's ally, France, was in the throes of revolution and could no longer help. In this situation Britain, customary ally of Russia and chronic antagonist of France, intervened to take France's place and prevent a Russian triumph: a classic instance of power politics and of Palmerston's dictum of "permanent interests."

The British, faithful to their interests and to keeping a "balance of power" on the Continent, had never accepted the Greek Project but had sought to use Catherine's infatuation with it for their own purposes. In the diplomatic reports mentioned earlier, Sir James Harris had written: ". . . she has been chimerical enough to christen the newborn Grand Duke, Constantine; to give him a Greek nurse, whose name was Helen; and to talk in her private society of placing him on the throne of the Eastern Empire. In the meanwhile, she is building a town at Tsarskoe Selo to be called Constantingorod. . . . I mention this . . . with a view of hinting to your Lordship that, if His Majesty could stand in indispensable need of assistance from this quarter, the only means of obtaining it is by encouraging this romantic idea . . . such a conduct, dexterously managed, would give us the first hold of this Court; and as its execution, whenever seriously planned, would instantly appear impracticable, we need not be apprehensive of having engaged ourselves too far in an unpleasant transaction."

When, on the contrary, Russian victories began to make the Greek Project apparently practicable, British policy made the necessary readjustments and served notice on Catherine that Britain would go to war to prevent her from taking Constantinople. In the circumstances there was not much she could do—for the time being—but make peace. The Turkish armies were tired, but so were hers; the cost of the war was becoming ruinous; to confront the recently bloodied but still enormous power of the British Empire would have been altogether imprudent—not least because so many of her senior commanders in the Black Sea (as noted in the affair of John Paul Jones) were British. She entered negotiations and, while Suvorov was still marching on Constantinople, the peace treaty was signed at Potemkin's old headquarters at Jassy.

Turkey acknowledged Russia's sovereignty over Crimea-Tauris and ceded the remainder of the northwest coast of the Black Sea all the way to the Dniester River, hundreds of miles beyond the outlet of the Dnieper-Borysthenes. So Catherine had a famous victory which fulfilled the defeated hopes of Peter the Great and, after a lapse of 600 years, restored to Russia all the Black Sea lands lost in the time of Kievan Russia.

She was far from satisfied. In her will, drawn in that same year (1792), she declared for her posterity: "My desire is to bring Constantine to the throne of the Great Eastern Empire." If she lived long enough she surely would try again; otherwise this would happen (a favorite phrase during these years) "in the time of Monsieur Alexander."

Catherine's relations with the French monarchy and its policies and delegates seldom had been better than mediocre and for the most part unfriendly or worse. On the other hand, as we have seen, she was devoted to Voltaire, Diderot, D'Alembert, and, in general, those leaders of the French Enlightenment whose doctrines and influence lit the long fuse that finally exploded the Revolution. And when the Revolution came, she was horrified.

Undoubtedly her own encounter with Pugachev's revolt had a great deal to do with this. Her near escape then from disaster at the hands of rebels had been so traumatic that when oppressed Frenchmen stormed the Bastille and the Jacobins defied the King, she saw herself in the same position. Her libertarian principles curdled. She forbade her subjects to travel to France and ordered home all those hundreds of students she had sent to be steeped in French arts and sciences and, especially, philosophy. In Russia she discouraged, then withdrew, the freedom of expression she had done so much to encourage. She imprisoned Alexander Radishchev and Nicholas Novikov, the two most eloquent literary spokesmen for Enlightened reform of the Russian social system. Finally, one day she, the most influential and reverent "Voltairian" of the age, smashed a marble bust of Voltaire that stood in her apartments at Tsarskoe Selo.

She offered sanctuary to the French aristocrats, and Petersburg began to fill with them. Her Hermitage evenings became a flotsam of elegant displaced personages. Through one of her confidential agents in Paris, a banker's wife, she smuggled Russian passports to Louis XVI and Marie Antoinette—both of whom, not long before, she had despised—and was devastated to learn that her plot had miscarried and their escape to Petersburg had failed. She railed against the revolutionists in tracts and diplomatic notes, tried to organize Europe against them, threatened to send Russia's armies against them. From having been (except perhaps for Joseph II) the most famously liberal monarch of Europe, she became in these last years the most vehemently reactionary.

This was a kind of hysteria. Yet at the same time, most of the time, her rational faculties were intact, analytical—and sometimes extraordinarily prescient. Much as the idea horrified her, she early predicted that Louis XVI would be executed. And when despite her efforts to save him, this did happen, she remarked of the revolutionary masses: "They will soon weary of this liberty, and then they will become as gentle and obedient as lambs. But a clever and courageous leader is needed, one who is far in advance of his fellow man and his age. A new Genghis Khan will arise. Does this man already exist? Will he soon appear?"

He existed and he appeared: ". . . in the time of Monsieur Alexander."

Her hatred of the Revolution did not, however, inhibit her in the least from making use of it for her and Russia's interests. In part because of her urgings and in expectation of her military support, England, Austria, and Prussia declared war on the French Republic, but despite her continuing anathemas Catherine delayed and delayed joining the common effort. She had, in fact, another quite separate and private tactical design, summed up in a remark she made to her private secretary: "I wish to keep Berlin and Vienna occupied, so that I may have free elbow-room. Do you understand me? There are certain plans I wish to complete and I do not want to be distracted." Berlin and Vienna had been the colleagues of Petersburg in the First Partition of Poland, and she had another "cake to bake" there.

When she last saw the hapless Poniatowski, King Stanislaus II Augustus, in that brief, chilling encounter on the Dnieper-Borysthenes, he was on the verge of convening a representative Parliament to reform the archaic Polish constitution. Catherine did not want this; she wanted a Poland crippled by internal problems and hence effectively dominated by Russia. To that end, she had notified Poniatowski a long time ago that Russia could not tolerate major changes in the Polish nonsystem of government.

Forced by reformist movements among the Polish intelligentsia and nobility and indeed by his own patriotic feelings and his own Enlightened convictions (ideas that he and Catherine had discussed when both were young and neither had a throne), Stanislaus had nevertheless prepared the way for just such changes. This was the principal reason for Catherine's treatment of him at their first personal reunion in thirty years. Soon afterward, as we saw, the Second Turkish War began and embroiled Catherine in more urgent problems, and the Poles used this time to accomplish what they desperately needed: a workable system of government.

It was to the destruction of this system that Catherine, her hands freed at last by peace and by the deep involvements of Berlin and Vienna in their operations against France, could now proceed.

It should be said on her behalf that this was not merely a matter of imperial vanity or of simple imperialism. Catherine knew Russian history. Large areas of onetime Russian territory—even after the First Partition of Poland—were still under the Polish flag: a good part of the center and western regions known later as White Russia, and practically all the regions west of the Dnieper-Borysthenes which six centuries earlier had been the hinterlands of Kiev. Catherine, the dramatist of Kievan Russia, the historian and maker of history, had coveted these areas for a long time because she had taken on her shoulders the task of undoing the misfortunes of Russian history.

The new Polish constitution was ratified a few months after her Second Turkish War ended, and by then her agents were long since busy organizing a faction of discontented conservatives. This "Confederation," emerging the following year, invited Russian intervention, which Catherine was pleased to supply. In the spring of 1792, Russian troops occupied Warsaw. The outcome was the Second Partition of Poland in 1793.

Catherine's well-prepared "elbow room" had found Austria so preoccupied that, this time, it got no part of the Polish "cake"; Prussia, more alert, was bought off with a substantial chunk of territory, including the port city of Danzig and a population of 1,000,000. Catherine took a great swath: most of White Russia and most of the western Ukraine, with a population of some 3,000,000. At her command, King Stanislaus revoked the new constitution. What remained of Poland was attached by treaty to Russia as a satellite state with its foreign relations under direct Russian control.

Little more than a year afterward there was a national uprising led by Thaddeus Kosciuszko, one of the notable foreign volunteers and heroes of the American Revolution, who made Stanislaus abdicate. With no chance at all against the combined invading forces of Russia and Prussia, Kosciuszko's army fought a suicide stand and survived only a few months. The Polish remnant of Poland disappeared in the Third Partition. Austria this time insisted on its share: 1,000,000 people. Prussia took an adjoining share: another 1,000,000. Again Catherine had the biggest portion: Courland and the rest of Lithuania and the western Ukraine: 1,200,000 people.

Having abdicated the throne he had never wanted, Stanislaus for a while went on living in Warsaw in the former royal palace, former king of a former country, protected by Catherine's sheltering armies from the hatred and contempt of his former subjects. Nothing could protect him, finally, from the knowledge of his own weakness, the dimensions of the catastrophe over which he had presided, the awful sickness of self-contempt. His lover's plaint of 1762—"What is left for me? Emptiness, and frightful weariness of heart. Sophie, Sophie, you make me suffer terribly!" —had acquired undreamed-of other dimensions.

The disappearance of Poland as a national state did, however, enable him to fulfill, in grotesque circumstances, the wish he had held ever since leaving Petersburg. For now at last Catherine did invite him to return. He did so early in 1796, accepting the pension and the palace she offered him. Numerous retainers and relatives arrived with him; so did his large and famous art collection, which included such delectations as Fragonard's "The Stolen Kiss" and which would in due course come to the Hermitage.

Catherine received him pleasantly and with comforting and reassuring words, and allowed him to attend some of her Hermitage evenings, where he could take some solace in the company of friends from former times, such as Leon Naryshkin, the busy, flibberty intriguer who long ago had smuggled him into Catherine's apartment to begin the affair and who was still amusing and still inconsequential and still intriguing.

Thus, surrounded by great masterpieces, luxuries, and sad memories, Poniatowski spent the next years, until his death in 1798—ruminating on the past and writing his memoirs.

She was literally a *femme fatale*: ruinous, almost without exception, to the men who were most important in her life. The morbid record: Peter III, her husband, murdered. Hanbury-Williams, insane and suicide. Serge Saltikov, discredited, disgraced, died in obscurity. Stanislaus Poniatowski, died convicted in the eyes of Polish patriots as chief accomplice in the murder of his own country. Gregory Orlov, died insane. Potemkin, died in despondency. And the list still was not complete.

Catherine herself, by the year of 1796, her thirty-fifth year on the throne of Russia, had without doubt become the preeminent royal personage of the whole world. No other contemporary monarch had reigned so long or done so much so successfully. None certainly had such personal power; in the twilight of autocracy, she was a colossus, a living monument. In Russia itself, among the vast bulk of the populace, the once-insignificant princess from Germany had become the apotheosis of *Matushka*: living icon, the very symbol and soul of Russia. She had always believed she knew best; now they believed her. She had come to seem to her subjects almost as naturally Russian as the forests and the steppes. Apparently, she had arrived at certain similar feelings about herself; at any rate, enough to becloud facts that she found it comfortable to ignore, such as her own origins. In the will already cited ("My desire is to bring Constantine to the throne of the Great Eastern Empire") she also wrote: "For the good of the Russian and Greek Empires I . . . advise avoiding consulting all Germans of both sexes."

As for the inevitability of her own death she could, with intellectual poise, accept and sometimes discuss that fact and the fact that Russia would exist and have a future history without her. But she was too much involved in life to reflect much on either fact. Her physical infirmities were an inconvenience and an affront to her vanity, but she was far from being immobilized. She made the seasonal rounds of her principal palaces. Tsarskoe Selo had become her summertime favorite. In the autumn and wintertime, in Petersburg, she now had a secondary residence, the Tauride Palace. She had bought it and its fabulous contents from Potemkin's heirs after his death. She lived there from time to time, warming herself with memories of that strange and gifted man —her husband, "hero," "idol." And, although she herself could no longer dance, she gave some of her most brilliant balls there in the lovely Catherine Hall. The Hermitage, however, remained her favorite and customary residence, office, salon.

As always, she arose at 6 A.M., consumed her enormous portion of strong coffee, and, with no noticeable diminution of either mental or physical energy, worked the day through at her vast official and personal correspondence. She remained "imperturbable": always pleasant and attentive to her visitors (who still sometimes included art dealers; she never stopped collecting). She was always prompt, never hurried, seemingly never tired. And somehow she found time to read the latest important books and journals, chat with her grandsons, frolic with her dogs, cuddle her pet monkey, feed the "beautiful, merry and friendly" white squirrel Potemkin had given her, and perhaps relax with billiards, needlework, or one or another of her many avocations.

In the evenings she had her familiar Hermitage gatherings under the familiar rules: Boredom, pride, ill-temper were forbidden, jokes were prized, and laughter was the greatest good. For as she had written to her friend Frau Mielke: "Madame, you must be gay; only thus can life be endured. I speak from experience, for I have had to endure much, and have only been able to endure it because I have always laughed whenever I had the occasion." And to Baron Grimm: "In spite of everything, I am as eager as a five-year old child to play blind-man's buff, and the young people, my grandchildren and great-grandchildren, say that their games are never so merry as when I play with them. In a word, I am their merrymaker. . . ." And, though she moved awkwardly and painfully: "I feel as agile as a water wagtail."

She remained insatiable in her political ambitions as in her appetites for life, art, love, and laughter. To one of her ministers she declared: "If I could live to be a hundred, I should wish to unite the whole of Europe under the scepter of Russia. But I have no intention of dying before I have driven the Turks out of Constantinople, broken the pride of the Chinese, and established commerce with India." Following the design of Peter the Great, she made war on Persia and annexed the southwest region around Baku, thus regaining another of Peter's lost conquests.

Then her attention focused on France. An upstart French Corsican general named Bonaparte had begun to stabilize and preserve the Revolution and to mold the Jacobin rabble into a powerful, aggressive military force. Her great Marshal Suvorov had been pleading: "Mother, let me march against France!" Catherine decided to send him with an army of 150,000 men. Suvorov was undoubtedly a military genius, and with such a force, at this stage in history, he might very well have subdued the French, broken Napoleon, and altered the whole subsequent course of Europe's history.

But the plan was canceled, for death took Catherine by surprise. The day Suvorov's army was to march, she had a massive stroke. She never regained consciousness.

Two days later, on November 16, 1796, Catherine died at the Hermitage—the scandal and glory of her age.

HERE LIES
CATHERINE THE SECOND

Born in Stettin on April 21, 1729.

She went to Russia in 1744 to marry Peter III. At the age of fourteen she made the threefold resolution to please her husband, Elizabeth and the nation. She neglected nothing in trying to achieve this. Eighteen years of tedium and loneliness gave her the opportunity to read many books.

On the throne of Russia she wanted to do what was good for her country and tried to bring happiness, liberty and prosperity to her subjects.

She forgave easily and hated no one. She was tolerant, understanding, and of happy disposition. She had a republican spirit and a kind heart.

She was sociable by nature.

She made many friends.

She took pleasure in her work.

She loved the arts.

This was Catherine's epitaph to herself, written in late 1791 or early 1792 at about the same time she wrote her will—presumably soon after Potemkin's death had brought her face to face with her own mortality. Her secretary, Khrapovsky, found it one day at the Hermitage on her bedside table—an ink-blotched, hastily written memorandum to herself, on a crumpled piece of paper—and had the sense of history to save it and put it in his archives. Obviously it is as much a declaration of good intentions as of good deeds. It has sometimes been presented as Catherine's last thoughts about herself, though it was not: Major events and transformations lay ahead of her; it was a provisional epitaph, a rough draft of her rights to self-esteem and the admiration of posterity. Even so it is a strikingly modest statement from a woman who, since girlhood, had felt destiny at her elbow and who would survive in history as Catherine the Great.

Epilogue

Among the Russian high officials who had been part of the Grand Tour, there was a glaring omission: Grand Duke Paul, heir to the throne, heir to all that New Russia. Catherine at that time was fifty-eight years old. Peter the Great had died at the age of fifty-three; Empress Elizabeth at fifty-two. Death was a fact of life that Catherine as a prudent ruler and Russian patriot could not ignore. Paul, the Czar-to-be, was now thirty-three. Where was he? Where had he been during these past years, during the many events narrated here that had such importance for Russia and Europe?

We have had earlier glimpses of him. He was the infant snatched away by Empress Elizabeth, who smothered him with her own thwarted mother love and allowed his mother only meagerly rationed times with him. He was the bewildered little boy that Count Nikita Panin, his tutor and a ringleader of the coup that deposed Peter III, brought to the Winter Palace balcony to share with Catherine the adulation of the guardsmen and the Petersburgers on that bravura morning of St. Peter's Day, June 29, 1762. He was the adolescent boy who, far worse than losing his childish charms, had begun to resemble his father of record, the deposed and murdered Peter III.

Catherine knew no love for this unappetizing, dull, and increasingly introverted youth. She was in fact repelled by him, and her vast ego was affronted by his defects. "My God," she once wrote to Baron von Grimm, "why do children so often resemble their fathers when it would be better to resemble their mothers? This is not common sense; Dame Nature is often a blockhead."

Paul showed every sign of disliking his mother as much as she disliked him. He had quite early encountered floating bits of court gossip that he gradually, and to his horror, put together in three mosaics of scandal about his parentage. They were: that he was actually a bastard; that his mother had conspired to depose, then murder, his legal father, Peter III; that his mother was an unbridled sensualist who had many lovers before his birth and during his childhood. In adolescence Paul began to loathe and fear his mother and to associate himself rather desperately, in his own thoughts, with Peter III. His need to believe that Peter III was his father was a conviction—shadowed then and always, however, by some agonizing penumbra of uncertainty, leaving him crippled by what nowadays might be called an identity crisis. In his mind, he constructed an idealized, heroic father image of a martyred Czar, a well-nigh saintly man sacrificed to the lusts and ambitions of a ruthless, deceitful, unnatural wife, Catherine, and her coteries of lovers—they, so very different from Paul himself, handsome and robust and confident men.

Paul imitated Peter in any trait he discovered: love of soldiers, uniforms, and drilling, admiration for Frederick the Great of Prussia, dislike of the church and the Russian gentry.

His tutor, Count Nikita Panin, remained in charge of Paul even after the count became Foreign Minister and had a great deal else to think about. Already neglected by his busy mother, Paul was considerably further neglected by his busy, dilatory, though well-meaning guardian. Having from birth lived among equivocal relationships, being uncertain of everything about himself, seeing himself soon enough as ugly and unworthy, being unloved he became more and more unlovable.

The reason for Paul's conception had been dynastic. In Catherine's eyes, regardless of everything else about him, he remained a dynastic implement. Remembering her frustrations with Peter III, she waited until Paul was nineteen and was physiologically mature before she set him to the essential business of procreation. In finding the right bride for him, Catherine characteristically sought one in her own image, a dutiful princess of a minor German state, and her choice settled on Wilhelmina of Hesse-Darmstadt, rechristened in the Orthodox Church as Natalya Alexeievna. The wedding took place in 1773. Catherine made it suitably lavish and as ornate as her own wedding to Peter had been.

The marriage turned out to be in part a bizarre reprise of Catherine and Peter's. Grand Duchess Natalya showed herself to be extravagant, self-centered, and ambitious—qualities for which Elizabeth had rebuked the young Grand Duchess Catherine. Indeed, for a respectably bred Lutheran princess, Natalya adapted to the excitements of Russian court life with a startling precocity that far out-Catherined Catherine. Within a few months she had taken a lover, Count Andry Razumovsky, Paul's best friend (and nephew of Elizabeth's Emperor of the Night Count Alexis Razumovsky) and soon was hatching a plot with him to overthrow Catherine.

Paul apparently was entirely ignorant of both these developments. But he knew at least that marriage, in which he had invested some hope for personal happiness, had only made him unhappier. His spells of morbid depression—the feelings to which he gave the name "black butterflies"—increased in frequency and depth; he retreated into himself; often he broke down in uncontrollable weeping. He had many complaints to make about Natalya. On the other hand and all at the same time, he seemed to be worshipfully in love with her. And when, three years after the marriage, she died in childbirth (the child was stillborn), he was paralyzed by grief.

Catherine was now confronted by a set of facts that were oddly reminiscent of those confronted by Empress Elizabeth. Three years of marriage had not provided an heir. And now the Grand Duke's emotional condition was such that there was no predicting when he could fulfill his dynastic duty.

Catherine had kept the young couple under a system of surveillance that, if more discreet, was no less effective than the one she and Grand Duke Peter had at first endured under Elizabeth. After Natalya's death she at once impounded the late Grand Duchess' papers. She was thus in a position to supply the most drastic medicine for Paul's incapacitating grief, taking the risk that although it might kill him, there was a better chance that it might cure him: She arranged that the love letters of Natalya and Count Razumovsky be placed where Paul would discover them.

Paul read them and, after his first agony and stupefaction, was filled with a cathartic rage. Within a week he was ready to put Natalya out of his mind and marry again. But for all his deep neuroticisms, Paul was not stupid, and it did not take him long to realize how the letters had been secured and by whose instructions they had come to him. He had resented and mistrusted his mother; perhaps it was at this point that he began to hate her. Nevertheless, at the age of twenty-two and emotionally unstable, he found himself—as much older, much more experienced men had found themselves—fulfilling her plans.

Catherine's choice for him this time was, as before, a German princess of modest circumstances, Sophia of Württemberg. She had been on Catherine's list the first time but was then only fourteen, which—again thinking of her own experiences—the once Princess Sophia of Anhalt-Zerbst felt was a bit too young. Now at seventeen she was a tall, blond, healthy girl, wholesome and rather pretty, who inconveniently had meanwhile become engaged to Natalya's brother, the young Duke of Württemberg. Catherine disposed of that obstacle by settling a life pension on him ("On condition that I shall never see or hear from him again") and then arranged for Paul to be invited to visit Germany to meet her and also, en route, to be received by Frederick the Great. By this time—1776—Catherine and Frederick had become close allies in Polish affairs and much else, so it was only natural that her heir should have a sojourn in Berlin.

Had she realized how deeply Paul revered the example of the dead Peter III and thus how susceptible he would be to Frederick, she would have avoided this meeting like the plague. A man of prodigious charm when it suited him to be charming, Frederick went to extraordinary lengths to impress, flatter, and beguile. It was the talk of the Prussian court that he actually, for the first time in a decade or so, had a new suit of clothes made for the occasion. Paul became a devotee of Frederick and of all things Prussian. He also found, in due course, that he liked Sophia of Württemberg very much and that she was willing to be his wife and next Empress of Russia.

In a jolly note to Baron von Grimm, Catherine wrote: "We shall have her here within ten days. As soon as we have her, we shall proceed with her conversion. To convince her, it ought to take about fifteen days I think. I do not know how long will be necessary to teach her to read intelligibly and correctly the confession of faith in Russian. But the faster this can be hurried through, the better it will be. To accelerate all that, N. Pastukov has gone to Memel to teach her the alphabet and the confession en route; conviction will follow afterwards. You see by this we are foresighted and cautious and this conversion and confession of faith travels by post. Eight days from this act, I fix the wedding. If you wish to dance at it, you will have to hasten." All this went as planned. Five months after the death of Natalya, Princess Sophia of Württemberg became Grand Duchess Maria Feodorovna.

She was a good choice, a very good wife for Paul, dutiful, loving, forebearing, and utterly domestic in the German tradition of *Kinder, Kirche und Küche*. She could sometimes make Paul's "black butterflies" vanish entirely and always could lessen them. She made him as happy as he could possibly be, and he adored her. She was his wife and also the mother he never had. Moreover, this domestic felicity produced a harvest of healthy, handsome royal children such as Russia had not seen for centuries.

The first child was born the year after the marriage, in mid-December of 1777; a Christmas blessing, it was a boy—and future Czar. Catherine was ecstatic. The second came eighteen months later, and Catherine's joy was profound. It was another healthy boy, insurance for the dynasty.

The Greek Project, as we saw, had been taking shape in her mind for a long time; by 1777 her hopes, if not her exact plans, had become well enough defined that she almost announced them in the name she gave the first baby. His name was Alexander. When the second came, she was already at war with Turkey and already had her first victories. The scent of destiny and glory was in the Petersburg air, and she named the second child Constantine. As if to advertise her plans to the whole world, in honor of his birth she ordered a commemorative medal with a view of Sancta Sophia, the great basilica and main landmark of Constantinople.

She named these children? As Empress and Autocrat, she could do so, and she could do and did far more than that. In one of the spectacular ironies of her life and of Russia's peculiar history, she made these two children her own. From infancy the two boys were under Catherine's close supervision and spent far more time with her than with their parents, who were allowed to see them only at her pleasure. She chose their nurses, decided their diets, designed their clothes (". . . the child scarcely knows that he is being dressed," she wrote. "The arms and legs go into the garment at the same time and lo! all is finished. It is a stroke of genius on my part, this outfit . . ."). She selected their tutors, ordained the course of instruction and herself wrote some of the textbooks, as well as moral fables, stories, and historical tales calculated to mold their minds to the destinies that she had set for them.

Constantine was to be the Emperor of the new Byzantium and therefore had a Greek nurse and Greek playmates. He was led through the history of Greece, Rome, Byzantium and Russia to make him know the meaning of his name and his assigned role in history. Alexander, future occupant of Catherine's own throne, was designed to be an ideal prince on the English model: the classics and sports; vigor and humor and poise; charm and courage and intellect; the Enlightenment. Not that recent English princes had been notable for any of these qualities, but Catherine had formed her opinion of the English character from English ambassadors and travelers, initially and indelibly from Hanbury-Williams.

Alexander was her favorite. His father had become an intolerable disappointment except in producing him; perhaps *he*, this boy, still an unknown quantity, would redeem her hopes. Soon she was convinced he would. In a letter to Grimm, when Alexander was four, she glowed with infatuated pride: "If you only knew what wonders Alexander achieves as a cook, a shopkeeper, an architect; how he paints, hangs paper, mixes colors . . . ; how he plays at being the groom and the coachman; how he is teaching himself to read, draw, calculate, and write!" And again: "I do not know, but there is a kind of profundity which springs up in the head of this little monkey." And: "He loves me instinctively." And: "I am crazy about him. . . . I am crazy about this child."

In truth Alexander was handsome, intelligent, responsive, wonderfully good-natured, loving, wanting to please and live up to all the great expectations that his instructors and his grandmother had of him. His grandmother was always busy but never too busy to stop whatever she was doing and give her undivided attention to him, play games with him, tell him stories, forgive his transgressions, admire him, embrace him. He became as devoted to her as she to him.

At the time of Catherine's coup it had been widely understood that she would hold the throne in escrow for Paul. When he reached manhood, she would either retire gracefully to the role of Dowager Empress or, at the very least, would enthrone him as junior co-ruler with large responsibilities. By the time Paul became twenty-one the somewhat analogous situation in Austria had been worked out to the reasonable satisfaction of Empress and male heir and had been a going concern and conspicuous example for close to fifteen years.

But Catherine allowed Paul no part in the government of Russia, no power at all. When Paul was twenty-one, Catherine had taken only some symbolic and, in the outcome, meaningless steps to bring him into the apparatus of rule. And when he was twenty-four, already remarried and the father of Alexander, he still had not the faintest sign that she ever intended to give him any authority.

Paul and Maria Feodorovna had more children—three daughters and, in the last year of Catherine's life, another son, Nicholas— these they were allowed to keep as their own. Catherine was fond of the granddaughters, was interested, had them visit her at the Hermitage, behaved altogether as a proper grandmother. In addition, of course, watching their developing beauty, she soon began calculating how their future marriages might best fit into her imperial policies, Russia's interests, her tactical plans. But Alexander and Constantine remained, beyond all comparison, her darlings, her joys, her instruments, her own.

Toward Paul she maintained, in public and to her correspondents, an attitude of optimism in which, however, any sign of intelligence was greeted with applause that implied surprise. She wanted him (as a public duty and a duty to herself) to be interested in art, and for that reason and in hopes of broadening his horizons generally, she sent him and Maria Feodorovna on a grand tour of Europe, officially incognito (he was the Duc du Nord), after the example of Peter the Great.

On this tour, Paul made a new pilgrimage to Berlin and Potsdam and was reinforced in his belief that Frederick of Prussia was the model monarch and greatest man of Europe. By then the First Turkish War, in which Prussia had supported Russia, had ended in an incomplete victory. Catherine and Potemkin were planning the second phase, the whole grandiose scheme of the Greek Project. Catherine's policy required a gradual disengagement from Prussia, and during this time Paul began to seem more and more a menace to the whole, carefully calculated design. He carried on private correspondence with Frederick—as Catherine's agents were able to inform her. He entertained himself at his palaces by forming nondescript recruits into squads and companies and drilling them in the Prussian manner.

Catherine began to smell the scent of treason.

History was repeating itself again.

By the time of the great expedition to New Russia, the estrangement between Catherine and Paul was complete. They preserved only some surface amenities. While the trip to the Black Sea was taking place, Grand Duke Paul and Grand Duchess Maria Feodorovna were as much under surveillance, in effect as much under house arrest, as Grand Duke Peter and Grand Duchess Catherine had ever been at Oranienbaum.

Peter the Great, having found his son Alexis unfit to rule, changed the law to allow the Czars to choose their own successors. But he was taken so suddenly by death he had been unable to make his choice known. Catherine's faithfulness to her model extended even to this.

The unfitness of her son Paul—whatever its origins in heredity and environment—became so increasingly evident with the years that it began to frighten even his dutifully loving wife, Maria Feodorovna. "There is no one," she once wrote, "who does not every day remark on the disorder of his faculties." It is certain that before she died, Catherine had decided to pass him over and name Alexander to the throne. But with faith in her own durability, she kept putting off a formal declaration. In her will she wrote:

"All my library and manuscripts and everything among my papers written in my hand I leave to my dear grandson Alexander Pavlovich, also my precious stones and I also bestow on him my blessing with my heart and my mind. The copy of this to be locked up in a secure place so that sooner or later shame and dishonor would strike those who would not see this testament carried out." But there was nothing explicitly making Alexander heir to the throne. She was actually preparing the manifesto during her last weeks. Even an oral declaration on her deathbed could have been enough. But by then she was unable to speak. Thus, Grand Duke Paul became Czar Paul I.

One of Paul's first official acts was to have the body of Peter III exhumed from its crypt at the Alexander Nevsky Monastery. Peter had been dead thirty-four years, and the remains were only a skeleton. Paul had it dressed in one of Peter's elaborate military uniforms, robed in ermine, and brought to the throne room at the Winter Palace. There the skeleton was placed on the throne. The scepter was placed by the bony hand, and the crown of Russia was put on the skull. Then the public was invited, the courtiers and high officials were required, to come and pay obeisance to the true Czar, rightful occupant of the throne usurped by the woman who had just died and who lay in state nearby in Kazan Cathedral. In this grisly fashion Paul "cleansed" the succession and made clear that he considered himself not the successor of his usurping mother but of his victimized father.

He then proceeded with a double funeral. In the doleful chanting procession down Nevsky Prospect toward the Neva and the Cathedral of Sts. Peter and Paul there were two royal corteges. By the side of Peter III's cortege walked an elderly man. This was Alexis Orlov, his murderer, dressed in deepest mourning. On a black velvet cushion he carried Peter III's crown.

In the cathedral, at the end of the funeral mass, the coffins were placed in two identical white marble sarcophagi, side by side. Thus, by the order of her son, Catherine was reunited with her husband.

This was merely the beginning. He had hated Potemkin. Now

he had Potemkin's body exhumed from its tomb at Kherson, brought to Petersburg, flung into the Moika Canal, where it would be carried to the Neva and the sea so "that no trace might remain of him." After removing all portable works of art from the Tauride Palace, Paul turned it over to the Horse Guards as a barracks and stable.

Among Catherine's advisers and friends he tolerated a few, accepted a few as his own (most remarkably including the Zubov brothers—a measure of their skill at manipulation), jailed some, banished some from Petersburg, and exiled a good many, including Princess Dashkov, from Russia.

He took pleasure in rehabilitating Catherine's foes and pardoning those she had punished. In his government policies, foreign and domestic, he operated by the same principle. What she had disliked, he approved.

Paul was not wholly mad. He had flashes of rationality and occasionally showed keenness. Moreover, even when his principal interior motive seemed to be a vengeful wish to change Catherine's policies, some of his policies worked, and some, in retrospect, seem admirable (not surprisingly, since some of hers were unadmirable). He revoked many of the special privileges she had given to the Russian gentry after the Pugachev revolt. And although he extended serfdom to New Russia and gave land and peasants to his supporters and sycophants as if giving largess from a bottomless bag of gold, "He tried for the first time to regulate and limit the obligations of the serfs to their masters," as the historian Riasonovsky wrote, "by proclaiming . . . that they should work three days a week for their landlords and three days for themselves, with Sunday sanctified as a day of rest. Although Paul's new law was not, and possibly could not be enforced, it did represent a turning point in the attitude of the Russian government toward serfdom. From that time on limitation and, eventually, abolition of serfdom became real issues of state policy."

Nevertheless, whatever his virtues were or could have been, they were soon obscured by his increasing dementia. In the image of his idealized Peter III, he changed the uniforms, drills, and formations of the Russian Army to the Prussian style, personally overseeing every detail to the last button, flew into rages at the smallest infraction, thrashed the men, and sent the officers to exile.

A cipher in Russian life until he was Czar, he became a paranoiac autocrat. "In Russia," he declared, "the only person of any importance is the one with whom I speak—and that only while I am speaking with him."

When he drove in his carriage, all other riders were required to dismount and salute. Anyone passing the Winter Palace had to stop and salute whether Paul happened to be in residence or not. He issued streams of ukases, directives, and state policies only to issue their opposites within days or weeks. A caricature circulated clandestinely at the time shows him with a document in either hand: one titled "Order," the other titled "Counter Order"; on his forehead was printed "Disorder." His officials lived in constant fear of being dismissed or imprisoned. This atmosphere increased Paul's own fears and suspicions. He lived in dread of treason and murder.

Paul decided he must build a fortress and live in it with only a few trusted friends. The site he chose was in Peter the Great's Summer Garden on land occupied by the New Summer Palace built by Rastrelli for Empress Elizabeth. That lovely structure, one of the jewels of Petersburg architecture, accordingly was demolished and replaced by a thick-walled "Gothic Renaissance" fort complete with battlements and a moat and drawbridge. This Michael Castle, as it was known, was completed in 1801. But by then Paul's fears were ready to be fulfilled. His closest friends had decided that for the safety of the nation he must abdicate in favor of his son Alexander.

The chief organizer of the conspiracy was Count Peter Pahlen, the military governor of Petersburg and thus responsible for the personal safety of the Czar. Another activist was Platon Zubov. Another was Count Nikita Panin, the man whose dearest enduring hope had been to see him on the throne. Another member—not an instigator, but one who had been informed of the plot and reluctantly had assented to it—was Alexander.

Paul moved into his fortress early in March, 1801. One night a week later a small group of officers entered his bedroom, confronted him with a proclamation of abdication and demanded he sign it. He refused. There were violent words, a scuffle—and Paul I, like Peter III, was strangled to death.

Bibliography

ALMEDINGEN, E. M., *The Emperor Alexander I*. New York, Vanguard, 1964.

——, *Catherine the Great*. London, Hutchinson, 1963.

ANDERSON, M. S., *Britain's Discovery of Russia 1553–1815*. New York, St. Martin's Press, 1958.

BAIN, R. NISBET, *The Daughter of Peter the Great*. Westminster, Constable, 1899.

——, *The Last King of Poland and His Contemporaries*. New York, Arno Press and the New York Times, 1971.

——, *Peter III, Emperor of Russia*. Westminster, Constable, 1902.

BILL, V. T., *The Russian People: A Reader on Their History and Culture*. Chicago, University of Chicago Press, 1959.

BILLINGTON, JAMES H., *The Icon and the Axe*. New York, Knopf, 1966.

CATHERINE II, *Letters to Field Marshal Count S. P. Saltykov, 1762–72*. Moscow, 1886.

——, *Memoirs*, translated and with notes by Katharine Anthony. New York, Knopf, 1927.

——, *Memoirs*, edited by Dominique Maroger, translated by Moura Budberg. New York, Macmillan, 1961.

DASHKOVA, PRINCESS CATHERINE, *Memoirs*, translated and edited by Kyril Fitzlyon. London, 1840.

DESCARGUES, PIERRE, *The Hermitage Museum*. New York, Abrams, 1961.

FEDOTOV, G. P., *The Russian Religious Mind: Kievan Christianity*. Cambridge, Harvard University Press, 1946.

FLORINSKY, M. T., *Russia: A History and an Appreciation*. New York, Macmillan, 1953.

GOOCH, G. P., *Catherine the Great and Other Studies*. London, Longmans, 1954.

GRUNWALD, CONSTANTIN DE, *Peter the Great*. New York, Macmillan, 1956.

GREY, IAN, *Catherine the Great*. Philadelphia, Lippincott, 1962.

——, *Peter the Great*. Philadelphia, Lippincott, 1960.

KERNER, R. J., *The Urge to the Sea*. Berkeley, University of California Press, 1942.

OLDENBOURG, ZOË, *Catherine the Great*, translated by Anne Carter. New York, Pantheon, 1965.

PARES, BERNARD, *A History of Russia*. New York, Knopf, 1953.

RADISCHEV, A., *A Journey from St. Petersburg to Moscow*, translated by L. Wiener, edited by R. P. Thaler. Cambridge, Harvard University Press, 1958.

REDDAWAY, W. F., *Cambridge History of Poland*. Cambridge, Cambridge University Press, 1950.

——, *Documents of Catherine the Great*. Cambridge, Cambridge University Press, 1931.

SUMNER, B. H., *Peter the Great and the Emergence of Russia*. New York, Macmillan, 1951.

——, *A Short History of Russia*. New York, Harcourt, Brace, 1949.

THOMPSON, G. S., *Catherine II and the Expansion of Russia*. New York, Macmillan, 1950.

VARNEKE, B. V., *History of the Russian Theater*. New York, Macmillan, 1951.

VERNADSKY, GEORGE, *A History of Russia*. New Haven, Yale University Press, 1929.

——, *Kievan Russia*. New Haven, Yale University Press, 1953.

——, *Political and Diplomatic History of Russia*. Boston, Little, Brown, 1936.

VOYCE, ARTHUR, *Russian Architecture*. New York, Philosophical Library, 1948.

Index

Q